THE LAST
MORNING
STAR

Talks on the enlightened woman mystic, Daya

OSHO

JAICO PUBLISHING HOUSE

Ahmedabad Bangalore Bhopal Chennai
Delhi Hyderabad Kolkata Lucknow Mumbai

Published by Jaico Publishing House
A-2 Jash Chambers, 7-A Sir Phirozshah Mehta Road
Fort, Mumbai - 400 001
jaicopub@jaicobooks.com
www.jaicobooks.com

THE LAST MORNING STAR
ISBN 978-81-8495-017-5

First Jaico Impression: 2009
Second Jaico Impression: 2010

Printed by
Snehesh Printers
320-A, Shah & Nahar Ind. Est. A-1
Lower Parel, Mumbai - 400 013.

Contents

Introduction

Every few thousand years an individual appears who irrevocably changes the world around them in ways that are never immediately apparent, except to the most perceptive.

Osho is one such individual: his spoken words will resonate for centuries to come.

All those words have been recorded and transcribed into books like this one, written words that can carry a transforming message to the reader.

For Osho, all change is individual. There is no "society" to change – it can only happen to each one of us, one at a time.

So, no matter what the subject matter of the book, the thread that runs through all Osho's words is like a love song that we can suddenly, mysteriously, hear at just the right moment. And strangely, no matter what the words seem to be referring to, they are really only referring to us.

And this is no ordinary love song, more an invitation to open our hearts to hear something beyond the words, beyond the heart…a silence beyond all understanding. Where we all belong.

I

REMEMBERING THE DIVINE

Remembering the divine,
The serpent of time and the creepers of sorrow
Do not bother you.
Hence, embrace the divine, says Daya,
Leave the net of the world behind.

Speak not to those who have no interest
In remembering the divine.
Open your heart to those
Who are in love with the divine.

The moment you utter the divine's name,
All your sins fall away.
O man, make the remembrance of the divine
A refrain in your heart.

Without this remembrance,
With only man, man, man in your mind,
In wretchedness will you weep and wail.
In the grip of maya,
Your mind will never be still.

Until the strings are ready to play
To become some new tune, some new rhythm,

One may pluck those strings ten thousand times
But there will be no resonance.

Until the black bee is drunk with nectar,
Until a melody arises in its own heart,
One may tease the bee a thousand times
But there will be no humming.

Until one awakens oneself with restlessness,
Until the fire to act ignites itself,
One may provoke a dead heart a hundred thousand times
But there will be no answering roar.

Until the strings are ready to play
To become some new tune, some new rhythm,
One may pluck those strings ten thousand times
But there will be no resonance.

An enlightened mystic is one whose strings have been awakened by the divine. An enlightened consciousness is one whose *veena* is no longer lying idle; the hand of the divine has touched it. To be an enlightened mystic means that the song this person was born to sing has burst forth, the fragrance that was hidden in this flower has been released to the winds. An enlightened consciousness means that you have become that which you were destined to be. And naturally, in the fulfillment of this destiny, there is supreme bliss.

A seed is unhappy and in anguish as long as it is a seed. The anguish lies in the very fact of being a seed. To be a seed means you are meant to become something which you have not yet become. To be a seed means you are meant to blossom but you have not yet blossomed. A seed is meant to grow but it has not yet done so, it has not yet fulfilled its potential. To be a seed means the waiting continues…the path is long, and you have not yet arrived at your destination.

The enlightened mystic is a human being who has become what he was destined to become. He is no longer a seed, now he is a flower: a lotus with its thousand petals blossoming, blissful like a flower. What is the bliss of a flower? Now there is nothing left to become, there is no place left to go. The journey is over, the full stop has come. Now there is the possibility of being at peace — because when there is somewhere to go you are always restless, when there is something to be done, you must plan. As long as you have to become something, success and failure will be following you. Who knows whether you will succeed or not? Doubts and misapprehensions will surround you… a thousand things. The mind will remain wavering, the mind will not be stable. "Which path should I choose? How to avoid a mistake? The path I choose may turn out not to be a path at all. Will the path I am choosing be in harmony with my ultimate destiny or not?" So doubt lives and burns inside us, filling us with despair.

And naturally there are the pains of the journey, the obstacles on the path. The biggest obstacle will be that the seed is not confident that it can become a flower. How can it be? It has never been a flower before. How can one have trust in what one has never been? "Other seeds have become flowers, but this does not prove that I will also become one. The other seeds were other seeds; they may have been different. This seed that I am may be just a pebble, it may not have anything inside it."

There is no way a seed can be confident about its future. Confidence comes only from experience. So a thousand doubts and misapprehensions surround it: Do I have a future? Does the direction in which I am heading exist? Is the idea of what I want to be simply a trick of my mind? Am I just dreaming? Am I creating some new kind of deception, some new illusion? All these things cause pain; they prick us like thorns.

The bliss of the flower is that it doesn't have to go anywhere; the future has ended for it. And when the future ends, the connection with the past also breaks. When nothing more has to happen, who needs to remember the past? We remember the past because something is about to happen, because our past experience might be useful. We gather from our past experiences for the journey ahead: they might be useful. When there is nowhere to go, when there is nothing left to become, when the future has come to an end, in that same moment we are free from the past. Now there is no need to carry the burden of memory. The test is over. Now there are no more trials.

So there is nothing to remember and no web of imagination to weave. The energy that was scattered into the past and the future is now concentrated into the tiny moment of the present. There is supreme bliss in this intensity and a sharp focus. It is in such a moment that *sat-chit-anand* – truth, consciousness and bliss – or what the devotees call God and the wise call truth or liberation, happens.

An enlightened consciousness means the flower of a person's life has blossomed. And when that flower blossoms its fragrance is bound to spread; when the flower blossoms there will be a celebration. All the enlightened mystics have expressed their celebration in poetry. Some did not write poetry as such, but there is a poetry in their speech. Even when they didn't compose poems or write verses, even if they only spoke in prose, their prose is still full of poetry. Buddha never composed any songs, but it makes no difference. Each and every one of his words is full of juice. Every word is imbued with juiciness, every word is extraordinarily poetic, every word is a burning lamp.

Before we turn to these songs of Daya's, we need to keep certain things in mind.

Firstly, enlightenment is a celebration, a great festival. No festival is greater than this. The supreme moment of life has arrived. There will be dancing, there will be singing, a thanksgiving, an expression of gratitude. How one does this is another matter. Meera danced, Daya sang, Sahajo hummed, Chaitanya danced, Kabir composed verses, Buddha spoke. Sometimes it also happens that one remains silent…but in this silence there will be a beauty.

Haven't you noticed the difference between the various types of silence? Sometimes a person becomes silent out of anger, so there is anger in his silence. He is silent, but he is not really silent; he is expressing his anger through silence. Sometimes a man is silent in his sadness. He is silent, but he is still saying something. Every fiber of his body is saying that he is sad. His face says it, his eyes say it, his gestures say it. When he sits he is sad, when he rises he is sad. The air that surrounds him is heavy and burdened. It is as if a thousand kilos were resting on his chest. Sometimes a person is silent because he has not got anything to say. There will be an emptiness in his silence, a vacuousness, a negativity. You will find that he is silent because his being is empty inside.

A pitcher doesn't make a sound when it is completely empty, and it also doesn't make a sound when it is completely full. But to be empty and to be full are two totally separate things. One person doesn't speak because he has nothing to say – you will experience it negatively, something there is missing – and another person doesn't speak because he has too much to say. How can he say it? There is too much to put into words so he will remain silent. Speech cannot contain what he wants to say, language is too weak. And because what he wants to say is so vast that it cannot be put into words, he remains silent. The pitcher is full, there is utter silence, but it is a very positive state. It is not a negative state. It is not an emptiness; no nothingness; a wholeness, a fullness reigns there. You will know that this man lacks nothing, that there is a divine richness around him.

This is what we mean by the word *Ishwara*, God. The presence of God can be felt in the presence of this person. He is abundantly full. He may be empty of himself, but he is full of the divine. And no one who is empty of himself is really empty. One is only empty when one is without the divine. The mystic, the sage has effaced himself and allowed God to enter; he has become the throne on which the divine is seated.

Sometimes such a person remains silent, but even in his silence there will be absolute poetry. If you listen carefully, you will hear a music in his silence. If you close your eyes and become silent, you will hear a sweet melody in his presence, you will feel the resonance of the soundless in his presence. There will be waves when he rises and sits down – waves from a faraway shore. If you taste him, you will find that there is a great nourishment in his presence, not a lack or an absence.

But when you are with a person who is silent because he is empty, you will come home empty; as though he has sucked you dry, as though he has soaked you up, as though he has robbed you. You must have experienced this many times. When you come home after being in a crowd you feel something has been taken away from you, you feel bruised. You need to rest for an hour or two so that you can recover. What has happened? There were so many hollow people there and they all plundered you, they robbed and sucked you. When someone is like an empty hole, your energy will flow into that person.

So you will return home shattered after visiting a person who is silent because of his emptiness. If he had been silent because of his fullness, then you would have returned home full – some of his energy would have entered your inner being, some of his light would have descended into your darkness. You would have inhaled his fragrance. You would have come back ecstatic from being near him – bearing a new melody, a new symphony. The strings which were asleep within you would have begun to resonate to the sound of his strings.

The enlightened mystic is a festival. An enlightened consciousness manifests itself in many ways: someone creates the statues of Khajuraho, someone carves out the caves of Ajanta and Ellora, someone dances, someone composes songs, someone remains silent. But one thing is certain: if you look deeply into them, they are all expressions of great poetry, unprecedented poetry. What form that poetry takes, what color — that is another matter. Most often, the sages have sung. They have sung what they wanted to say; they have not just said what they wanted to say, they have sung it, hummed it, ecstatically. There is a difference between the two.

When you speak prose you use logic. When you speak poetry you rely on feeling. When you have to prove an argument, it can't be done in poetry, when you have to prove something, you have to use prose. The language of logic must be highly polished. Logic requires an unblemished mathematical approach. But devotees and sages do not need to prove anything. They have experienced the divine. It is not just a hypothesis; it is already proved to them. No more evidence needs to be gathered. An enlightened mystic does not need to prove that the divine exists. When he speaks to you, it is not to prove something to you. It has already been proved to him; he speaks as an expression of his fulfillment. He says: "It has happened to me. I am dancing because of what has happened to me. If you can understand my dancing — fine. If you do not understand — that is your misfortune!"

An enlightened person does not need to prove anything, so you will not find the word "therefore" in his language. He does not say: "The world exists, therefore God exists, because there has to be someone who created the world." This is nonsense! To prove God by logic is a kind of atheism. It means that God is smaller than logic; he can be proved by logic. What can be proved by logic can also be disproved by logic.

So bear it in mind that a mystic is no *pundit*. He is a man of feeling, filled with feelings, moved by feelings. The mystic has known: now, how to make you know? He has experienced something unprecedented – how to convey this good news to you? His eyes have opened, he has seen the light – the same light that you have been longing to see for many lives. How to tell you that the light exists? Should he argue, teach you doctrine, try to explain to your intellect?

The enlightened mystic has no such function. No one has ever been able to convey understanding through the intellect. An enlightened person tickles your heart, he awakens your feelings. He says: "Come and dance with me! Sing with me! Abandon all logic and thought – come, immerse yourself with me in this juice, perhaps you will be touched by the same thing that has touched me. And there is no reason why not. I am a sinner just like you, I am a human being just like you. I have made mistakes as you have. I have the same limitations as you. I am in no way different from you, I am in no way more special than you are. You are the same as I am. Perhaps the divine came into me because my doors were open – and your doors are shut, so he is unable to come in. Just become like me! Look! When I dance, my doors open. You can also open your doors. If you taste it once, you will find this out too."

It is not the purpose of the mystic to explain: he makes you taste. It is not the function of the mystic to make your intellect agree with his: he wants to color your feelings. This is a completely different process. It is as if he is drunk – thoroughly intoxicated and dancing with unrestrained ecstasy – while you are sitting dry, devoid of all juices, like a desert. An oasis has never happened in the desert of your

life, so what can he do? Can he dance, and hope you will see
his dance? Can he ask you to look into his eyes, to see his
ecstasy – the ecstasy which is a part of his life and can be a
part of yours? Can he say, "I am swaying in bliss, why can't
you also sway in bliss?"

Understand this difference. A pundit explains the existence
of God; a mystic explains the existence of ecstasy. And when
you are ecstatic, you begin to see God. A pundit explains that
if you believe in God, you can be ecstatic. But *how* to believe
in God? Who does not want to believe in the divine and who
does not want to be ecstatic? But this is a very strange
condition – that first you believe in God and then ecstasy
will come. And this is where the obstacle arises. How can you
accept God? How can you believe in what you cannot see?
How can you believe in what you have not known? How can
you believe in what you have never tasted? So there is a
falseness in the way that those who do believe in God, believe.

The earth is full of believers – false believers. They believe
because of their greed – thinking that believing will bring
them bliss. So far, this hasn't happened. Many lifetimes have
passed. They have worshipped in temples, they have placed
offerings of flowers on stones, they have made pilgrimages,
they have visited Kaaba and Kashi – they have been through
the whole complicated business, but there is still something
basically wrong in it. Their belief is false. True belief is a
product of your experience, it cannot precede it. You are
approaching things the wrong way around. You are tying the
bullock behind the bullock cart. Right now, you are dragging
the cart, but it doesn't move, the journey doesn't happen and
you are upset. Your pundits have told you that you should
believe first and then you will know the divine. This is the

wrong way around. When you know, then belief comes.

The sages say: "Just know. Don't be in a hurry to accept."
How can you believe? If you believe, it will be just a
hypocrisy. If you believe, it will be just a lie. And don't form
a relationship based on lies, at least not with God. At least
with God be truthful. At least don't extend your hypocrisy
and deceitful behavior in his direction. At least be truthful
towards him in this respect — "I will believe in you only when
I come to know you." How can I believe? How can I force
myself to believe? Shall I believe out of the fear of hell or
out of my greed for heaven, or because I am not very skilled
in logic and someone intimidates me with it? Shall I believe
for that reason?"

Have you seen? No one ever agrees because of logic; at the
most you can silence him. It is possible that you may be more
skilled in logic and so you can silence someone else. You may
stubbornly persist and the other person may not be able to
reply to you. But one who has been silenced is never really
satisfied. The person who has been silenced has not
agreed; he burns within himself, he smolders. He searches
for arguments and waits until he can find ones that are better
than yours. Even if he does not find better arguments, his
life will still not be transformed. This earth is full of false
believers. Temples, mosques, *gurudwaras* — all are full of
false believers, who have simply believed.

The enlightened mystics say: "Believing won't do. Taste it!"
An enlightened mystic makes that taste available to you. He
pours forth the sweet honey in which he himself is drowning.
That is why there is so much emphasis on *satsang*, on sitting
near an enlightened mystic.

What is the meaning of satsang? A master, an enlightened
mystic, has drunk from the divine wine; you can take a little
of it from him. Even if you drink water from the earthenware
cup that is him, you will still become intoxicated – because
the sediment of that divine wine is still there. Even if you
are just sitting near him, tomorrow if not today, the day
after tomorrow if not tomorrow, you will begin to sway –
something will start resonating in your heart. This resonance
is totally illogical! It is beyond your intellect, it is not
something your mind can grasp.

Enlightened consciousness is when a person has tasted the
divine, is when a person's window has opened, is when his
eyes have known. You have to come a little closer to such a
person's eyes. You have to use his eyes as a telescope. You
have to get a glimpse through his eyes. That is the meaning
of a master. A master is one who has known. A master is the
mystic whom you have begun to taste, through whose
medium you have begun to know.

There is a saying in Tibet: "If you want to find your way
around the mountains, then ask someone who walks to and
fro on them daily." Don't ask the people who have never been
to the hills, who have always lived in the valley – even if they
have studied many maps or have knowledge of the great
scriptures. If you ask them, you will wander aimlessly and
get lost. Ask the person who comes and goes every day: the
postman, the man who collects the mail and delivers it
around. He may not be a great pundit, he may not have any
maps, but you should ask him.

Now Dayabai is not a very wise person – wise in the sense
of being a pundit. She does not know the scriptures. Still, I

have chosen to speak on her. I will speak on her instead of
the great pundits. It is unlikely that she was educated at all,
but she has traveled on the path, she is familiar with the path.
She has breathed much dust from the path. She is colored
by that dust. By constantly walking on that path, traveling
on that path, she has become a void as far she herself is
concerned. Now only the fragrance of that path exists. That
fragrance has manifested itself in these verses.

There are three kinds of poets. One: those who have a
glimpse of the divine in dreams. They are the ones we
ordinarily call poets: Kalidas, Shakespeare, Milton,
Ezra Pound, Sumitranandan Pant or Mahadevi. We call them
poets: they have had glimpses in their dreams. They have not
seen the divine in their waking state; just a faint whisper has
reached their ears while they were lying down asleep. They
turn that whisper into a song. Still, there is a sweetness in
their song. God has not entered their lives, but at times they
have had a faint glimpse of him in a rose, they have heard a
distant sound of his footsteps. At times they have heard his
sound in the moon, in the stars. At times they have heard
his sound in the murmuring of a river or a stream. At times
his beauty has shimmered in the lofty waves of the ocean....
But they have not seen him directly; all this has happened
in their sleep. They live in sleep, they are unconscious — but
still there is an unprecedented juice in their poetry.

Poetry belongs to God — all poetry is God's, because
all beauty is his. Poetry means a eulogy to beauty, the praise
of beauty, a panegyric to beauty, a description of the
majesty of beauty. Poetry means the science of beauty. And
all beauty is God's. They have had occasional glimpses of
him, they have seen his footsteps in a few places — not in a
waking state, because they have done nothing about waking

up. They have not wept for their waking, they have not suffered for their waking. It is only the devotee who wakes up.

So the second kind of poet is the devotee, an enlightened mystic. He has not just seen beauty, he has seen what is most beautiful. He has not just heard an echo, he has seen the source of it. It is like this: someone sings a song on a mountaintop and his sound echoes in the valleys. The poets have heard the echo, the mystics have seen the musician himself. The poets have captured the echo, the resonance of the music which rises in the valleys; the mystics have absorbed it by sitting directly in his company. Naturally, the power of their speech is unprecedented. A poet is more skilled in an artistic sense because he has a talent for poetry. A mystic is not so skilled in an artistic sense because he has never learned the art of poetry. So from the point of view of poetic artistry the words of the mystics may not be great poetry, but from the viewpoint of truth they are supreme poetry.

Then there is the third kind of poet who is neither a sage nor a poet; he only has the knowledge of poetic artistry. He knows everything about figures of speech and meter. He just rhymes his verses on this basis. He hasn't seen the truth, or even the shadow of the truth, but he knows linguistics, he knows grammar. He is a rhymer. He can rhyme words.

Ninety out of a hundred poets are rhymers. Sometimes they rhyme very well, verses that charm the heart. But they are rhymes; there is no life in them, there is no experience in those verses. Their words are clever: they have counted their syllables, they have observed the rules of meter and its teachings. Ninety out of a hundred are rhymers. Of the remaining ten, nine are poets and one is a true sage.

Daya is such a one: a devotee and an enlightened mystic. Not much is known about her. Devotees never leave much information about themselves. They become so engrossed in singing the song of the divine that they never have time to leave any information about themselves. We only know her name. What is so special about a name? Any name would have served the purpose. One thing we know for sure: that she meditated upon the name of her master. Her master was Charandas. He had two female disciples – Sahajo and Daya. I have spoken on Sahajo. Charandas has said, "They are like my two eyes."

Both were devoted to serving him throughout their whole lives. If one finds a master, then service is a *sadhana*, a spiritual discipline; it is enough to be close to him. There is no information about their having practiced some other spiritual discipline, but this was enough. If someone has found the truth, it is enough to stay near him. If you pass through a garden, your clothes will catch the fragrance of the flowers. If you live near a person who has known the truth, his fragrance will enter into your being too. That fragrance floats in the air, it spreads everywhere. They must have massaged their master's feet, they must have cooked for him, they must have brought water for him.... They must have done many small acts like this for him.

There is not much difference in the poetry of the two either – because when the master is the same, what flowed into them both cannot be very different. They have both drunk from the same well, they have both known the same taste.

Both appear to have been uneducated. Sometimes it is a blessing to be uneducated. Educated people cannot bow down because of their education. Education gives rise to egotism. "I am somebody! I am educated, how can I bow down to someone else?" They are uneducated. They come from the same region that Meera came from.

It often happens…. If a soul has been born in a particular region, if the divine has been seen, sparks are left there. The very air of that region becomes contagious. One wave awakens another wave: with one wave another arises, with the second wave a third arises. There are windstorms of enlightenment too. Once in a while these typhoons will strike. Such a storm came during the time of Buddha and Mahavira. Enlightenment reached such heights the whole world over – heights that had never been touched before, and have never been touched since. Tens of thousands of people were carried off towards enlightenment, they rode the storm. When one person becomes enlightened, it is the beginning of a chain. This is what the scientists call a chain reaction. When a house is on fire, the whole area is endangered. The flames leap from one house to the second and from the second house to the third. There is a chain, a series. If the houses are very close together, the whole village can be burned to ashes.

Enlightenment is a similar phenomenon. One heart catches fire with the divine, one heart is lit up by the fire of the divine, and then those flames begin to jump… invisible flames, but whosoever comes close will be caught by those flames. So Daya and Sahajo came from the same region that Meera came from. Blessed is that place, because no other region has the good fortune of having given birth to three enlightened female mystics.

The verses that they both wrote were born at the feet of the same master, so their songs have the same color, the same melody. Of course there are a few minor differences, differences because of their different personalities. The differences are so few that when I gave the first series of discourses on Sahajo, I used Daya's verse to name them. Daya's verse is:

There is much light without lightning,
And it is showering without clouds.
Watching this, ceaselessly
My heart is delighted, says Daya.

The verses for that series of talks were Sahajo's, but I gave them a title from Daya's verse. The verses for this new series that we are beginning today are Daya's, and I am giving them a title from Sahajo's verse:

The world is like the last morning star.
Sahajo says: It is fast disappearing
Like a pearl of dew,
Like water held in the hollow of your hands.

Just as the last morning star does not remain for long, so the world is the star of the dawn. All the other stars have set. The moon has set, the stars have gone, the sun is about to rise, day is breaking, the last star twinkles and then is gone. You hardly see it – one moment it is here and then it is gone. One moment it is here, the next it has vanished. The world is like the last morning star: that's what it is – the last morning star! Now it is here, now it is not. Don't rely on it too much. Search for that which always is – for the polestar, not for the last morning star. Seek refuge in that which is immovable, eternal, immortal; that which always was, which always is, and which always will be – because you can transcend death only by seeking refuge in this.

If someone clings to the last morning star, how long will their happiness last? It is like catching a bubble of water. The bubble will burst before you can even hold it.

The world is like the last morning star.
Sahajo says: It is fast disappearing...

You can try in thousands of ways to make it stay, but it will not stay. And this is what we are always doing – the whole world does it. What are the things that we try to hold on to? Relationships, attachments, love, our husband or wife, sons and daughters, wealth and riches, fame, position, prestige. *The world is like the last morning star.* It will vanish before you are able to hold it. It will pass in the time you waste in holding it. You cannot hold these waves. The world is unstable, fickle. Whosoever wants to hold on to it will be unhappy.

Why are we unhappy? What is the root cause of our sorrow? The root cause is only this much: that we try to grasp things which do not endure. But we want them to last, we want the impossible and therefore we are unhappy. We rely on water bubbles, we build our houses on sand, we erect a house of cards. A small gust of wind comes and everything falls down. Then we cry, we weep and wail. Then we are very unhappy and we say, "What a misfortune." It is not misfortune, only stupidity. We say that God is displeased with us. No one is displeased with us, it is only our lack of understanding.

If you make a house of cards, of course it will fall down. The surprising thing is that it stayed up while you were making it. That was very good. Usually it will fall down before you finish making it. You must have made such houses when you were a child – they always fell down before you finished building them. It didn't even take a gust of wind. Perhaps you touched it, and that was enough. Perhaps you breathed on it, and that was enough. Once one card moves, the whole palace will collapse.

The world is like the last morning star.
Sahajo says: It is fast disappearing...

One who has seen all this and is no longer building a palace from cards, who is no longer floating paper boats, who is no longer building houses on sand, who is no longer relying on dreams – only he will be able to know the eternal. As long as your eyes are filled with the transitory, you will not be able to see the eternal. The waves of the transient hide the eternal. The transient covers the screen and you invest your whole energy in trying to catch it, in trying to keep it together. It never comes together, it always falls apart. This has happened many times, life after life,...*like a pearl of dew.* You have seen dewdrops in the morning glistening like pearls in the early sunlight: on the grass, on the trees, on the lotus leaves. Even pearls do not glisten like this. But keep well away, don't get too close, don't touch them, don't start trying to gather these pearls – otherwise they will become like water in your cupped hands; just pearls of dew, water in your hollowed hands. If you try to pick them up, to gather them, to hoard them in your iron safe, you will be left with wet hands, but no pearls. These pearls are deceptive. And the world is like this too, as if someone were trying to hold water in his fist. It escapes time and time again, it slips from your hands again and again.

This is the name I am giving to this series on the verses of
Daya: *The Last Morning Star*. The wise have tried to say so many
things, but perhaps there is no sweeter statement than this:
The world is like the last morning star. What more straightforward
statement can there be? All the scriptures, all the lengthy
dissertations, all are contained in this small phrase.

It is said of Buddha's life that he attained enlightenment as
he watched the setting of the last morning star. Perhaps his
inner state at that moment was like that of Sahajo's when
she wrote *The world is like the last morning star*. He was sitting
under the bodhi tree, his eyes wide open, the last star was
setting…setting…setting…and then it was gone. As the last
star set, in that same moment something within him also set.
With that setting star all that he had thought he was up until
then came to an end. In a split second a fire was aflame, a
lamp was lit. Buddha has not said it anywhere, but if he ever
met with Sahajo he would certainly agree with this verse:

The world is like the last morning star.
Sahajo says: It is fast disappearing
Like a pearl of dew,
Like water held in the hollow of your hands.

When Buddha saw the last morning star setting, he
understood the whole nature of the world. Now there was
nothing left here to cling to, there was nothing left to hold
in his hands. The person who understands the fickle nature
of the world will be freed from the world, and *only* the person
who understands the fickle nature of the world is able to raise
his eyes towards the divine. All of these things are connected
with one another.

Why does it happen
Oh, why does it happen?
Life passes in searching,
Yet one does not find a soul mate.
In the absence of a single touch,
The flower of the heart
Takes one through so many seasons
Without blossoming.
The heart, smiling on the outside,
Is weeping silently within.
Why does it happen
Oh, why does it happen?
For how long will things go on
In this unlikely way?
When will my hands meet other hands
In lasting love?
When will my eyes understand
The language of other eyes?
When will the path of truth
Be free of thorns?
Why does the heart that is longing to gain
Forever lose?

Why does it happen
Oh, why does it happen?
Life passes in searching
Yet one does not find a soul mate.
In the absence of a single touch,
The flower of the heart
Takes one through so many seasons
Without blossoming.
Why does this happen,
Oh, why does this happen?

The reason why this happens is simple. We are trying to hold back something whose nature is not to stop, trying to hold back something which must keep moving – which *has* to keep moving, its very nature is movement. We are trying to catch hold of something which cannot, by its very nature, be caught. It is like someone trying to grasp mercury. The mercury spreads. We are chasing the world in the same way as someone chases mercury. The mercury scatters.

But we haven't even looked at the one who is always present, at the one who stands beyond all these games that we play; at the one who is standing inside us, who is standing outside us. We have not even looked at the one under whose gaze all this play takes place, the one who is a witness. We have not gazed at the divine. That is why we have found no soul mate. Many people seemed to be our soul mates, but not even one truly was. Many a time we thought that we had found a soul mate, only to lose them again and again.

How many friendships have you forged, how many loves have you formed, how many threads of attachment have you tied – and every time you have lost everything. All that came into your hands was anguish and sorrow. But still you did not wake up. Still you hoped you would find someone somewhere else: "Let me search a little more, just a little more!" Hope never dies. Experience tells us that we will not find what we want, but hope goes on winning over experience. Hope goes on weaving new dreams. Only the person who awakens from hope awakens from the world and becomes free.

No, there is no soul mate here, and the inner flower of the heart never blossoms here. It can only blossom with the touch of the divine. Seasons will come and go but this flower within you will never blossom, never. It can only blossom when the season of the divine comes. That is its spring; the rest is autumn. You can wait as long as you like, but sooner or later you will have to return. An intelligent person returns sooner, a foolish person takes longer. An intelligent person learns after even a little experience, a foolish person makes the same mistakes again and again — and gradually becomes used to these mistakes. Rather than waking up and learning, he goes on becoming skilled at making mistakes. He repeats them more and more, he becomes skilled at this.

Wake up! Don't repeat your mistakes. If you have tried something and gained nothing, don't rack your brains about why this happened — why? It happens because of a very simple law. If you try to walk through a wall, you will bang your head. Why does that happen? Go through the door, the door is there. All the sages are talking about this door, this doorway.

Remembering the divine,
The serpent of time and the creepers of sorrow
Do not bother you.
Hence, embrace the divine, says Daya,
Leave the net of the world behind.

The world is a net. You have preserved it for a long time, but nothing has come into your hands. How many times have you cast this net without catching any fish? You have sat on the shore, life after life, sad, utterly weary; weaving the same net again and again, casting the same net again and again, and still not catching any fish.

Jesus saw a fisherman catching fish. It was morning and he

put his hand on the fisherman's shoulder and said, "Look at me. How long will you go on catching useless fish? Come, follow me. I'll teach you the secret of catching real fish."

The fisherman looked into Jesus' eyes – it was really strange, a complete stranger walking up from behind you and putting his hand on your shoulder – but the fisherman left his fishing net there and then and set off to follow Jesus.

His brother shouted, "Where are you going?" His brother was on the boat. He was fishing too. "Where are you going?" The fisherman replied that he had had enough of casting his fishing net, he had spent a lifetime doing that. Even if he had sometimes caught a few fish, what had he really caught? Sometimes they had caught fish, sometimes not, but what had they really caught? He was empty and he had remained empty. "Today I have looked into this man's eyes. I have faith in what he says. No harm will be done, we have nothing to lose. If we get something, good. If not, that will also be all right. I will go with him."

All the mystics are saying this same thing to you. With their hand on your shoulder they are saying, "How long will you continue casting this net?"

Hence, embrace the divine, says Daya,
Leave the net of the world behind.

You have cast this net many times. Sometimes you caught something and at other times there was nothing. But if you look more deeply, you will find that the net always came back empty, that nothing was caught in it. Whatever you caught was worthless, it had no value. Sometimes you found a little money, sometimes some position, sometimes a little prestige, but what were they all worth? One day you will leave them all behind you: your position, your prestige, your wealth. You will not be their master – you are not their master. They were here before you came, they will still be here after you are gone. Prestige and position will remain, but you will go. And you will return as empty-handed as you came.

Remembering the divine,
The serpent of time and the creepers of sorrow
Do not bother you.

Daya says, if you remember the divine, then all of life's sorrows, the whole conflagration of life's sorrows, will be soothed. Then nothing will be able to burn you. Right now, everything burns you. Right now, what you call life is not life, it is a funeral pyre. You are burning in all sorts of ways. Sometimes you burn with fury, sometimes you burn in a funeral pyre, but you are burning the whole time. Sometimes the funeral pyre is obvious, sometimes it is hidden; sometimes it is visible, sometimes invisible – but you continue to burn. Have you ever known taste of nectar in your life? Have you ever known a moment when your heart did not burn, when the burning was completely alleviated? Sometimes the burning is intense, sometimes it is less intense, sometimes the burn marks go away, sometimes not, but have you ever known a moment of peace, have you ever known a moment of bliss? Did the door ever open? Never!

Remembering the divine,
The serpent of time and the creepers of sorrow
Do not bother you.

But only he who remembers the divine attains to that supreme peace and goes beyond the raging flames of the world.

What is meant by remembering the divine?

If man considers himself to be the peak as he is, he will live in sorrow and then be finished — just as no flowers will ever blossom if a seed assumes itself to be the end of things. A seed has to transcend, it has to go beyond itself. It is when man also tries to go beyond himself that he remembers the divine.

What does remembering the divine mean? It does not mean sitting down and saying "Rama Rama, Rama Rama," or covering yourself with a shawl which has the name of Rama printed on it. This matter is not so cheap! Remembrance of the divine means that you have begun to go beyond yourself, that you have begun to raise your eyes upwards, that the seed has begun to search for the flower.... It is not a flower yet, but it can become one.... The seed has begun to search for the flower, the flame of the lamp has begun to rise towards the sky, towards the sun. The journey has begun: the seed has burst, the sprout has emerged and has started its journey towards the sky.

As long as you think: "Whatever I am, whoever I am, I am a human being, and there the matter is finished," there is no door within you that opens beyond you. You are without a door. A man without a door is sad, sorrowful; he is closed within himself, locked up in a prison.

Believing in God does not mean that there is a God sitting

up in the sky, running the world. Don't fall into these childish notions. Believing in God simply means…if you understand it rightly, then it simply means: "I don't end at myself, more is possible." Let me repeat this: "More than myself is possible. My circumference is not the ultimate circumference of my existence. I can be big, I can be vast, I can expand." Simply remembering this is remembering the divine.

Remembering the divine is merely a symbol. When a person sits down, deeply engrossed in chanting the name of the divine, what is he saying? He is saying: "I invoke you, Oh my future, I call on you, Oh my potentiality! What I am right now is just a seed, but I am remembering the flower so that this becomes a journey within me. I will walk, I won't sit down now. I will rise, I will journey. I have to search, I have to find my destination. What can happen by idly sitting down?" One who becomes spiritually discontented is already religious. To be satisfied in worldly matters and to be dissatisfied in the spiritual sense is the characteristic of a religious person.

At the moment the situation is the opposite. Right now you are dissatisfied in the worldly sense. You have wealth, but it is not enough. You have a house, but it is too small. You have a car, but it is old; you bought it from a scrap merchant, you want a new one, a proper one. You have a safe, but it is too small. You have a position, but it doesn't satisfy you, you want a higher position. Right now you are dissatisfied with the world. And the funny thing is, you are completely satisfied with yourself! There is nothing that needs to be done inside you. Your discontents are all about outer things: your safe has to be larger, you have to buy a new car, your

house has to be bigger, you need to increase your wealth a
little, to find a better wife or husband.... These are the sorts
of things you are involved with. You are expanding, but you
are expanding your world and not your self.

This is the only difference between a worldly person and a
spiritual person. You want to expand your world; a spiritual
person expands himself. You are completely satisfied with
yourself. You are content with yourself as you are; you are
not at all concerned that you can be quite different, that a
Buddha can descend within you, that a Mahavira can be born
within you, that a Jesus can be born within you. No, you are
not worried about this. You are very discontented about small
things and not at all discontented about great matters.

Bear this in mind: when the dissatisfaction you have with
things begins to move inwards and the contentment that you
have towards the inner moves outwards, you have already
become a religious person. You only have to make this small
change. Contentment has to be turned outwards: if the house
is small, it will still do. Life lasts for such a short number
of days: it won't make much difference whether you live in
a big house or in a small one. Life is transient: make do with
what you have. The outer lasts for only a short time. The
outer life is like someone sitting in a railway station, in
the waiting room. You don't start changing the waiting room:
painting it a little, cleaning it a little, hanging up a picture,
decorating it — just because you have to sit there for three
hours! You tell yourself, "This is a waiting room, I don't have
to become too involved. I am sitting here peacefully reading
my newspapers. As soon as the train comes, I will be gone."

The outer life is an overnight inn. In the morning, you will have to leave. There is no need to be too worried about this. To be satisfied with this outer life is the sign of a religious person. Of course, if you want to be dissatisfied about something, then the inner journey is vast. It is a long journey, it is an eternal journey: there, you have to explore the truth. So put your discontent to work there, draw the whole fire of your discontent inwards and let all your contentment rest on the outer. As soon as you do this, you are a sannyasin; you are religious, spiritual.

Remembering the divine, the serpent of time and the creepers of sorrow do not bother you. And whoever remembers the divine.... Remembering the divine means moving towards being the divine. But first you must remember. First, you must remember what you have to become.

Have you ever tried to understand the nature of thinking? You want to build a house, but first of all the thought is born — that you want to build a house. You plan it in your mind, you stretch your imagination, perhaps you even draw a sketch on a piece of paper to show what kind of a house is to be built. And then perhaps you go to an architect so that the plan can be arranged even better. The house will be built later on, but first it is built in your mind, in your remembrance.

Whatever happens in this world happens first in thoughts and then in the world; first in thoughts and then in its actual reality. The meaning of remembering the divine is that you have begun your inner journey. Now you know that you have to become full of the divine, that you have to dive into the divine. You have seen the world, the last morning star, now you have to move towards it. Now you have begun to write letters; the destination is still far away, but you have begun to send messages ahead of you.

He forgot me so totally,
That he didn't even send me a letter.
The time of the rains has gone,
The lovers' meeting season has passed,
The pleasing dense-dark cloud thunders
But my water-pot remains empty still.
Not a drop has touched my lips,
I have quenched my thirst with more thirst.
He forgot me so totally,
That he didn't even send me a letter.
Every morning I entreated the crows to fly away,
Every morning I created welcoming ornamental patterns.
Sometimes in the dark, sometimes in the light,
I wore down the dust of many paths.
I became the object of people's ridicule and laughter.
He forgot me so totally,
That he didn't even send me a letter.

Remembering the divine means you have begun to write
letters. God is far away: right now his chariot is not even
visible, you cannot even see the dust rising on its path. Right
now, the divine is only a dream, a mere thought, a ripple – a
ripple arising from the thought that it is not enough to be
as I am, that there is no peace in being what I am, no bliss,
that there is no time for relaxing as I am right now, that I
still have to travel. Are you content with who you are? Are
you truly content? Don't you want something to happen
inside you – for a lamp to be lit, a melody to arise, a flower
to blossom, a fragrance to be released? If this desire, this
longing for the flower, for the fragrance, for the light is awakening in you, then you have begun to write letters, then you
have remembered.

Remembering the divine,
The serpent of time and the creepers of sorrow
Do not bother you.

A memory of the divine has come back to you. You have recalled the home you came from, the home from where you were sent. Here, is a foreign land. You have come here, but you were not here before you were born and you will not be here after your death. When you begin to remember your home — where you have come from, who is your original source, what is your point of origin, where you were before your birth, which gigantic ocean of milk you were sleeping in, where you will be after your death, which ocean your stream will fall into, who or what you were, where you were before your birth and where you will be after your death — when you begin to remember all this, then the transformation has begun, then your eyes have started to turn withinwards. Your eyelids have started closing to the outer and your eyes have started to move inwards.

You will still live on the outside, but like someone who is living in a foreign country but who still remembers his home. He lives there, he keeps things moving: he goes to his shop, he moves around in the marketplace, he goes to his office, he does everything.... There is a husband, a wife, children, he looks after everyone, everything is all right, but now an inner memory, an irrepressible inner memory has begun to arise. It is as if someone has started pulling him. Your real life force has begun to turn inside. It is only nominally outside. Abundant streams of life begin to gather inside you, the energy begins to crystallize.

And remember, we return to where we came from. A river

comes from the ocean, it rises up into the sky, it turns into
clouds, it rains on the Himalayas, it becomes a river, and it
runs back towards the ocean. The source is the goal. We
return to where we come from. Where we were before our
birth is where we are after our death. Eternity is in that
original source. Rest is there. Here, there are only hustle and
bustle, running around.

He forgot me so totally,
That he didn't even send me a letter.
The time of the rains has gone,
The lovers' meeting season has passed,
The pleasing, dense-dark cloud thunders,
But my water-pot remains empty still.
Not a drop has touched my lips,
I have quenched my thirst with more thirst.
He forgot me so totally,
That he didn't even send me a letter.

This is how things are. Right now, you are quenching your
thirst with more thirst. There is not even one drop of water.
You are just trying to console yourself. However much you
try to console, your mind is not consoled. Has thirst ever
quenched thirst?

Have you noticed one surprising thing: before one desire is
satisfied, you create another desire. Why? – because if one
desire is not satisfied, you feel despair and your mind has
to be engaged somewhere else. What will you do if your mind
is not involved? So you create another desire at once –
quenching thirst with more thirst. One desire caused you
sorrow, so you bring in another desire.

Have you ever observed that when you have some sorrow and another, really big sorrow comes along, the smaller sorrow is quickly forgotten? It is like when you have a headache and you go to the doctor and say, "My head hurts a lot, it is about to split," and the doctor replies, "Wait a moment. Your head is all right. Let me examine your heart." And he listens to your heartbeat and says, "Why are you worried about your headache? There is a possibility of a heart attack!" At that moment your headache will completely disappear. You might even forget your head, let alone your headache!

What has happened? The bigger sorrow took over from the smaller sorrow. The bigger worry takes over from the smaller worry. The bigger despair represses the smaller despair. This is your device. There is one sorrow. What do you do to forget it? — invent a bigger sorrow. There was a small trouble, you bring a bigger trouble home. The smaller trouble will be forgotten, now that you are engaged with the bigger one.

You will be entangled in the big problem for a while. Then, when you begin to get bored with even that one, you get an even a bigger problem. In this way man keeps enlarging his problems. This is what Daya calls "the net of the world."

"…quench thirst with more thirst." Has thirst ever quenched thirst? Are you mad? Not even a drop has fallen on your lips, the season is quickly passing, the opportunity that this life brings is being lost.

Remembering the divine,
The serpent of time and the creepers of sorrow
Do not bother you.
Hence, embrace the divine, says Daya,
Leave the net of the world behind.

Change the direction of your dissatisfaction — *Hence, embrace the divine*...remember the divine. Take care of that which will take care of everything. Allow the remembrance of that which is your original source. Remember that which is your original nature so that a thirst for it, an intensity for it may awaken a longing — in you. Hence, remember the divine.

Remember, you should not conclude from the words of the devotees that you just begin to recite "Rama Rama, Rama Rama" and you have done all you have to do. To chant "Rama Rama" is part of a larger process. If this larger process is a part of you, then it will be meaningful to recite "Rama Rama." If the process is not there, chanting is useless. Think of it like this: when you press a switch, the electric light comes on. But don't think that all you have to do is buy a switch from the market, stick it onto the wall, press it, and everything will light up. Electricity is part of a large network. One switch alone won't do the job.

There was a wonderful man by the name of T.E. Lawrence. He lived in Arabia and served the Muslims. He was a very brave man. Although he was an Englishman, he fell in love with the Arabs and he spent his whole life in Arabia.

Once, a large exhibition was held in France — a world exhibition. He took ten or twelve Arab friends to France so that they could see the world. "The place where you live, the things that you do in the desert of Arabia are stagnant. You must see the world!" So he took them to see the exhibition. He was puzzled to see that they had no interest in the exhibition. But whenever they entered a bathroom, they would not come out again. Their sole interest was the bathroom! He asked them several times about what they did there for so long. For hours! They were people thirsty for water. They had never had a decent bath. Here, they would sit under the shower or lie in the tub for hours, they were not interested in anything else. He would take them to the exhibition, but they would soon say, "Let's go back to the hotel."

When the day of departure, the day of farewells arrived and all the luggage was put in the vehicles, Lawrence realized that those ten or twelve Arabs had disappeared. He could not understand where they had gone. He was very puzzled. They were going to miss their flight. Then he thought that maybe they had gone to the bathroom again. So he went upstairs and all ten or twelve of them were in the bathroom. One was trying to unscrew the shower, another was taking off the taps – with no success. He asked them, "What are you doing?"

They said, "We thought we should take these home. We will enjoy them there. If we can take these taps to Arabia, we can use them at home."

They didn't know that the tap, which was all they could see, was just the part that was visible. Behind this was a huge network. Huge pipelines are connected to a source of water far away. The tap is merely the final end. "Rama Rama" is just like this. Don't think that if you sit down and continuously recite "Rama Rama" that you will turn on the tap and take a bath. This won't work. Behind it is a vast backdrop of consciousness, a long process.

The first stage in this process is not being content with yourself. The second stage is being content with the world: it is all right as it is. You accept it if it is like this, and you accept it if it is like that. But now you are not content with what you are like inside yourself. All your longings, desires and passions have begun to flow into one single stream and that stream belongs to your innermost being. But this stream has to flow as far as the divine. You have to seek out the infinite, because sooner or later the finite will be destroyed by death, the body will be destroyed. You have seen the funerals of other people; one day your funeral will also take place. You have seen other people's funeral pyres; one day you will also burn on a pyre. The finite body will have to go.

Before your finite body goes, recognize the infinite. Otherwise, your life will have passed in vain. The opportunity came and went and you could not recognize the infinite, you could not find a soul mate and the lotus of your heart did not blossom.

The infinite has to be recognized. And the call towards recognition of the infinite is the divine's name. The nameless has to be recognized. So far you have thought that you are what your name is. How are you connected with your name? You can be given any name. Names are always borrowed. You came without a name and you will go without a name. So before the moment of departure comes, you must recognize the nameless. We have called this nameless "Hari." We have to call the nameless something too! We will have to give it some name, otherwise how can we address it? So "Hari"!

The word *Hari* is very charming. It means a thief – the one who captivates, the one who steals, the one who takes away your heart. In this world there are no people as wonderful as the Hindus. People have given many names to God – but Hari! Only the Hindus could do that. And it is right too.

Love is a kind of theft. He will steal your heart. One day you will discover that you remain, but your heart has gone. Now Hari reigns where your heart used to be, he has taken possession of everything. He has stolen it all. He is "Hari" because he has stolen your heart. He won't leave anything for you. He will absorb everything that is yours into himself. He will drink every drop and not leave you a thing.

One night, some thieves entered the house of a Sufi *fakir*. The *fakir* was lying on his blanket – he had only one blanket. He watched and watched and saw that they were working very hard. "What will they find?" he thought to himself. They were working very hard gathering the few broken old pots and pans that were there.

After they had tied them up and were starting to leave, the *fakir* began to leave with them. They asked him, "Why are you coming with us? Where are you going?" They were a bit frightened: why was this man going with them?

He replied, "Friends, as you are taking everything away, I thought I should come too. Why leave me behind? I will live there as I have lived here. It won't hurt you to have me there."

Immediately they put his things back saying, "Dear sir, take your things; they aren't much anyway. And who wants to take all this responsibility for you?"

When Hari steals you and takes you away, he leaves nothing behind. What do you have that can be stolen anyway? When Hari is taking your heart away, remember this Sufi *fakir*. Go with Hari and say, "Dear Sir, take me along too. You are taking away all my goods – my thoughts, my emotions. This

is fine, but take me too. What will I do here now?" And Hari
does take everything. When he steals, he steals everything.
He doesn't leave anything behind.

Remembering the divine,
The serpent of time and the creepers of sorrow
Do not bother you.
Hence, embrace the divine, says Daya,
Leave the net of the world behind.

Speak not to those who have no interest
In remembering the divine.

Daya says that she won't explain to those who are not
interested in Hari. What is the point of doing that? They
wouldn't understand anyway. They would only misunderstand.

Speak not to those who have no interest
In remembering the divine.

And she says that you too shouldn't bother about them. They
are against the divine, so let them stay that way. When the
divine itself cannot explain things to them, how can you?
They are falsifying the divine, they will certainly falsify
you! They have become stubborn. Let them take care of
themselves.

...those who have no interest
In remembering the divine.

This has been my experience as well. Only those who have
turned towards the divine can understand. This understanding cannot be forced, it comes only when there is

an intense desire in you. When you hear me, if you listen with sympathy, with deep interest and love, with devotion, then what I say will shower like nectar inside you. If you argue with what I say, if you are closed to me, in opposition to me, then what I am saying will prick you like a thorn.

To those who are still entangled in the world, the words of the mystics are like thorns. They will say, "What is this? 'The world is like the last morning star'? We have just finished our election campaign and you say, 'The world is like the last morning star'! Don't bother our voters with 'The world is like the last morning star'! Let me get to Delhi first! Then you can say whatever you like. But first, let me reach the goal."

Those who are still interested in the world will find these words very poisonous. The one who is running madly after the world will find even the name of the divine bitter, it pours poison in his ear. Keep this in mind: it all depends on you. If you are full of poison, then even precious words like "the name of the divine" instill only poison in you. If your vessel is full of poison, then nectar cannot be poured into it.

...*Those who have no interest in remembering the divine.* Don't talk about the divine to those who have not yet remembered it, who have never thought about it, who do not even understand that there is something like the divine and that one has to search for it, to those who are, as yet, intoxicated with the world. They are asleep. Don't disturb their dreams, or they will get angry.

Open your heart to those
Who are in love with the divine.

Daya says, the person who is in love with the beauty of the divine, the person who has begun to dive into the divine, the person who has opened the door of his heart towards the divine — *Open your heart to those who are in love with the divine* — only talk to that person. These matters are very inner.

People come to me and ask, "Why can't everyone enter here?" Only those whose minds have clearly begun to search can enter. Why should everyone come here? This is not a theater! No one should come here simply out of curiosity. This is not a lecture going on here. Here, the heart is being exposed. Only those who are prepared, who are eager to open up their hearts can come. The only point of coming here is if our hearts can meet, otherwise your time will be wasted and all my work will be in vain. And on the contrary, you will leave here angrily saying, "What kind of talk was this? He should have explained something. He should have explained something useful."

When you go to a saint, you go to get something. People come to me and say, "Give us your blessings." What are you asking my blessings for? At least tell me that much.

They say, "You know everything." No, no, tell me exactly. I don't want to be in trouble afterwards, because I will be responsible if the blessing bears fruit.

They say that there is a lawsuit going on in the courthouse. It has been going on for a long time, so "Please help me to win it." There is a lawsuit, and you have come to me for *that* ! But your so-called saints do that sort of work! You call them saints, but they bless you if there is a lawsuit, they bless if you want to win in the elections, they give you a talisman if there is some sickness.

Know well that anyone who helps you with your world in any way cannot be a saint, he is simply a part of your businessman's world. He is a shopkeeper of religion. He also is a business-man — just like you. But he is a more skillful businessman than you are. You sell visible goods, he sells invisible goods. And you cannot even catch hold of this invisible merchandise. Beware of him!

A real saint will startle you. A true saint will hit you. You will writhe with impotent anger in his presence. Many times you will be angry with him, many times you will want to run away from him. You will fear the sage. You will think a thousand times before going near him. Because going near an enlightened person means change, transformation.

Open your heart to those
Who are in love with the divine.

The heart can be opened up only in the presence of such a person. These matters of the heart can only be revealed to someone who has fallen for the beauty of the divine, who has fallen in love with the divine, to those...*who are in love with the divine*, who have found joy in the countenance of the divine, in whom the inner madness has awakened.

Open your heart to those
Who are in love with the divine.

...To those who have begun to be a little aware of the beauty of the divine, within whom a new thirst has begun to arise, to a person who says, "It is all right. Whatsoever is here is all right, but there is no reason to be satisfied with just this. If this is all there is, then life makes no sense." You get up every morning, go to the office, return home in the evening, eat, drink, sleep, and then get up again in the morning, then go to the office.... If this is all there is, then life is meaningless. Something more is needed. Some absolute meaning is required. Some other world of light is needed, some new expanse of consciousness, some new sky.

If this is all that there is – crawling along on the ground every day, morning and evening – if this living like an insect is all there is, then life is futile. Whosoever has understood this, open your heart to such a person – tell that person what is in your heart, bare the strings of your heart. Put your diamond in front of that person. This is what the enlightened mystics do. They don't just give discourses, they display the diamond that they have found in front of you. But your eye can see those diamonds only when you have been able to see that there are no diamonds in the world. There is nothing but dirt here. If you still see pebbles and stones as diamonds, then it is better not to show you this diamond. You will think it is another pebble or stone.

When you have learned to recognize the diamond, to test it, if you have become a connoisseur – *Open your heart to those who are in love with the divine.* Share what is in your heart with the person whose life has begun to be an awaiting for the divine. Open your heart to that person. Show that person everything. Show him your entire treasure. Invite him into your innermost heart, invite him into your temple. Say, "Come inside, be my guest. See what has happened inside me, test it, recognize it, enjoy it, taste it." Tell him that what has happened to you can also happen to him."

A tender red plant,
Waiting, waiting.
Beloved,
A tender red plant.
Keep the doors open;
Clouds of colors will come
Bearing banners of fragrance.
Long may you live
Oh bridges to smiles.
A tender morning
Waiting, waiting.
Beloved,
A tender morning.
Keep watch on the light
Keep the lamp aflame – oh!
Pass the night hours
Like the rajanigandha flower,
Quietly, oh so quietly.
A glowing glance
Waiting, waiting.
Beloved,
A glowing glance.
Beloved,
A tender red plant.
Waiting, waiting.

Keep the doors open – keep watch on the light. Keep the lamp alive. The master invites you into his heart and says to you: "Just look at what has happened inside me. And now it becomes a waiting for you. You have to wait just a little longer and then what has happened in me can also happen to you. I am just like you, an incarnation of bones, flesh and marrow. I am burdened by my limitations, just as you are. I

have wandered in the darkness, just as you do. The lamp that
has been lit in me, you too have such a lamp. Yesterday I was
where you are today. Tomorrow you can be where I am today.
Just a little waiting."

Keep the doors open;
Clouds of colors will come
Bearing banners of fragrance.
Long may you live
Oh bridges to smiles.
A tender morning
Waiting, waiting.
Beloved,
A tender morning.
Keep watch on the light
Keep the lamp aflame, oh!
Pass the night hours
Like the rajanigandha flower,
Quietly, oh so quietly.
A glowing glance
Waiting, waiting.

It becomes easy to wait once you have met an enlightened
mystic, a master – very easy. There is no longer any pain in
waiting. Waiting becomes very enjoyable, because now there
is trust, now there is also faith.

People ask me the definition of an enlightened mystic. I tell
them that the person who arouses faith in your heart, the
person in whose company your waiting becomes easier,
the one near whom you feel that it will happen, it will
certainly happen, it will not stop until it has happened,
is an mystic. Whether it happens sooner or later – that is

another matter – but it will happen, that is absolutely certain. If it happens today, well and good. If it happens tomorrow, so be it. Now you will be able to wait patiently. There is no more doubt. The enlightened mystic is one in whose presence your doubts drop.

The moment you utter the divine's name,
All your sins fall away.

Daya says, *The moment you utter the divine's name....* One in whose life a deep awaiting, a remembrance has entered, in whose innermost heart the name of the divine has begun to echo, who has begun to sway in the enjoyment of the divine; one who has fallen in love with the beauty of the divine, in love with the divine.... *The moment you utter the divine's name, all your sins fall away.* All your sins are burned away by uttering this one name. Remember this. You too have uttered the name, but your sins did not burn away. So you didn't *really* say the name. Know this.

You have uttered the name before, you have invoked it many times, but you didn't really mean it. You uttered it casually, superficially; it didn't sink into your depths, you didn't wager your whole life for it, the arrow didn't penetrate your heart. You said it in a routine way. You uttered the name because people told you that it would be beneficial to do so, but it was not your search. You had not fallen in love, you had not been possessed by madness.

The moment you utter the divine's name,
All your sins fall away.

All your sins will be burned. They should burn away; there

is no reason why they should survive. All darkness is dispelled
as soon as the lamp is lit. In the same way, as soon as one
gives birth to remembering the name of the divine, one's
entire world is as good as gone. Your entire world will go
and all the deeds you have done in the world will fly away.
It was all a dream, it was all a darkness.

O man, make the remembrance of the divine
A refrain in your heart.

"Refrain" means that whatever you do or say – whether you
get up or sit down, walk or not walk, eat or sleep – the whole
time the name of the divine remains with you like a support.
You lean on it. Don't let that support go.

O man, make the remembrance of the divine
A refrain in your heart.

We see this in songs, don't we? One line keeps recurring and
it is called the refrain. The same line recurs again and again.
Let the divine's name become your refrain. Whatever you do
– whether you are running your shop, your bazaar, or doing
your household chores – let the refrain of the divine's name
be there in all your activities, let its remembrance be inside
you. Seeing your son, remember the divine. Seeing your wife,
remember the divine. Washing your husband's feet, remember
the divine. Feeding your guest, remember the divine. From
everywhere the window of the divine opens for you – that is
the meaning of "a refrain."

And only then will you be caught up with the divine twenty-
four hours a day. Otherwise, you will sit in a temple for a
few hours, for five minutes, chant the divine's name and run

away. You will be in a hurry — there are thousands of other jobs to do. If remembering the divine is just one of the thousand other things you have to do, it will never go deep within you. Let the divine's name be your refrain. Let it be the core of all you do. When you go to the bazaar, go in such a way that you meet the divine in each and every customer. You will still go to your shop, but you will feel that the divine is coming to you in the form of your customers.

This is what Kabir used to do. They say that when Kabir went to sell his cloth in Kashi, he would go dancing. And when people asked him why he was so happy when his job was so ordinary, just selling cloth, he would reply that Rama had come, that the divine was there and would be waiting for him. Perhaps he would be disappointed that the weaver Kabir had not yet come, that he was late that day.

When Kabir sold something to a customer, he would say, "Rama, take good care of it. I have worked very hard spinning this. It is a fine delicate sheet I have woven, I have woven it with great love. I have woven it in remembrance of Rama — look after it well. I have woven it in such a way that it should give you good service throughout your whole life. It should serve your children as well."

Let Rama be your refrain. Kabir would weave cloth and say "Rama." The thread could be going vertically or horizontally, but Rama's name was in every thread. Let Rama become your very humming: like your breath, like your heartbeat. *O man, make the remembrance of the divine a refrain in your heart.*

Without this remembrance,
With only man, man, man in your mind...

This is what I have been saying to you for so long. Until one
has remembered the divine, there is nothing more than "man"
in man. And when there is nothing more than "man" in a
man, there is nothing in him. Think a little: if there is
nothing inside you but you, what is there?

Without this remembrance,
With only man, man, man in your mind...

There is nothing but man, nothing but man inside your
head, there is nothing else. Just you, and your mind. That
is why you are empty of meaning. The meaning comes from
beyond you. The meaning comes from afar. The meaning
comes from above. You are meaningless. Meaning can never
be in you, meaning always comes from beyond you.

Have you seen? When a woman cooks for herself there will
be no joy in her cooking. It will be all right – she has to cook.
But when her beloved is coming home after many years, then
there will be a thrill in her, then she will dance, then she will
hum to herself, then there will be great enjoyment in her
cooking! Someone beyond her has added something extra to
the process. And when a woman becomes a mother, another
fragrance, something extraordinary, comes into her life. A
woman is a woman. As soon as a child is born, new meaning
comes into her life, now there is a purpose in her life. A man
lives for himself, and that is all right, but then he falls in
love with a woman and his walk changes. A radiance appears
on his face. Something beyond him has been added to his
life.

And all these are very small matters. They are certainly not
the most important things to come from the beyond. They

are very small indeed. But you do not end at your small circumference. Another circumference has joined it and has given it meaning.

When an artist creates a painting, his life has meaning. He is totally devoted to the beauty of that painting. He is making something bigger than himself. The artist will die, but his painting will remain. The sculptor may make a statue, a statue of Buddha. The sculptor will die, but his statue will remain for centuries after him. Something bigger than him is being added. Whenever you allow something beyond yourself to enter into you, then the fragrance of meaning enters your life.

So these are very small matters. The divine is the great event. On the day the ocean of the divine is added to your tiny drop, infinite meaning enters your life, eternal sky, eternal space enters your life. You have expanded. Then you have no boundary.

When there are limitations, there is sorrow. With the limitless, there is bliss. Wherever there is a boundary there is a prison, there is a wall. When there is no boundary — and as soon as one unites with the divine one has no boundary — there is bliss.

Without this remembrance,
With only man, man, man in your mind,
In wretchedness will you weep and wail.
In the grip of maya,
Your mind will never be still.

And when there is nothing but man inside you, you will weep

and wail, you will continually be a beggar crying and whining —...*in the grip of maya, your mind will never be still.* And in this turmoil, this crying, this dejection, this beggarliness, your mind can never be still. You will go on wandering from door to door, begging:

...In wretchedness will you weep and wail.
In the grip of maya,
Your mind will never be still.

And as long as illusion resides in your heart, you will be a beggar, your mind will never be still, will never be peaceful. It won't come to a stop, it won't find rest. All stillness lives in the divine, all rest dwells in the divine.

In this country for centuries the place where one explores the divine has been called an *ashram*. "Ashram" means where rest resides. "Ashram" means where you can pause, where there is peace, where your mind will become still. If you remain attached to that which changes, you will continue to weep and wail. You will cry, you will lament. Become attached to the eternal, to that which does not change. If you have to marry, if you have to follow the rituals of marriage, then says Kabir, marry the bride called the divine. Then who cares about lesser brides and lesser bridegrooms? Then let the great wedding take place:

...In wretchedness you will weep and wail.
In the grip of maya,
Your mind will never be still.

The mind rests when it remembers the divine,
Life has a meaning with his name.

"The mind rests when it remembers the divine...." You will reach this state of rest only when you reach the state of remembering the divine: "...life has a meaning with his name." And only when you are joined with him does your life have meaning — not before that.

Remember that life is an opportunity to wed the divine. Don't die a bachelor, like you are now.

Life wanders through the dark desert,
What has happened to the stars
That appeared on the horizon?

...Otherwise you will sink just like the stars that rise and set on the horizon. They rise with no meaning and they set with no meaning. The flowers that blossom today wither tomorrow. "Life wanders through the dark desert." Life wanders aimlessly in this desert of life. Flowers blossom, wither and fall. You are born, you die, you are born again and die again. This is what has been happening with you. You arose, you set; you arose and set. Morning came, then the evening; this has been happening for life after life. How long, for how long will you go on rising and setting like this? If you had become one with the divine, then you would have risen forever. Then there is only the rising, there is never any setting.

And sooner or later the present intoxications that appear to be giving some meaning to your life are snatched away. Some intoxications are from childhood and they are taken away by youth. Youth has its own intoxications, and old age takes them away. A few dead and withered intoxications still remain in your old age, and death takes them away.

Childhood has many intoxications: "One day I will become this, one day I will become that."

Mulla Nasruddin was telling me, "When I was young I swore I wouldn't rest until I was a millionaire."

So I asked him, "Then what happened?"

He said, "Well, when I was eighteen I saw that it is easier to forget a vow than to keep it."

A millionaire! It is easier to change the vow. In childhood everyone has their dreams. Who knows what those dreams want him to be? But youth takes those dreams away. Then in youth there are other dreams – the dreams of love. Old age takes them away. A few dreams still remain in old age – of respectability, of honor – and death snatches even those away. In this world, your intoxications are continually snatched away. The person who doesn't wait for the arrival of death to take them away is wise. A discerning person understands the future. There is no wisdom in understanding the past. Absolutely no wisdom is required to understand the past. One who sees what is going to happen in advance, who wakes up to it before its time comes, is wise.

Alas, there was a time
When I was intoxicated without drinking,
Alas, now I am not even drunk after drinking.

There was a time in your life when you could be drunk without wine – you were young and always intoxicated. Then there will come a time when you are never intoxicated, no matter how much you drink. Drop all intoxications before this time comes! And I am not asking you just to drop all intoxications, I am telling you that there is one intoxication after which you will never be sober again. That is the intoxication which comes from drinking the divine.

This is what Daya has said,...*those who are in love with the divine.* It is the intoxication which never allows you to be sober again. It is the unrestrained ecstasy which never leaves you. It is an eternal intoxication.

We will try to find the same unrestrained ecstasy in these small couplets of Daya. But keep in mind the first clue:

The world is like the last morning star.
Sahajo says: It is fast disappearing.
Like a pearl of dew,
Like water held in the hollow of your hands.

The first step lies in realizing that the world is futile, that it has no substance. Then we can take the second step towards finding the substantial, the meaningful. To recognize untruth as untruth is to take the first step towards the truth.

Enough for today.

2

LOVE CAN WAIT FOR LIFETIMES

The first question

Osho,

The thirst doesn't arise and my doors don't open.

No one can make himself thirsty. You may search for water, but you cannot make yourself thirsty. If the thirst is there, it is there. If it is not there, you must wait. You cannot force yourself to be thirsty, and there is no need. When the right time comes, your very being will be ripe and the thirst will arise. And it is good that nothing happens before its time.

Your mind is greedy. For example a young child who hears about love, about sexual intercourse, or who gets hold of Vatsyayana's Kamasutra begins to wonder how he too could feel such sexual passions, and a greed arises in him. But a young child cannot feel sexual passion; he must wait. His passions will come when his sexual energy ripens. And the passion for the divine ripens in the same way as our sexual energy ripens. There is no other way. And there is no need to make it happen earlier either.

But when you hear others talk, you feel greedy, you start to wonder when you will meet with the divine. You have seen Daya singing about the divine, you have seen Meera swaying with unrestrained ecstasy — and your greed quivers inside you. You want to have the same unrestrained joy. You don't care about the divine, it is this uninhibited joy which attracts you. You want this ecstasy. You see a divine drunkard swaying along the road and you want to experience a similar state of drunkenness. Your concern is not about the divine wine — perhaps you are not even aware of the wine — but this man's uninhibited ecstasy triggers a jealousy in you.

Remember: coming close to an enlightened mystic can trigger jealousy in you in the same way as it can trigger prayerfulness. It will be difficult if jealousy arises. A great uneasiness can be born in you because you have no thirst. And when there is no thirst, a stream of water may be flowing by your side, but what are you supposed to do with it? When your throat is not dry, what do you care about a river? And even if you do drink, you won't experience contentment, because contentment comes only when first there is discontent — otherwise you may even feel like vomiting.

No. Never hurry. Be patient, be trusting. When the time comes you will be ready, you will be ripe. And understand what that ripening means. To be ripe means that all the pleasures of the world now seem pointless to you. Only then will the thirst for the divine arise in you. You have not yet known the futility of worldly pleasures. They won't be seen as futile to you just because I have told you that they are. How can they become futile to you just because I say so? Old people go on telling children: "Toys are useless. Why are you wasting your time with useless toys? There is no point in them" — but children go on seeing a significance in their toys.

A young child was talking to his doll. His mother said, "Stop this silly chatter." He ran away. His mother didn't understand why he ran away so quickly.

He came back shortly afterwards and said, "What were you saying?" He had come back without his doll.

So his mother asked, "Why did you run away so fast?"

He replied, "The doll would have been sad if she had heard what you were saying, so I have put her to sleep. Now, tell me what you wanted to say."

It may seem to you that the child is talking nonsense, but in that moment the doll is alive for him, the doll will be hurt. For him, the very idea of not talking to the doll will offend her, will annoy her.

The child's truth is not the same as an old man's truth, and an old man's truth is not the same as a child's truth. And if a child is forced to throw away his doll because he thinks that what the old people say must be right because they are adults, he will not be able to sleep at night. His sleep will be continually disturbed. "What is happening to my doll? I hope no one is tormenting her in the dark! She may be scared of the dark! It rains at night – maybe she is getting wet! Maybe some animal or some wicked person is torturing her!" He won't be able to sleep. He will dream of the doll the whole night. The time for him to let go of his doll has not yet come.

One day that time comes. One day the child suddenly sees that the doll is only a doll, that there is no sense in talking

to it. The doll has never heard anything he has said. Smiling
and laughing at his own foolishness, he will put the doll in
a corner and move on. After that he will not even look at it
again. It is the same with life.

I understand your difficulty. You are greedy for happiness. You are seeking happiness in wealth, in power —
everywhere. You haven't found it yet, but you have also not
yet realized that happiness cannot be found there.

This is your dilemma. You have not found happiness. It
cannot be found. No one has ever found it. No matter how
young you are and no matter how much faith you have that
the doll will answer you; it never does, it never speaks. There
is no way it can. No one has ever found happiness in this
way. You haven't found it either, but your hope has not yet
died. You think it is possible to find it, you think that the
doll will speak: "Let me try a little harder. Let me try to
persuade it a little more, let me wait a little longer. Perhaps
I didn't work hard enough; perhaps I didn't work as much
as I should have done. Perhaps my race is half-hearted.
Perhaps I didn't run properly, I didn't stake my life totally.
Let me stake it one more time."

Your hopes have not yet died. Your hopes are fully alive. And
this is where the world exists — in those hopes. When your
hopes are shattered...and this doesn't mean that they will
be shattered by simply listening to someone else — otherwise
a child would become old by simply listening to an old man
talking. If they are shattered by listening to someone else,
they have not really been shattered. You will go and sit in a
temple but you will think about the marketplace. You may
become an ascetic, renounce the world and sit in a cave in

the Himalayas, but you will still be thinking about your wife and children. And there is nothing wrong in that, it is completely natural. I don't even say that you will be making a mistake by doing this.

One day Mulla Nasruddin took his battered watch to be repaired. It was in such a state that it was difficult to recognize that it had once been a watch. He had dropped it from the seventh floor of a building. He had leaned over to look at something below, stretched out too far, and the watch had slipped out of his pocket.

Because it fell so far, it was completely ruined. When he put the many broken bits and pieces of metal on the watch-maker's table, the watchmaker looked at them carefully and then adjusted his glasses, as if trying to see what this object was. Finally he asked, "What is it, good sir?"

Nasruddin said, "This is the limit! Can't you see that it's a pocket watch?"

The watchmaker exclaimed, "Why did you...?" That was all he said, "Why did you...?"

Mulla thought he was about to ask, "Why did you drop it?" so he replied, "What could I do? It just fell. I was looking out from a seventh story window and I made a mistake."

The watchmaker said, "I am not asking you why you dropped it. I want to know why you picked it up? Why did you bother?"

The day you wake up, you will find that there was nothing to life. On that day you will not worry about letting go, you will wonder why you held on for so long! "Why did I pick up the watch?" It is not that you will think about the greatness of renouncing. On that day you will wonder why you were engrossed in pleasures for so long. "How did this happen? Why was I so blind? Why was I in such ignorance? Why was I so unconscious when there was nothing there?"

There is a saying in the West that a philosopher is a man who is looking for a black cat on a pitch black night, in a room without a light – looking for a cat which is not even there in the first place. This is the story of your life. You are looking for a black cat in a dark room on a dark night, and the cat is not even there in the first place. There is no way you can find it. But it is pitch dark and you think that the cat is black, so you keep looking for it. You cannot see it at the moment, but if you keep looking for it you might just find it. No one has ever found it.

But don't leave the room just because someone else tells you all this, otherwise you will keep wandering, you will keep coming back to the same room again and again. Even if you don't come back physically your mind will come back, your thinking processes will come back, your thoughts will come back, your dreams will come back. It makes no difference whether you sit with a woman with your eyes open or shut. What difference does it make if you count real money or imaginary coins? It makes no difference. Wealth as such is mere imagination. Apparently real coins, those that jingle when you throw them down on a stone, are just as imaginary as the ones you count with your eyes shut. Both are figments of the imagination. But it cannot become a fiction to you just because I say so. Experiences cannot be borrowed.

I understand your difficulty. You say: "The thirst doesn't arise and my doors don't open." You are looking for a borrowed experience. Avoid borrowing. It is the borrowing that has destroyed you. It is this borrowing that has led you astray for so long. Now, stop borrowing. Now, if you feel that there is some happiness in this world, then try your utmost for it. Try for it – with your whole body, mind and soul. Don't leave a single stone unturned – because it is the untried that will torment you, it is the untried that will pursue you. The world itself doesn't pursue you, but those corners in the world that you have not entered, those corners that are unlived, unvisited, are the ones that pursue you. You are free from what you have known. You remain tied to the unknown.

So come down a few steps. If the thirst doesn't arise in you, why try to awaken it? You might still be thirsty for the world. Both thirsts cannot exist together. Until you have a thirst for the unreal there cannot be a thirst for the real in you. Until you are interested in drinking untruth, there can be no interest in drinking the truth. There is still interest in the unreal, there is still interest in egoism. Egoism means the false. Right now you want position, prestige, the throne – you have an interest in your egoism. Go through these pleasures. And there is nothing to be afraid of, because these pleasures are not really there. The cat is not in the room. That's why I say to search with courage, to search in every nook and corner. Search inch by inch.

Your so-called saints are tremendously afraid. Your so-called saints also seem to have borrowed everything. They say to you, "Don't go into the world, you will become entangled." I say to you: Go! How can you become entangled? What is there to entangle you? Yes, if you don't go totally, then you will remain entangled. Then your mind will always say, "If only I had gone! Perhaps I would have found it...who knows? Some parts have remained unknown, the treasure might just be there, that might be exactly the place – and I missed!" How can you be absolutely sure that there was no truth there, that there was nothing but falsehood, that there was only delusion there?

So I say to you: Go. Go where your interest takes you. Don't try to convert your interest. The interest must be there somewhere. There is no one who doesn't have an interest somewhere. Such a person couldn't live, not even for one moment. Why should a person who has no interest anywhere want to continue breathing? Why should he get up in the morning again and again? Why should he walk anywhere? Why should he open his eyes? A man who has no interests at all will be dead in that same moment, in that very moment! There is no way for him to live even a moment longer. If the desire to live goes, then life also goes.

So you must have an interest somewhere or other. I understand your difficulty. Your interest drives you towards wealth, towards position, and your so-called holy men are holding you back. They are saying, "Where are you going? There is nothing there." You fall into a dilemma: "Should I listen to the holy ones? What they are saying seems to be right – they are nice, decent people...." But your heart tells you, "Look for it, right now."

A *maulvi* spoke in the mosque. After his speech he said, "All those who want to go to heaven, please stand up." Everyone except Mulla Nasruddin stood up. The *maulvi* was a little perplexed. When everyone sat down again, the *maulvi* said, "Now please stand up all those who want to go to hell." No one stood up, and Mulla still remained seated. Then the *maulvi* said, "Mulla, what do you want? Don't you want to go anywhere?"

Mulla replied, "I do want to go to heaven, but not right now. And you are talking as if the bus is waiting outside and everyone has to get ready to go. Not yet! I want to go to heaven, but not yet. There is still plenty to do here. My desires are not yet fulfilled."

The Mulla is a more honest person. If all the people who stood up knew that a bus was actually waiting outside, they would sit down again. They want to express their desire to go to heaven, but not yet. Who wants to go to heaven right now? Right now, there is plenty left to do in this world. You have plans, you have ambitions. Your dreams haven't been shattered yet. Right now, your dreams are spread out like rainbows – tremendous rainbow bridges are there. Right now, you can see mirages on the distant horizon. Right now, you think, "We are almost there. We have nearly arrived. However far it may be to Delhi, it is not really that far. It seems we are very close – we have almost reached it. We are about to arrive. Two more steps, or four more steps…we will soon be there. A little more hard work, a little more toil, a little more waiting…." Your mind continues to tell you these things.

Your interest is in the world. But when you look at the faces of the worldly people, it begins to seem improbable that you will ever get what you desire because none of them seem to have got what they wanted. Then you look at the holy men, at the sages – it seems that they may have found what they wanted…peaceful, blissful…but your experience within you says, "Not yet, not right now; search a little more. Who knows, I might be able to find what no one else has ever found."

One of the most basic things about the mind is that it always tells you that you may be an exception. Although no one else ever got what he wanted, does this prove that you also won't get what you want? One rule about the mind is that it always exempts you. It says, "You may be different." Everyone dies, the earth is a graveyard, someone dies every day, but your mind still says to you, "It is others who die. That doesn't mean that you will die. Have you died yet? When did you die? Have you ever seen yourself dead? Maybe you won't die!"

Until the very last moment man continues to think that death always happens to other people but not to himself. It is always someone else's coffin you see being taken away, not yours. You have been in other people's funeral processions. Has anyone ever taken you to the cremation ground? A hope remains inside you that maybe God will spare you from this rule.

When a thief goes out to steal he also knows that thieves get caught, but he still thinks, "Perhaps I won't get caught. Others get caught: they must get caught because they are not skillful enough. Perhaps they don't know the art of stealing."

When a murderer kills someone he knows what the consequences of a murder are, but he thinks, "Will I get caught? No. I will do it so skillfully and with such attention to every detail that they won't be able to catch me."

You use this rule every day. You were angry yesterday, you were angry the day before – and every time you were angry you felt sad. But today you are being angry again. You think that maybe it won't bring sadness this time, maybe it won't bring regrets this time. How many times have your hands been pricked by thorns and bled? But you still want to play with the thorn just one more time – perhaps this time the thorn will turn into a flower, perhaps this time the thorn will have mercy, perhaps because you have learned so much from life the thorn will not trouble you any more. In this way your mind continues to exempt you.

One who starts seeing the eternal rule of life, which is that: I am no exception. I too will die, I too will become dust and remain as dust; all my positions and prestige will not save me. No matter how much wealth I may have, there is no safety from death. The day a person has seen this clearly, a revolution takes place in his life. On that day the same thirst that was directed towards the world, towards the outer, turns towards the inner, towards the divine. Wait!

Love is restless but also patience-testing.
The soul is bliss-nourishing and pain-loving too.

Love is always eager to obtain its object: "Love is restless but also patience-testing." Love is eager to obtain its object; and yet it is patient, capable of waiting. These are the two contradictory aspects of love. Love is restless, it is eager to obtain its object, and yet at the same time it is capable of waiting. Love can wait for lifetimes. This is its contradiction; you won't understand it outwardly.

Have you seen a beloved waiting at the door for her lover?

How restless she is! Even the rustle of a dry leaf makes her jump up, hoping that her lover has come. When a gust of wind touches the door, she runs to open the door – perhaps her lover has come.

Don't you remember a time when you were waiting for a letter? Someone passed by on the road and you ran out in case it was the postman. You might be engaged in a thousand jobs but your heart remains at the door waiting for the guest, hoping you have not missed him. You are afraid that you might not be there to welcome him. There is quite an uneasiness, an eagerness – but also a great patience. You are very restless, eager; but you are also very patient. Even if you have to wait for lifetime after lifetime, there will be joy in your waiting. You will wait.

So there is impatience in love and there is also patience. Love is a meeting of the opposites.

So one thing: if the thirst has not yet arisen don't worry, don't be hasty. Enjoy the experiences of life. If you think that you are freed from your interest with the world – not by listening to someone, but through experiencing – if you think that the world has become insipid, then be a little patient. Something is on its way, some other interest must be on its way. Be a little patient. Sometimes there is a small interval between the two. Sometimes there is a short rest between one journey and another. One race ends and there is a short stopover before the next race begins.

It is possible that you may be really finished with this world. Then there is nothing to worry about. Then a little endurance, a little patience, little wait...soon, the new race will begin. You have always been running on the outside, now it has stopped. So give your energy a chance – to turn around, to go back, to form a new habit, to learn a new style and a new way, to find a new direction. Give it a chance.

Ordinarily man is like this. When Ford made his first car, it didn't have a reverse gear. He hadn't thought of it. There was a forward gear, but there was no reverse gear. It took experience to realize that this was a problem. People would go a little too far beyond their house and then they would have to go around many miles to return home as there was no way for them to turn around. Even if you just took the car out of the garage, you could not put it back in without making a trip around the whole village. So a reverse gear was installed.

The car of your mind has been going forward for many lives with no reverse gear. It only goes forward, outwards. It only goes towards the other. There is no provision for bringing it back to yourself. You have never even thought about coming back into your garage. As it is, the only way for you to come back to yourself is to travel around the world. And the world is big: even after many lifetimes, your journey does not finish. It is vast.

So sometimes it is possible that one's interest in the outer has truly finished, but it will take a while before one can add the reverse gear. The provision is there, but the gear has become rusty. It is there inside you – because the divine didn't make you capable of going in only one direction, it has made you so that you can go inwards as well as outwards. In the end you have to go inwards. There is nothing wrong with your mechanism, but because you have not used it for so long…for lifetime upon lifetime you haven't tried turning inwards, you haven't looked within.

If a man never looks behind, his neck will become stiff. Then later, when he tries to look back after years and years, his muscles will have hardened and his neck will snap. This is exactly the way your mind is. So have a little patience, wait a little….

"The thirst doesn't arise and my doors don't open." How can the doors open? It is thirst that knocks at the door. When you writhe in agony because you are thirsty, when you writhe like a fish because you are thirsty – like a fish taken out of water and thrown onto the shore – when you feel the world in the same way that the fish feels the burning sand and when you writhe in longing for the divine like a fish wanting to go back into the ocean, then you begin to knock at the door.

Jesus has said: "Knock and the doors shall be opened." But what does it mean to knock? Of course, there are no physical doors there; you cannot take hold of the bell and ring it. We are talking about the inner door. There, there is no physical door and no bell. This will happen when longing arises from your whole being. Just as you longed for your wife, for your child, for wealth and position, for the world – on the day when all your longings merge into one single stream and become a longing for the divine, on that day the door will open by itself. What door can remain standing, remain shut in the face of such a mighty stream? The stream is full, it is in flood; your whole energy is in a mighty flow…. The doors will collapse. And in reality there are no closed or locked doors. The divine is not hiding itself from you. The divine is calling you – it is you who doesn't want to hear. The

divine is knocking at your door every day – but until you
begin to knock at its door there can be no meeting, no union.
How can there be? So if the thirst doesn't arise, certainly the
doors won't open.

So, there are two things here. The first is: if you still have
some interest in the world, then don't be in a hurry. The divine
has given you the world for this very reason, so that you can
experience it fully, so that this experience can tell you
that there is nothing outside of you, that nothing worth
obtaining is outside of you. This is an empty, meaningless
race. Your hands remain empty as they always were and your
life is never fulfilled.

The world is there so you can gain experience.

One day Mulla Nasruddin told his young son to climb a
ladder. The boy climbed the ladder. Then Mulla asked him
to jump down: "Jump into my arms." The son was a little
scared. If he jumped from such a height he might slip out
of his father's reach and fall. Mulla said: "Why are you afraid?
Don't you trust me?"

The son jumped and Mulla moved away. The boy crashed on
the earth. He began to cry and said, "Why did you do that?"

Mulla said, "I wanted to teach you a lesson. Don't even trust
your own father. Don't ever trust anyone. That is the characteristic of a wise man. Do you understand?"

The divine has created the world for you to experience. But
don't depend on the outer. There are many beautiful tempta-
tions here. The music of distant drums feels very hypnotic,

but they are hypnotic only at a distance. As you get closer their charm vanishes. When you finally reach them, their charm is just a mirage.

And the world was created so that you can come to know that the real wealth is inside you. As long as you keep searching for it outside yourself you will remain poor. On the day you are tired of searching outside yourself and you quit the search...closing your eyes, diving within yourself, you will find that the wealth of all wealths was always present inside you.

You were sent here to be an emperor. But you can only be an emperor after you have experienced all the outer poverties. Without knowing that poverty, the experience of being an emperor doesn't happen. If you haven't seen the darkness, you cannot see the light. If you haven't known the thorn, you cannot know the beauty of a flower. If you haven't experienced the futile, meaningfulness cannot descend in your life.

People ask me: Why does the world exist in the first place? The world exists so that you can have the experience of opposites. We can see that in our schools. When we teach children, we write with white chalk on a black board. We could write on a white board, but our writing wouldn't be legible. You never ask why one writes on a blackboard. You can see the letters clearly on a blackboard. If you want to write on a white board, you must use black chalk.

This world is a blackboard: on it your life energy can manifest at its purest, its brightest. This cannot happen without it.

The sorrow of this world is the background, and it is on this background that the ultimate bliss of life manifests itself. There is no other way. Life manifests itself against the background of death. One finds out about success through failure, about bliss through anguish, about attainment through loss. The throat will only know what it is to be quenched through being thirsty. You can only be replete when you are hungry.

This world is a device created by the divine. You will never reach your self unless you enter this world. If you have not yet entered this world, if there is still some interest and pull in your heart – go out! Go, without any hesitation. Don't listen to anyone else. Even if you do listen, do only what you want to do. Go! When you yourself find that the world is nothing but sand, and that oil cannot be squeezed from sand, then you will begin coming home. Only on that day will you understand what the scriptures say. Only on that day will the doors open. Only on that day will you find no resistance at the door. In fact, the doors are already open.

The gardens ran wild, the buds blossomed,
The courtyards hummed, the lanes danced in delight,
But my doors didn't open.
A lifetime has passed trying to open the door,
What chains did you place there?
You forgot. You didn't even send me a letter.
The dwelling that is my heart is empty.
The sweet-smelling sandalwood fire is lit,
Beloved, enough of these games of hide and seek.
Hear me now.
The morning has turned to evening.
You forgot. You didn't even send me a letter!

When your morning turns to evening, when you have been endlessly searching and searching, when you are tired and defeated, when you stop running and fall down, the door will open of its own accord, the lock will turn. In that moment the divine descends.

An intense experience of the world is an essential part in the search for the divine. The world is not the opposite of the divine; the world is the backdrop in the search for the divine. Knowing this will change your entire outlook.

There is not much value in what your so-called saints tell you. They explain to you that the world is the enemy of the divine and that the divine is the enemy of the world. This is very strange – and you never ask them about it, even though they are the ones who also tell you that the divine created the world. The divine is the creator, and then they convince you that the world is the enemy of the divine. Both of these things cannot be correct. If the divine is the one who created the world, how can he be its enemy? And if he is its enemy, how could he have created it?

No! The world is not the enemy of the divine. The world is the compulsory journey towards the divine. You must go through it; it is a compulsory journey. If you escape from it, if you quit in the middle and run away, you won't be able to find the divine. It is a test. You must pass through it.

The second question:

Osho,

You are in the sun, you are in the moon. You are all around. Without my knowing and without my asking, I have found such a spring of bliss in you that I have drowned in it. But you say that one has to be free of this as well. Why should I deliberately throw away such bliss?

Nirupama has asked this. What she is saying is right. When one is in bliss why should one want to throw it away? But you must understand this.

There is one happiness which the world keeps promising, but you will never get it. One hopes for happiness, but all you find is sorrow. The door is marked "happiness," but once you are inside all you will find is sorrow. There is the happiness of the world which is false. There is the bliss of the divine which is real. Between these two stands the master. The master is the door. The master is where you enter the divine from the side of the world. The master is the shade of a tree which is available to the wayfarer who is tired of walking in the sun and wants to rest. The master is that shade.

But he is only a resting place, a stopover, not your final destination. You will receive happiness, much happiness. And you have never known any happiness in the world, so you will find great happiness in the presence of the master, in his love, in his blessing. And you have never known any other happiness, you have never known anything greater than this. So your heart will say, "Why should we let go of this? Let us hold tightly onto it." But if the master is a true master, he will tell you that there is the possibility of a still greater happiness, he will tell you not to be in such a hurry to hold on to it. He will say: "Look. When you left the world, you found me. If you leave me as well, you will find the ultimate reality. You listened to me and found so much happiness when you left the world. Now listen to me a little more; if you let go of me too you will find eternal happiness."

But I understand the devotee's distress. He has never found a garden in the desert of this world. There was nothing but thirst, there was only hunger, nothing but a burning. He was continually lost. Now he has found somewhere to rest, tranquillity, a spring, a cascading waterfall, with green trees besides the waterfall, and green grass. He has begun to rest on the green grass. He has drunk from the waterfall, he has sat in the shade of the trees. How can he give this up just because someone asks him to? He knows only two options. If he leaves the oasis he will be back in the desert again. He knows only these two things. To leave the oasis means going back to the desert. There is no third choice.

But what does the master say? The master says that the small waterfall flowing here is connected to the ocean. This stream is not here by itself. Left to itself, all waterfalls will dry up. How long can they last if their source is in themselves, not in the ocean? They will soon run out of water. A waterfall is not like a pond. A pond is closed, it has nothing beyond itself; its water soon becomes stagnant and decays. It is soon exhausted. The water of the pond is always dead.

This is the difference between an enlightened mystic and a *pundit*. A *pundit* is a pond. The water in the pond appears to be the same as that of the waterfall, but its water is dead, borrowed, stagnant, rotting. There is no living source to keep it fresh, alive, clean. When water flows it is clean; when it stops flowing it becomes dirty.

The master is a waterfall. The enlightened one is one in whom the divine is cascading down. What you see in the master is the *Gomukh* at Gangotri, the source point of the Ganges. When the Ganges descends at Gangotri, it comes from a small gorge called Gomukh, which means "the mouth of a cow."

The master is like that mouth: he is the mouth, but what is falling, cascading through him is the divine. Now don't sit down and cling to this small stream. There is a happiness in this stream, but compared to the boundlessness from where this stream comes, this happiness is nothing.

So a master who makes you stay with him is not really a master. The true master says to you: Come to me and go beyond me. Take hold of me and then let go of me. Make a ladder of me, climb on it, but don't stop.

What do you do with a ladder? You climb it. But then you don't sit on the ladder thinking, "The ladder has brought me so far, lifted me so high, how can I ever abandon it?"

You sit in a boat.... Buddha often said that the master is like a boat. You sit in a boat; you use it to go from this shore to the other shore. When you arrive, you don't carry the boat on your head. You don't say, "This boat brought me to this shore, gave me such happiness, helped me to leave the darkness and reach to the light. Now I will carry it on my head, I will turn it into a deity, I will worship it and never abandon it." Then it becomes a complication.

Buddha tells this story:

Once four fools crossed a river and carried the boat on their heads to the marketplace. People asked them, "What are you doing? We have seen people inside boats, but never a boat on top of people."

But the four men said, "We will never leave this boat. It is so dear to us. We could only reach this shore because of the boat. It was very dangerous on the other shore. It was night, very dark, there were wild animals all around, but this boat saved us. We are so grateful, we will never leave it. We have set it over us. It is our crowning glory. It is so precious, we will guard it with our lives."

Buddha has said, "Someone should explain to those madmen that one uses a boat to cross over and then be thankful that there has been something to take you across — but there is absolutely no need to carry the boat on your head. That is stupidity."

So I can understand. Nirupama is right when she says, "In finding you, I have found happiness, shade, and shelter. Now you tell me to go beyond you." It is painful. I understand that too. It hurts. I can understand that as well, because there are only two experiences that you know — the first is your experience before you met your master and the second is the experience after meeting the master.

But I have three experiences. Keep remembrance of the third one too which lies ahead. And when the master asks you to let go of him so that you can move ahead, please have trust in what someone who has given you so much happiness has to say. You can have even greater happiness in the future.

The divine is the ultimate master. For this reason, we also call the master the divine, because the master is nothing but a representative of the ultimate reality in a small form. And the divine is an expansion of the master in a vast form.

When I ask you to let go of me, you will not really be leaving me. When I ask you to let go of me, you will find me in an even bigger form, in a vast form — where there will be no boundary, where the waterfall will no longer be a waterfall, where it will be the ocean. Even the smallest of small waterfalls is connected with the ocean. Its water comes from the ocean, its water belongs to the ocean.

Wherever there is knowing and wherever there is light, it all flows from existence, the divine.

So the master is "Gomukh" — the cow's mouth from where the Ganges flows. Drink to your heart's content; bathe, dive deeply into it. But learn only this much from all this experience — that you have to go forward, you have to keep moving on ahead. You should not stop anywhere until you have reached the ultimate point beyond which there is nowhere else to go. That is what we call the divine — the ultimate point beyond which there is no longer anywhere else to go. Beyond the master, there is still one place more to reach to.

That is why Nanak called the Sikh temple a *gurudwara*. The word is appropriate. It means: "The *guru* is a door." One doesn't stop at the door, one only passes through the door. You don't remain sitting at the door. If you sit at the threshold you are mad. You will be neither inside nor outside. You will simply be like the washerman's donkey which it is said belongs neither at home nor at the washing *ghats*. You must go in. You must cross the threshold, you must pass beyond the door.

There are so many words for temples — a mosque, a Buddhist *chaityalaya*, a church, a synagogue — but there is no word more beautiful than the one used by the Sikhs: a gurudwara. It is very profound. It means the master is the door. Take his support, but go beyond him. This doesn't mean that you have not been grateful. Once you cross over, you will be even more grateful. Understand this. If you have received so much happiness from being with the master, if you are so grateful, then you will experience supreme gratitude when you go beyond him.

This is why Kabir has said: *Guru Govind doi khare, kake lagun paon?* "The master and God are both in front of me. Whose feet should I touch first?" – whose feet should I bow down to first? Both are standing in front of me. I am afraid I may insult the master if I touch God's feet first! I am afraid I may insult God if I touch the master's feet first! It is a great dilemma.

The person who faces such a difficulty one day is fortunate indeed. The day you face it, how fortunate you will be! It will be a difficult moment, but a great blessing when it happens to you. "The master and God are both in front of me, whose feet should I touch first?" Who should I go to first? I intend no disrespect to either, I am simply afraid I may do the wrong thing.

Of course Kabir was nervous. On one side was Ramananda, his master, and on the other was Rama. Whose feet should he touch first?

Kabir's lines are wonderful:

The master and God both stand in front of me.
Whose feet should I touch first?
I offer myself to you, my master,
You pointed me towards God.

The master says: "Don't hesitate. Don't deliberate anymore. Touch the feet of God."

This is what the couplet says. It can have many meanings, but I believe that Kabir fell at the feet of the master first. This meaning seems to be more significant. Because when he says, "I offer myself to you, my master," he must have hesitated, seeing them both in front of him and wondered, "Whose feet should I touch first?" The master must then have pointed towards God, "Touch his feet, don't worry about me."

But how could he touch the feet of God first? When the compassion of the master is so great that he helps to release us even from himself, one has to touch his feet first. This is why Kabir says, "I offer myself to you, my master" – how great of you to show me what to do, otherwise I would have been in great difficulty. You gave the final hint too, you told me to leave you.

So I believe he must have touched the master's feet first, because one has to express gratitude for this. The very meaning of "the master" is one who brings you out of the world and takes you to the divine.

So Nirupama...so far, I have taken you out of the world. This is half of the journey. Your journey is not yet over. And such bliss from only half of the journey, such intoxication! When such a song emanates from half the journey, when such a joyous fragrance is spread, then imagine what the complete journey must offer. You have not yet reached the destination, you are only at a resting place midway. Don't let any attachment grow. Don't cling and stop here. It is natural to want to stop, even though you know this.

Because you have come, the house has a beauty,
How colorful my evening is becoming.

Even if the master comes at the twilight of your life, even if
he comes in the last moments of your life – "How colorful
my evening is becoming"–your evening will become morning,
your old age will become your childhood. Flowers will
blossom, lotuses will bloom, spring will come again.

So I think that your distress is quite natural.

From the distance,
Ringing reverberations of lightbeams' strings,
Melodies of dreams drowning in the earth's song,
Million upon million of lamp-like stars vanishing
Into the faint smile on the lips of the eastern sky.
It is dawn: the flutes of the trees begin to sway,
The leaves rustle,
And each and every branch begin to dance.

Your life energy will delight. The touch of the master will
fill every pore of your body with an unprecedented bliss. A
new dance will be born. In your innermost being you will
begin to hear a song that you have never sung. A flute
will begin to play which has never been played before, but
which you have been longing for for lifetimes. Something
will start to become faintly visible. The destination may still
be far away, but it will begin to shimmer into sight. You
will be able to catch a glimpse of it. It is like the lofty peaks
of the Himalayas seen from far away: from thousands of
miles away the white, snow-capped lofty peaks of the
Himalayas have started to become visible. They will still be
hazy, covered by clouds. Sometimes you won't be able to see

them, and then you will find them again. Sometimes you will
see them, sometimes you won't. These things will happen.

But you shouldn't stop. You have to take the glimpse you
have seen to the point where it becomes the reality of your
life. The happiness you have received so far has come through
me. You will have to reach the point where the divine showers
directly onto your life and you don't need me as a medium
anymore. Even if I remain between you and the divine that
much hindrance, that much of a veil will still be there. It
might be a beautiful veil, it might be a veil of gold and silver,
a veil studded with gems and diamonds – but it will still be
a veil. You are not to keep even that much of a screen. You
have to take away the master's veil as well.

You have taken me by the hand,
This much support is enough.

This is what one will feel like saying – because so much
happens that you will wonder what more can happen.
If a single drop of the elixir of immortality touches your lips,
you will feel that nothing more than that is possible.

You have taken me by the hand,
This much support is enough.
You look at me with loving glances,
This much giving is enough.

Even if the lamp of beauty burns in the far distance,
At least it is burning.
By taking it as a beacon,
At least the traveler called life-breath
Can travel on his arduous path.
To brighten my path,
This much light is enough.

Long had my loneliness pined
For someone to be intimate.
Now, since you came into my life
The whole world seems to be mine.
You are in some way mine,
This much privilege is enough.

My lips are soaked with laughter,
The garden of my heart is fragrant,
The lovelorn crested cuckoo of my being warbles,
The deepest monsoon month of remembrance showers
To keep my whole life green.
This much juice is enough.

How very fortunate is my heart –
I have received the gift of lifetimes,
I have found a sweet song to sing,
I have found a God to worship.
I can never repay this debt,
This much love is enough.

I understand. I understand what you are saying. If I was in
your place I would also say the same:

You have taken me by the hand,
This much support is enough.

But there is still much more to happen. Why look at the lamp
from a distance? One has to come close to it. Not only does
one need to come close, one has to immerse oneself in the
lamp, to become one with it.

Have you seen how the moth dies on a lamp? In the same

way the devotee merges one day with the divine. Only then has the whole phenomenon happened – don't rest before that. Many times before that you will feel like settling: you have reached the most beautiful place, what more beautiful place than this can there be? But don't stop. Keep walking.

There is an old Sufi story. Every day a *fakir* used to meditate in the forest and a woodcutter would come to chop wood. The *fakir* felt sorry for this man. The woodcutter was old – he must have been seventy years old – but still he chopped wood and carried it home. He was nothing but bones! His body was weak, his back was bent.

One day the *fakir* said, "Listen, you crazy man! You have cut wood all your life, now go a little further."

That woodcutter replied, "What is there ahead of me? Nothing but forest. I am old, I cannot walk much. It is difficult to walk even this far. What shall I gain by going further into the forest?"

The *fakir* said, "Listen to me – go further. There is a mine in there. You will get more from it in one day than you can get from chopping wood for seven days."

The old man went further. He found a copper mine. Now he could take all the copper he could carry and sell it. It earned him enough for seven days. He was delighted. He didn't need to go back for seven days. He returned each week.

Then the *fakir* said, "Listen. Don't stop – go still further. There is another mine in the forest."

The old man said, "What shall I do with it?"

The *fakir* said, "If you go further, you will earn enough in one day to keep you for a whole month. There is a silver mine in the forest."

He had to listen to the *fakir*. At first he felt like saying, "Why should I bother? Why should I take the trouble? My life is fine. This is enough. I just want to be left alone. Once I cut wood from the forest every day so that I could buy bread. Things are even better now – I can come to the forest only once a week and enjoy myself for the rest of the time. I can rest, I can live in comfort."

He said to the *fakir*, "Please don't confuse me."

The *fakir* said, "As you wish, but try just once more."

The woodcutter became curious and he went further into the forest. There he found a silver mine. So he began to go to the forest only once a month.

The *fakir* said, "There is still more I need to tell you. Go further into the forest. You will find a gold mine. Then you can have enough for the whole year."

The old man didn't want to make any more effort. He was too old for any complications.... But he had begun to have faith in what the *fakir* said. The *fakir* had been proved right twice, he must be right again. "Once a year! I have wasted my whole life. I should have gone further much earlier. This forest was always mine; I came here, cut wood and went back again. I stopped at the edge of the forest and then went home.

I never even thought that there might be other riches in the forest."

So he went deeper and found a gold mine. Now he only came to the forest once or twice a year. The *fakir* said, "You are getting very old. Go a bit deeper. You fool! — why don't you keep on going by yourself?"

The old man said, "What more can there be? Nothing is better than gold."

The *fakir* replied, "There is more. Go further."

He went further and found a diamond mine. What he gathered in one day was enough for an entire life. Now he no longer came back at all. So one day the *fakir* came to his house and said, "Are you mad? Why haven't you come back to the forest?"

The old man said, "Why should I? I have enough, not just for myself but for my children too. Once was enough."

The *fakir* said, "Go deeper."

The old man replied, "What can there be beyond diamonds?"

The *fakir* replied, "I am beyond diamonds. Come."

When he came, he found that the *fakir* was sitting beyond diamonds, sitting in absolute peace. His peace was unprecedented. The woodcutter forgot everything. When he bowed down at the *fakir*'s feet, he couldn't get up again. Hours passed. He had never known such peace, such bliss. It was a living stream.

The *fakir* shouted, "You madman, have you stopped again? Go further."

The old man asked, "But what more can there be? I have never experienced more bliss than this."

The *fakir* said, "Go further. The divine awaits you."

This is what I say to Nirupama: go further, go further.

There is a happiness in being at the feet of the master. If you weigh it against the world, it is like nothing you have ever known before. But if you weigh it against the divine, it is trivial. You should not stop before you reach the divine.

I say this in spite of knowing your difficulty. It is very difficult to let go of the master. First of all, it is hard to find the master. Only after lifetimes does it click with someone. One meets many teachers through many lives, but nothing clicks. The teacher with whom it clicks for you then becomes your master. The person with whom it doesn't click remains merely a teacher for you – no matter how great a master he may be for everybody else.

You may go to Buddha. If it clicks for you, he is your master. If not, he is only a teacher. You came to me. If you felt the click, then I am your master; otherwise I am only a teacher. You will learn something from me and move on. If the click happens, all moving on is over. Then you will drown in me. Things will not end with you learning from me, you will start becoming one with me.

This is the meaning of sannyas. Those for whom the click

happens will be eager for sannyas. Some people will come, they will hear me, they will like what I say and will pick up a few things, and then they will be gone. They will look after those things carefully, they will arrange them beautifully – occasionally they will even remember their existence – but they have not drowned in me. They have not become moths, they were not intoxicated. Their intellect collected some wealth, but nothing happened in their hearts, the juices didn't flow there.

Sannyas means that you have drowned yourself. Such people say, "Now that we have found these lotus-feet, we will not let go of them. Now we are ready to be mad for these lotus-feet."

First, it is difficult to find a master. And when you find him then the second, even more difficult thing comes sooner or later when he says, "Now you must let go of me too. My only use was that I held your hand and led you to the divine. I am the door – now you have reached the inner sanctuary. Now you must forget me and immerse yourself in the divine." This is much harder. First, it is difficult to find the master, then it is even harder to let go of him.

You ordered me to simply let go of love,
With what heart can one sigh and accomplish this?

You simply said to let go of love, to give up my attachments. "You ordered me to simply let go of love…." You just said, gave the order, to let go of this love.

You ordered me to simply let go of love,
With what heart can one sigh and accomplish this?

But how can the heart do this, how will it be possible? How can one become so unfeeling as to let go of love?

I long for her to lift the veil herself,
She waits for me to entreat her.

In the last moment, the very last moment, the moment of meeting the divine..." I long for her to lift the veil herself..." for the divine to reveal itself.

...She waits for me to entreat her.

And the divine waits for you to express your desire: that you pray, that you ask, that you insist. Then the veil will lift.

Better not to have the courage to see the divine,
But if you do, better to go on seeing with my eyes.

Either let no madness arise in you to see the divine, let no stubbornness arise in you to see the divine....

Better not to have the courage to see the divine...

One should not dare.

...But if you do, better to go on seeing with my eyes.

If you have been courageous so far, then gather a little more courage — to see through my eyes.

When I ask you to let go of me, please pay a little attention to what I am seeing through my eyes. I am seeing something which you cannot see yet. You have listened to me and come this far: I told you about the copper mine and you went there; I told you about the silver mine and you went there; I told you about the gold mine and you went there; I told you about the diamond mine and you went there...you have come this far.

When I told you about the mine of meditation, you entered it willingly. Now go a little further. Everything ends there. There, there will be no meditator and no meditation, no disciple and no master, no seeker and nothing to search for. There, everything becomes one. The river meets with the ocean. There is supreme bliss. What you have found near the master is only a tiny echo of that supreme bliss.

It is like the fragrance of a flower riding the wind to your nostrils. You have not seen the flower yet. Certainly, it must be there somewhere – the fragrance has drifted towards you. The master is nothing but the fragrance of the divine.

Take hold of this clue of the fragrance of the divine. Slowly, using it as a thread, seek out the flower. Taking hold of the master one has to seek out the flower.

You have shown courage once. It requires great courage to take hold of the master – because taking hold of the master means letting go of yourself. Taking hold of the master means surrendering your ego. You have shown courage once in letting go of yourself and taking hold of the master. Now show even greater courage, now let go of the master as well. Then all holding is finished. This is the point where there is no one who can hold on and there is nothing to be held on to. This is the point where the divine descends.

The last question:

Osho,

It is difficult to become a witness. Is there no other way to the divine than this?

There is. Every day we have been talking about it. Daya's words are the other way. Devotion is that other path. There are two ways: witnessing – witnessing is meditation – and devotion, which is your feelings. To witness means to see with alertness. And devotion means to drown, to stop looking and doing all those other things. Devotion means drowning into oblivion in every possible way; drowning in devotional singing, in dancing, in songs – as though you were drunk. You just forget everything, you just forget yourself.

Forgetting yourself is one way, and remembering yourself is the other. The processes are different, but the outcome is the same. The paths are different, but the destination is the same. Remembering yourself: that is witnessing. But you must remember yourself, and not forget even for a single moment. Distance yourself, distance yourself from everything. "Whatever I see is apart from me." Keep this in your remembrance. Don't allow any identification to take place. No matter what the situation, the witness must remain a witness. Even if the divine appears in front of you the witness will remain a witness, it will not want to merge with it. Merging is not part of the path of witnessing. It will continue to observe.

Do you know what the followers of the path of witnessing have said? The Buddhists have said: "If the witness meets even the Buddha on the path, he must take up his sword and

cut him in two." Witnessing means that whatsoever becomes
the object of your senses — you are not that. If Krishna stands
in front of you, playing his flute when you close your eyes
and sit down to meditate, then take your sword and cut him
into pieces — "This is not 'I.' I am the one who sees."
Through practicing this *neti-neti*, not this, not this, through
constantly denying by saying "I am not this" and "I am not
that," then when all the objects disappear, when the mind is
without objects, without thoughts, without any options;
when there are no alternatives, when there is supreme
stillness, when you are alone as the knower and nothing
remains there to be known — on that day you have arrived,
you have reached the journey's end.

So one who follows the journey of witnessing will not see
the divine in front of him. One who follows this path will
simply experience that "I am the divine." The Upanishads
say: I am the ultimate divine! That is the path of the witness.
Mansoor says, *Ana'l haq!* "I am the truth." That is the path
of the witness.

On the day that all your mind's agitation has been dissolved
on the path of witnessing, then you yourself will become a
manifestation of the divine.

You have said: "It is difficult to become a witness."

Don't be worried. There is another path — and it is exactly
the opposite of the path of witnessing. For those whom the
path of witnessing does not suit there is this other path
which will. There are only two kinds of people. Just as there
are men and women on the physical level, there are also men
and women at the level of consciousness. A "man" is a

witness. Male consciousness is part of the path of the witness. The male mind – and remember, when I say "the male mind," I don't mean that all men are male: there are many men for whom the term "male-consciousness" is not appropriate. And when I say "woman," remember that not all women are women. There are many women for whom witnessing is appropriate. So don't limit my differentiation to the physical level. This is an inner difference. A man can have a female mind and a woman can have a male mind. But the difference between the two is clear.

A female mind relies on devotion, feeling, oblivion. And what is the difference? What is seen on the path of the witness has to be eliminated, separated off – only the seer is to be saved. And what is seen on the path of devotion has to be saved and the seer has to be dissolved. They are very different, exact opposites. Krishna appears... the image of Krishna appears in your feelings and you have to dissolve yourself and save Krishna. You have to pour your very life into him. You have to pour your very life into him in such a way that his image comes to life, that his image blossoms into life. You have to pour yourself into him so totally that your own life energy plays Krishna's flute. That is what the devotee does.

The paths of the devotee and the witness are so different that even the language they use is different. A devotee says: "Self-forgetfulness. Forget yourself. Drown yourself in the ecstasy, in the remembrance of the divine. Forget yourself in the way a drunkard forgets himself. Turn the divine's name into wine and be drunk. Make your own wine and be drunk. Be ecstatically mad."

If the path of the witness is difficult for you, don't be worried — the path of devotion is your path. Ecstasy, drunkenness... go that way. Dance, sing, drown in the remembrance of the divine. This is Daya's message. This is the message of Sahajo and Meera.

On a vine in the desolate forest
She slept, full of wedded bliss,
Immersed in the dreams of love,
A delicate innocent young woman —
A jasmine bud.
She slept.
How could she know of her beloved's arrival?
The hero kissed her cheek,
The vine swayed like a swing,
And still she did not awake.
An omission — and no apology was given.
She kept her drowsy curved eyes closed...
Or was she drunk?
Drinking the wine of youth, who can say?
That ruthless hero
Showed such complete callousness
That he shook her beautiful soft body
With a succession of gusts,
Thus pressing her fair round cheeks.
The maiden was startled.
Casting astonished glances around her,
And finding her beloved near the love-bed,
The soft-lipped one laughed, blossomed,
And played colorful games with him.

Devotion is a search for the beloved. Devotion doesn't see the divine in the form of truth. The divine is the beloved, dearer than anything else. Devotion is the search for that precious beloved.

And finding her beloved near the love-bed,
The soft-lipped one laughed, blossomed,
And played colorful games with him.

The path of devotion is very colorful. It is the path of spring. An overabundance of flowers blossom on this path. The *veena* plays, the *mridang* drums beat. The path of devotion is the path of ankle bells: there is dancing, singing, there are hymns, there is love and passion. And all this love, all this devotion is offered at the feet of the divine. The entire water-pot is filled again and again with love and poured out at the feet of the divine. One must pour oneself out so totally that nothing is left behind. And when everything has been poured out, you have arrived.

The path of the witness is for those who find the path of devotion difficult. First search for devotion, because devotion is easier for most people. It is also juicier. When it is possible to dance your way to somewhere, why walk? Why go somewhere with a sad face when you can reach there singing? Why get mixed up with the practices of the *mahatmas* and the renouncers, when you can reach the divine in a delightful way, playing your drum; when your joy can remain with you? Leave renouncing and all of this to those whom devotion does not suit. If devotion does suit, if love suits, then everything has fallen into place and there will be nothing more to be done.

But I know, the problem is such that if I say devotion, people get nervous. They come to me and say: "We don't have the courage for devotion. We dare not be so mad." People even go mad in a calculated way — mad only up to a certain point....

Mulla Nasruddin's wife was lying on her deathbed. As she was dying, she said, "Nasruddin, what will you do when I am dead?"

The Mulla replied, "I will go mad."

His wife said, "Don't lie. I know you. You will be married as soon as I am dead."

The Mulla said, "I will go mad, but I won't go that mad."

People even want to go mad in a calculating way. They calculate how far they should go! If I mention devotion, people come to me and tell me that this path is the path of madness. In dancing, singing, *kirtan*, as Meera has said, one loses all the respect of the society: "I am a deputy-collector or the sub-collector of revenue, or an engineer, or a doctor — and this will only cause chaos!"

A doctor used to visit me once. I had a problem with my thumb and he operated on me. He was a dear man. By chance, when he came to do the operation, he fell in love with me. He said, "I will follow you, but not yet. I will come. I must follow you one day, but right now I am afraid."

I asked him, "What are you afraid of?"

He said, "I am afraid that if all this singing, dancing, celebrating appeals to me — and I am sure it will, because I have always wanted to be that way — then I will be in trouble.

On the day I operated on your hand, that night I dreamed that I was dancing in orange robes.... Don't do this to me. Not yet. Please excuse me for the moment. I have a wife and children to support and everything is going very well for me. Right now I need order in my life...I must certainly come one day, but right now I am afraid."

There are many such people who are frightened of the path of devotion. But if you tell them about witnessing that does not appeal to them either, because the path of witnessing is arduous — a path of austere disciplines, of effort. It is dry. The harsh conditions there make people nervous. But where there is a stream of love, one becomes afraid of madness.

The path of devotion is the path of the madman. There can be no calculations in madness. If you want to move in a calculated way, witnessing is the path for you. It is mathematical, it is pure mathematics. It has no place for madness. Madness never arises there. It is a very scientific process. So whichever one interests you....But sooner or later, you will have to decide.

My experience is that if you tell people about devotion they prefer to think of witnessing, because they are frightened of devotion. If you mention witnessing, they prefer to think of devotion, because witnessing seems to be a very harsh path. They begin to be afraid of this harshness. "No...we don't feel capable of following such a strict path."

As you move into witnessing, all the joys will begin to disappear from your life. If you experiment with witnessing, you will see your wife, but you will be unable to see that she is yours. The sense of "I" starts dissolving, you remain a mere witness. If someone abuses you, you will hear him abusing you, but you will not feel insulted. How can a witness be insulted? If someone puts a garland of flowers around your neck, you will feel it happening, and that is okay, but you will not feel honored by it.

This creates a difficulty. In this way your whole lifestyle will be changed. At present, at least you have a little joy when someone puts a garland of flowers around your neck. In fact, so far you have never received a garland of flowers – you are still waiting! And before this can happen you have begun to become a witness – so there is a little difficulty. Right now, you know how to retaliate against someone who abuses you – witnessing will destroy all that. The very meaning of witnessing is that you live in the world, but you will be completely untouched by it. Nothing touches a witness. You are like a lotus in the water. But one doesn't gather even that much courage.

There is nothing in devotion that should cause you any worry. But there is something else about devotion: if you look at your wife with the eyes of devotion, you will see the divine in her. If you look at your husband with the eyes of devotion, you will see the divine in him. You will see the divine in your son. All this seems like madness. The divine in your wife – it doesn't seem right! To some women it may even seem right to see the divine in their husbands, because they have been told to do so for thousands of years – but to see the divine in one's wife? So the god who is a husband will feel some difficulty. But with devotion, one day you will find yourself placing your head at your wife's feet.

I have a friend, a very simple man. One night, we talked

together until late, and what I said struck him deeply. In some context about feeling the divine everywhere, I told him that the divine is in everyone, even in your wife. I simply said this to illustrate a point, but it struck him as right. He went home and bowed down at the feet of his wife. She became very puzzled. She woke up the other members of the household, afraid that there was something wrong with him. And my friend was feeling such joy from bowing down at his wife's feet, that he bowed down at the feet of whoever he could find in his house. The servants, anyone at all…. The members of his household thought that he had gone mad, that he had completely lost his mind.

They woke me up at two o'clock in the night and said, "What have you done?"

I said, "What is wrong in it? Wives have always touched their husband's feet and you never thought they were mad. Now if the husband does it, what harm is there in it?"

They said, "What are you talking about? We always tried to persuade him not to come to you."

And he was having so much fun with all that was happening around him that he kept doing it ecstatically for three months. His family pursued him with various treatments, medicines and charms — even incantations to cast out the evil spirits. And he would laugh and tell them, "I am not mad." His family were afraid that some ghost was troubling him and they began trying to cast out the demons from him. Finally they didn't even listen to me and they sent him for electric shock treatment. Things became worse and worse. And my friend was in such a state of unrestrained ecstasy that he began to touch the feet of any passer by. And there was nothing wrong with him, nothing. He was a very simple-hearted, innocent person.

So people are afraid of devotion too, because it unleashes an altogether different world. This often happens here. When I explain witnessing, people come and say it will create all sorts of problems for them, and when I explain devotion, people come and say it will create all sorts of problems. So decide once and for all. And remember, when you decide, don't calculate the problems involved. There should be only one consideration: which do you feel more in harmony with? Nothing else is important. All other things are secondary. If you feel that devotion is juicy for you, then gather your courage and dive into it. Don't say that you will start one day, because that day will never come. If you don't start today, you will never start. Tomorrow never comes – and who knows, death may come even before that.

So whichever stirs your heart, touches a chord within your heart…. When you think of Meera dancing, does a tune arise in your heart, do you want to dance like her? Or when you see Buddha sitting in peaceful meditation, witnessing, when you see a statue of Buddha, do you feel that you would love to be like that, do you feel that you would like to sit like that? Which one do you feel most in harmony with?

Nothing else is worth considering. The family in which you were born is not worth considering. Maybe the family in which you were born follows the path of devotion, the path of Vallabha or of Ramanuja, but if you find joy in Buddha or Mahavira and their statues call you, then don't worry. The family you were born into has nothing to do with it. In such a situation, the path for you is meditation. And if you were born into a Jaina or a Buddhist household, or if you are a Vedantin, that makes no difference either. Look into your own heart. If you feel that something sways inside you when you hear one of Meera's songs; that when you see the veena in Meera's hand, someone begins to pick up a veena in your own dreams; if a desire arises in you that one day, you too would like to dance like her, completely engrossed, ecstatic, forgetting everything.... And if you begin to feel a stream of joy arising, flowing in you from such imaginings and a fragrance spreading around you – then don't worry that you have been born into a Jaina family or a Buddhist family or a Vedantin one, or whatsoever. All of these are worthless considerations. It is a matter of coincidence which family you were born into.

Listen to your own heart. That is your only true home. Take your clue from there, and realize that difficulties will come on all paths. Do you think there should be a path on which no difficulties arise at all? There is no such path. If you think that, then you won't be able to move a single step. Difficulties will come on all paths. What these difficulties mean is that you have followed a lifestyle up to this point, you have built a certain structure, and that must now be changed. This causes difficulty. So far you have shown one aspect of yourself to people, and now it will be difficult to manifest a different side. But these difficulties are easily solved. All you need is courage.

That is why I call courage the first quality of a religious person. The person who has no courage cannot be religious. Religion is not for cowards.

So I will say to you that if you cannot manage witnessing
don't be sad, don't be disappointed. If it has become clear
to you that witnessing is not for you, then the other path is
clear. There is no third path — and one of the two is bound
to suit you. It has to. There are only two types of people in
the world. So now sing, hum and immerse yourself in the
beauty of the divine.

The rich have millions of riches
But you are the only wealth of a poor man like me.

Sing! Bow down at the feet of the divine. And his feet are
all around, in every direction. Wherever you bow down, there
are his feet.

Someone wears a diamond necklace,
Someone has a ruby-studded one.
Another decorates her feet with scarlet dye,
Patterns her hands with henna,
And has pearls braided in her hair.
There are a million adornments for the body,
Made from gold, from silver,
From gems, from stones.
But for my heart, you are the only jewel.

Say it, say it to the divine....

Someone goes to Puri or to Dwarka,
Another adores Kashi,
Someone practices austerities at Triveni,
Another dwells in Mathura.
North, south, east and west,
Within, without, throughout the known world.
For others there are a hundred places of pilgrimage,
But you alone are my Vrindavan.

Make a request: "For others there are a hundred places of pilgrimage, but you alone are my Vrindavan."

Someone is proud of his beauty,
Another swaggers his strength,
Someone brags of his knowledge,
Another flaunts his wealth.
Body, wealth, wife and house,
Glory, shame, happiness and sorrow,
Physical, mental and incidental sufferings,
This world lives and dies in a hundred ways
But you alone are my life and death.

Search. If meditation doesn't suit you, search through love. If meditation doesn't suit you, search through devotion. But search you must. Don't console yourself by elaborating on the difficulties and saying you cannot start because of these difficulties. If one has to start, one has to start – and then who cares about such difficulties? We worry about difficulties only when we don't have the courage to start. You weave a web out of your difficulties.

I have heard:

Emperor Akbar was returning home after a hunting expedition. At dusk, he sat down at the outskirts of a village and spread out his mat under a tree to recite his prayers. He had hardly started when a woman came running towards him – a young, ecstatic, carefree, almost mad woman. As she ran over his mat, her *sari* brushed against him. Akbar was deeply disturbed. He was very angry. But he couldn't say anything because he was in the middle of reciting his prayers.

He quickly finished his prayers and started to get his horse ready so that he could look for the woman. What rudeness! To do such a thing to anyone who is praying is wrong, and then to do this to the emperor! But there was no need for him to look for her. She was coming back again. The emperor stopped her and said, "You are rude, woman! Have you no consideration? Don't you know that when someone is praying, you shouldn't disturb that person? And couldn't you see that the emperor himself was praying?"

The woman looked at him carefully. She said, "Now that you mention it, I do remember that someone was praying as I ran along this path. And I remember that the border of my sari touched him. You are right. But my beloved was coming and I was running to meet him. I couldn't see or think of anything else. Please forgive me.

"But there is one thing I want to ask you. You were going to meet the divine, the ultimate beloved — and yet you still felt the border of my sari touch you? I was going to meet an earthly lover, and I didn't notice you. You felt my touch, I didn't feel you at all. This doesn't sound right, your majesty — what kind of prayers were you involved in?"

The emperor has written in his autobiography, "I will never forgot this blow to my ego. Truly, my prayer was no prayer. A small disturbance, like someone passing by, should not hinder true prayers. There can be no disturbance if there is love! The touch of someone's clothes cannot disturb you if there is an inner absorption in blissfulness."

You too sit down to meditate, but small things keep disturbing you. They disturb you because your meditation is not yet meditation. You sit down in remembrance of the divine and trivial things keep disturbing you because your remembrance is not remembrance yet.

If you are only pretending, everything can disturb you. Be authentic. Decide which thing suits your heart, which is in harmony with you. Then walk that path, and walk it wholeheartedly. Immerse yourself in it completely. Without complete dedication neither the witness nor the devotee will ever arrive, neither the meditator nor the lover. You must immerse yourself. If you think it will be difficult to immerse yourself, then you will never be able to progress. Immersion is a must! Immerse yourself either in meditation or in devotion — but immersion cannot be avoided.

Both paths have their difficulties. Both paths have their beauties. There is no path which is absolutely free of difficulties. What kind of a path would that be? If you walk, there will be difficulties. If you take on a journey, you must suffer the sun and the dust. There are rocks and stones on the path, and thorns as well.

But when remembrance of the divine enters your life, when this quest starts in your life, you will forget all difficulties. Then even difficulties become a stepping stone.

Enough for today.

3

THE LAST MORNING STAR

The state of the sadhus when immersed in love
Is indescribable.
They cry while they sing and they laugh,
This is very paradoxical, says Daya.

Drunk with the nectar of the divine,
Their state of knowing is unfathomable.
The riches of the three worlds are but worthless
For a sadhu, says Daya.

He puts his feet in one spot, but they land elsewhere,
His body is ecstatic with delight.
The more he drowns in the beauty of godliness
The more his love grows, says Daya.

He laughs, he sings, he cries; he rises and falls again and again,
He is ever-restless.
But once he has tasted the nectar of the divine, says Daya,
He can endure all pain of separation.

The flame of the anguish of separation is born in my heart,
Come, O divine, come my beloved,
Come, O enchanter of hearts,
Come, O Krishna, O simple one,
I long to see you.

My hands are tired of shooing crows,
My eyes of looking expectantly at the path.
My heart has fallen into the ocean of love,
And there is no shore, no exit.

Look! Anyone look! says Shakeel,
Is this not madness?
That I became his who could not be mine?

The path of love in the search for godliness is the path of
the mad ones. You can belong to the divine, but it will never
be yours – because if it is to be yours one thing is required:
that you should exist. Someone can be yours only if you exist.
But the essential condition for meeting the divine is that you
should be no more. It will appear only when you disappear;
only when you no longer are will it be there.

So one thing is certain: you can belong to the divine but it
can never be yours. Who can make such a claim when you
are no longer there? "My" can exist only when "I" exists.
When "I" no longer is, what relevance is there to "My"?

On the path to godliness, there is nothing for the lover but
to lose and lose; any talk of gain is futile. And the interesting
thing is, it is in this losing that everything is gained. There
is nothing else but to drown and to go on drowning; any talk
of being saved is useless. And it is in this drowning that the
saving happens. The bank of the river is found midstream.
One needs to have the courage to disappear, and the first step
in gathering that courage to disappear is to let go of your
intellect, to let go of your cautiousness, your cleverness; to
let go of all mathematics, calculation and logic.

This is why the path of love is the path of the mad, the path

of the carefree, the path of the courageous. Even a businessman can travel on the path of knowledge, because there the
arithmetic is neat and clean. But only gamblers can walk on
the path of love, because there you have to lose everything,
and with no certainty of gain. There nothing can be
gained, and everything will be lost. If your heart is big enough
to accept defeat as victory, death as life, your disappearance
as an arriving – only then does the door to the path of love
open. The path of love is closed to the prudent, so we call
it the path to the tavern, the path of the drunkard.

Love is a wine. The reality is that you are looking for all kinds
of wine, because you have not yet learned how to pour the
wine of love. You go to the tavern because your temple has
not yet become your tavern. You drink the wine made from
grapes because you are not yet capable of drinking the wine
of the soul. You look for small and cheap escapes because
you have forgotten the language of true drunkenness.

The divine is absolute drunkenness.

Today's sutras are marvelous. They have come straight from
a devotee's heart, they are the blossoming of a devotee's heart.
Each sutra is a lotus petal. Understand them carefully.

The state of the *sadhus* when immersed in love
Is indescribable.
They cry while they sing and they laugh,
This is very paradoxical, says Daya.

Paradoxical! A paradoxical statement means when something
doesn't fit with our logic, doesn't fit with our mathematics,
when it escapes the grasp of arithmetic. A paradoxical
statement means inverse talk. In order to attain you have to
lose, in order to arrive you have to disappear, the only way

to find the shore is for the boat to sink in midstream...this kind of inverse talk.

Kabir has composed many paradoxical verses. A paradoxical verse contains statements which cannot happen in logic but do happen in life. Kabir has said: *Nadia lagi aag!* "The river is on fire!" Now a river doesn't catch fire. If a river could catch fire, there would be no means to put the fire out. A river doesn't catch fire – it can't. This is contrary to all logic, mathematics and science. But Kabir says that it happens in life. What cannot happen happens. Man is God and he behaves like a beggar – "The river is on fire!" Man is immortal and he trembles in the face of death – "The river is on fire!" Man is indestructible, eternal; he has always been and will always be. The divine itself is present within him and he is begging for things that are not worth even two cents, he is holding out his begging bowl and wailing. It is like an emperor begging with a begging-bowl. "The river is on fire!" What shouldn't happen is happening. And where everything has become so topsy-turvy, you cannot reach the divine through mathematics. You will have to find some other way – a way that is as paradoxical as your life has become. This is the path that will take you out of your confusion.

Understand this. Paradoxical speech means.... When you see the sun rising in the morning, you never have any doubts about the sun. Have you ever met anyone who told you that they believe in the existence of the sun? No. You never meet anyone who believes in the existence of the sun and you never meet anyone who doesn't believe in the existence of the sun. The sun exists: this is the experience of us all. So there are no believers and no non-believers regarding this. The sun is. We all agree that the world exists, because it is in our experience. It is right there in front of our eyes. Our hands can touch it, our ears can hear it, our tongues can taste it. It is within the grasp of our senses.

The divine is not within the grasp of our senses in this way; it is not visible to the eye, we cannot touch it with our hands or hear it with our ears. So the person who has faith in the divine seems to be very incoherent. It is not absurd to have faith in the world – that is mathematical, logical – but to have faith in the divine is completely absurd. To have faith in one you have never seen or touched or experienced! Gamblers have that faith. Trusting the unknown…it requires great courage.

You don't need any courage to have faith in the sun, but you need extraordinary courage to have faith in the divine – a courage which sweeps away the entire web of logic.

In life there is only one such door: it is in your heart and it is the door of love. Only in love can you put aside your web of logic for a short time. When you fall in love with someone you give up all calculation. Then you say, "I am in love. This has nothing to do with bookkeeping." You are willing to wager everything. Majnu staked everything, didn't he? Become a Majnu. Then you will stop thinking, then you will say it is simply a matter of the heart, that thinking isn't allowed in here.

A young man went to the father of the girl he was in love with and said, "Sir, I would like to marry your daughter."

Her father was a calculating man – as fathers should be. He looked at the young man carefully and said, "Why do you want to marry my daughter?"

The young man said, "Forgive me, I can give you no reason. I love her. There is no other reason."

Love is not a reason. Love is something that destroys all reasons when it manifests. Love is not a reason. Love comes from the unknown. You have no control over it, you are helpless. So the lover is under someone else's control, he is helpless. Something happens which is beyond his limits, beyond his control.

Even love in ordinary life is beyond your control.... When you fall in love with a man or a woman, even that is beyond your limitations, beyond your control. It is bigger than you, it engulfs you. You cannot envelop it: your fist is too small, your fist cannot hold it. It grabs your fist. What then can one say about the love for the divine? It is love for the vast, for the eternal. When the ray of love for the divine descends into your life, it is a state of paradox – something which does not ordinarily happen.

Meera danced from village to village. She forgot the normal order of things. She was a lady of the royal household, but she began to dance like a mad woman on the streets, in the crowded bazaars, in the temples.

The members of her family must have become disturbed. When they sent her a cup of poison it was an act of prudence, it was not out of enmity – bear this in mind. They had no reason to be her enemy. They sent her the poison because, to them, Meera had now become a disgrace to the family, a dishonor. Better that she were dead.

The divine manifests in her and the members of Meera's

household are disturbed! Take this as a symbol. When a ray of the divine descends into your heart, your intellect will be disturbed. Your intellect is like the members of the household. The intellect is calculating, the intellect means logic. When a ray of love descends into your heart, stay with it, help it, because the intellect is very strong. It can kill the light. It can shut the door completely.

This often happens. You must have experienced it many times. It sometimes happens that when something begins to take hold of you you become nervous. You immediately cling to your intellect. You ask yourself, "What is this? How did it happen?"

People often come to me and say, "A moment comes during the meditations when we feel as though we are possessed with a dance, but then something from inside gets a hold on us. It is as if chains have suddenly been put on our feet. We stop just as we are about to start. A feeling arises somewhere as if to say, 'What are you doing? This is madness.'"

The intellect is the opposite to the heart. For the intellect, love is madness. So those who only listen to the intellect live lives which are empty of love: paradox never enters their lives. And when there is no paradox, no lotuses ever blossom in their lives either.

The lotus flower is a great paradox. It blossoms in the mud. What could be more paradoxical than that? In filth! Such a beautiful flower, yet it blossoms in the ugly mud. That is why it is called *pankaj. Pank* means mud. A lotus is known as "pankaj" – one that is born from the mud. It would still be a miracle if the lotus blossomed out of gold, but when it grows out of mud – what to say of such a miracle? It would still be a miracle if the lotus blossomed out of diamonds and gems, because they are dead and the lotus is alive. But it grows in mud, where there is nothing but stench and filth. When you walk past the mud, you have to cover your nose with a handkerchief. And the lotus has an unparalleled beauty and fragrance. It really is a paradoxical phenomenon.

One day the lotus of the divine will blossom in the mud of your body. It is a paradox. The lotus of love blossoms in the mud of lust. It is a paradox. When I first said to people that it is from sex that one rises to superconsciousness.... People are still angry with me, they say it is not right to say such a thing. All I am saying is that the lotus blossoms in the mud, nothing else. I am bringing the symbol of the lotus and the mud to a human level. And if the lotus does not blossom in the mud, then there is no hope for you. Then your lotus can never blossom – because you are nothing but mud. No one is anything but mud. But the lotus blossoms in this mud.

What has really happened when a buddha becomes enlightened? The lotus has blossomed in the mud. Right now you are mud and Buddha has become a lotus. Today, the difference is obvious, but when your lotus blossoms tomorrow you too will become like Buddha. And once Buddha was mud, just like you are.

When I say that sex becomes superconsciousness, that the mud becomes a lotus, that the passions become the divine, I am simply stating that the paradox happens. It is not logical. If the logicians had been consulted as to whether the lotus would be able to blossom in the mud, they would have said that it was impossible. How could it? The lotus

and the mud have nothing in common. If you didn't know
that a lotus grows in the mud, if you were born in a country
where there are no lotuses, and one day a heap of mud was
placed on one side of you and a bunch of lotuses on the other
side, would you even be able to imagine that this mud has
become lotuses? Impossible! It is totally illogical, paradoxical.

The state of the *sadhus* when immersed in love
Is indescribable.
They cry while they sing and they laugh,
This is very paradoxical, says Daya.

The state of the sadhus when immersed in love.... The *sadhjan* who
have become immersed in love.... This word sadh, is very
charming. It has become corrupted. If you look it up in a
dictionary, you will find that it means a monk, an ascetic.
But the correct meaning is: simple, plain. It means a man who
is so plain, so simple that his life is free of the web of the
intellect, of the web of logic. The intellect is very crooked,
very cunning. It is deceitful. It does one thing but shows
something else on the surface. What is happening on the
inside is different from what it does on the outside. The
intellect is a hypocrite.

The one who has become free of the hypocrisy of the intellect
is a *sadhu*, a *sadhjan*. He is the same on the outside as on the
inside. He is one in whom there is no disparity between
the outside and the inside. What he is, he says; what he says,
he is. You can taste him in any place, and he will always taste
the same.

Buddha has said that a *sadhu* is like the ocean; it is
always salty wherever you drink it, whenever you drink it.
It makes no difference whether you drink it in the day or at

night, in the morning or in the evening, in the darkness or in the light, on this shore or that shore. A *sadhu* is like the ocean; he always tastes the same.

The cunning person has many different tastes. The cunning person wears many masks to hide his face. He puts on his masks according to the needs of the time.

A *sadhu* is one who has revealed his face. He looks as he is.

You are used to the opposite meaning of the word *sadhu*. You think that a *sadhu* means one who has done great spiritual disciplines, one who is making great spiritual efforts. But if he is making an effort he won't be simple anymore. Only one who is not simple must learn spiritual practices. Do you think that the simple person ever has to practice? Children are *sadhus*. What have they practiced? They are simply natural.

A person who is natural is a *sadhu*. The one who practices will become something quite different. Practicing, making an effort, means that there is something inside you and you cover it with something else. There is anger inside you and you show compassion outside. There is sexuality inside and you show celibacy outside. There is greed, great greed inside, but on the outside you renounce everything. Inside, you burn with some desire, but on the outside you manage to conduct yourself quite differently. This is what you have been calling a *sadhu*!

Daya does not call a person like that a *sadhu*. Daya's definition of a *sadhu* is... *the sadhus... immersed in love....* Those who are immersed in love, who are simple in their love, who dive into love, who are willing to descend into the madness of love –

their state...*is indescribable*. It is very difficult to describe their state: their feet sway and stagger like the feet of a drunkard. There is an ecstasy in every pore of their body. There is a song in their standing up and their sitting down. There is music in their every breath.

And you will find no consistency in their lives...but you will certainly find music. Consistency is to be found in the lives of those who have disciplined their behavior. You will not find consistency in the life of a *sadhu*, but you will find music – each moment you will find fresh music playing. And you won't find that he does the same thing today as he did yesterday. Yesterday was yesterday and today is today. Today, he will do what the divine makes him do today: there is no bond with yesterday. Hence you cannot predict what a *sadhu* will do; you cannot prophesy what he will say or do tomorrow. You will find out when tomorrow comes. The *sadhu* himself doesn't know what will happen tomorrow. Tomorrow he will do what the divine makes him do, he will see what the divine shows him, he will dance when the divine makes him dance.

A *sadhu*, an enlightened mystic, is one who has surrendered himself into the hands of the divine, who has stopped controlling his own life, who has simply become an instrument, who says, "Do as you please. A leaf will shake if you move it; it won't shake if you don't move it."

A *sadhu* is one who has given up living his life according to his own will and has begun to live according to the will of the divine. That is why his state is "indescribable." The *sadhu*'s state becomes as paradoxical as the state of the divine. A real *sadhu* becomes a smaller version of the divine – new flowers are blossoming every day, new songs appearing every day. If you look for consistency on the outside you won't find it. But you will find such consistency in your so-called *sadhus*. They have a set structure to their lives, their framework is fixed.

I have heard about Eknath. There was an atheist in a particular village and the whole village was fed up with him. They tried in every possible way to make him understand, but he wouldn't. Not only did he not understand, but he even tried to make them understand that there is no God. The villagers began to feel very uneasy about him so they told him, "A supreme *sadhu* has incarnated. His name is Eknath. Go to him. If anyone can make you understand about the divine, it will be Eknath."

The atheist went to visit Eknath. When he reached him, he found that Eknath was staying in a temple in the village – in a Shiva temple. When he reached the temple the man was perplexed, very troubled. He was an atheist, yet he wouldn't have done what Eknath was doing. Eknath was lying down, resting, with his feet on the statue of Shiva. The man was an atheist and didn't believe in Shiva, but his heart trembled and he thought, "This man appears to be very strange. Resting his feet on Shiva! What a great atheist! Even though I say that God doesn't exist, if someone asked me to kick Shiva's statue my heart would tremble and I would worry about whether God really did exist after all. He might! And I wouldn't want any trouble to follow my actions. And here is this man, lying down without a care, with his feet on the statue of Shiva...."

The atheist asked, "What are you doing, sir? I am an atheist. I have come to you in search of God. The stupid villagers have sent me to you. But what are you doing?"

Eknath replied, "Any time, wherever you place your feet, he is there. Wherever you rest your feet, they rest on him. Who supports us but him? So this is not a problem."

What Eknath said was paradoxical but it was very meaningful. It was as if this man had really seen something: if there is only God, then where can you place your feet? He is wherever you put them. In every situation your feet are resting on him. So what is the difference? You might as well rest them on Shiva's statue.

"Well," thought the man, "this *sadhu* has some depth. Let me stay and watch him. I want to see what else he does."

Eknath remained lying down; the morning came and the sun climbed higher and higher into the sky. The man said, "Sir, I have heard that the *sadhus* get up in the early hours of the morning, the *brahmamuhurt* – but you are still resting!"

Eknath said, "*Brahmamuhurt* is whenever a *sadhu* gets up – when else can it be? It is not that *sadhus* wake up at brahmamuhurt, it is *brahmamuhurt* when the *sadhu* gets up. Why should I come in between? God gets up whenever he wants and sleeps whenever he pleases."

Understand this – the divine gets up when it wants to. The divine is within you. If it doesn't want to get up yet, who are you to make it get up? Such a feeling of being only an instrument, such complete surrender.... But there can be no consistency in the behavior of such a man.

Eknath got up. Later, he came back from begging and began to make bread. When the loaves were cooked and he was just tapping them to knock off the ashes, a dog suddenly came along and ran away with one piece. The man sat there, watching. Eknath ran after the dog. The man thought, "This is the limit. A minute ago, this man was saying that the divine is everywhere and now he is chasing a poor dog!" So he ran after Eknath to see what would happen next.

Two miles later, Eknath caught the dog. He had also brought a pot of butter with him. Eknath got hold of the dog's mouth and said, "You fool! I have told you a thousand times not to run away with the bread until I have buttered it. Don't do this again! You are God and I don't like to see that you eat bread without butter."

He took the bread out of the dog's mouth, dipped it in the butter pot, gave it back to the dog and said, "Now, Rama, please enjoy this."

The behavior of a *sadhu* will be simple, childlike. The behavior of a *sadhu* doesn't arise out of any spiritual discipline, it arises out of simplicity. It is not disciplined, cultivated — it is natural, and there is a new joy each moment. You cannot predict how a *sadhu* will act. If you can predict how someone will behave, he will be like a machine. The same yesterday, the same the day before, the same today and tomorrow.... Such a man is dead. A *sadhu* is alive. Hence the life of a *sadhu* will be very paradoxical.

The state of the sadhus when immersed in love
Is indescribable.

Their actions cannot be talked about because they cannot be

predicted. No one knows what they will do. They themselves don't know: whatever will be, will be. If you know what you will do tomorrow, your tomorrow is already dead, it has died before it is born. If you know what you are going to do when someone abuses you, you are not giving the divine a chance, you have already decided everything. No, let the abuse come. Afterwards, tell the divine that this man has abused you and "Now do what you want to do about it." You will find that a new response arises every time. Then, there won't simply be reactions in your life, there will be a sensitivity instead. You will not behave mechanically.

Right now, it is as though someone presses a button and you become angry, and then he presses another button and you are happy. It is just like turning on switches. You press one switch and the light comes on. You press another switch and the fan starts. Right now, you are a machine, a slave. And anyone who knows your life just a little becomes your master. You are a slave to whoever has recognized your buttons and begins to push them.

Have you seen that this is what people normally do? A wife knows which of her husband's buttons to press. A husband knows which of his wife's buttons to press. And even small children know which of their father's buttons they need to press, and when. A beggar knows this too. If you are alone he will not ask you for money. He knows your button won't work if he presses it at a certain moment, so he catches you when you are standing in the bazaar, talking to some other people. He turns it into a question of honor. If you don't give him a few coins now, what will these other people say? You don't want to, you don't feel like giving him anything – you feel like splitting his head open! You won't

give him anything out of a sense of compassion, you will only
give him something to get out of the situation. You have your
prestige: what will these people think of you? So you smile
and give him some coins. The beggar also knows that
you are not giving these coins to him, that you are putting
them into your prestige account. He is pressing one of your
buttons.

If you examine yourself, you will find that you press other
people's buttons all the time. And you will also find that
other people press your buttons all the time. People are just
like machines.

A *sadhu's* response cannot be predicted, because he has no
buttons. And it will make no difference to him if you try to
press his buttons or not. A *sadhu* is an awakened person. He
has stopped living according to codes of conduct; he lives
through simplicity, he lives through naturalness.

They cry while they sing and they laugh...

A *sadhu's* state is hard to grasp. Sometimes he cries, sometimes he laughs, sometimes he does both things at the same
time. Only madmen ever cry and sing at the same time –
because it is completely illogical. When a man cries, you
understand that he is sad. When someone laughs, you understand that he is happy. But if someone cries and laughs at
the same time, this is difficult. It is hard to understand, it
is a riddle. If he is unhappy, he should cry; if he is happy, he
should laugh. Why is he doing both these things at the same
time?

This is the situation of the *sadhu*. On the one hand he sees

the world and cries, and on the other hand he sees the divine
and laughs. He stands in the middle, at the door. On the one
side he sees unfathomable sorrow and pain, people writhing
like insects, and he cries. On the other side he sees the
supreme gift of the divine, a showering of bliss, so he laughs.
He laughs and he cries.

They cry while they sing and they laugh,
This is very paradoxical, says Daya.

So if you have set out to find a *sadhu*, keep a few things
in mind. A *sadhu* is intoxicated, he is ecstatic. He is drunk
without drinking.

Without even drinking, people call me a drunkard,
Oh rapture! You gave me a bad name for nothing.

And the *sadhu* sits there without drinking. But he will appear
drunk to you.

This is my condition now…a toast to your beauty!
I can no longer distinguish
Between awareness and intoxication.

To him there is no difference anymore between what is
consciousness and what is unconsciousness. Both have
mingled together. Opposites have dissolved into one another,
opposites have drowned into each other. In this way, laughter
and tears go together. He can cry and he can sing at the same
time.

The way we are living, we divide up our lives. We divide
everything in life. We put life here and death there, happiness

here and sorrow there, heaven here and hell there, love here and hatred there. Our near ones are put here and strangers there, our friends here and our enemies there. We divide everything – but life itself is undivided. A *sadhu* does not divide; he lives the indivisibility of life. Life is non-dual; a *sadhu* lives life in its totality.

Life and death are not separate – you have just believed they are. You started dying the day you were born. Your first breath was also the beginning of your last breath. You don't suddenly die one day after seventy years. Does anything ever happen suddenly? It takes seventy years to die – slowly, slowly, dying, dying. You finally die after seventy years.

So life and death are not two separate things. Life and death are like your right and left feet walking together. They move together. Like the incoming and the outgoing breath.... If life is the incoming breath, death is the outgoing breath. Both move together. Your feet move together; these wings move together.

Sometimes your behavior perplexes you. If you are crying and you suddenly feel like laughing, you will control yourself. Otherwise you fear that people will say that you are mad.

One of my teachers died. He was a very dear man, very fat and strong. Our Taru is nothing compared to him! He was also very innocent. You could be moved to laughter just by looking at his face – there was such an innocence in it. And it used to provoke him when people called him Bholenath, "the Lord of Simpletons." It was enough to keep him upset for the whole hour if you wrote the word "Bholenath" on the blackboard in the classroom. He would remain annoyed for the whole hour. He would jump up and down and leap about, he would be angry, he would beat his stick on the table, his whole body would be covered in sweat....

When he died, all his pupils went to his house. I was standing very close to his dead body. Looking at his face, I felt like laughing. My tears were falling as well. I tried hard to stop myself from laughing, because it was inappropriate. A man has died and someone else is laughing.... I felt sad and I was crying too. I was the one who had tormented him the most and I was the saddest person there. I had lost more than anyone else. I would never experience that kind of happiness again. So in this way there was a deep connection between the two of us.

Just then, his wife came out and, overcome by grief, prostrated herself over him and said, "Alas, my Bholenath...." Then I couldn't stop myself. All his life we had teased him by calling him Bholenath, and today his own wife was calling him that. If his soul was somewhere nearby, it must have started to jump up and down. I continued crying, but I also burst out laughing.

Back at my home, people rebuked me severely. They said, "Don't ever go to another wake."

I asked them, "But what is wrong? Can't these things happen together?"

They replied, "Stop your nonsense!" They all explained, "Whether they can happen together or not is not even the point. When someone dies, it is appropriate to cry and it is inappropriate to laugh. And then to do both together is sheer madness."

But have you ever seen young children cry? If a child laughs too much, his laughter will slowly change to tears. That is why village mothers say, "Don't laugh too much, my son, otherwise you will start crying" – because the division is still not very clear to a young child. He still lives in non-duality. When he laughs, his laughter gradually becomes tears. When he cries, it gradually turns into laughter. Opposites are not yet opposite to him. All things are still one for him in some way. A sage becomes one again, he becomes like a small child again.

Jesus has said, "Only those who are like small children will be able to enter the kingdom of God." Like small children....

Don't think *"sadhu"* means a seeker, a disciplinarian. A *sadhu* means: one has become a child again, innocent again.

I am not aware of my condition,
I have only heard it from others
That I am in deep distress.

A *sadhu* has no awareness of his own condition; he disappears. Just as the divine is a missing entity without an address, the *sadhu* is also a missing entity. If you unite with one who has no home, you will have no home. If you unite with an unknown entity, you will become unknown too.

I am not aware of my condition,
I have only heard it from others
That I am in deep distress.

A *sadhu*, an enlightened mystic, comes to know of his own actions through others: that he was laughing or crying, that he had gone mad or was dancing on the streets. He finds out about it when people talk of it, because when he is doing something he is totally in it, he does not stand back and watch. This is the difference between the paths of meditation and devotion. On the path of meditation you stand at a distance, you stand back and watch; you are always the watcher. No matter what is happening you remain apart; you stand at a distance, untouched. You are not in the action.

Devotion means you are not to stand at a distance, you are not the watcher; you are the doer. Devotion is to have become totally the doer, to have become immersed in whatsoever is happening, to have become so totally immersed that no crevice or corner of yourself remains untouched — every pore of your body is drowned in it.

An action is total only when your consciousness is completely immersed in it. When you are not the watcher but the doer, when you are so totally a doer that you no longer remain separate, when only the act remains, then this absolute act is called devotion. And when you have completely disappeared into the act...while singing a song only the singing remains and not the singer, only the dancing remains and not the dancer, only the devotional chanting remains and not the chanter.... When the devotee bows down at the feet of the divine there is only bowing, there is no part of him standing back watching: "I am bowing." If you are seeing yourself bowing, you are not bowing; your ego has remained standing. The body has bowed down but not you.

I have heard that a *fakir* came to see Bayazid. He bowed down as was the custom. Then he got up and asked Bayazid a question.

Bayazid said, "Bow down first!"

The *fakir* said: "I have just bowed down, and you are asking me to first bow down – didn't you see me bowing down?

Bayazid said: "Your body bowed down, but you did not. Bow down!"

A similar thing happened in Buddha's life. An emperor came to him with diamonds and gems in one hand and lotuses in the other, even though it was not the season for lotuses. He thought, "Buddha might not like it if I offer him diamonds and gems. What will he do with diamonds and gems? If so, I will offer him flowers. Surely he will like flowers instead!" He was just about to offer his handful of diamonds and gems to Buddha when Buddha said, "Don't offer like that, just drop it!"

The emperor hesitated – because there is a joy of its own in offering: the joy of egoism, of having offered such precious gems. And Buddha simply says, "Drop it!" But when Buddha says to drop them.... The emperor hesitated for a moment, and then dropped them, afraid he would have lost face in front of the assembly. There were so many people present, and Buddha is asking him to drop them on the ground. If he didn't.... So he dropped them on the ground.

And then the emperor got ready to offer the flowers. Again Buddha said, "Drop it." So he dropped the flowers as well. Then he was about to bow down with both his empty hands when the Buddha repeated, "Drop it!"

He stood up. He said, "Are you out of your mind? I have

nothing in my hands to drop anymore."

Buddha replied, "We are not talking about dropping what was
in your hands, we are talking about the one who was standing
holding things in his hands. What is the point of dropping
flowers, diamonds and gems? You must drop! You have come
with these flowers, these diamonds and gems to show what
a great emperor you are – you can offer such precious
things! On the outside you appear to be offering them to
me, but inside you are standing tall in your arrogance."

When a devotee bows down, there is only bowing down, there
is no one there who is bowing down. And when the devotee
dances, there is only the dancing, there is no one there who
is dancing. Only the act remains, not the one who is doing
it. The doer drowns completely in the act. Only the experiencing remains, the experiencer merges completely into the
experiencing. This merger is called simplicity. This merger
is surrender.

They cry while they sing and they laugh,
This is very paradoxical, says Daya.

He laughs when the divine makes him laugh, he cries when
the divine makes him cry; he does not laugh or cry of his
own accord. He goes wherever the divine takes him. He does
what the divine makes him do; when he is not made to do
anything, he doesn't do anything. He has let go of his own
will, he has dropped his own plans. Now he is simply an
instrument in the hands of the divine. So it looks very
paradoxical.

Drunk with the nectar of the divine,
Their state of knowing is unfathomable.
The riches of the three worlds are but worthless
For a sadhu, says Daya.

Drunk with the nectar of the divine.... It is a lovely expression:
Drunk with the nectar of the divine.... Those who have drunk the
nectar of the divine are intoxicated, ecstatic. *Drunk with the*
nectar of the divine.... Those who have tasted the nectar of the
divine no longer have any sense of themselves, no awareness,
no consciousness of themselves.

Always remember that as long as you are conscious of
yourself you cannot be aware of the divine. These two swords
don't fit into the same sheath. As long as "I" is there, the
divine is not. The divine appears only when the "I" has gone
away. *Drunk with the nectar of the divine....* Those who are...

Drunk with the nectar of the divine,
Their state of knowing is unfathomable.

Their consciousness is unfathomable, boundless – because
as soon as you surrender, all your boundaries disappear. You
are limited because *you* are there. The divine is limitless.

Understand this. The Ganges flows to the sea – it is a big
river but it still has its banks. When it enters the ocean, the
banks disappear. People are like small waterfalls; when they
enter the ocean all their boundaries vanish. A drop is no
longer a drop when it enters the ocean – it becomes the ocean
itself. It ceases to be a drop and becomes the ocean.

Drunk with the nectar of the divine,
Their state of knowing is unfathomable.

Their consciousness, their perception, their state of enlightenment becomes simply unfathomable. They are intoxicated
with the taste of the divine.

In his *Rubaiyat*, Omar Khayyam is talking about this elixir
of the divine. Fitzgerald, who translated Omar Khayyam into
English, didn't understand him. He thought that Omar
Khayyam was talking about wine. This was a great injustice
to the Sufi, Omar Khayyam. People think that Omar
Khayyam was talking about wine, bars, barmaids – things of
that sort – so you will find taverns named "Omar Khayyam"
or "The Rubaiyat." But Omar Khayyam was talking about
the wine of the divine. He was a Sufi *fakir*. He never tasted
wine, he never went to a tavern. All the pictures of Omar
Khayyam show him sitting with a wine jug by his side. This
jug is a symbol. It refers to another place. This jug is not of
this world, it is not made from earthly clay, and the wine
being poured is the divine wine.

The enlightened ones have often suffered from injustice in
this world, but none as great as that done to Omar Khayyam
– because each time his work was translated into another
language, the same mistake occurred. Fitzgerald was a great
and important poet. He added a feather to Omar Khayyam's
cap, but he got it all wrong. There is no comparison between
the wine of love and the wine of the divine. The poem was
ruined. It became a poem about a tavern.

But the symbol of wine is very significant. It is significant
because what happens with wine on a very small scale happens
with the divine on a very large scale, on a vast scale.

Drunk with the nectar of the divine,
Their state of knowing is unfathomable.
The riches of the three worlds are but worthless
For a sadhu, says Daya.

To a *sadhu*, to one who has become simple, all the riches of
the world seem worthless. Why? Don't misunderstand this.
People have explained it to you wrongly in the past. They
have been telling you to regard the riches of the world as
worthless. Daya's sutra doesn't say that. Daya's sutra tells
you that a *sadhu knows* that the riches of the three worlds are
worthless. It is not a matter of thinking like this, of thinking
that you hoard gold and then think of it as clay. How can
you? You may tell yourself a million times that it is clay, but
you will still know that it is gold. You don't put clay in front
of you and tell yourself over and over again that it is clay;
you put gold there and remind yourself that it is clay. You
know the difference very well. You are just trying to falsify
that difference; you are just trying to convince yourself that
it is clay, that it is not worth anything at all.

Who are you trying to convince? Inside, your mind knows
that it is gold, that it is very valuable.... You are only trying
to suppress that mind by saying that it is clay, that it is
nothing; that it is here today and gone tomorrow, that
all this pomp and show will be left behind here when you
leave this world. But as things are, you *do* think that it is
valuable. You will leave it behind here – but if it were in your
power, you wouldn't leave it here, you would take it with you.
You will miss it when you leave.

You are only trying to console yourself. Please note this
point: a *sadhu* is not one who thinks of gold as nothing more

than clay, a *sadhu* is one who *knows* that the gold is clay. And what is the difference between knowing and thinking? Thinking is borrowed. You take others' knowing to be your knowing, but it is stale, not worth a penny. And in this way you will create a false way of being; you will become a hypocrite – not a *sadhu*, not an enlightened one.

How does a *sadhu* know that riches are worthless? His art of knowing is quite different. Until you know the wealth of the divine, the riches of this world cannot become worthless. How can they? Only when you have known the larger can the smaller be known as small.

You may have heard the story about Akbar. One day he came to his court and drew a line. He challenged his courtiers to make the line smaller without touching it. The courtiers racked their brains, but no one knew how to do it without touching the line.

Birbal got up and drew a bigger line next to Akbar's line. He didn't touch the first line, but it was immediately shorter.

You have been taught to take the riches of this world to be clay. I don't say this, neither does Daya. Those who know have never said such a thing and never will. How can they say such a foolish thing? But ninety-nine out of a hundred of your *mahatmas* are as foolish as you are – sometimes even more foolish.

Draw the larger line first; there will be no need to even touch the smaller one. Experience the wealth of the divine, and the entire wealth of this world will become worthless. It is like a man walking with a stone in his hand – a colored stone that shines in the sunlight. He thinks the stone is precious. If he finds a diamond, the Kohinoor for example, he will no longer think that his shining stone is so precious. He won't have to drop the stone, he won't have to renounce it – he will simply forget it. He won't even notice when it slips out of his hands, he won't even turn back to look. Which will he keep – the diamond or the stone? He will have to empty his fist to make room for the diamond. He will need to make room for the diamond.

I tell you to search for the divine, but not to renounce the world. The day the ray of the divine descends on you the world will begin to be left behind. That is why I have not given my sannyasins a system that renounces the world. Sannyas does not mean dropping anything. Sannyas is not renunciation, sannyas is not escapism. Sannyas is an invitation to the divine, sannyas is a call to the divine: "O beloved guest, come! Be seated. I will wait. I will worship, pray, call and meditate. Come!" The day the divine comes, the larger line is drawn – it is a boundless line, it has neither beginning nor end. One doesn't even notice when or where the smaller line of this world fades and then disappears.

You can never claim to have renounced after this happens – how can you? If you have never renounced anything, how can you claim to be a renunciate? If someone claims to have renounced, know well that he has missed. If someone tells you that he has renounced millions of rupees, you can be sure he is still holding on to them, the counting is still carrying on inside him. If someone boasts about how much he has renounced, you should understand that the larger line has not yet entered his life, he is still struggling with the first line. He is still trying to do everything he can to make it

shorter. And the line cannot be shortened that easily. Even
if you try to rub it out you cannot erase it – because the
trivial doesn't disappear without the presence of the vast.

Can you take the darkness out of a room without bringing
in a light? How can you do that? You can fight with the
darkness, you can close your eyes and pretend that the
darkness has gone, but when you open your eyes again you
will find that it is still there. Once light comes darkness has
no existence.

The world is darkness, the divine is light. Search for the light,
don't fight with the darkness.

Drunk with the nectar of the divine,
Their state of knowing is unfathomable.

Drown yourself in the wine of the divine, drink it to your
heart's content, let every pore of your body be ecstatically
intoxicated with it.

The riches of the three worlds are but worthless
For a sadhu, says Daya.

He knows it to be so, he doesn't believe it to be so. Believing
doesn't help in any way. Belief is very weak, impotent. One
must experience that the world is futile. When you experience
this, all clinging drops. You don't have to drop it, it drops
of its own accord. The world vanishes – just like a dry leaf
falling silently from a tree. Then you will not wander around
telling people, "I have renounced." Others may say, "Look
how much he has renounced!" but you will be surprised:
"What renunciation? Renunciation in what way?"

One day a man went to Ramakrishna and said to him, "You are a great renunciate."

Ramakrishna began to laugh, "What a great joke!" he said. "I thought you were the great renunciate."

The man replied, "Surely you are joking. But you never joke. What do you mean? I, a renunciate? I am a worldly creature, completely immersed in this world – twenty-four hours a day. I gather these worthless objects twenty-four hours a day – and you call me a renunciate?"

Ramakrishna replied, "Yes, I do indeed. I call you a renunciate. Never call me a renunciate, even by mistake, because I am enjoying the divine. How can I be a renunciate? You are gathering worthless worldly objects, and you have abandoned the divine. Your renunciation is great! You are the one who is truly selfless. We are mere pleasure-seekers enjoying the divine. What have we renounced? We have renounced a penny and found a diamond. Is that renunciation? You have renounced a diamond and kept a penny: your renunciation is greater than mine, it is certainly far greater."

The worldly man is a great renunciate. He picks and sifts through the rubbish, finding and keeping junk. If a diamond or a gem accidentally appears, he moves it to one side. If occasionally, meditation finds its way into his life, he moves it to one side, thinking, "How can I do that now? Right now I am too busy getting rich. Meditation? – not yet!" If sannyas raises its head, he ignores it, saying, "Not yet, there is still the rest of my life. I have so much to achieve. I must prove myself." If occasionally he remembers the divine, if the divine's waves stir in him, he shakes himself and brushes it away. "This is a dangerous business," he says. "Don't get ensnared in such things."

The true renunciate is not even aware of the place of renunciation in his life.

I am not in my normal senses,
But perhaps you may know...
People say that you have ruined me.

One day the devotee will say to the divine, "People are simply unbelievable: they tell me that I have been ruined, that I have renounced the world, that I have given up everything and am a fool, that I am mad."

I am not in my normal senses,
But perhaps you may know...

The devotee will say to the divine: "Maybe you know – I have no idea what happened or when, what took place or how! I am totally intoxicated."

People say that you have destroyed me.

He puts his feet in one spot, but they land elsewhere,
His body is ecstatic with delight.
The more he drowns in the beauty of godliness
The more his love grows, says Daya.

He puts his feet in one spot, but they land elsewhere... this is the condition of the devotee. He puts his feet in one place but they land elsewhere. He aims for one place and arrives at another. He is not in control of himself, he is under the control of the divine. He has no control over himself.

Remember, as long as you are in control, ego is there. Ego

is another name for your control. The day you surrender your mastery at the feet of the divine, the day you offer it saying, "Now you take care of me, now thy will be done" – then your feet may land wherever they want, however they wish. You don't control your feet.

He puts his feet in one spot, but they land elsewhere...

And then there is such ecstatic intoxication! If such a vast immensity descends into your small courtyard, won't you become drunk? Won't you start dancing if the spring of such bliss begins to flow into your miserable life, if such a stream of divine nectar flows across your despairing, sad and anguished desert and an oasis blossoms? Will your feet know where they are landing now? Will your feet choose where they are going?

He puts his feet in one spot, but they land elsewhere,
His body is ecstatic with delight.

It is marvelous.... *His body is ecstatic with delight.* Every pore of his body has filled with delight, with celebration. The vastness has arrived, the beloved has come. Light has descended into the darkness, life dances where once there was only death. *His body is ecstatic with delight....* Every pore is thrilled, dancing. Every pore is filled with music. The veena of the heart is playing. There is happiness, delight, real celebration.

The life of a devotee is the life of celebration.

For too long a sense of sadness has prevailed in the name of religion. The temples, the mosques and the churches have become very gray. Dance, celebration and exultation have all been lost. The so-called saints sit like heavy rocks on your chests. True religiousness is very joyful, very ecstatic. True religiousness is not stony; it is like flowers. It is not sad; it is exultation and celebration.

A few days ago an old, traditional sannyasin came to see me. He said, "What is all this? What kind of an ashram is this? People dancing, joyful, happy.... People are ecstatic – as if they were drunk. They should be serious. A seeker of truth should always be serious. The search for truth is a very serious affair."

I said to him, "Here, we are not searching for the truth; we are searching for the divine, for God." The very word truth becomes too serious. It has become dry and juiceless. The desert has entered into it.

Do you see the difference? "The search for the truth" – it sounds as though you will have to spread a web of logic, you will have to use your intellect, to torture yourself. "The search for God, for the beloved, for your very dear friend," is quite a different matter. Philosophers search for the truth, religious people search for the divine. Philosophers call the divine the truth, and in this way they even make the divine sad. Religious people call even the truth "lord," the beloved. They create a relationship of love. This relationship is not based on logic; it is a relationship of love, of affection and of attachment.

His body is ecstatic with delight.

When your body and heart begin to dance, when your body and heart are united in one celebration.... And remember what Daya says: *His body is ecstatic with delight...* that not only your soul is dancing, because the idea that only the soul is ecstatic is an incomplete view – it is a judgment against the body. When your soul dances, your mind also dances, and when your mind dances, your body dances too. Your totality will dance, every part of you will dance. When the divine comes, not just the soul receives its wealth, but your mind, your state of consciousness will also expand without limits.

Their state of knowing is unfathomable.

And when the divine comes, your body will also become sacred; it will become divine, you will become "a divine body." When the divine comes, all will turn to gold; when it comes, all will become nectar. The flowers will certainly blossom – even the thorns will blossom.

He puts his feet in one spot, but they land elsewhere,
His body is ecstatic with delight.
The more he drowns in the beauty of godliness
The more his love grows, says Daya.

And the more you immerse yourself in the beauty of *godliness...the more his love grows....* In the same proportion your love grows.

The characteristic of a religious person is the stream of love which flows from him. That is the only touchstone for testing whether someone is religious or not. The more your love, your affection increases, the more you begin to give love unconditionally – loving those who need it and those who don't, those who ask for it and those who don't – the more you start going to people and filling their receptacles with your love, the more you spread your love around you as you walk, the more you give it to friends and to strangers without any reason, without calculation.... It is like "baling out with both hands," like trying to get rid of water flooding into a boat....

Kabir has said: "When water starts filling the boat, you must bale it out with both hands." Similarly, when love starts filling your heart, "bale it out with both hands." This is the task of the *sadhu*.

When you are baling out love, distributing it, when love starts flowing from you and you become a temple from which unending streams of love flow, then you should know that the divine has been realized in you. Claims about this mean nothing. If you say that you have found God, that means nothing. What matters is: how much are you sharing love, how much does your life move along the path of love?

In India the situation is just the opposite. The mess of thousands of years, and what the *pundits* and priests have promoted in the name of religion, means that we call someone a *sadhu* whose love has dried up completely, who is like wood, like a dry log. Even if you burn him, he doesn't give off any smoke because there is no juice, no sap left in him. But we call such a person a saint, we say that he has arrived. He has not reached to God — he seems to have arrived somewhere else! He must be somewhere else — because the divine is very juicy. Your saints are absolutely juiceless, and the divine is very juicy.

Just think: if the saints were given the job of running the world, what sort of a state would it be in? Would the flowers blossom? No. Would the trees turn green? No. Would a man love a woman? No. Would a mother love her son? No. Would a friend live or die for another? No. If this world were in the hands of the saints, your entire life would become machine-like. It would be there, but minus one thing – love. There would be no love.

Hence Gurdjieff used to say that the so-called saints seem to be against existence, because existence is so full of juice. Existence is flowing with tremendous juice – in the moon and the stars, in the rocks and the mountains, in every direction, in endless ways. Existence is a dancer, a singer, a lover! And the same will happen to you when religion grows in your life.

The more he drowns in the beauty of godliness,
The more his love grows, says Daya.

This is the symptom. Accept this as a touchstone – that if your love grows each day at every step, then know that you are coming close to the divine, that you are moving ahead, that you are on the right path. If your love begins to decrease, then know that you are missing something, that somewhere you are going astray.

When you come near a garden, you start feeling a cool breeze and a fleeting fragrance of flowers in the air. Even if the garden has not yet become visible, you still know that the air is becoming fragrant, cooler. You know that you are moving in the right direction, towards the garden. In the same way, when your love begins to grow – *His body is ecstatic with delight* – and your affection is growing each moment and you begin sharing it unconditionally; when it is not a trading but a gift, then you should know that you have begun to approach the divine, that the temple is not very far away, that it is very close. Perhaps you are already standing on the steps.

He laughs, he sings, he cries; he rises and falls again and again,
He is ever-restless.
But once he has tasted the nectar of the divine, says Daya,
He can endure all pain of separation.

Let these words sink deeply into you:

He laughs, he sings, he cries; he rises and falls again and again,
He is ever-restless.

The man who is thirsty for the divine, laughs, sings, cries, rises and falls. He is delighted that a light shower has begun to fall. He is also restless in his desire for more. He is content because the divine has manifest itself a little, but he is impatient for the divine to descend completely. He is satisfied that a ray has come, but he is also dissatisfied in a way which he never was before, when he did not know any ray. Now that he has felt one ray, he wants the whole sun. He waits for the union with the supreme sun.

He laughs, he sings, he cries; he rises and falls again and again,
He is ever-restless.
But once he has tasted the nectar of the divine, says Daya,
He can endure all ·pain of separation.

But once a person is addicted to the taste of the divine, once he has tasted it, once he has had a sip of its wine....

But once he has tasted the nectar of the divine, says Daya,
He can endure all pain of separation.

No matter how much pain there is in his life, no matter how much his separation from the beloved inflames and burns him — even if every pore of his body is yearning and crying out — if he has tasted it even once he cannot turn back. Now, there is no way to turn back.

The devotee thinks of turning back many times. You may not understand this. Many times the devotee thinks of turning back, because along with bliss he is also experiencing tremendous pain.

Look at it this way. You have heard the story of the problem of the ninety-nine, haven't you? The same thing which occurs in this world also occurs in spiritual matters.

An emperor once had a barber who also massaged him every day and received one rupee for his work. It was a long time ago and one rupee was worth a lot then. It was enough for a whole month. How to tell of the barber's joy? He enjoyed life to the full and often invited his friends to eat with him. The whole village called him a generous man. One rupee was really something in those days. And he simply had fun — he would massage the emperor once in the morning and then enjoy the rest of the day. He held card-playing sessions where his friends played dice and chess and sang songs, and at night they danced. He was a very happy man.

The emperor began to feel jealous. He was jealous of the barber's joy. The emperor had everything, but he was not as carefree as the barber. The barber had nothing but his joy, which was beyond all words. He worked for about an hour in the morning and then enjoyed himself for the rest of the day.

The emperor asked his minister the secret of the barber's happiness. The minister replied, "It is not much of a secret. We will cure him."

From the very next day the barber appeared to be recovering. "Recovering," meaning that he began to feel miserable. In less than a week, he was in very bad shape.

The emperor asked him, "What is wrong? Why are you wasting away like this? You no longer have your gambling and chess sessions. I don't hear the sound of music coming from your house at night. What is the matter?"

The barber said, "Because you have asked me, your majesty, I will have to tell you. The riddle of ninety-nine has arisen in my life."

"What is wrong? What do you mean?" asked the emperor.

The barber replied, "Someone threw a bag of ninety-nine rupees into my house."

The emperor asked him, "Why does that upset you? Enjoy them!"

The barber explained, "It has spoiled all my fun. The next day, when I received my rupee from you, I thought that if I saved it, then I would have a hundred rupees. It was just a matter of one day. I would do without pudding, milk and the games for just one day. I fasted. Things have become very bad since then. I saved one rupee. The next day it occurred to me that if I continued to save in this way, I would be rich in a few days. I had a hundred, so I changed the figure to one hundred and one. This continuing preoccupation is destroying my life."

What happens in the world also happens in your spiritual life. When the first ray of the divine descends into your life, you suddenly realize for the first time what you have been missing, what you have been lacking so far. What you called life was not really life; for the first time you have tasted life. Now a great desire arises within you, a longing to have the whole thing. You have had a taste, you are addicted. Daya has used the right words:

But once he has tasted the nectar of the divine, says Daya,
He can endure all pain of separation.

On the one hand you have begun to enjoy greatly, but on the other hand you feel a pain because you want more and more — you want all of it! When such a small ray has intoxicated you, when one small sip has filled you with such bliss, you want to drown yourself in it completely.

At such moments, one feels many difficulties. Many times the devotee will start thinking, "Lord, I want to go back. This pain is so intense that I cannot bear it any longer. I cannot endure this waiting for a moment longer."

The strength to abandon love came not even once,
The thought to abandon love came again and again.

The thought comes many times, "I am tired of this trouble, I want to get out of this intoxication of love."

"The strength to abandon love came not even once" — one

could not gather the courage to leave. "The thought to abandon love came again and again" – but this thought has occurred time and again: "I am tired of this trouble, I want to go back to the old days. In some ways they were better; I was lost in darkness, but at least I was oblivious of things." You had not experienced the taste, so in a way you were at ease, you were happy, you were at peace. You didn't have this problem, this restlessness. You were not crying day in, day out. You didn't spend every moment with your eyes fixed on the path. Now it doesn't feel right to sleep and it doesn't feel right to be awake – there is only this restlessness all around.

"The strength to abandon love came not even once." You couldn't find the courage to drop love, to renounce love. "The thought to abandon love came again and again." Many times you wanted to drop love, you wanted to go back.

On this path of loving you
Came that step which is taken with a heavy heart,
Came that point of letting go of love.

There are times when one wonders: In the journey of loving you, do there come stages when one has also to let go of love? Many times one feels like quitting and running away. Many times one feels like going back. If so much pain is coming with just the little that has happened so far…. Of course, happiness has begun to enter one's life, but it is because of this that you also start to feel an immense pain. One has started to see a little bit, but because of that, the darkness has also become visible.

Understand it this way. A blind man lives in darkness, he

becomes at ease with it. But when his eyes begin to recover he can see a few blurred objects. Because he can see these things dimly, he can also see the darkness. Before that, he couldn't see the darkness either.

Remember this: a blind person cannot see the darkness either – because to see darkness eyes are needed. Without eyes, you cannot see either light or darkness. You are mistaken if you think that a blind person sees only darkness. That is your experience. When you shut your eyes you see darkness, but it is so only because you have eyes to see. A blind person doesn't even see darkness. But if his eyesight recovers a little he is greatly afflicted; he sees things dimly, and in that haze he can also see the darkness. And then an intense desire arises in him to be able to see properly, to be able to see completely.

But although you want to go back a million times, you cannot. The devotee quits many times; sits down and closes his doors. But then again and again he opens them.

Many are faithful, but none is a beauty,
Come, let us talk of that unfaithful one again.

Many times the devotee thinks, "Enough, forget it! The journey is too difficult. I have got myself into so much trouble – it was a mistake ever to have begun this journey. Worldly people are better off than I am – at least they are living a life of ease. They go to the shop, they come home, they carry on with their businesses, the law courts, their law cases…they keep going perfectly oblivious of anything else. What a misfortune it was to become aware of what I have become aware of! How did I become so addicted to this?"

Satsang, a heart-to-heart communion with a master, is an addiction. You will want to run away many times. You *will* feel like quitting many times. You will quit many times. But you won't really be able to give it up.

"Many are faithful, but none is a beauty…." Once you have seen the beauty of the divine, nothing else in the world is as beautiful. You might try to engage yourself a million times with other things, but you won't be able to.

Come, let us talk of that unfaithful one again.

Again and again you will come back to your devotional songs, to your worship and remembrance of the divine, "that unfaithful one."

There have been but two arduous times in my life:

One – before you came,
The other – after you left.

But you will only find this out when the first ray of the divine has come to you, when you have heard its footsteps. Then you will know that your life before this was also a time of suffering. There was no substance in it, it was worthless. And now a time of even greater suffering is with you.

There have been but two arduous times in my life:

One – before you came,
The other – after you left.

But slowly, slowly the door opens, slowly, slowly the light begins to shine.

The sadness of separating from you
Has saved me from all other afflictions.
None dares to approach me now.

In time, only one memory will remain – that of the divine.
Only the fire of separation from the divine remains. The
thousand afflictions you have known disappear, leaving just
this one. All afflictions – of wealth, of position, of prestige,
of this and that – they all leave you and only one problem
remains. And there is no way you can escape from this one
problem.

But once he has tasted the nectar of the divine, says Daya,
He can endure all pain of separation.

The flame of the anguish of separation is born in my heart,
Come, O divine, come my beloved.

And now something blazes like a fire in your heart.

The flame of the anguish of separation is born in my heart,
Come, O divine, come my beloved.

Now you wait for the divine to come, for the beloved to
come. The fire is so intense that you want it to rain, you want
his raincloud to come and cool you.

The flame of the anguish of separation is born in my heart,
Come, O divine, come my beloved.
Come, O enchanter of hearts,
Come, O Krishna, O simple one,
I long to see you.

There is only one desire, one longing left – *I long to see you,* I
yearn to see you. The whole search has moved to his eyes;

everything in him becomes a waiting. The whole energy of
the devotee turns into prayer and waiting.

I remember neither the cruelties of the world
Nor my own faithfulness.
Except love, I remember nothing now.

...Just a madness, an intense madness, an intoxication which
you will not be able to explain to anyone. Yes, when two mad
people meet, they will understand it. That is why Daya says,
*Speak not to those who have no interest in remembering the divine. Open
your heart to those who are in love with the divine.* Only they will be
able to understand your pain.

The flame of the anguish of separation is born in my heart,
Come, O divine, come my beloved.
Come, O enchanter of hearts,
Come, O Krishna, O simple one,
I long to see you.

The eyes of the devotee are completely focused. His whole
energy moves slowly to his eyes. And the day that your
whole energy becomes the eyes, the ultimate happens... in
that very moment.

Our relationship was only of the eyes,
Now this matter is reaching to the heart.
What until yesterday I was hiding from my heart,
Is now reaching to my lips as a melody.
I could see you but once, and never again more,
But still no eyes can contain your loveliness.
I want to sing of your full, graceful beauty,
But no melody can do it justice.

Tying the sacred knot, it feels as if
My heart has walked around the wedding fire,
The bride of love has mounted the palanquin,
Dreams are its bearers.
The golden palanquin turns towards her beloved's home.
With red-patterned feet and henna-patterned hands,
Love knocks at the door of the heart.
Our relationship was only of the eyes,
Now the matter is reaching to the heart.

Slowly, slowly your energy begins to pulsate at only one
point: you want to find the beloved, you want to see him,
to meet him. When you have no other melody inside you,
there remains no obstacle to your union. But until that union
has happened, know that your longing is unfulfilled, your
thirst is unquenched, and that there are also other thirsts in
you. As long as there are also other things on the laundry
list of your life, as long as finding the divine is only one
amongst the many other items to be attained, you will never
reach to the divine. When all your energy crystallizes into
only one desire, that desire is called a longing.

Right now our desires are many: to find wealth, to find
position, to find love, to find prestige, to find this and that,
to find a big house.... Your desires are many; you are divided
between them. The horses of your desires are galloping in
different directions. When all these horses are harnessed
together and run in only one direction, that of meeting the
divine....

Jesus has said: "First seek ye the Lord, and all else will come
by itself." If you run after everything else, not only will you
not attain them, you will also not attain the Lord. The person

who runs after many things, misses this one thing too.

Rahim says: "By attaining the one all else is attained." The person who attains this one thing attains everything. What higher prestige can there be than finding the divine? What better position can be attained after attaining to the divine? What wealth will there be left for you to find after you have found the divine? In finding the divine all other attainments have already happened.

My hands are tired of shooing crows,
My eyes of looking expectantly at the path.
My heart has fallen into the ocean of love,
And there is no shore, no exit.

There is no way back. The river has entered the ocean, now how can it return?

My hands are tired of shooing crows...

The crow is symbolic. Crows are the futile thoughts moving in the sky of your mind. You have never invited them, but they come anyway, like crows, and they caw all the time....

All the crows of India live at the place where Krishnamurti speaks in Bombay. They like that place. You can hardly hear Krishnamurti, because those crows are so noisy. But Krishnamurti insists. He says, "Let the crows caw, you just listen...."

Such is the state of the mind – cawing all the time. You call on the Lord, and the crows caw. Each thought is a crow. And it is meaningful to call them crows because firstly, they come uninvited and secondly, their cawing is very discordant. There is no melodiousness in it at all. It is great crowd, full of noise, complete turmoil, but without even one shred of music.

My hands are tired of shooing crows....

Daya says, "I am watching the path for you. I am afraid that some crow may come, interfering, and I may miss you; that some crow of a thought may come between us, that you may arrive and I may not see you.... So my hands are tired of shooing the crows away."

My hands are tired of shooing crows,
My eyes of looking expectantly at the path.

"And my eyes are fixed on the door, on the path. They are open, watching, waiting in deep welcome. My eyes are getting tired, my hands are getting tired."

My heart has fallen into the ocean of love...

And her heart is like a river that has fallen into the ocean.

...And there is no shore, no exit.

"How nicely you have got me entangled," complains Daya. "You have spread your net well, you have left no way to escape"...*and there is no shore, no exit.* Now there is no way out. When the river enters the ocean, it enters completely and cannot go back: "There is no way back and you are taking so long to come. There is no news of your coming. My hands are tired, my eyes are swollen. You have left me with nowhere to go back to. What a trap, what a conspiracy against me!"

This is a lover's complaint. Many times the devotee complains – only a devotee can do that. Others cannot even dare
to do so. The devotee even fights with God; he becomes
angry. Many times he will clearly say, "I refuse to worship, I
will stop all offerings now. There is a limit to everything!"

Only a lover will dare to speak like this – because love is
courage. And the lover knows that even such rashness will
be forgiven. A pundit cannot dare like this, neither can a
priest.

Sometimes Ramakrishna worshipped in his temple, sometimes he didn't. And his worship too was very strange.
Sometimes it went on for hours and sometimes it ended
within a few minutes. Sometimes the entire day would pass
in worship. And there were some other interesting things. He
would taste the food himself first and only then would he
offer it to the deity.

People complained. The temple committee summoned
Ramakrishna and asked him what sort of worship he was
performing, saying that there should be a certain discipline
in it.

Ramakrishna said, "Whoever heard of love having a discipline? How can love exist where there are rules? And where
there is love, how can rules exist? These two things don't
belong together. If you want someone to follow rules, find
yourself a priest. I am a lover. I will worship but it cannot
be confined by rules. If I don't feel like worshipping, I won't
pretend. Should I stand here and offer false worship? How
can I worship when I am angry? I won't do it – there can't
be any worship.

"Let God wait! If he torments me, I will torment him. The doors will remain closed – let him suffer, let him remember me just as I remember him. And as to offering food, my mother always tasted food before she gave it to me, so I cannot offer him food without tasting it first to make sure that it is worthy of him. First I have to taste it. If you want rules, find a priest!"

Ramakrishna was a true priest. Now this is totally different, this is a state of feeling. The devotee will complain many times, even become angry. After all, there are limits to everything....

I am afraid this pain is becoming incurable.
I am afraid this pain is becoming incurable,
Even for you.

The devotee realizes many times that his suffering is getting out of hand, that his pain is continually increasing.

I am afraid this pain is becoming incurable...

He is afraid that even the beloved may not have the cure but is nevertheless getting him more and more entangled – only to say in the end that there *is* no cure. It is becoming difficult to turn back.

I am afraid this pain is becoming incurable.
I am afraid this pain is becoming incurable,
Even for you.

"My suffering is so intense that I am afraid that in the end you may not be able to treat it. Then I will be stuck. Going back is not possible... because I have tasted love:

But once he has tasted the nectar of the divine, says Daya,
...there is no shore, no exit.

You have tricked me so well!"

The devotee will fight many times, will quarrel many times.
When the quarrel is full of love, that too is a form of prayer.
If you don't have the courage to quarrel with the divine, you
don't know anything about devotion yet. Your love is still
weak if you cannot fight with the beloved. True love endures
a million fights and still survives. No fight can break it. The
truth is it becomes even deeper, even more refined and
shining after every fight. The devotee is angry with God, but
then again he persuades him. And if a devotee is really angry,
then God also makes an effort to persuade him!

So those moments do come when your quarreling is really
authentic and your prayer is really true; when your impatience
is real and your heart is one burning flame. Then it happens,
then the rains come.

The universe is not indifferent towards you. Existence is not
unconcerned about you. Existence is as interested in you as
you are in it. Keep this key in your heart. If you feel that
existence is unconcerned about you, that it is indifferent to
you, that it has no interest in you, then this means only one
thing: that, as yet, you have not taken any interest
in existence. You are standing aloof from existence and in
return existence is remaining aloof from you.

As you come closer to existence, it comes closer to you. It
hums when you hum. It embraces you when you embrace
it. As you move courageously towards existence, it responds
to the same degree towards you.

Existence is not unresponsive. This is the whole science of
devotion. A response is intrinsic to existence. If you call, the
response comes. If you don't receive a response, know well
that something somewhere is lacking in your calling.

Oh thou beloved with the parched lips,
Let your thirst so awaken,
That yonder dark cloud cannot depart without raining.

The dense clouds thunder and rain
A hundred times on this earth,
The joyous strains of the monsoon raga
Echo in the lanes and alleyways,
But whenever I meet you coming and going
I see only an empty water-pot in your hands.
While everyone else is full, you are thirsty,
While the world is cheerful, you are sad.

The song of the beloved dances delicately
In the throat of the papiha bird,
The low, dark cloud plays pitter-patter on its flute,
It is time to meet, the earth is in a fresh embrace.
Why is it that the lamp on your balcony
Appears to be running out?

While the honeyed garden hums, you are dejected.
While it is raining gold, you are in poverty.
Oh you who puts the moon to shame,
Light such lamps,
That a falling tear may smile like a star.

Oh thou beloved with the parched lips,
Let your thirst so awaken,
That yonder dark cloud cannot depart without raining.

It does rain, it has rained. It has rained on Daya, it has rained on Sahajo, it has rained on Meera. Why can't it rain on you? It has rained and it will rain – again and again.

Thirst is needed, a deep thirst is needed. The day your thirst is total, the rain comes out of that total thirst. Your total thirst becomes the rain-cloud. There is no other cloud. The day your call is total, the day your call is from your whole being, the day you stake everything in your call, holding nothing back, the divine appears.

Enough for today.

4

A PURE FLAME OF LOVE

The first question:

Osho,

What does devotion mean?

Devotion means that you are beginning to experience the divine in matter, that you are beginning to perceive the unmanifest in the manifest, that the formless has begun to be glimpsed shimmering in form.

Devotion means that whatever is visible to you, a shadow of the invisible has also begun to appear within it. If you stop at what is visible, devotion will never be born in you. You must listen for the sound of the invisible approaching, you must hear the footsteps of that which cannot be heard. Your senses have to become ecstatic, they have to be thrilled with the joy of that which is beyond all your senses. You begin to perceive the invisible through some hitherto unfamiliar medium — and the name of this medium is devotion. That which cannot be seen directly, which cannot be perceived by the eyes — that too can be seen, the invisible can become visible. The miracle of making the invisible visible is called devotion. Devotion is a kind of alchemy, a kind of science.

Perhaps you have never even thought about what happens when you fall in love. When you fall in love, do you see only the bones, the flesh and the marrow of your lover? If that is all you see, then one day you might just as well fall in love with a corpse. No, you have had a glimpse of something else too. Your eyes have begun to enter deep within that person; the inner image of that person has begun to surface. This is what it means whenever you fall in love – whether you understand it or not. The divine has called you from some window.

So the first glimpse of the divine always comes through your lover. And one who has never loved can never know devotion, because devotion is love in full flood. Love is like a light shower of rain, devotion is a flood – but the basic natures of both love and devotion are the same. Love has limits, devotion has no limits. Love ends: it is here today, maybe not tomorrow; it comes for a moment and is then lost. It is ephemeral. *The world is like the last morning star.* Once devotion comes, it stays. Then there is no way to get out of it. Once you have entered it, you have entered it forever. It is not possible to turn back. In love it is possible to turn back, because love is always a little hazy, a little superficial. Devotion goes very deep.

So you must understand devotion through love. Love is the first lesson in devotion. You are a husband: you love your wife. You are a father: you love your son. You are a wife: you love your husband. You love your friends…. Wheresoever there is love, use it to search further.

Love is like a diamond in a mine; it has not yet been cleaned, it is still covered with dirt. For centuries it has lain together with pebbles and stones – its shine is lost. Love is like a diamond which has just been taken from a mine – it has not yet been cleaned, it has not yet been in the hands of a jeweler, it has not yet been touched by a chisel. Right now, only someone who is capable of looking at it very deeply can realize that it is a diamond. You cannot see what it is yet. This is why devotion is not seen in love – because love is like an uncut diamond. The same diamond has come to its refinement in a Meera, in a Daya, in a Sahajo; there is a shine on it, it has received the art of a jeweler's hands. *Then* it glitters. Much needs to be cut away.

The Kohinoor is the biggest diamond in the world. It weighed three times more on the day it was found. Only a third of it has remained after all the cutting, trimming and polishing. But its value has increased every time it has been trimmed. It has become more beautiful as new facets have emerged. Because it weighs only a third of its original weight, it should be less valuable today than on the day it was found – if you were to look from the point of view of weight. But it had no value on the day it was found. Its value has come through its refinement, through being polished.

There was a famous Western sculptor, Michelangelo. One day, as he was walking along, he noticed a large piece of marble lying by the side of the road near a marble shop. He had seen it many times, it had simply been dumped by the side of the road. He went into the shop and asked the shopkeeper the price of this abandoned piece of rock. The shopkeeper said, "It has no price. It is completely worthless. No sculptor wants to buy it. Take it if you want, we will be glad to be rid of it. You can have it free of charge, as long as you pay to take it away."

Michelangelo took the stone away. As he was taking it, the shopkeeper asked him, "What will you do with this worthless piece of rock? It is useless."

Michelangelo said, "I will let you know in a few months." After some time, he invited the shopkeeper to come to his home. There was a statue of Jesus lying in Mary's lap. The shopkeeper was spellbound. He said, "I have seen many statues, but where were you able to find this rare piece of marble?"

Michelangelo replied, "This is the same stone that you threw away and I took for nothing."

The shopkeeper could not believe him, "That crude piece of rock has nothing in common with this statue. They have nothing in common at all. How did you realize that such a worthless stone could be turned into this statue?"

Michelangelo replied, "Whenever I passed your shop, this statue used to call out to me from inside the rock. It asked me to free it, to take it out of its prison, to release it from its bondage."

I want to tell you that devotion lies imprisoned within the prison of love. And love calls out for its release. The day devotion is released from love, the day it emerges refined and purified, you find the divine. Love is like a nugget of gold which is full of impurities; devotion is gold which has passed through fire and been refined and cleansed. All the rubbish has been burned away, only the pure gold remains. Devotion is the purest form of love and love is an impure form of devotion.

So there are two things in love. Devotion is a part of love
and so is the world. The impurity in love is the world, and
the pure devotion hidden in that love is the divine. So a
discerning person will seek out the divine in love, and a fool
will descend into the world. Love is a ladder: the world is
below, the divine is above. If you go on purifying love you
will move towards the divine; if you go on polluting it,
you will descend into the world. Love becomes nothing more
than a dream when it gets too polluted, love becomes the
truth when its purity shines out.

Godliness is hidden in love – release it. And in love you have
had glimpses of godliness many times, but you didn't know
how to free it. Make your love more like a prayer and less of
a physical passion. Don't demand in love, give. Don't be a
beggar in love, become an emperor. Share in love, don't hoard.
Gradually you will begin to discover that the impurities in
your love are melting away. And as these impurities melt, a
pure flame of light begins to manifest. This flame is called
devotion.

I cannot forget your remembrance,
It is as if someone is forever pinching at my heart.

Every love pinches because it is nothing but a remembrance
of the divine. A dim remembrance – very dim, buried under
many layers – but it is a remembrance of the divine all the
same. That is why you become mad when you fall in love –
just a little mad, but mad nevertheless.

No face resembles yours,
I keep wandering this world, carrying your picture.

And that is why although every love gives you the promise of contentment, it never delivers it. When you fall in love with someone, in the beginning the beauty of that love is unsurpassed. But soon the ashes settle. Love rusts very quickly. Soon strife, conflict and turmoil begin. No one knows what has happened to those heights of love. Soon every love turns into a conflict. But in those first moments, when your eyes were fresh and everything was new, you had a glimpse – otherwise how could you have fallen in love? Someone had called out to you, something had thrown out the challenge to your being. Whose challenge was it? Whose glimpse was it? You felt as if you had found the ultimate. You felt as if you had found that which you have been searching for; the lover that you have been looking for!

But soon everything is lost again. The smoke of physical passion, the self-seeking, all the pettiness of life, the anger, the dirt... all these soon take you over. Soon you begin to drown again. For a brief moment you rose up from under the water and saw the sky – but this proved to be very momentary. It was only the wedding night. You start drowning again.Whenever you have experienced this nectar in love, it is because...

No face resembles yours,
I keep wandering this world, carrying your picture.

Understand this. A picture of the divine is hidden inside everyone's heart. We wander, carrying this picture within us, hoping to find someone who resembles it, hoping to find someone on the outside to match this picture, to find the one whose picture it is. Until we meet that beloved of our very soul we will remain distressed, in pain; searching and pining for something. Sometimes you will find a face which, just for a moment, seems to resemble the one you are seeking and you call that love. But when you look more closely, things fall apart again. No, the resemblance was just an illusion. In the dim light, in the darkness, you felt there was a resemblance, but there never really was. You have missed again.

So when you see the lover, the vessel of love, at a distance, everything looks fine. But as soon as you come closer everything begins to go wrong — because no one's face resembles the divine's, even though the divine is hidden in all faces. No one's face resembles the divine's one hundred percent: perhaps one percent resembles it and the ninety-nine percent does not. It is this one percent that you see at the beginning of love, but then gradually the remaining ninety-nine percent emerge.

It is only through losing out in love again and again that a person enters into devotion one day. The failure of love proves the fact that, "I searched for you outside of myself and didn't find you. Now I will search within. I searched for you in the body, in matter, in form, in beauty, and you were not there. Now I will search for you beyond beauty, in the formless. I searched for you in the ephemeral and…."

Just imagine: the moon is in the sky, it is night, the full moon is shining and you are sitting beside a lake. The lake is still. You feel that the moon is inside the lake. If you don't look up, you will believe that the moon is in the lake.

I have heard:

It was the fasting month of Ramadan. Mulla Nasruddin was
sitting beside a well. He was thirsty, so he peeped into the
well to see how far down the water was. It was a full-moon
night, and he saw the moon in the well. "Poor thing," he said,
"How did you get stuck in this well? Someone should get
you out!"

There was no one else around. It was a very lonely place. He
forgot all about his thirst and threw a rope into the well to
catch the moon and to pull it out in some way – because
otherwise what would become of the world? The rope became
stuck on a rock somewhere in the well, but Mulla thought
that things were going well, that the rope had attached itself
to the moon, so he pulled with all his might.

The rope broke and he fell on his back with a thud. As he
fell, he saw the moon in the sky, "It doesn't matter," he said.
"I hurt myself a little but you have been rescued, oh Master
Moon. That's enough for me."

What we have seen in the world is just the reflection of the
moon in the well. What we have seen in the world is just a
reflection of the divine. We have not yet raised our eyes to
the divine. We don't even know how to raise our eyes. In
all the religions of the world, people raise their eyes towards
the sky when they pray. This is symbolic. The divine is not
in the sky, but we must rise up, we must look up. The divine
is somewhere beyond us, above us, but we have no idea of
how to look upwards, beyond ourselves. We are so used to
looking down. That is much easier.

Whenever you look at someone with physical desire, you are looking down. And when you look at someone with eyes full of prayer, you are looking upwards. This looking upwards is devotion, and that looking downward is love. The two are related. Both are connected, it is the same energy: when it goes down it becomes love, when it goes up it becomes devotion.

And the heart burns in devotion in exactly the same way that it burns in love. There is a difference – they are certainly different kinds of burning. There is a kind of fever in the burning of love and there is a kind of coolness in the burning of devotion – a cool fire. In the burning of love there is only burning: as though someone is sprinkling acid on a wound. In the burning of devotion, yes, the burning is there – the pain, the writhing of separation – but it is very cool, very calming.

My heart is on fire, Shefta,
Perhaps this is what they call love.

Love burns, devotion burns too. But there is a great difference between them. The fire of love burns you, the fire of devotion not only burns you, it also wakes you up. The fire of love puts you to sleep, the fire of devotion pulls you out of your sleep, it awakens you. In the fire of love you remain only your body, in the fire of devotion your body is lost and only the waking consciousness remains.

Devotion means:

I search for my maker;
I want to meet the one from whom I came.

I search for my source,
As hidden there
Is my final destiny.
I search for the ultimate,
For when that is found
No other search remains.

The learned person searches just as the devotee does, but the learned person's search depends only on himself. The devotee says, "How can I accomplish the search by myself? You must help me." He tells God, "I don't have your address, but you must have mine. I may not know you, but you must know me. I may not have seen you, but you must have seen me. So when I search for you my search is one-sided, because I will be groping in the dark like a blind person. Please take my hand, please hold my hand in your hand."

The learned person relies on himself. The path of the learned person is determination, will. The path of the devotee is surrender. The devotee says, "I will search, I will search with my whole life; but one thing is certain — that our meeting will only happen when you allow it. So please take care of this, don't leave it to my searching alone."

O my heart, my emotional heart,
I am calling him...
But let something happen to him
So he cannot help but come.
I invite him, but of what use is that?

But let something happen to him
So he cannot help but come.

...That he will have to come! Only when the fire burns on both sides will something happen, and it *is* burning on both sides. God is searching for you with the same eagerness as you are searching for him – perhaps with even more.

Look at it this way: a child is lost in the bazaar, at a fair, or in some other crowd, and he is running around looking for his mother. Do you think the mother doesn't look for her child? And the child may be distracted many times – he may see some toys, he may hear some drums, he may watch a conjurer showing tricks and stand there, forgetting all about his mother. But no drum, no conjurer, no game, no spectacle will stop the mother. She will keep searching like a mad woman. The child will forget all about her in this world he is in. *The world is like the last morning star.* But to him all these things he sees will appear to be real. He will stop in front of the toy shop, or someone may give him some sweets and he may think that all is well. How much can a child understand? Even if he searches, what kind of a search will it be? And if he doesn't find his mother, in a few days he will begin to forget her. A month or two later, and he won't even remember her. After a year or two, he will forget what she looks like. But the mother will keep searching, writhing in agony.

Remember this second point: the divine is also searching for you.

When you search only with your own strength, you are on the path of knowledge. When you say, "I will search, I will put all my energy into it, but unless you also search for me, one thing is certain, our meeting will never happen...."

O my heart, my emotional heart,
I am calling him...
But let something happen to him
So he cannot help but come.

I will continue to call you. But let something happen to you
too so that you cannot help coming to me, so that you have
to come to me.

Devotion is surrender.
Devotion is the total letting go of oneself.

The man on the path of knowledge renounces the world; a
devotee renounces himself. The man on the path of
knowledge lets go of other things; a devotee lets go of his
ego.

Sometimes in moments of love you may have felt that your
ego has disappeared. Sometimes, if you have ever truly loved,
for brief moments you must have experienced the ego
disappearing. For a few moments it *does* disappear. You
remain, but there is no sense of "I." When the "I" disappears,
the temple comes closer. When the "I" disappears, the curtain
lifts, the door opens. It is the lock of "I" that is on the door.

The second question:

Beloved Osho,

*The way you are teaching is absolutely the right kind of education. But
it is doubtful whether the politicians and the bureaucrats will regard it
as right education.*

It is not doubtful, it is certain that they won't consider it as right education! It is certain that what I am teaching will seem like wrong education to them. They will feel that it should be stopped – because a politician lives on people's lack of intelligence.

If people become more intelligent then the politician cannot exist. The politician's entire power rests on your ignorance. The more ignorant you are, the more powerful the politician can be. The day there is a little more intelligence on this earth, the day that people are a little more alert, the first thing to disappear will be politics.

The very meaning of politics is that you are not intelligent, that others tell you: "You are not intelligent, but we are. We will give you a code of laws to help you organize your life. You are not intelligent enough to organize your own life; give us power and we will give you a system. You cannot be your own master; make us your master and we will take care of you. You cannot look after your own interests; we will look after them for you."

This is the whole meaning of politics. You need a leader only when you cannot work out what to do on your own. So politics will never want people to become aware – they should remain asleep. Politics will never want people to become meditative – because the moment people become meditative they begin to drop out of the circle of politics. The circle of politics requires anger, hostility, jealousy, envy, spite, conflict. Only as long as these flames are burning within you are you able to remain in politics. Violence, the urge to dominate others, the desire to oppress others, competition, rivalry...all these are needed in politics. Politics is a kind of struggle.

So as your meditation grows, your sensitivity, your love and your peace will also grow and you will begin to drop politics. You will not want any wars in this world.

A politician feeds on war. If wars were to disappear, the politician would have no power. When there is a war a politician becomes a great leader. Have you noticed? The greatness of any great political leader in the world depends on there being a war. If there isn't a war, a politician cannot become a great leader in his lifetime. So every politician wants a big war to take place during his lifetime so that he can be victorious and can prove that he was the right man.

Politics is an expansion of the ego. Meditation is the dissolution of the ego. Politics is a fraud, a hypocrisy.

I have heard:

A miracle that took place in a dense forest: the lion suddenly became very ordinary and humble, he began to go around greeting all the animals with folded paws. The animals of the forest were all astonished about what was happening! He stopped snarling and roaring; he talked about brotherhood to whomsoever he met on his way.

One day he was hungry and for a short while he forgot to be humble...in politics, people wear superficial masks. He saw a donkey standing under a tree. Normally, the donkey would have run away, but because the lion had been completely non-violent for the past fifteen or twenty days – a Gandhian trying to improve every single person's lot – the donkey wasn't scared and continued to stand where he was. Within a split second the lion's inner reality manifested itself and he pounced on the donkey. But as soon as he did it, he realized what he was doing. Instantly he fell at the donkey's feet, saying, "Forgive me, father, I made a mistake!"

The donkey couldn't believe what he was hearing — a lion calling a donkey "father"?

An owl was sitting on a tree, watching. The donkey went away, and the owl asked, "What is the matter? This is the limit! I had heard rumors that you had become simple and virtuous, but this is a little too much — falling at the feet of a donkey and calling him 'father'."

The lion replied, "Because you are an owl, you are nothing but an idiot. The elections are coming soon. Do you think that I want to lose my deposit by displeasing that donkey?"

A politician has only one ambition: to become powerful over as many people as possible. Politics feeds on the ego; hence politics can never be in favor of right education. Politics is hypocrisy; there is no greater fraud. Politics is a business based on telling lies. Politics means showing how skilled you are at telling lies.

I was only reading yesterday:

A politician was giving a speech, telling people to be just a little more patient, because socialism was on the way. One man stood up and cried out that socialism would never come, that he had been hearing that it was coming for the past thirty years.

The politician replied, "Believe me, it isn't very far off now, it has almost come. It won't be long now – just a little more patience. One more election and then socialism will be with us."

Some other members of the audience stood up and said, "Socialism will never come! In the club last night, your secretary said that socialism will never happen."

The crowd that stood up was large and so noisy that the politician was disconcerted. He said, "How could my secretary have said that? He wrote my speech! I want to tell you one more time that socialism is nearly with us."

But more and more people stood up saying, "Socialism will never come. Stop this nonsense, we have listened to you for long enough."

The politician realized that things were getting out of hand, so he stood humbly before them, and said, "I thought socialism was coming. But if you say so, maybe it is not coming after all. I will try to find out the truth…perhaps the agenda has been changed."

Politics is exploitation, empty words and slick phrases. And naturally if a man begins to be complete unto himself, then not only will he lose his own political attitude, he will also be able to see right through the politics of others.

The day the world becomes a little more intelligent there will be no room left for politics – and there shouldn't be any place for it either. There is no need for politics. Politics lives on ignorance. And what politics teaches you only goes so far – and to a place where a revolution cannot happen in your life.

Politicians want you to remain crippled and dependent on them so that you don't become independent. Politicians don't want any more people like Buddha, Mahavira, Krishna, Kabir and Christ in this world. They will never want that, because these are dangerous people. Politics could not tolerate Jesus, he was crucified. Politics could not tolerate Socrates, he was made to drink poison. They are dangerous people!

What danger do these people pose? Their danger is that they are honest and authentic people. They speak the truth, they have no hidden agendas, they don't lie, they are not opportunists. They will only talk about what is of most benefit to all mankind, and they will talk about that benefit even if everyone turns against them. These are the characteristics of an enlightened one.

A friend has asked another question:

Who is an enlightened one? What are his characteristics?

An enlightened one is someone who calls a spade a spade, who shows people how to live that which is, who doesn't make even the slightest alteration to it. And that which is a so revolutionary, that if you enter into a relationship with it your whole life will be radically transformed.

Politicians have always been angry with the enlightened ones. They like all kinds of priests and *pundits*, but they don't like enlightened people. Priests and pundits have always conspired with the politicians. They join religion and politics together, they put religion in the service of politics.

An enlightened one is one who lives his life in godliness and doesn't accept any conditions. An enlightened one is one who doesn't fix any limits and who doesn't accept any limits. An enlightened state means rebellion, it is like a burning red coal: it will burn you and turn you to ash. And it is out of your ashes that the divine will arise. The more people the divine enters, the more people will get out of the web of politics. If a large number of people immerse themselves in meditation and devotion, there will be a tremendous change throughout the whole world. Such people will not accept your so-called leaders — even as followers. They are blind people leading the blind.

So what you ask is right. The politicians are not prepared to accept what I call education as education. They are trying their best to stop my message from reaching to people. They keep trying to stop you from reaching me and to stop me from reaching you. It is in the politicians' greatest interest that what I am saying reaches to the minimum number of people.

And the hilarious thing is that not just one kind of politician is against me, all kinds of politicians are against me. This is extremely interesting. Ordinarily, if someone is speaking against the Congress party, then the Janata party will support him. If someone is speaking against the Janata party, then the Congress party will support him. But you will find that whenever enlightenment manifests somewhere, *all* the politicians will be against that person. About this they will all be in agreement — because enlightenment pulls away the very cornerstone of politics.

The world can live in only two ways: one way is the way of politics, and the other way is the way of religiousness. So far, the world has not lived the way of religiousness; it has only lived the way of politics. No wonder it has never lived! It has not lived at all: it has always been dying, it has always been rotting. So far, no society has ever dared to live religiously. And politicians will not let this happen. Why should they want to lose their power, their strength, their respect, honor and position?

If the number of awakened, enlightened people were to increase, if the level of meditative energy were to rise even a little in this country, many things would change instantly. One of the biggest things would be that this enormous tide of competition — so much force, such aggression and personal rivalry, so much pulling of one another's legs, such respect for status — all this would disappear. The person who has become enthroned on the seat of his inner self needs no other status. Such a person has found the throne — there is no greater throne. All journeys of the ego come to an immediate halt for the person in whose life even a small stream of the divine has begun to flow. And politics, wealth, position and respectability are all journeys of the ego.

The basic principle of right education is that of dissolving the ego. And the basic principle of wrong education is the cultivation of the ego. Your schools, your colleges and universities all teach you everything except how to drop the ego. Rather, they teach you how to enhance your ego. Whoever comes first is awarded a gold medal, whoever comes at the top of the list is praised. Whoever gains a first-class degree will get a job faster. This is teaching you competition.

In admitting thirty small children to a class, the first thing you do is to commit a political act. Now you have put them to compete against one another. Each one is set against the other twenty-nine. Each one feels that he has to come first, that he must defeat all the others. They have become his enemies: politics has entered their lives. They will learn to become skilled in politics, to be cunning and dishonest.

And yet later on, you yourself will say such extraordinary things! Whenever some educated person is found to be dishonest, you will say, "What kind of an education did he receive?" For twenty to twenty-five years you teach every person to be dishonest, and then, when he finally returns and begins to pick pockets, when he begins to be dishonest, when he begins to cheat, you will say, "What is going on here? It would have been better for him to have remained uneducated – at least uneducated people are not dishonest." An uneducated person cannot be dishonest. You need some skills, even for this – otherwise you will be caught cheating in the smallest way. You need some skill even for this, you need a university degree even for this.

What you call education is just a glorification of the ego. What I call education means the total dissolution of the ego. The universities will only become real on the day that they no longer teach ambition, on the day that a person leaves them having become humble – living as though he does not exist, happy to be nothing.

The third question:

Osho,

I find no joy in the world and my life is not joyful, but I am afraid of death. What sort of irony is this?

If you are afraid of death, there can only be one reason, simply one reason. The reason is that you have not yet lived life and you are afraid that you may die before you do. You think it is ironical, you think that it is an incomprehensible, paradoxical situation – you don't enjoy life, your life is not happy, so why is it that you are afraid of death? Your mind tells you that the logical thing would be for you not to be afraid of death because you don't enjoy the world, because your life is not at all joyful.

No. It won't happen this way. You are not aware of the deeper fundamentals of life. You will not be rid of the fear of death until you come to realize that, *The world is like the last morning star.*

There *is* no joy in life. *You* have no joy in life, but deep down you believe that it must exist somewhere, and that it is just not coming your way because there are some obstacles in its way at the moment. You don't yet have the clear understanding that there is no joy in life. Such an awareness has not yet deepened in you. Your life is not joyous, that is true, but this vast life that surrounds you is also devoid of any joy. Such an experience, such a realization has not happened to you yet so you remain afraid that death may come before you have lived and have found that joy. You don't want to die before you have tasted that joy – otherwise you will feel you have not lived at all, that you have died in the middle, before ever having lived.

Your fear of death reveals only one thing – that you are still interested in life. I agree with you: your life might not be joyful, but you still have hopes, you have not given up hoping, the thread of hope is still there. It is a weak thread, but it is still intact. You still think, "There must be some way, the path must lead from somewhere. If I am not on the right path, then there must be another way which is the right way." Your interest in the world is still there.

You are still running. You have not arrived anywhere, but that doesn't prove that there is nowhere to reach to. On the day you feel that there is nothing in life to attain, that there simply is no joy in life, that as Buddha said, life as such is sorrow....

Buddha said that there are Four Noble Truths. The first noble truth is that life is sorrow. He called this The First Noble Truth, the first great truth. The person who knows that life is sorrow is noble, is a true human being. The Second Noble Truth is that there is a way in which one can be freed from life, from the sorrow of life. The Third Noble Truth is that there is an emancipated state of mind, there is a state of consciousness that is free from the sorrows of life. The Fourth Noble Truth is that this state is not simply imagination, it has happened to others and it can happen to you too.

Buddha proclaimed these Four Noble Truths, and the first of them is that life is sorrow: the whole of life is sorrow, from beginning to end, life is sorrow.

You haven't seen this yet – and the reason? The reason can only be this: that you have become entangled with the scriptures, the sages and their teachings before your time. You have heard these words too soon. You have not realized from the experience of your own life that life is meaningless, you have only heard someone else say it. Your heart continues to tell you that life is delightful. You have heard from somewhere, from some saint or another, that life is futile. And now you are in a dilemma; one door calls you back, the other door beckons you forward. You are in a difficulty.

I say to you: forget your saints and sages, enter into life. Wander a little more, stumble around a little more, bang your head a little more. Life is like a wall; it won't open, there isn't a door. But until you have covered yourself with blood you won't be convinced. Buddha must have said that life is sorrow, but how can you accept this? How can you accept that life is sorrow? If someone else had told Buddha this, he would not have accepted it either. He accepted it only when he knew it for himself. You too will accept it only when you know it for yourself.

I tell you not to turn away from life while you are still immature just because of what the *mahatmas* say. If you do, it will never be possible for religion to become the truth of your life – because you will have missed the very first truth. How can you build a temple with no foundations? Don't come back after only having gone halfway because you have heard the words of the mahatmas. Don't return until you have had your own experience, until your heart has broken to pieces in every possible place and is weeping bitterly, otherwise you will become a hypocrite. You will be turning back after having gone only halfway and will start pretending to be something that is not your inner reality. You may sit down like a saint, but your mind will still be in the world – in the shop, in the marketplace. You may close your eyes and try to remember the divine, but the divine won't come. Something else will be there – the snares of the world.

We are sulking with ourselves,
We are broken, damaged people,
So false
That truth must cast its eyes away.
Taking this, gathering that,
Such pegs are we.
What can those swords,
The hilt of which we are,
Ever do to us?
In every gathering of drunkards
We are the empty sips.
Put us in a museum,
We are very unique people.
People who can never become signatures,
Only thumbprints.

Don't become false by listening to what others say. Don't become a thumbprint by listening to others. Live your life! This is *your* life, it has been given to you. It has been given to you so that you may travel to its very end, so that you may seek it to its ultimate depths. If you find joy, you are fortunate. If you don't, then you are still blessed – because if you don't find joy then you will be able to move inwards, free of doubts and cares. No doubt will surround you, there will be nothing outside to call you, to invite you. You have turned back after knowing. You have turned back after recognizing. Consider this my basic teaching.

This is why I say that even if you become a sannyasin, don't renounce the world – live life where you are, wake up where you are, experience where you are! To be an escapist means that there is still some fear in you. A person only runs away from what he is afraid of, otherwise why would you run

away? A person who renounces his shop to go to the jungle
is afraid of his shop. He is afraid that if he sits in front of
his safe he may start being interested in it. The man who
runs away from his wife is afraid that if he holds her hand
it may awaken his passions. The man who runs away and
leaves his son behind is scared that if he looks into his son's
eyes he may feel attached to him. All this means is that he
has not yet experienced the first truth of life. He has not
yet experienced that, *The world is like the last morning star.*

So I say to you: go fully into life, don't be afraid, don't be
frightened. This is the task that the divine has given you.
You must ripen with experience, you will come back home
only after having experienced. When you come back having
experienced, your hands will be full of pearls. If you return
after just having heard what other people say, you will only
bring pebbles with you. Pebbles cannot bring you contentment.

I also tell you that life has no juice, but please don't turn back
simply because of what I say. Life is futile: I also tell you that.
But my knowing is my knowing, how can it become your
knowing? You cannot see with my eyes, you cannot walk with
my feet, and my experience cannot become your experience.
You must make it your own experience. Keep this as a deep
remembrance: "Someone has said that life is futile — but now
I will look into it."

I may be wrong, Buddha may be wrong. You can count the
number of enlightened ones on your fingers, and these few
people may all have been wrong — because after all, the
majority consists of people who have not renounced life.
Only a few people have said, "Beyond life...." They may have

made a mistake. Don't turn back because of what they have said. Return only because of your own experience.

I say to you, that if you dive in totally and go down to the rock-bottom of life, you will find nothing there. From there you will return empty-handed in one sense, but in another sense your hands will be full. You will be empty-handed because you will have realized that there is nothing in life. Your hands will be full in the sense that now you can search for the divine – carefree, devoid of all doubt. There remains no obstacle now in your search for the divine. No new alternatives will arise before you. The crows of your thoughts and desire will not caw at you. Now you can walk on. Now the stream of your life can become one and fall into the ocean of the divine.

The fourth question:

Osho,

A few days ago you were beating the drum of Ashtavakra's "witnessing." Now you are playing Daya's tunes on "devotion." Between these two, Mr. Lieh Tzu neither said nor heard anything – he just rode about on the white clouds. Is it possible that riding the white cloud of Tao someone can travel on the path of devotion today and on the path of witnessing tomorrow...wherever the winds carry him?

Krishna Mohammed has asked this. You see this every day; this is what is happening here all the time. Sometimes I am Lieh Tzu, sometimes Ashtavakra, sometimes Kabir, sometimes Meera, sometimes Mohammed. I don't have the slightest difficulty with this. It doesn't worry me at all that yesterday I was talking about witnessing and now I am talking about devotion. As far as I can see there are many paths, but the destination is always one and the same.

It is like climbing a mountain. You can come from many different directions, on many separate paths, but from the peak you can see that everyone is moving towards the same point. If you can't see this, then you have not really reached the peak yet. If even at the peak a Jaina remains a Jaina, a Hindu remains a Hindu and a Muslim still remains a Muslim, then this means that you have not really reached the peak. Hinduism, Islam, Jainism, Christianity...it is all about paths. It's okay: one has to walk on some path, so you have to chose one way or the other. Even if there are fifty paths to the summit, you can only go on one. You cannot walk on fifty different paths at the same time. If you did, you would go mad. If you did, you would never get there. How could you even walk? You would be in great difficulty.

I have heard about a fat lady who was going to the cinema. She gave the usher two tickets. The usher asked, "Where is the other person?"

The lady replied, "I am sorry, I am a little fat so I have booked two seats for myself."

The usher said, "As you please madam, but you will find this rather difficult."

The woman asked, "What is so difficult?"

The usher replied, "The first seat is number fifty-one and the second seat is number sixty-one. You can sit on both if you wish, but it will be very difficult."

You cannot sit on two chairs at the same time.

A politician came to meet Mulla Nasruddin. Mulla was just sitting by himself, and he didn't even invite the politician to sit down. During the elections no one bothers to ask a politician to sit down. The Mulla looked at him with the same look that people use for beggars, as if to say, "Go away! Go somewhere else and don't waste my time!"

The politician was angry. He said, "Don't you know that I am an MP?"

Then Mulla replied, "All right, please sit down." The political leader continued, "I am not just an MP, I hope to be in the cabinet after this election. I will be part of the ministry."

Then Mulla said, "In that case, take two chairs! How else can I help you?"

It is not possible to sit on two chairs, even if you are a minister. Nor is it possible to walk on two paths, or to ride on two horses, or to sit in two boats at the same time. You will be facing a difficulty.

So as long as you are still on your journey, you will have to choose between one of the two paths. As long as you have still not arrived, choose one. If witnessing appeals to you, follow the path of witnessing. If devotion appeals to you, then follow the path of devotion. If Mohammed stirs your heart, follow him; if Mahavira stirs your heart, follow him.

I have opened all the doors for you. Don't try to pass through all of the doors at the same time. Just use one door. But all of the doors have been opened so that you don't face any problems. Whosoever appeals to you, with whomsoever you can attain to joy – follow that path, certainly. But once you have reached the inner sanctum of the temple you will find that all the doors would have brought you to the same place inside the temple. When you reach the summit of the mountain, you will find that those who were climbing from the east and from the west have also reached there. Those who were climbing from the south have also arrived, and so have those who travel in palanquins. Those who came on foot are there, and also those who came on horseback. Those who came singing have arrived, and those who walked in silence are there as well. All have arrived.

From where I am, there is no difference between Lieh Tzu, Daya, Sahajo and Ashtavakra: Lieh Tzu dissolves into Ashtavakra, Ashtavakra dissolves into Daya, Daya is immersed in Kabir. All become one. The rivers are separate, but when they enter the ocean they all become one. Every river has a different taste, its ways and looks are different, but once the rivers enter the ocean they all taste the same.

The fifth question:

Osho,

People drink and stagger,
And then there is me.
I come thirsty and I go away thirsty.

As you wish; it is every person's choice! If you have decided not to drink, if you have sworn an oath to abstain, then there is no way that I can help you.

There is a saying: "You can take a horse to water, but you can't make it drink." I take you to the river, but the rest is up to you. If you enjoy this coming and going, then please keep coming and going. You are welcome. But for how long can you go on doing this? And what is the sense in coming and going all the time? Taste something! Don't make any more excuses. Man is very clever, he always throws the responsibility onto somebody else.

Your question seems to indicate that you feel that you are not at fault at all.

Destiny has its place
In the bazaar of love.
Just as the deal of my heart
Is about to come through,
It is bungled.

Sometimes you blame your luck or the circumstances, and sometimes you find some other reason. All of them are simply excuses and evasions. If you don't want to drink then don't, but don't look for excuses. One needs courage to drink.

You say: "People drink and stagger..."

You are probably scared of staggering about. You seem to be interested in drinking, otherwise why would you bother to ask this question, why would you bother to come here? You must be afraid of staggering about. You want to drink, but you don't want to stagger. This can't happen. If you drink, you will stagger. You must be trying to work out some way in your mind to drink without staggering about.

People often come to me…. Just a few days ago, a gentleman came and asked me to give him *sannyas* – but he wanted "inner sannyas." I asked him, "What is that? What is inner sannyas?"

He said, "No one should know. Sannyas should just be something between you and me."

Now he is finding a tricky way: "No one should know! I don't want anyone to find out! Not my wife, not my children – no one should find out when I go back home."

I told him, "In that case, you don't really need sannyas. With me, if you want to drink you will have to stagger about. Everyone will know. You will be the laughingstock of the whole world."

He said, "Well then, I will just wear the beads, the mala. Can I wear them inside my clothes, or will I have to wear them on the outside?"

Man has lost his courage, he has become very weak. Those who took off their clothes and followed Mahavira must have been very courageous people. They didn't say, "Master, will it be enough if we are naked inside our clothes?" It could have been enough – because inside their clothes everyone is naked. Where is the difficulty in that? They must have been very courageous people. They must have been very daring. They staggered a lot.

There is a story in the scriptures about a young man who came home after listening to Mahavira. He was in his bathroom, and his wife was bathing him. She anointed his body with turmeric paste and with oil and perfume. She rubbed his body well and then washed him. Then they both began to talk.

His wife said, "So, you have been listening to Mahavira. My brother listens to him too. He too is thinking about taking initiation and renouncing the world."

The young man said, "He is thinking? That means he doesn't want to do it. What is there to think about? If something has appealed to him, it has appealed. What is there to think about? What does thinking mean? It means, 'I might do it tomorrow,' or 'I might do it the day after that.'"

The wife was hurt, feeling that her brother was being insulted. She said, "No, he will definitely do it, in a year."

Her husband said, "He might die before the year is over. And how can you be sure that he won't change his mind? He doesn't have the courage to do it. He is a *kshatriya*, of the warrior caste, and he is behaving like this? In a year? So right now, don't talk of it and we can come back to this topic in a year's time."

The wife was even more hurt. She said, "Go and listen to him! Do you think you could become a sannyasin just like that?"

The husband got up and began walking out of the bathroom. His wife asked him, "Where are you going?"

He said, "The point has been made."

She said, "At least put some clothes on."

He said, "Why should I? Mahavira will only make me take them off again."

His wife screamed, she began to cry; all the members of the family came running. He stood near the door on the street. His parents tried to advise him, "You are crazy. This was just a conversation...."

He said, "It is not a conversation. The point has been made. Now I understand that what I was saying about someone else — that there is nothing to think about — it is my situation too. The point has been nailed to the target."

People were so courageous in those days. Gradually, people have become very weak — so weak that they are afraid to wear ochre clothes, afraid to wear beads outside of their clothes for fear that someone might say, "What's come over you?" — that someone might think they are mad.

You have come here so you are certainly interested, you have certainly developed an addiction. You might not have drunk it, but the fragrance of the wine that is being served here is in the air. It must have touched your nostrils. And those who drink here and become ecstatic create a milieu around them. That too must have touched you. You must want to drink — otherwise why would you bother coming here? But you are afraid of staggering. Gather courage to stagger too. What fun is there in drinking if you don't stagger? If that is the case it makes no difference whether you drink or not.

Sannyas means that your old life will be demolished and a new way of life will take root. Sannyas is a revolution. Your life will be uprooted from its old place and new ground will have to be searched for.

There will be difficult days in between. The period of transition will be a time of difficulty. People will laugh, they will make sarcastic comments about you. People have always done this, and it is not their fault that they do. When they are being sarcastic and laughing, don't think that they are laughing at you. They are just protecting themselves – they are scared too. When you put on ochre robes and start dancing ecstatically, the person who laughs at you is afraid. He can see that if he doesn't oppose you, this same pull may take hold of him. He opposes you to protect himself. He says that you are wrong; he shouts that you are wrong, that you have gone mad. In reality, he is saying that he is afraid that this madness will possess him too.

When you oppose someone, look carefully at yourself. Somewhere you must be attracted to going in the same direction, that is why you are opposed to him – otherwise you wouldn't bother. Those who oppose you will follow in your footsteps, but then you must stagger a little.

It is not easy to plunder the heart, O tyrant!
And it is not easy to inhabit it.
Creating a settlement is no game,
It happens gradually.

It takes some time. Even staggering develops a certain discipline, even ecstasy has a certain rule, a golden rule. There is a method – even in this madness. At first it all seems to be madness, but then gradually everything settles down. And then for the first time you know that everything before this was madness. Now for the first time you have become sensible. The world will call you mad, but you will know that up until now you *were* mad but now you are not. For the first time, a ray of light has descended into your life and erased all your madness.

Gather a little courage — sannyas means courage. And this is a tavern. This time, go back staggering. If you have the courage, I am always ready to bless you.

Who knows what fears and apprehensions we have?
Helplessly doing what we do not want to do,
Only pretending to live,
And dying every step of our lives.

What are you so nervous about? What have you got to lose? What will you lose? What is the fear? What are you protecting? You don't have anything, but you continue to do what you don't want to do, and you are too scared to do what you do want to do. Recognize this. Don't look for excuses. And if you can have just a little courage, the journey into the unknown begins.

I repeat the word courage again and again, because the divine is still unknown. It is an unknown wine, like no other, and you have never tasted it. It is an unknown path, and you have never traveled on it. The divine is not a highway; it is a path through the forest. There, you will find yourself alone. The crowd will be left behind on the main road. The political leaders, the crowds, the agitators, all sorts of processions and floats — all will be left behind on the highway.

The journey of sannyas is about being alone. Meditation is the process through which you become alone. Immersing yourself in devotion means that you begin to forget the world, and your entire awareness becomes focused on that distant star. One day only that one star will remain inside you, everything else will be gradually lost. That is why one becomes frightened – going into that much aloneness, going into that much of solitude, transcending all relationships….

Hence, courage is a compulsory requirement for a religious person. A violent person can become religious, an angry person can become religious, a sexual person can become religious, but a coward can never become religious. Think about this, meditate on it.

All your religious scriptures tell you to give up violence, to give up anger, to give up passion. I tell you to give up cowardice. Because if you don't give up cowardice, you cannot give up violence. If you don't give up cowardice, you cannot give up anger. If you don't give up cowardice, you cannot give up money. If you don't give up cowardice, you cannot give up relationships. Take the first step by giving up cowardice. Then you have become strong, then you can give up anything.

Yesterday's total stranger,
Has become my life's support today.

Have courage! When you dare, you suddenly discover that some very powerful hand has taken your hand.

Yesterday's total stranger,
Has become my life's support today.

You become helpless and you will find that the divine has become your help.

Yesterday's total stranger,
Has become my life's support today.
The golden chain of memory
Binds the lonely heart,
Sleepy eyelids lose
The silvery estate of dreams,
Every pore of the body
Is guarded by some sweet unknown quiver.
One who was nowhere in the radius of my sight
Has become the very source of my breaths.

The one we had never even seen, the one we had never heard
about....

One who was nowhere in the radius of my sight
Has become the very source of my breaths.

This one will pervade your every breath.

Words of assurance are like birds
Singing on the branches of promises.
In the lotus-forests of my longing
The fragrance of patience lingers at every step.
These first utterances of love have grown
In the innocent courtyard of loving tenderness.
Without my knowing, someone's name
Has become the recipient of my songs.

The name which you are so far unfamiliar with, that which
so far is nameless....

Without my knowing, someone's name
Has become the recipient of my songs.

In the mirror of my soul,
I captured a light-delighting form,
But it is not easy to confine the inconfinable,
Hence my defeat.
Naked, unsuccessful lines
Raise their hands and gaze at the sky.
O, my unknown life,
Someone's picture
Has become my own sketch.

Have a little courage, be daring, accept the challenge to enter
into the unknown and unfamiliar a little and you will not
be alone. The divine is with you. But before it can be truly
with you, you must show the courage to be alone. The divine
is with those who are alone.

The last question:

Osho,

What loss is there if one does not attain to the divine?

There is no loss in it at all, because you will only become
aware of the loss after you have attained to the divine. You
understand a loss only when you lose something that
you have had. How can you know what you have lost
unless you have had it? You cannot even guess what will
happen when you attain something – whether it will be a loss
or a gain – until you attain it.

What can you tell a child who asks what is the harm if he
does not grow up to become a youth? It is difficult to explain
the loss to him. It is like a blind person asking what is the
harm in his not having eyes. A blind person has never known

light so he will never know that he is being deprived of the whole luminous empire of light, of the whole playful interweaving of colors of light; that he is being deprived of the rainbows, the sun, the moon, the stars, the flowers and the trees. This incomparable world of light is completely lost to him, but he doesn't know this. If he asks what is the harm if his eyes are not cured, how can you explain this loss? – because there is only one way to explain a loss. Only if you have had something and then lose it, can you know what the loss is.

You ask, "What loss is there if one does not attain to the divine?" I know what the loss is…but your question is also relevant. You haven't known the divine, so how can you understand what the loss is? Let us approach this question from the other side.

What is there in what you call life right now? Is there a single thing that seems worth living for? Is there anything in your life that makes you want to live it a second time? If existence were to offer you this life again, would you like to live it in the same way as you are living it right now? Would you like to live it in exactly the same way?

Think about it: you wouldn't like to live it in exactly the same way because there is nothing in your life. It is empty, dry. No flowers bloom anywhere, no veena plays. Your heart doesn't pick up its flute, no music arises in your heart. There is nothing in this life, not anywhere. You go on living, being pushed this way and that. You keep going because there is nothing else you can do. You keep going because you have found yourself in this life and so you just keep going. Death will come one day, and then you will be finished. Perhaps knowingly or unknowingly, man even awaits death.

Sigmund Freud has said that there are two basic human desires: sexual desire and the desire for death. This is a rare insight. One is sexual desire that keeps pushing a person on. And Freud says that somewhere, far deeper, a hope remains that because life is utterly useless, death will come – if not today then tomorrow – and everything will be all right.

Have you ever looked at it? Is there anything else in your life except waiting for death? What would matter if this dried and withered tree fell down?

I look at it from the other side. I ask: If this is life, what does it matter if you lose it? Getting up every day, going to the office, returning home, going to sleep, quarreling again, fighting again…. If this is life, what does it matter if you lose it? The greatest thinkers of the world have asked the same question.

There is a great Western thinker, Jean-Paul Sartre. He asks: "If this is all there is to life, what is the harm in committing suicide?" This is not a foolish suggestion. Suicide is the greatest question ever, because if this is what you call life and then someone wants to commit suicide, why should that surprise you? You will do exactly the same things again tomorrow, won't you? – get up in the morning, drink tea, fight with your wife, read the newspaper, and go to your office. It is just like a broken gramophone record. The needle is stuck and it keeps repeating the same music again and again – the same groove, the same groove, the same groove! Your life the same – an old broken gramophone record.

You ask, "What loss is there if one does not attain to the divine?" So far what is there in your life anyway?

The whole purpose of attaining to the divine is to bring meaning into your life. There is no other purpose. The purpose of attaining to godliness is so that a fragrance can come into your life, a perfume, a music. A celebration, an elation can come, so that your life does not remain stale, borrowed; so that it becomes fresh – as fresh as the morning, as fresh as the morning dewdrops – virgin. The whole purpose of attaining to the divine is so that your life can have the shine of the moon and the shine of the stars. It should have, because man possesses the most unique thing in the whole of the existence: consciousness. You have been given such a precious treasure, but what have you attained with all your running around? Your salary may go up a little, you may accumulate some more money in your safe, you may get a bigger car in place of a smaller car, a bigger house in place of a smaller house....

But having been given this supreme consciousness, what are you really doing with it? What are you really attaining through this supreme consciousness? The bliss of the entire universe can be contained in it.

Finding the divine means only one thing: that your doors can become open to bliss, that the whole festival of life can penetrate you, that you can rise up dancing. Otherwise it will be like this:

Today, the Kachnar tree blossoms,
But my beloved is not in the palace.
My girlfriends dress me in spring attire,
And put vermilion in my hair.

Laughing with the moon, and chatting,
They of a sudden pause
Link arms, hold, embrace, and then let go.
Like the fragrance of madhukamini blossom,
Youth cannot be contained in golden scarves of silk.

Today, the Kachnar tree blossoms,
But my beloved is not in the palace.

When the flowers are in blossom and the lover is not home,
it means nothing to the beloved....

Today, the Kachnar tree blossoms,
But my beloved is not in the palace.
The breeze blows
Cooling my body.
My eyes are dry and lifeless,
The bloom of spring fades fast,
Night-time passes in waking.

Today, the Kachnar tree blossoms,
But my beloved is not in the palace.

Her lover is not there, the moon is in the sky and the Kachnar
tree is full of blossom. A cool breeze blows, there is a
fragrance all around and the moonlight is spreading everywhere, but what is the point of it all? — her lover is not in
the palace. The condition of the human heart is just like this.
Until the divine, the lover, graces your heart of hearts, your
whole life will be dry, empty, lifeless, dead.

Searching for the divine means enthroning the beloved, the
divine in your heart, or whatsoever name you want to give
to it. Right now the throne of your heart is empty. There is
a palace, but the emperor is nowhere to be seen.

Even from death I have received the gift of life,
But my entreaty was not heard at your door.
The universe has changed,
Life has changed, kingdoms have changed,
The earth and the sky have changed,
The seasons of spring and rain have changed.
I do not know what bracelet you have tied on me,
So that my wrist is still not free.

Sometimes I called your name on the ocean's shores,
Sometimes I called you in the deserts like a cloud.
Like a game I searched for you in crowds and fairs,
Enshrouded, I called your name in the crematoriums.
While measuring the tracks, the traveler disappeared,
The feet of breath grew tired, the journey ended.

But my body and soul know not the smallest respite
From this agonizing prison.
I know not from which window you may be glancing.
Remembering this, I bow my head at every temple gate.
Who knows when you may knock at my door?
With this anxiety, I have not slept my whole life.
My eyes are always full and half-open.
Diminishing part by part,
My body wastes away, my water-pot lies empty.
But, oh my moon, without you in this world,
The night of my life knows no moonlight.

Without the divine man is a dark night: there is no moonlight,
the moon doesn't rise. Without the divine, man is only a seed,
closed and inert. This seed can only sprout in the presence
of the divine and then life's journey of blossoming and
becoming fruitful can begin. Without the divine, there is a

temple but no deity. You are empty, unfulfilled. The beloved
is not in the palace – and you know it.

Don't ask what you will lose if you don't attain to the divine.
Start by asking what you have right now. If you don't attain
to the divine, then what have you attained? It will be
more meaningful and more relevant to ask this: If you don't
attain to the divine, then what will you have attained in this
life? Ask this question. Then you have started your search
from the right place.

The only meaning of "the divine" is that the truth of your
life becomes manifest, the destiny that you are carrying
within you is revealed, your inner lotus blossoms. When such
a lotus blossoms, it is the ultimate celebration. The only
meaning of the divine is that this ultimate celebration within
you is realized. That is why we depict Buddha on a lotus,
Vishnu on a lotus, and why meditators have named the
ultimate source of man's energy *sahasrar* – the thousand-
petaled lotus. When your consciousness blossoms fully it is
as if a lotus with a thousand petals has opened. Only on that
day will you realize what were you missing. Only on that day
will you realize that what you were calling life was no life at
all.

Shri Aurobindo has said that only when he became
enlightened did he realize that what he had been calling life
was worse than death; that what he had been seeing
as light was a mighty darkness, and what he had been
drinking – believing it to be the nectar of immortality – was
really poison.

There is a Tibetan story. A Buddhist monk had lost his way.

Night was falling and a few stars were twinkling in the sky, so there was a little light. He was thirsty because he hadn't had anything to drink all day. He searched all around, but he couldn't see even one faint light. He was thirsty, hungry.... Tired and exhausted, he fell down on his knees and remembered Buddha. He meditated, "Oh Lord, help me now or I will die. I need water immediately, my throat is completely dry."

Just as he fell to the ground, he saw a golden bowl in front of him filled with water. He picked it up and drank the water. Then he put the bowl down and fell asleep, so happy that he had received the Buddha's grace.

When he awoke the next morning, he had a great shock. There was no bowl. In front of him was a human skull. And it was no ordinary skull; the person must have died very recently, he must have been killed by some wild beast because the skull still had blood on it and bits of flesh. The flesh was rotting and contained maggots. And in that skull was a little water. He had drunk from that water in the night.

Because he was so thirsty and tired, because the night was so dark, the skull had seemed like a golden bowl. In the light of the day, there was no golden bowl, only a human skull; a rotten, decaying skull. Upset and horrified, the monk vomited. He had slept comfortably all night, without vomiting or anything like that, but now he vomited. And according to the story, as he was vomiting he became enlightened, he entered the state of self-realization. He understood everything, he understood the secret of the entire universe.

You are just as unconscious. What you take to be a golden

bowl is as dirty as a human skull. What you think of as love in this moment, is still something which is full of mud. What you understand to be life is not life at all. On the day that your eyes open – the divine means nothing but the opening of your eyes – on the day that your eyes open, you will be amazed to see that the life you have been living up until now was worse than death.

But this will occur at a later date. What about now? How can you understand this now? So leave all this behind for the moment. Right now, think about what there really is in your life. If you find that there is nothing in your life, then seeking becomes a necessity. Use this time that you have in your hands.

I say only this to you: Whosoever seeks, certainly finds; whosoever seeks, attains. Doors open for the one who knocks on them. A seeker never returns empty-handed: search with courage. There is nothing in your life right now, so don't ask such topsy-turvy questions like "What is the loss in not attaining to the divine," just to console yourself that there is no point in attaining to it, so that you can go on doing exactly what you have always been doing up until now.

People come to me and ask, "What is to be gained from meditation?" I ask them: "Until now you have been an angry person, but did you ever ask, "What is to be gained from being angry?" You have never asked that. But you ask me, "What is the benefit of meditation?" So far you have been violent, envious, jealous – did you ever ask what is to be gained from that?

They reply, "No, we never asked." So I tell them to ask

themselves right now: "What good has come from my being angry so far in this life?" They reply that no good has come from it. So I ask if they will still be angry in the future. They begin to get nervous, because no good comes from it, and so then...?

If you are only living with an idea of gain in your mind, then give up anger, lust and jealousy — you have not benefited from any of these things. And if you give up anger, lust, jealousy, greed and attachment, you will immediately see the benefits of meditation.

You will discover the benefits of meditation only when you enter meditation. How can you know beforehand? It is as Kabir says, *Gunge keri sarkara!* — a dumb person's sweetmeat! Those who have tasted it, even they cannot explain it. All they can say to you is that you should taste it too.

This is what I am saying to you. It is only after finding the divine that we discover that there is only one thing of benefit in the whole world — and that is the divine itself. Everything else is useless. But this realization comes only after you have tasted it. Right now, all you should do is to ask again and again, "What do I have in my life right now?" Take your life and examine everything. Open up everything and see what is there. You will find that there is nothing there, that there is a dead silence there, an absolutely blank silence! It is because of this emptiness that you become ambitious and you want to fill it with wealth, with high position — with anything at all. You are empty, and you want to fill yourself with anything you can find.

This inner emptiness gnaws at you. You can try to fill it as

much as you want, but you won't be able to — because you
cannot take the outer wealth inside, you cannot take
your status, your position inside. However big your house
may be, however big your shop may be, you cannot take it
inside you. The only one who can go inside you is the divine,
because it is already there. And once you begin to see it, then
you will start feeling the pull to go within yourself.

To be full within is to have attained to the divine. And when
you are completely full inside, totally full, then there is
contentment, satisfaction, satiation, truth, consciousness and
bliss.

Enough for today.

5

GOING BEYOND TIME

No one remains forever in this world,
O princess Daya,
Life in this world is but a one night's stay
At an inn.

Like a pearl of dew,
It is in a moment gone.
O Daya,
Carry the divine in your heart.

Your father and your mother have departed,
Now you too are preparing to go.
It may be today, it may be tomorrow,
Be astute, oh Daya.

Time has a big belly,
It is never satiated.
Kings, princes and emperors,
It swallows them all.

As the winds blow through the sky-borne clouds,
Unmaking them in myriad ways,
Man's life is in the hands of death,
And he knows no peace.

There is a famous statement by Karl Marx that religion is the opium of the people. Karl Marx knew nothing about religion, because everything *but* religion is an intoxicating opium. The race for wealth, the race for high position – these are all drugs. Religion is the only way of waking up from their intoxication.

We live in dreams, and because of this we don't become acquainted with the truth. Happiness is not possible unless we know truth; happiness is the fragrance which comes from our beginning to know truth. If we live in dreams, we will only create sorrow – because happiness cannot be born out of something that doesn't exist. These dreams which have no existence will cause us pain time and again. You can try to be happy in a million different ways, but it will not happen. That which is not is not. Only that which is, is.

"Religion" means the search for that which is. "Non-religion" means the desire for that which is not.

Man asks for many things which have no existence, and there is no way they can exist. And even if you do manage in some way to arrange your dreams, you will still remain empty inside because who has ever been satisfied by dream food? How can you ever quench your thirst with dreams? You can delude yourself with your dreams, you can become entangled with them, you can manage to pass your life in dreams, they will keep you busy – but you will never attain anything, you will never reach the shore.

A dream has no shores. Truth has a shore. The difficulty is that when someone is running around in dreams he is moving away from the truth. Dreams are the opposite of truth. So when you run around in dreams you are depriving yourself of the truth day after day. These dreams can never be fulfilled and you remain deprived of that which could have been fulfilled. Because of your demands, you are unable to become what you could have become.

You can only become that which you already are on some deep level. A seed will become a flower, but only the flower that is inherent in the seed. Right now it is hidden, one day it will manifest.

The divine means that which is already hidden within man. Once in a while, that which is hidden becomes manifest – in a devotee, in an enlightened mystic. Every human being is a seed of godliness, but our energy flows in a thousand and one other directions; hence the seed doesn't receive any energy and isn't nourished.

Have you ever noticed that you don't go to the temple with the same enthusiasm with which you go to the marketplace? You don't turn your rosary with the same devotion that you count your money. You have never wanted the divine with the same passion that you want a high position. Even at the door of the divine you ask for worldly things – there is no limit to your stupidity. You only go – even to the door of the divine – to ask for worldly things. The truth is you only ever go there when you need something to do with the world – wealth, fame, prestige, high position. Even from the divine you are asking for those same things that you have been wanting all along and have never had. You seek the divine's help even for your dreams.

Your eyes will only turn towards the divine when it becomes absolutely clear to you that whatsoever you ask for is useless – simply rubbish – and that even if you get it you will gain nothing. In the first place, you are not going to get it; but even if you did, you would still gain nothing. Even if you were the emperor of the whole world and the whole earth belonged to you, what would you really gain? Inside, you would still be exactly the same as you are right now – just as miserable, just as worried, just as agitated and suffering, just as harassed. Perhaps you would even have a few more problems – because you would be carrying the troubles of the whole world on your shoulders. You wouldn't have less trouble.

Religion is not an intoxication, an opium. Everything *but* religion is an intoxicating opium. Religion, religiousness, is the only way to take one out of these intoxications: religiousness is the only way to detoxify.

So the first thing to be taken note of: What is a dream and what is the truth? Where is the touchstone? How can we know that what we are seeing is a dream? How can we recognize that the things we are asking for are nothing but a part of our dreams?

The first thing about this is: one does not have to ask for the truth in any way. Whatsoever you can ask for has to be a dream. It is only untruth that needs to be asked for. Truth simply is. For truth, it is enough that you just open your eyes; you don't have to ask for it.

Pablo Picasso, a great Western artist, used to say one thing again and again. People thought he was being egotistical, proud. I don't think so. His manner of speaking may have been arrogant, but what he said is very much in accordance with the truth. It is utterly incomprehensible, very paradoxical. Sometimes artists, sculptors, musicians and poets utter something which comes very close to the paradoxical nature of religion, very close — because sometimes poets, sculptors and artists get a glimpse of the truth. When their link with the intellect breaks and they enter deep into the heart, some doors, some windows open.

What an enlightened mystic attains limitlessly, a poet gets occasionally, as a small fragment. What a mystic attains forever, a poet gets an occasional glimpse of, a wave.

Pablo Picasso used to say: "I don't seek, I find" — I don't search, I find it!

People thought this was a very egotistical statement: "I don't seek, I find." But it is a charming statement, it is very significant. You don't have to seek for truth — you have to find it.

There is a famous statement by Lao Tzu: As soon as you begin to search, you lose it...because the very meaning of searching is that you are looking for something that you don't have. That which is, is surrounding you from all sides. It is within and without — everywhere, and it is inside the seeker too. The one you want to search for abides within you, it is seeing through your eyes. You will not only see it outside of yourself, it pervades every pore of your body, it pervades your every breath. Why search for something that you already have? You only need to find it.

I say the same to you: that you only need to claim the divine; you don't need to search for it. The moment you search you have missed. To search merely means that you are searching for a Hindu God, a Muslim God or a Christian God. To search means that you are looking for some human

conception of a god. If you want to find God, let go of all
your notions about it. Let go – even of the search. Sit down,
be empty. The divine is revealed in a consciousness that is
empty of the search, because there are no waves in a consciousness which is free of searching. When there is no desire,
how can there be any waves? When there is nothing to
be attained, when there is nowhere to go, how can there be
tension, restlessness? In this ultimate state of tranquillity,
godliness surrounds you from all the sides. It was already
surrounding you, but you have only become aware of it in
this state of tranquillity.

But far from searching for the divine, we only go to ask for
trifles. If you ever ask for something when you are praying,
you are committing a sin. It would be better not to pray than
to pray and make demands, because that only shows that, as
yet, you don't know anything about the divine, you only want
to make use of it for your own petty desires. Someone must
win a court case, someone's business is not going so well,
someone's shop is about to go bankrupt, someone else cannot find a wife…. Never go to the divine to ask for such
things.

I read a short satirical poem yesterday:

A hippy-style devotee
Was devoutly praying to God,
Obstinately remaining in front of his statue,
Obstinately standing on just one foot,
Until the Lord was well pleased with him.
Having to honor his indebtedness for such devotion,
God was compelled to appear.
"O devotee," saith the Lord,

"I am happy with you,
"I stand here, before you.
"Wake up this very moment,
"And whatever you desire,
"Ask for it with one *var*, one wish."
Replied the devotee, "O my Lord,
"Be thou not deceived
"By my bell-bottom trousers and long hair.
"I myself am a var, a bridegroom,
"So please just find me a bride."

But whenever you have asked for something, whatever you have been asking for is just as ridiculous, just as laughable. To demand something from the divine only shows your lack of intelligence. What you ask for makes no difference.

Vivekananda lived with Ramakrishna. When Vivekananda's father passed away, he left things in a pretty bad state. The family was deeply in debt, and there was no way to pay back what they owed. At home, there was not enough flour to make bread twice a day. When Ramakrishna saw that Vivekananda was sad, distressed and hungry, he said, "You fool, there is no need for you to be distressed. Why don't you go and ask the Mother Goddess? Go inside the temple and ask for what you need. You will get whatever you ask for."

Vivekananda went into the temple because Ramakrishna had told him to go, but he was still very hesitant. He couldn't say no, because Ramakrishna had told him to go. He had to go.

After an hour or so he returned, ecstatic. Ramakrishna asked him, "Did you ask for what you wanted?"

Vivekananda replied, "What was I supposed to ask for?"

Ramakrishna said, "You fool, I sent you into the temple because you were so distressed. You should have asked for what you needed."

Vivekananda said, "Oh Paramahansa, I forgot!"

"Go back again," said Ramakrishna.

Vivekananda replied, "I will forget again."

Ramakrishna said, "Your memory is not that bad. Why should you forget?"

Vivekananda explained, "I am sure I will forget again. As soon as I went in there, tears began to fall from my eyes. As soon as I went in, my meditation began to ripen. I started swaying. In that ecstasy, I was not hungry, I was not poor, I was not needy, I was not poverty-stricken. I was an emperor. The divine began to shower upon me. It seemed so petty to ask for anything, let alone money! When the divine is showering on me, how can I ask for money? I can't do it."

Because Ramakrishna didn't want to listen to him, Vivekananda went back inside again. But once again he came out empty-handed and very ecstatic. Ramakrishna sent him in three times, and he came back three times. He couldn't make the request to ask for money. He prayed, he drowned, he was overwhelmed with ecstasy, but he didn't beg. In that moment Ramakrishna embraced Vivekananda and said, "If you had begged today, your relationship with me would have been broken for ever. The test is over — you have been tested and proved authentic, true. To beg is to spoil your prayer."

…But you are always begging. You have never prayed without begging. When you don't have anything to ask for, you don't pray because you think, "What is the need? Everything is going so well." That is why you don't remember the divine when you are happy, only when you are sad. I want to tell you that God is only really remembered when he is remembered in your happiness. What you remember when you are sad is not the real God, because when you are sad, you start asking for your sorrow to be taken away. When you are happy, there is nothing to ask for, there is something to give.

Pour yourself into prayer, don't ask for anything. Give, don't ask. In the ultimate moment of prayer, a devotee lets go of himself at the divine's feet; he gives himself, he offers himself.

As soon as you begin to search, you have lost. Everything is just here to be had, but in order to have it, one needs a mind that is not the mind of a beggar.

Your prayer and worship, your homage and reverence – they all become meaningless because your beggar's mind keeps following you there too. To beg while you pray means to drench the seed you have just sowed with poison. You turn everything upside down: you want to do one thing and something else happens. It is better not to ask for anything – at least then the seed will be safe. Don't worship – at least then the seed will not be poisoned. Save your prayers for the day when you can pray with thankfulness, with gratitude; for the day when you realize that the divine's compassion is infinite: "You have given me so much. You have given me everything without my asking. You have given to me for no reason at all. I am not worthy, but still you have given me everything. Even though I am not worthy, still you have showered on this unworthy person. You have given me life, you have given me love, you have given me the capacity to experience bliss, you have given me the sensitivity to see beauty. You have given me all of this!" When you go to pray, go to give thanks for all of this.

On the day your prayer becomes a thanksgiving you will find that the divine has begun to descend into your prayers. As long as your prayers ask for something, you are standing in the world. Whether you are in a temple, in a mosque, or in a *gurudwara* – it makes no difference – you are standing in the marketplace.

And this marketplace is not something that is outside you. Don't think that it is outside: that too creates a big fallacy. This marketplace is within you, this jostling crowd of thoughts is within you, this carnival of dreams is within you. This you, who is riding on dream horses in so many different directions, is within you. The outer marketplace is only a shadow of the marketplace within. The real marketplace is inside you.

So it sometimes happens that becoming tired of the outer marketplace, you start running towards the jungle, or you become a *sannyasin*. You have missed again...you have missed again. The outer marketplace was simply a projection of the inner one. The real marketplace is within. Drop this inner market! Then you will find that even the outer market is nothing but a temple. Even when you are sitting in your shop you will be in the temple.

Marx had to say that religion is the opium of the people because all the people he saw were pseudo-religious people. And it was not really his fault either, because out of a thousand people, nine hundred and ninety-nine are pseudo religious, are beggars – they grovel like beggars. They never even think of thanking the divine; they are too full of complaints and more complaints. And Marx must have seen these people going to the temple and returning home with the hope that now they will get something soon. This hope of receiving something *is* the opium – opium in the sense that things are not all right today but they will be tomorrow. This is the pure opium essence – its extract, its concentrate – and if you coagulate it, it will turn into an opium tablet.

Opium means the hope that today is a suffering, but tomorrow will be happiness – that happiness will certainly come tomorrow. There is sorrow in this life, but there will be happiness in the next life. There may be sorrow in this body, but once we are released from this body, once the soul is bodiless, there will be nothing but happiness. There is sorrow on earth, but there will be happiness in heaven.

Opium means hope. Opium means being reassured about tomorrow: that we can suffer today as long as we have hope for tomorrow; that we can say, "Just one more day, just get through today in some small way. Just a little further, just a little longer. You are tired, but just go a little further. Everything will be fine tomorrow."

And it was no different yesterday, or the day before – and nothing will ever come right. Tomorrow will come and still nothing will be any better. Tomorrow you will think about the day after tomorrow: that soon things will be better, that soon everything will be all right. You pass your child-hood believing that everything will be all right by the time you are a youth, and you pass your youth believing that everything will be all right by the time you reach your old age. You pass your old age in the same way, believing that everything will be all right after death. But nothing ever becomes all right.

If anything is ever going to be all right, it will have to be so now – it will not happen tomorrow. "Tomorrow" is the opium. The person who avoids, postpones, is like an opium addict. What does an addict do? He tries to avoid. His wife is lying in bed, sick. He can't bear it, so he takes opium and forgets his wife and everything else. Now things are going well! He will remember his situation again when his intoxication wears off, but when that time comes he will see to it – he will take another tablet. His business is making a loss, his business has failed – he will get drunk, perhaps on alcohol. At least for one night he will have no cares because of his intoxication. He will worry about tomorrow in the morning. For now everything is all right, the rest he can worry about tomorrow. Everything is postponed. There is sorrow: it is postponed until tomorrow. Opium or alcohol provide excuses to forget your problems, to overlook them.

The foolish indulge in crude forms of intoxication. The so-called wise go for subtler intoxications. There is intense pain: you go to the temple and pray to God. When you come back, you will be full of hope that now everything will be all right because you have told God – as if God didn't know and needed to be told by you, as if God wouldn't know unless you had told him, as if some divine person sits up there listening to you! You are just talking to the walls.

So in a way, what Marx said is correct. For nine hundred and
ninety-nine people, religion is a form of intoxication. But
those nine hundred and ninety-nine people know nothing
about religion. That is why I say that Karl Marx was wrong,
and that he is still wrong. The person who knows religiousness is one in a thousand — a Buddha, a Meera, a Daya, a
Sahajo, a Krishna, a Christ. Only this one in a thousand
knows. Only such a person should be investigated — what is
religion to him. His religiousness is a thanksgiving.

If you mix things up, if they are half wrong and half right,
that creates a great difficulty. Your prayers are buried underneath and your demands are sitting on top of them. The
truth is that you have begged so many times that prayer has
come to mean asking; the word prayer has become synonymous with asking. You have asked many times that even the
word prayer has been turned upside down.

You need to rearrange your life rightly. Keep things where
they belong. Don't turn them upside down — it causes great
difficulty.

I was reading a satirical song:

On the borders of our city,
On the banks of the river,
An ascetic of the Kaliyuga
Lights the fire of mortification.
He makes amulets —
A modern-day creator of destiny.
A few days ago, a boy came to him
Weeping as he spoke:
"I have addled my brain

For three years past
And still I have failed my BA.
Give me a talisman, please,
So this year I may succeed."
The *fakir* replied:
"Drink milk to bring more sharpness to your brain,
Live life a little more fittingly."
The boy answered:
"Milk! Ah, milk should be easy,
Because we have a cow,
But for the past three years
She too gives no milk."
The *fakir* replied:
"My dear friend!
Take these two talismans,
Put one around your neck,
And the other around the cow's."
The boy departed.
But by sheer coincidence
The lockets were somehow exchanged.
The cow wore the boy's locket,
And the boy wore the cow's.
This mistake was the ruin of the boy,
The cow passed her BA.
But the boy weeps to this very day
While in Moradabad, in the sweetmakers' shops
He carries the milk pails.

Keep things in their right place, otherwise the same mistake
that happened with the amulets will cause you great difficulty
and trouble. Your shop has entered uninvited into your temple,
begging has become a part of your meditation, your prayer
has become corrupted and defiled. Purify your prayers. Don't

worry about the divine, first purify your prayers. Don't even ask whether the divine exists or not. Just purify your prayers.

On the day that your prayer is pure, you will gain eyes. On that day you will come to know that the divine exists – and not only that the divine exists; you will come to know that *only* the divine exists, that there is nothing else but the divine. On that day, its message will come to you from every direction. You will find the divine in life, and even in death you will only see its presence. It will be present in your happiness, in your sorrow, in your defeat, and in your victory; it will be present in the flowers and in the thorns. On the day you begin to see godliness all around you, life starts happening to you for the first time. On that day you are born.

Don't consider your physical birth to be your true birth. Being born from your mother's womb has fulfilled only the primary condition. Your real birth has yet to happen. On the day of your real birth.... In India we call such a man a *dwija*, the twice born. He is the true *brahmin*; he is born again, he is born a second time, he has given himself a new life, a new meaning, a new expression. His life is colored by prayer, he has remembered the divine – for no reason at all, just out of bliss, just out of total joy. He doesn't call the divine and say, "I need a few things done. Please come." He calls because calling the divine is the joy of his heart. He finds a bliss in calling. He prays, and praying gives him tremendous joy. When prayer is its own reward, it is true prayer. If the reward is to come afterwards, then it is a false prayer.

Today's sutras by Daya are sweet. Each one is worth understanding.

No one remains forever in this world,
O princess Daya,
Life in this world is but a one night's stay
At an inn.

This world is a dream. *Life in this world is but a one night's stay at an inn.* It is like staying in an inn overnight and setting off again in the morning. Don't think that the inn is your home. Don't tie yourself to a post. Don't form attachments, don't be bound by your attachments. You shouldn't be crying, weeping and wailing and forever looking backwards when you leave the inn in the morning.

The inn is not your home. You still have to find your home. How can a person who believes that the inn is his home search for his true home? He has understood things differently from what they really are. He believes that a stone is a diamond. His search for gold has stopped: he has taken brass for gold. His search for truth has stopped: he has taken dreams for truth and his search for truth has stopped.

In millions and millions of people's lives in this world, there is no longing for truth. What could the reason be? How can this be? How does this unlikely thing happen? So many people – with no desire for truth! How can they live with no yearning for truth, with no roots in truth, without raising their eyes towards truth? Try to understand the reason for such a way of living. The reason that they are living like this is that they have accepted the untruth as truth and so now there is no reason to search for the truth. When you accept that rubbish is diamonds and gems, and you carefully lock this rubbish in your safe, then why should you go to the diamond mines? Why do all that work, why bother?

So in order to awaken this thirst, it is necessary to know that:

No one remains forever in this world,
O princess Daya,
Life in this world is but a one night's stay
At an inn.

Remember one thing, use it as a touchstone every day: Is this lasting? will it last? In a jeweler's shop, there is a stone used for testing gold – a touchstone. Whenever someone comes to buy or sell gold, the jeweler tests it on his touchstone. Let this understanding be your touchstone. Whatever you do: Will it be enduring? will it stay? will it last? If you write poems on water you are bound to weep because they will be gone even before you can write them. Or if you write your poems on sand...they may last slightly longer, for at least as long as it takes you to write them, but then the winds will come and blow them all away.

Jesus said to his disciples to build the house of their lives upon a rock. Jesus called his most beloved disciple Peter. "Peter" means a rock. He said that Peter would be the rock of his temple, that his temple would be built on Peter. The name was appropriate; it was a significant name.

Don't write on sand, don't write on water. Write the story of your life on rock. Rock signifies the eternal: it lasts, it remains. If what you are doing is ephemeral, don't worry too much about it. If it gets done, fine; if it doesn't, fine. It is all the same: what has happened will unhappen, what you have done will be undone – and all in a short time. But we are so mad after what is ephemeral! We draw lines on water and then we wait for them to last. No one else's lines have lasted, but we think that perhaps ours might.

What are you doing with your life? Are you looking for status? Does anyone's position ever last? If someone has a position today, he will lose it tomorrow. While a person has a position people sing his praises, but as soon as he loses it, people forget him. They don't even remember who he was, they don't even remember what has happened to him. Those who used to salute him pass him by as though they have not even seen him. And you are going mad after such a position, you are devoting your whole life to it. There is no substance to it; it is like a bubble of water.

Very few people truly mature.

Have you seen young children making bubbles from soapy water? They are so happy, so excited. But old people are doing the same thing. Their soapy water is a little more subtle, but nevertheless they are also blowing bubbles. Until the day they die, their only concern is how to leave a well-known name behind them.

When you yourself can't survive, what is the point of fame? If you cannot survive, how will your name survive? Do you know how many people have been born into this world? The scientists say that there are at least ten bodies buried beneath where you are sitting right now. The whole earth is a grave-yard. There is no need to be scared of graveyards, because wherever you are you are in a graveyard. People are buried everywhere. Man has been on the earth for millions of years.

Today's settlements used to be crematoriums. Today's crematoriums used to be settlements. There is no piece of land where man is not buried. Today's ruins used to be great capitals.

I had a meditation camp in Mandu, near Indore. A friend of mine who was having a house built, was staying with me. He had only come to tell me about the plans for his house. He was not interested in the meditation camp, but because I was going to be there, he thought I would be easily available and he would be able to tell me all about it.

He was going to build a big house, and he wanted my blessings. I told him, "I have no problem with that. It costs me nothing to give my blessings. That is why your so-called saints go on bestowing blessings – the poor things have nothing else to give, and blessings cost nothing. If you want, I can even write out my blessings and put my signature to them – there is no problem in that. But I suggest you look around here first and look into what you can see."

He asked, "What is there to see here?"

I said, "Go outside and look."

Once, Mandu used to be a great capital. They say that nine hundred thousand people used to live there. And now nine hundred people live there. And nine hundred thousand people must have been living there.... "Do you see how vast Mandu is? There are such big and grand ruins here! There are ruins of mosques where ten thousand people could pray in together. There are ruins of *caravanserais*, where ten thousand camels could be stabled at one time."

It was a great city. Caravans to and from all over Asia passed through Mandu. Today it is known as Mandu; in those days its name was Mandavgarh, the fort city of Mandav. Mandavgarh became Mandu. Just as the Honorable Chandulal becomes Chandu when he is bankrupt, so Mandavgarh becomes Mandu. It would not seem right to call it Mandavgarh now. Where is the castle? Where is the fort now? Even to call it Mandav would be out of proportion.

I said, "Look at the plaque at the bus station. It says that nine hundred people live here, nine hundred and something! Once nine hundred thousand people lived here, today only nine hundred are left. What were once great palaces stand as ruins today. Once the city spread for miles. Go outside and look, and then receive my blessings. I will give you my blessings when you come back."

He went outside and returned with his eyes full of tears. "Give me the plans," he said. "I want to tear them up. There is no substance to them."

I said, "This is a more appropriate blessing. It is all right to build a house and live in it. But don't create such fantasies. Those who built these grand palaces must have had grand fantasies too. Neither the owners nor the palaces have remained; all have become ruins. Owls live in these ruins now. And no matter how much I bless you, owls will rest in your palace one day too."

We should keep a touchstone in our lives: whatsoever we are doing, will it last? We may acquire great wealth, but will it last? Will our fame, our position, our prestige remain? Will the body which we are so mad about last, will it remain? It will go tomorrow, or even today. Don't entangle your heart too much in things which are sure to go. Live with them as one lives in an inn. One gets up in the morning and leaves without even looking backwards.

All the world's carnivals, all the gatherings of people,
Are mere show.
I have been alone
In a crowded assembly.

You are surrounded by a large crowd, but you are still alone. In reality, you are alone, you *are* really alone. These shows and worldly crowds of desires have no value, no eternal value. And something without eternal value has no value at all.

But you plan for the future. And not just for the future, but even for the past: that if you had done this and this, things would have turned out differently.

Think about man's madness. The past is gone, nothing can be done about it now. But how many times have you caught yourself trying to change the past? Something that has already happened, about which nothing can be changed now.... Once somebody abused you, and now you curse yourself because in that moment you couldn't come up with the particular type of response that you have now....

Mark Twain was a prominent Western writer. After one lecture he was on his way home – his wife had come to take him home. On the way, his wife asked him how his lecture had gone. Mark Twain said, "Which one? The one I had prepared, the one I actually gave, or the one I am now wishing that I had given? Which lecture do you mean? There are so many lectures. And the one I had prepared was wasted."

When you face a crowd of people, all preparation goes to waste. You start saying things differently from how you intended: "I gave one lecture and now I am thinking about another one which would have been much better. Which lecture do you mean?"

Many times you will find yourself changing the past, whitewashing it: "If only I had said this, if only I had done that! Again, I missed out." Can you understand how mad this is? The past has gone. Nothing can be done about it now; what has happened has happened and cannot be undone. Now there is no way to go back to the past. The bird of time has flown from your hands. The bird has eaten your crops — there is nothing you can do about it now.

But man keeps thinking, even about the past. And he also thinks about the future, and that too is madness, because what can you achieve by thinking about what has not yet happened? What can you achieve by thinking about what has already gone? Live what is. Live the moment that you have been given. And live in that moment as though it were...*a one night's stay at an inn.*

When desires fail, the heart lives on with the thought:
Had this been so, what might have happened?
Had that been so, what might have happened?

We continue to think in this manner: "Had this been so, what might have happened; had that been so, what might have happened?" Or, "If only this could happen...." Sometimes you think of such crazy things...you have not even filed your nomination to run for the election and you keep thinking "If I win the election...." You have not even bought a lottery ticket and you keep thinking, "What if I win the lottery?" And you are not only thinking about winning, sometimes you believe you have already won it and wonder what to do: "What shall I do with all of this money? Shall I buy a house? a car? What shall I do with all this money?"

Many times you will find yourself thinking in this way. And you shouldn't — because if this continues to be your state of mind, you will never wake up, you will remain buried in these lies, in this opium. You are never finished with this opium, so you never wake up.

Buddha says: self-remembrance, right-remembering.

Kabir says: *surati*, be mindful.

Nanak too says: surati, be mindful.

Wake up! Remember. What are you doing? What are you thinking? If you think with even a little awareness, you will realize that ninety-nine out of a hundred things that you are thinking about are madness. At least cut them out and throw them away. Don't waste your time with them. That will leave you with the one thing which won't be useless, but won't be fully meaningful in the absolute sense either. It is functional for the time being. Just use it and get out of the inn.

See the unseeable,
Forget not yourself.
Explore the truth,
Don't lull your dreams to sleep.

Don't keep calling on dreams, don't keep decorating them. Don't keep singing lullabies – get out of your childishness. Don't sit clutching your toys to your chest – drop these toys! The name of these toys is the world.

Like a pearl of dew,
It is in a moment gone,
O Daya,
Carry the divine in your heart.

Like a pearl of dew.... We see it in the morning – how this pearl shines, how colorful it is, how rainbow-like! Sometimes, if it catches a ray of sun, it defeats the beauty of any diamond. But it is a pearl of dew – now it is here, now it is gone. As soon as the sun rises, this pearl will begin to evaporate. As soon as the sun awakens, all these pearls will disappear; all the dew will evaporate, will turn to vapor.

Like a pearl of dew.... The world is just like that.

Mahavira also said that the world is like a dewdrop on a blade of grass. With the slightest breeze, the blade of grass will tremble and the dewdrop will slip to the ground and be lost. It is the same for human beings – you are lodged on a blade of grass for a short time, a very short time, and then the wind will blow, death will come, and you will slip away and be lost. How many people were lost before you? Don't these forgotten people give you a reminder?

Chuang Tzu always kept a skull beside him. He was a great man, a wise man. His disciples used to ask him, "Everything else is okay, oh master, but why do you keep this skull near you? We feel disgusted when we see it, we feel sad."

Chuang Tzu used to reply, "That is why! Whenever wrong or untrue things begin to move in my own skull, I just look at this skull and see that one day, this will be the condition of my skull too. There is no need to be deluded by what your skull tells you. As soon as I look at this skull, I regain my awareness. I always keep it with me: it is my master — because sooner or later this is going to be my condition, and sooner or later my skull will be lying on the ground, being kicked around.

"This skull saved me once. One day I had it here with me when a man came. He was angry with me and picked up his shoe to beat me. I was also about to lose my temper when, by chance, I saw the skull. I immediately softened. I reminded myself that I too will be dead tomorrow, and what will I do then if people beat my head with shoes? So I said to the man, 'My brother, go ahead and beat me to your heart's content.'

"He was startled. He asked, 'What do you mean?'

"I told him, 'This skull has reminded me that one day other shoes will be walking on my head. For how long can I prevent this? Sooner or later my skull will lie in the burial ground, being kicked around by everyone. It will lie in the dirt for centuries with people walking on it. This is bound to happen. So, my brother, beat me to your heart's content! Before this skull falls, let your heart be at peace. If you are satisfied, it is no mean achievement. I will lose nothing and your heart will be content.'"

The man threw away his shoe and fell at Chuang Tzu's feet. He said, "What an extraordinary skull you keep! You are quite right — what is there to hit, what is there to protect? I came here angry. What substance is there in my anger? We have but a brief stay in the world: what is the point of quarreling or of being angry with someone; of making someone angry? The situation will pass."

If someone lives consciously, then the dirt of life will not stick to him. If someone passes through life consciously, then the purity of his life will remain intact.

Like a pearl of dew...

This world is a dream that you watch with open eyes. And there is nothing that is yours in your dreams; your dreams are not your own. To find oneself, one must look beyond the dreams. One must see the witness — the one hiding behind the dreams. The witness is hidden in your crowd of dreams, and you don't remember who you are. You have forgotten yourself.

It is in a moment gone.
O Daya,
Carry the divine in your heart.

So Daya says that it will all be destroyed in a moment. Even if that moment is seventy years long what difference does it make? — it will be destroyed in a moment. One thing is certain: it *will* be destroyed. This practice — of keeping those things in your heart which will sooner or later be destroyed — defiles the heart. So why defile your heart for such transient guests? Take into your heart the one who always remains:

O Daya,
Carry the divine in your heart.

So now rather take the divine into your heart: it will always remain there.

Embrace the eternal. Take hold of that which has existed from time immemorial: which has always been, which still is and which will always be there. Don't grab at straws – nothing remains when you grab at straws. Don't sail in paper boats. If you must make a boat, make it out of the divine's name. If you must grab hold of something, take hold of the divine's feet. If you must grab something, grab that which will never leave you, which cannot be taken away from you.

O Daya,
Carry the divine in your heart.

And in this way if your stream begins to flow towards the divine, away from the world and towards godliness, away from the meaningless and towards the meaningful – and then you will arrive at the highest peaks.

Taking the support of the flame,
Soot turns into kohl.

If you can take the support of this flame of remembrance, of the awareness that now you will dedicate yourself only to the eternal and not to the momentary, then even soot becomes *kohl*, then even the impure becomes pure, then even the profane becomes sacred. And whereas now nothing can be seen except flesh, bones and marrow, soon the hidden inner stream will be seen, soon an unprecedented beauty will be born, and an unprecedented bliss too.

Bliss is the shadow of truth, happiness is the outcome of truth.

Your father and your mother have departed,
Now you too are preparing to go.
It may be today, it may be tomorrow.
Be astute, O Daya.

Your father and your mother have departed, now you too are preparing to go. What we call life is really nothing but a queue at the door of death. The queue moves forward every day, because every day a few more people enter that door. You are getting closer. Soon your turn will also come.

Before death grabs you, surrender yourself completely to the divine. Then there will be no death for you. If you yourself have surrendered everything, then there is nothing left for death to take away from you. Death only snatches the ephemeral. Death's power is only against the ephemeral. Death cannot touch the eternal, it cannot touch the eternal that is hidden within you. It will take away your body, it will take away your wealth, your position, your fame, your prestige – everything – but your stream of consciousness within will remain untouched. But you have no acquaintance with it whatsoever. You have turned your back on it, you have forgotten the source.

Your father and your mother have departed,
Now you too are preparing to go.
It may be today, it may be tomorrow.
Be astute, oh Daya.

Understand this word astute. You call those people astute

who are cunning. You call those people astute who are skilled in worldly matters. A wise person will not call them astute. A wise man calls them great fools, because what will their cleverness bring them? – a few fragments of clay. What will their cleverness bring them? – a few soap bubbles. What is the final outcome of all their cleverness? Death will snatch away all the wealth they have acquired through their cunning. This is not cleverness. They are deceiving others. Not only that, they are deceiving themselves as well.

You call those people who simply increase their misfortune in the name of fortune "astute." You call those people who never knew fortune, who take their misfortune to be wealth and prosperity "astute."

The really clever, the really astute person is the one who moves in the direction of the real wealth:

...Be astute, O Daya.

What does Daya say? What does she mean by asking to be astute? There is only one intelligence: becoming aware of death. It will not be long before the one who awakens to death, awakens to the divine. He will have to!

Without death, there would have been no religion in the world. People would not have woken up; there would have been no way to wake people. Just look: even though death exists, people still don't wake up. No one would ever wake up if there were no death. The slight possibility of awakening that exists in this world is only because of death – because with the existence of death only a complete idiot can go on deluding himself.

Anyone with even the smallest sense will see that his death keeps moving towards him, that it can happen at any moment. Whether the next morning will come or not is not certain. Whether or not you have one more moment in your hands is uncertain. Why build a house when there is so much uncertainty? How can there be any rest when change occurs so swiftly, so quickly; when it is not possible to step into the same river twice? What bliss can there be? There is no way of staying here.

So an astute person is one who listens to what death is hinting at and immediately sets off in search of the eternal. You can see that all the people who have become enlightened in this world became so basically because of the awareness of death.

Buddha saw a dead man and asked his charioteer, "What has happened to him?" Until that time he had never been allowed to see a dead man. He had been made to live an artificial life hidden within the palaces.

When he was a small child, the astrologers had told his father to shelter him from certain things, otherwise he would become a *sannyasin*. What were those things? The astrologers said to protect the boy from the fact of old age by not letting any old person come before him. Secondly, no sick person should be allowed to be seen by him. Thirdly, he should not see a corpse. And fourthly, no sannyasin should ever come into his sight.

His father was puzzled. He said that he understood all they said except one statement. It seemed right that his son should not see old age, sickness or death — because these things shock a person, and the astrologers had told the king that his son would leave home if he was shocked. And Shuddhodana, the king, had only this one son, who had been born in his old age and was the successor to the kingdom. The king was scared. The astrologers had also told him that if he stayed his son would become a chakravartin, a world ruler, but if he left home he would become a great sannyasin. These were the two possibilities. The astrologers told the king, "Make him stay."

So Buddha's father made every arrangement to keep him hidden in the palace. But he questioned the astrologers about one point. He understood everything else, but why should the boy avoid seeing a sannyasin?

They told him, "A sannyasin? Only a man who becomes aware of death takes *sannyas*, renounces the world. Seeing a sannyasin, the question will arise in his mind, 'What has happened to this man? He doesn't appear to be like other people. He is not interested in accumulating wealth, position, or prestige. This is a different kind of man. What has happened to him?' And if he decides to understand the sannyasin, then he will have to understand what death is, because no one ever becomes a sannyasin without becoming aware of death. It is only after a man has seen death that he becomes a sannyasin."

In the past, sannyasins were not invited to weddings and celebrations because it was thought dangerous to invite someone who had seen death to such festivities. A sannyasin is a dead man. He has already died, died to the old world. That is why, in the past, a sannyasin's head was shaved – just like the head of a dead person. He was actually laid on a

funeral pyre, and a fire was set. Then the master would recite
the mantra and say, "All your past has died, all your past has
been destroyed, has turned to ashes. You are no longer what
you were until yesterday. You are no one's father, no one's
husband, no one's brother, no one's son. The man who
existed until a moment ago is now gone. We have placed him
on the funeral pyre; he has been cremated. Now you can get
up. You are another man, you are a *dwija* – a twice born."

That is why they are given ochre robes. Ochre clothes
symbolize fire: this man has passed through fire, he has died.
The ochre clothes are the flames – the flames of the funeral
pyre.

So the astrologers said that Buddha should not be allowed
to see a sannyasin, because a sannyasin is proof of the fact
that there is death in this world. Otherwise, why would
anyone take sannyas? Sannyas is proof of the fact that the
person has seen death and has been shocked by it: he has been
shocked and he has become shrewd.

Buddha's father hid everything for long time, but for how
long could he manage this? These things cannot be hidden.
And it is not just Buddha's father who hides them, you also
hide them; all fathers and mothers hide them. If a funeral
procession passes outside the door of their house, the mother
will call her son inside and shut the door. You have seen this
happening, haven't you? – "Come inside, someone has died."
She is afraid that her son might see it. All parents are afraid
that if their child sees death prematurely, their child might
become a sannyasin.

As soon as you reflect on death, you will begin the journey
of sannyas. Only idiots can carry on without becoming

sannyasins. Those who have some awareness cannot stop themselves.

Sannyas simply means that this life is not the true life. This life is held in the hands of death. We are being tightly held in the jaws of death: its mouth can close at any time and we will be finished. But still we want to enjoy life for a short time, to hum a song, to dance a little, to forget the reality for a short time.

There is an ancient Buddhist story. It has many meanings. One of them is as follows:

A man is running. A lion is following him and as he becomes more and more frightened, he reaches a place beyond which he can go no further – he reaches a pit, a gigantic ravine. He looks down and knows he cannot jump. But even if he could jump – perhaps he has the faint hope that he may be saved, lame and crippled – he realizes that there are two lions down below, looking up at him. And the lion behind him keeps roaring and coming closer.

So he hangs on to the roots of a tree. This is the only way left. That lion comes and stands above him, roaring. Down below him are two more lions, also roaring. And the man is hanging on to the roots of the tree – and the roots are weak, worn with age; they may snap at any moment. Not only that, when he looks carefully, he finds two rats gnawing at the roots. One rat is white and the other is black – just like day and night! Time is cutting the roots, and there is not much time left, and his hands are beginning to ache. It is a cold morning and his hands are getting cold and stiff.

Soon he realizes that his hands won't be able to hold on for much longer; they are already beginning to slip. And just then he happens to glance upwards. The honey bees have made a hive in the tree and a drop of honey is about to fall. So he spreads out his tongue and catches that drop of honey. When the honey drops on to his tongue, it tastes very sweet, "Oh! What sweetness!" In that moment he forgets everything else. The lion is not roaring above him, there are no lions below him, and no rats gnawing. For one moment, he is very happy. And then he begins to hope for another drop of honey, because another drop is about to fall.

This Buddhist parable is important. The state of man is just like this. Death here, death there, death all around you. Every now and then a drop falls from a beehive and you are very happy, you are blissful. And the rats of time keep gnawing at the roots. There is no way for you to be saved. You cannot escape, because no one has ever escaped. Escape is impossible, escape never happens. It is not in the laws of nature that anyone can escape. You will have to die.

The fool keeps death hidden. He says, "It will come when it comes. Right now let us taste some honey."

The intelligent person looks at death carefully. He says, "It is a false pleasure to waste my time tasting these drops of honey. I must do something before death appears before me. I must do something, I must find some way."

There is no outward escape, that is true. The man is hanging there. If someone were to ask you what you would do in the same situation, how would you escape? There is a lion above you and lions below you. The rats are gnawing at the roots, the roots are old and about to snap, and your hands are getting cold. What would you do? Where could you run to?

The Zen masters in Japan use this as a method for meditation. The master tells the disciple, "Imagine that this is your situation. Sit down and meditate on yourself suspended like that man was and find a way out. You must find the way. There has to be some way."

So the disciple sits down with eyes closed, and thinks and thinks. Every day he comes back with an answer and says this is the way out. But the master always denies him, saying that these ways are no ways at all. "Find another way." Sometimes, the disciple will say that there are other roots nearby, he will take hold of them. The master will tell him that these roots will not last for long either. The rats are chewing at them as well. After all, there are many rats in this world, many more rats than people! The rats are chewing at these roots too. Time is gnawing away everywhere.

You will find other ways, "I will rub my hands, warm my hands somehow...or I will hang by my feet, like people in a circus." These are the sorts of things you will come up with. Month after month, the disciple will think of doing this or that and the master will always say, "This is foolishness, this will not achieve anything. If you cannot save yourself with your hands, how long can you hang by your feet? After all, this is not a circus. There is no net below to save you if you fall. This is not a circus — it is life." And the disciple continues searching and coming up with all sorts of solutions and all of them prove to be worthless.

The master simply waits until the disciple finds the real solution. And what is the real solution? The day he says, "I will close my eyes and go inside. There is no way to escape outside. There is nowhere to go outside. But there is somewhere to go inside. Death is coming closer, I will shut my eyes and descend into meditation. I will enter into the state of nothingness. I will begin to go inwards. There is no lion there, no rats cutting the roots. There is no question of my hands and my feet getting cold. The eternal reigns within me."

To embrace the divine means to slip within oneself.

...Now you too are preparing to go.
It may be today, it may be tomorrow.
Be astute, O Daya.

Astuteness means meditation, awareness, alertness.

The offsprings of knowledge are distress and disease,
The glory of meditation is eternal at-easeness, samadhi.

Samadhi is the door. Samadhi means the solution. This is why we have given samadhi the name "samadhi." Samadhi is the state in which everything is resolved, in which all problems vanish. Knowledge cannot solve anything: "The offsprings of knowledge are distress and disease." Through knowledge, other complications, new questions, new problems, new difficulties, new mental and physical sufferings arise. "The glory of meditation is eternal at-easeness, samadhi." If you enter meditation, then whether you call it prayer, the divine, or the universal self – these are all just names – if you proceed on the inner journey, then all solutions will be available to you and all your problems will disappear.

Time has a big belly,
It is never satiated.
Kings, princes and emperors,
It swallows them all.

Time has a big belly, it is never satiated. Understand this too, India is the only country where we have given the same name to death and time: kaal. This hasn't been done without a reason. This is the only country where the same word is used for time and death – kaal. Time is known as kaal and death is known as kaal, because time itself is death. Whosoever lives in time lives in the clutches of death. Whosoever has escaped time has escaped death.

In India "yesterday" is *kal,* and so is "tomorrow." It is this way only in this country. In all the other languages of the world there are two separate words. When they first hear this, people are a little startled and ask how we know what we are talking about when there is only one word for both. But that which is past is kal; it has gone into the hands of death and become a morsel of kaal – kal. And that which has not yet happened – right now, it too is in the jaws of death. It is in the mouth of time, of death. Only the present moment is outside death. Yesterday has disappeared into the mouth of death and tomorrow is also hidden there. The past is dead, the future is also dead. Only in the present is there no death. Only this moment, this present moment, exists outside of death. If someone makes the right use of this moment – and this moment is the key – if he opens the door with it, then he enters into the eternal.

The present is not a part of time. Ordinarily you say that time is divided into three parts: past, present and future. That is wrong. The present is not part of time. The past and the future are parts of time. The present is part of the eternal; it is beyond time, it is transcendental to time, it is beyond death.

Time has a big belly.... The stream of time is transitory. It has a big belly. It holds an endless number of people in it. Time is never satisfied, it is continually swallowing everything. Whosoever is born will die, whatever is created will be erased, whatever has a beginning will come to an end. All processes and actions will be lost into nothingness. Therefore, don't be too eager about time, don't take too much interest in time. Go beyond time.

You must have noticed there is a great deal of time consciousness in Western countries. Why? Because the more materialistic a country becomes, the more time-conscious it becomes. The more spiritual a person becomes, the less time-conscious he becomes. The very meaning of spirituality is that we have begun to move outside of time, to slip outside of time.

Have you ever known some moments when time has disappeared? These alone are the divine moments. Sometimes, watching the sun rise, you disappeared into meditation so deeply, your joy within settled so deeply...to the point that you forgot time, that you didn't remember how much time had passed. Or once, while you were looking at the moon or listening to music or sitting next to your beloved holding hands, you forgot time. Or once, even in your aloneness, without any reason, sitting down doing nothing, you forgot all about time, you didn't remember how much time had passed, how much time had gone. When did the moments come and go? It is in these moments that you have the first taste of samadhi, of no-mind.

If you slip out of time for even a brief moment, you have slipped into the divine. The world means time. The divine means timelessness, eternity.

Time has a big belly,
It is never satiated.
Kings, princes and emperors,
It swallows them all.

And don't think...the stream of time doesn't bother about who is poor or who is rich. Death is a great socialist! It doesn't worry about who is rich or who is poor; who has a position, who doesn't have a position. It doesn't see who is moral and who is immoral. It doesn't see who is holy and who is unholy. Death treats everyone equally. In this way, death is a true socialist – king or pauper, it carries them both off in exactly the same way.

Kings, princes and emperors,
It swallows them all.

And don't think that there is a way out! Alexander the Great had every means with which to protect himself, but still he could not save himself. How many emperors have there been in this world who had all the means – huge armies and great walls around their forts? But still death came and took them away.

I have heard that an emperor built a palace to protect himself. He had a single door made to the palace. There was not even one window, so no enemy could break in — no thief, no scoundrel, no murderer. No one could enter there. It was closed on all sides; the palace was completely sealed. There was only one door through which the emperor could come and go.

A neighboring king had heard about the building of this most wonderful palace and came to look at it. He was greatly impressed. There was one door with five hundred guards, who were lined up one after another, one behind the other. It was impossible for anyone to enter. The ruler of the neighboring kingdom came to see the palace and as he was getting ready to return home and was about to get into his chariot, he said to the emperor, "I really like your palace. It is completely safe. No enemy can enter here, no rebel, no murderer. I think I will build a palace like yours."

As this conversation was taking place, a beggar who was sitting by the roadside burst out laughing. The emperor said, "Why are you laughing, you madman? What is causing your laughter? Answer me, or prepare to die! One should not laugh when two emperors are speaking. Didn't you know that?"

The beggar said, "Yes, I am laughing — I am laughing because of death. And now my death is also approaching, and that is okay."

The emperor ordered, "Explain yourself."

The beggar replied, "I laughed because this one door will be very dangerous, death can enter from there. Do this: go inside and have this door bricked up as well. Then even death will not be able to enter. At the moment it is not yet completely safe, there is still some risk. These guards are fine; they can stop the people, but can they stop death? Their swords can't, their bayonets can't. Five hundred, or even five hundred thousand men will not be able to stop death from breaking in. Do this: go inside, have the door bricked up from the outside, and close the wall. Then you will be completely safe."

The emperor said, "You are mad. If I do this I am already dead! If I go inside and have the wall bricked up, what is the point of being safe? With this solution one is already dead – right now. Death will come when it comes, but you are telling me how to be already dead, right now."

The *fakir* said, "That is why I am laughing – you are already dead. Ninety-nine percent of you has already died. Only one percent of you is alive – because of this one door. If there were a hundred doors, you would be one hundred percent alive, according to your own mathematics. You have said that when this last door is closed, you will be already dead. So to a great extent you are already dead – because there is only one door left. You are one percent alive. Is this the way to avoid death?"

The *fakir* continued, "Once I was an emperor too. Realizing that money cannot stop death, I began searching for meditation. Power cannot stop death, so I am searching for nothingness. I also want to go beyond death, but my journey is different from yours."

The *fakir* was right. No one can escape death. But some people have escaped: no one escapes the ordinary, physical death, but some people have been alert and awake even in their dying moments. Everything else has died, but consciousness never dies, and because of their consciousness they have entered the universal self through the door of death. The door of death becomes the door of a new birth for an unconscious person, and the door of ultimate liberation for a conscious one. Then, there is no new birth. Then, there is no coming and going – Be astute, O Daya.

As the winds blow through the sky-borne clouds,
Unmaking them in myriad ways,
Man's life is in the hands of death,
And he knows no peace.

As the winds blow through the sky-borne clouds, unmaking them in myriad ways.... Have you ever noticed the way the clouds gather in the sky and the wind keeps changing them? Have you ever noticed that the clouds' form never stays the same – even for one moment? The winds keep them in a flux, moving. For one moment a cloud looks like an elephant, and even before that moment has passed, its trunk has disappeared, its feet are missing and it no longer looks like an elephant at all. It has become all topsy-turvy. If you continue watching it for some time, you will see that the cloud keeps on changing. A cloud is only smoke. The winds keep tossing it. Just as the waves toss on the surface of the ocean – the winds keep tossing them – in the same way the winds keep scattering the clouds and reshaping them.

As the winds blow through the sky-borne clouds,
Unmaking them in myriad ways...

The clouds are destroyed because of the winds, they are

continually being made and unmade. The winds destroy them in so many ways in the sky.

...Man's life is in the hands of death,
And he knows no peace.

And in the same way, a human being is made and unmade by the winds of death. *Man's life is in the hands of death....* A man is made or unmade by the winds of kaal, of death. You were once an elephant, once a horse; you have been a bird, a tree; sometimes a man, then a woman; sometimes beautiful, sometimes ugly.... Who knows how many shapes your cloud has already assumed? You are not new at all. This is a unique Indian discovery – that every person has had countless births. He has been born as every species; he has wandered through eight hundred and forty million species. Death has kept pushing him around and the cloud has continued to take innumerable forms.

Daya has chosen a very sweet symbol:

As the winds blow through the sky-borne clouds
Unmaking them in myriad ways...

And just as the gusts of wind change the clouds in the sky:

Man's life is in the hands of death,
And he knows no peace.

In the same way a man is continually pushed around by death; becoming this and then that. And as long as this keeps happening, how is peace possible? Until you are stable, how can you know peace? Until the gusts of winds stop, how can bliss take possession of you? Who knows in how many forms you have suffered; sometimes as a horse, sometimes as an elephant, sometimes as an ant, sometimes as a human being – as a woman, as a man...and you have gained nothing but sorrow. All of life's species are species of sorrow.

There is a way to be outside death: *Be astute, O Daya....* Train your awareness a little. This means to wake up and see that "I am not the body," to wake up and see that "I am not the mind." Awareness means to wake up and see that "I am the state of witnessing, I am merely a witness." As soon as you start getting the knack of this awareness, you will find that although death still unsettles your body and shakes your mind, it is unable to shake your state of witnessing. The state of witnessing is beyond death; death does not reach there. And the divine resides where death cannot reach. Truth resides where death cannot reach. That conscious state where death cannot reach is called *moksha*, ultimate liberation.

Moksha is not part of any geography. So don't think that moksha is some geographical location, and that sooner or later scientists will reach it in their spaceships. Moksha is your inner state: it is not a geographical location, it is the sky of your consciousness.

On the day that you begin to know, on the day that you begin to awaken to the fact that you are not the body, that you are not the mind, you will have gone beyond. Understand the difference. The clouds gather in the sky, form and dissolve, come and go; they gather when it is the rainy season and then disappear – but the sky is always there. The clouds come and go, but the sky is always there. The wind can only change the clouds, not the sky. How can it change the sky? The wind cannot have any effect on the sky. The wind blows, it continues to move, but the sky remains untouched, virgin, undefiled by any contact.

The soul inside is like the sky outside. The soul is the name for the inner sky. The sky is the name for the soul spread outside. On the day that you realize that there is no division, on the day that the body disappears from the middle, on the day you realize that "I am not the body," on that day the inner and outer sky merge. The moment of this merging of the inner and outer skies is samadhi, union with *brahman*, union with the divine – or whatsoever name appeals to you.

Always remember one thing: until you have realized this sky you cannot be at peace...*he knows no peace.* You are not at peace because you are identified with the cloud. And the cloud changes every moment, so you cry. It changes – again and again! Just now you thought everything was going well, and in less than a minute it has been spoilt.

Attachment to *maya* deceives us day and night.
Let go of the world so the fires may cool.

The fires will cool only when you wake up and see that you are not the world, you are not the body, you are not the mind; that you are beyond all of these. There is only one way to peace: in some way you have to find that which is eternal, that which never changes into something else.

When unfolded wings fold,
Prose turns into poetry.

When the wings of the bird of your desires close, when you

don't want to fly in the world of desires anymore, when
the crows of your thoughts cease their cawing, when you know
that "I am not this," that I am merely a watcher, a witness,
then suddenly you will find that prose has turned into poetry!
There will flow within you a stream of bliss, of songs, of
music, of celebration. Every pore of your being will be thrilled.
And when this bliss arises within you, it will not merely stay
in your soul, it will spread throughout your mind and
your heart as well, it will color them. It will spread
throughout your body and color your body. It will
start jumping out of your body and coloring others as well.

This is why so many people who were close to Buddha, close
to Mahavira were transformed, colored. Whosoever came to
them was colored by their presence. Once you have discovered
this wealth, you will find that it is an unprecedented wealth,
an infinite source.

The cup has broken,
Now I will scoop up the water of life,
And drink to my heart's content.

Right now you are drinking the water of life in a tiny
measuring cup. The body and the mind are tiny vessels. You
are trying to drink the vast ocean of life with this small cup.
The head cannot be satisfied in this way. On the day that
the body and the mind are left behind, on the day that the
measuring cup is broken, you are a part of the ocean itself.

I have heard about the Greek mystic, Diogenes, who let go
of everything – even his clothes – and became naked, just like
Mahavira. There has been only one man in the West
comparable to Mahavira, and that is Diogenes. He kept a

small cup for drinking water and for such things. One day, he was so thirsty that he went to the river with his cup. He arrived at the riverbank and was cleaning his cup so he could drink from it when a dog came running by. The dog was so thirsty, it leaped into the water, quickly drank, and then went away again. Diogenes had not yet finished cleaning his cup. He was amazed to realize that he had been defeated by a dog! He wondered why he had been so attached to the cup and so he threw it away. "If a dog can live without a cup, why should I be so tied to this cup? I have to clean it, to do this and that — so much nonsense! I am even afraid of it being stolen, so when I sleep at night I keep touching it to make sure that no one has taken it." In that very moment, he threw the cup away and prostrated himself in front of the dog. "You are my master," he said. "The cup was my last attachment."

The cup has broken,
Now I will scoop up the water of life,
And drink to my heart's content.

Now no barrier remains. When you leave the vessel of the mind and the body you have entered the ocean of life.

Placing the arrow of time
On the bow of nothingness,
The destructible is pierced
And the indestructible liberated.

You must balance the bow of nothingness, place the arrow of time on it and release it, so that you can be free of time and time can be free of you.

The destructible is pierced
And the indestructible liberated.

As soon as your awareness pierces the destructible, indestructible within you, the sky within you, is experienced, realized. Only he who has known this sky that is hidden within has known life. He who has not known it, has lived in vain.

What is the point of meeting
If our hearts do not meet?
What joy is there in the journey
If one does not reach the destination?
It is better to drown in the middle of the ocean
Than to sail near to the shore but never find it.

Those who live without knowing this inner sky – better they drown in the ocean, because even though they may come close to the shore, they will never find it.

What is the point of meeting
If our hearts do not meet?

If you do not find your innermost core, your inner soul...
"What joy is there in the journey if one does not reach the destination?" You have been walking for a long time, you have journeyed for lifetimes, and yet you have still not had even a glimpse of your destination.

What joy is there in the journey
If one does not reach the destination?
It is better to drown in the middle of the ocean
Than to sail near to the coast but never find it.

Every day you feel that you are coming closer, but as you come closer you feel that there is no shore ahead of you. You come closer and your destination moves further away, just like the horizon. Life is like a mirage, so it is better to drown.

But if you have the courage to drown, the meeting happens. If you have the guts to drown, no one can stop you from finding the divine – because whosoever is ready to drown is ready to die. Such a person says, "I am ready to die." This is what sannyas means. Sannyas means that, "I voluntarily let go of everything which will die; I separate myself from all that which will be erased. I have severed my relationship with the ephemeral. Now I will live in this world, but I will not take it as more than an inn."

People often ask me what is the meaning of sannyas. I tell them it means to consider the world, to take the world as an inn. You have to live here, there is nowhere else you can go, but there is a way of living in the world so that you are free of it even while you are living in it – as if you were living in an inn. Live with awareness: *Be astute, O Daya.*

Fame needs no search,
But first you must do something.
Before you make a name for yourself,
First find solitude and rest.
Do not fill every spare moment with visitors, other people,
Nor place a flowerpot in every empty spot.
There must be moments when
You talk with your god.
Gods come only when there is silence,
And if the heart is noisy
They quietly turn away.

Become silent. Find moments of peace. Descend a little into the state of no thought. Sometimes, sitting peacefully, not doing anything, you will suddenly find that you have become blessed – blessings will shower upon you. The divine will surround you from every direction. This is not something you have to do. It is not something that will be accomplished when you perform great gymnastic feats. It will not happen at all when you do something for it, because then you will be present there in your doing. Doing is the ego, I.

The divine is not found through effort but through grace. Sometimes, sitting silently, make time for doing nothing. Sitting under a tree in the garden or on the bank of a river; at night under the open sky, below the stars, sit and do nothing, be empty, silent. Your thoughts will come and go. Let them come and go. Don't take any interest in them; neither in them nor against them. If they come, good; if they don't come, that is also good. It is like being near a busy pathway: it is noisy, but let it be so; just sit at a distance, indifferently. Be empty.

And sometimes it will happen that your thoughts will stop for a moment – and it is in such moments that a ray of light will descend upon you, as if someone had shaken the dark- ness, destroyed it. In such moments you will feel a drop of immortal nectar falling on you; you will glimpse something that is beyond death. Gradually these moments will go on increasing. Gradually, as you acquire the taste, your inner journey will start becoming more crystallized and easier. Then one day it happens that wherever you want, whenever you want – even if you don't close your eyes – the divine is continually surrounding you. Then, everything is filled with its presence. Until this happens, know that you have not found your destination.

And the destination has to be found. Finding your destination means finding the divine in such a way that there remains no way of losing it again.

Know this world as something which can be destroyed in an instant:

...It is in a moment gone,
O Daya,
Carry the divine in your heart.

Know this world as a queue at the door of death:

Your father and your mother have departed,
Now you too are preparing to go.
It may be today, it may be tomorrow,
Be astute, O Daya.

Enough for today.

6

RECEIVING YOUR SOUL

The first question

Osho,

Having managed to make it here for the meditation camp, why do I notice some discrimination? Does becoming a sannyasin immediately do away with the gap? Is your blessing only for sannyasins? Isn't it for all living beings?

The blessing is for everyone, but it is not that you will receive it just by my giving it. You will receive it only if you take it. The river is flowing, and it flows for everyone. The trees will drink its water, the birds and the animals will drink its water, and so will human beings, but whosoever drinks it has to want to drink it. If you stand on the bank, stiff and arrogant, the river will not jump into your hands. You will have to bend down and fill your cupped hands with water in order to drink. Don't complain about the river if you aren't drinking the water. The river is always flowing.

But man is upside down. If he does not receive the blessing, he thinks that perhaps the blessing has not been given. But is he capable of receiving the blessing? Will he accept the blessing? A blessing is not a cheap matter. You might think that it is cheap, that it is to be had for free. But a blessing is a fire – it will burn you, it will change and transform you. Courage is needed.

What else can *sannyas* mean? It simply means that someone has bent down, made a cup with his hands and agreed to enter into a relationship with the river. Sannyas only means that you have shown the willingness to receive the blessing, that you have held out your vessel, that you have held out your receptacle. Blessings are continuously showering, but if you don't hold out your vessel to catch them, you will never receive any.

It rains. It rains on the mountains as well, but the mountains remain unfilled – they are already so full of themselves. When it rains on the mountains, the water runs towards the hollows and the ravines; it runs, filling them completely and forming lakes. Would you say that the rain was falling only for the sake of the lakes and not for the mountains? It was raining on everything, but the mountains were too full of themselves, there was no room for water. The lakes were empty, there was room there. They eagerly opened themselves to the rain and the water poured in.

This blessing rains continuously – on you, on the sannyasins, on these trees. But who receives it and how much they will receive, depends entirely on the individual.

This is all sannyas means – nothing else. It means that you are ready to go along with me.

But you want to receive these blessings for nothing. You don't want to change your position at all. You don't want to empty yourself even one little bit — even though you want to be a lake. Your ambition says you want to be a Mansarovar, the sacred lake and pilgrimage place on mount Kailash, and you don't have the courage to empty yourself just one little bit.

Sannyas is another name for courage. Why are you scared? Who is stopping you from taking sannyas? What is the fear? The fears involved are trifling. But man is cunning. He whitewashes his fears with his cunningness. It seems difficult to even accept fear as fear, because to accept fear hurts your ego.

One night Mulla Nasruddin began to leave the tavern early. His friends asked, "Where are you going?"

Mulla said, "I won't be able to stay long tonight. My wife told me to come home before ten o'clock."

His friends began to laugh. They said, "We have wives too. Why are you so afraid, Mulla? Are you a man or a mouse?"

The Mulla puffed out his chest and stood up. He beat his chest and said, "I am a real tough guy, a true he-man! Never say such a thing again."

Then a friend asked him, "Show us the proof! If you are such a tough guy, show us the proof."

The Mulla said, "Proof? The self-evident proof is that my wife is scared of mice and she is not afraid of me."

No man ever wants to admit that he is frightened.

You ask: "Having managed to make it here for the meditation camp, why do I notice some discrimination?"

Because the discrimination is there. And the discrimination comes from your side; you are the one who sees it. The one who is not a sannyasin is shriveled up, on his own; he is timid and isolated. He is unable to open up, unable to relax, unable to connect. He is scared. He is afraid that if he mixes too much with the others here, if he drowns himself deeply, if he goes out beyond his limits and suddenly becomes a sannyasin, then what will happen to his house? his wife? the marketplace? his shop? the society...? So he moves very carefully. He keeps his cunning, his calculations; he goes this far – and no further. And he maintains his distance even with these drunken orange-colored people. He steps to one side. It is not safe to come too close to them because this disease is contagious. If you stay too long with these ochre-colored people, dreams for this ochre color will begin to arise in your mind too.

So *you* are creating the discrimination. You are afraid, that is why the discrimination is there. It is there because of your fear. Then you feel that no blessings are showering on you. Why do you feel that way? You feel that way because you look at the others and they are so blissful, so entranced – and you are not blissful, you are not entranced – so they must be receiving the blessing, and you are not. They must be receiving something special which is not being given to you.

What is available to them is exactly the same as is available to you. But they drink, while you have closed your throat. They are bending down and are filling their water carriers, but you are afraid to do so. The difference comes because of your fear, simply because of your fear.

You ask, "Does becoming a sannyasin immediately do away with the gap?"

All distance does not immediately vanish when you become a sannyasin, but the beginning of those distances disappearing is certainly triggered. All distances will be gradually eliminated. These distances have been formed during many, many lifetimes. They cannot be eliminated in one moment; it will take time. One will have to have patience, but the beginning of all these distances disappearing has started to take place.

One man sits, another stands, another walks. Right now, they are all in the same place. One man sits, another man stands, and the third one starts taking the first step forward. Right now, they are all in the same spot, on the same line, but there is already a great difference between them. The one sitting down has not even started to erase the distance. The one standing up is at least in the middle state – he might set off somewhere. The one sitting down must first stand up – only then he can walk. He can't walk sitting down! The person standing up is closer to the one who walks than to the one who is still sitting down, because if he wants to walk, he can begin right away. And the man who has only lifted his foot has not yet reached any destination – he is still where the other two are, but he has already begun to shorten the distance. If a person has taken even one step, then he is closer by at least one step.

Sannyas is the first step; it is the first step in erasing the distances. And the first step is the most difficult. After that, the steps keep following one after another. The first step is the hardest; hence you should see the first step as half of the journey.

There is a famous saying of Mahavira's: He who has begun walking has already arrived. This saying is not factually true. A person doesn't necessarily reach the destination simply because he has begun; he may stop halfway and turn back. His feelings may change, his views may change. So the statement that he who has started walking has already arrived is not altogether true — but there is a deep meaning in it. There is some intrinsic truth hidden in it. Mahavira states this so emphatically because the one who has begun has completed half the journey already. Half the journey is over with the first step. The first step is the most difficult step.

When you bring the cup to your lips, the cup that I am giving you and asking you to drink from, then the matter is almost completed. How great is the distance between your lips and your throat? If the cup touches your lips, its contents will reach to your throat. But if it doesn't touch your lips, if you don't even hold it, how can the contents reach your throat?

You ask: "Is your blessing only for sannyasins?" My blessing is for everyone, but only sannyasins are able to receive it. Understand this rightly: it is going over your head.

An emperor came to meet Buddha. He asked some questions. Buddha replied, "Come back in a year or two. Now, I will give you a meditation technique. Do this first."

The emperor felt a little unhappy. He said, "I have come such a long way, and I am no ordinary man. I have asked you some

questions, and I have thought about these things for a long
time. I have asked many others these same questions and they
have all answered me. You have not even bothered to answer
me. And now you want me to go away and meditate. Your
attitude is very offensive. Do you mean to insult me?"

Buddha said, "No." He told the emperor to understand it
in the following way. If a pitcher is placed upside down in
the rain, not even a single drop can fall into it. If another
pitcher is placed the right way up but is full of holes, it will
fill up with rain, but then it will empty itself again. As soon
as the rain stops, the pitcher will be empty. It may seem
full, but it can never be full because it has so many holes and
everything will flow out of it again. And think of a third
pitcher with no holes, which is placed the right way up, but
is full of rubbish. When it rains, the pure water will be sullied
and become poisonous. You shouldn't drink it. If you do,
even by mistake, you will not find life – rather you will die.

"You are all these three pitchers in one," said Buddha. "Who
knows how much poisonous, impure rubbish from your many
previous lives is inside you! And you are also the upside-
down pitcher and you are the pitcher filled with holes. I have
asked you to meditate for a year or two so that you can clean
out your pitcher a little before you come back to me; so that
you can fill the holes and put your pitcher upright. I am ready
to shower upon you, but right now it will serve no purpose.
It is not necessary that answers should be given just because
you have asked questions. The first thing is whether you have
the capacity to receive my answers or not."

You may think that what Buddha said is harsh. But he said
it out of the utmost compassion – that you can come after

a little preparation. Sannyas is that preparation.

Here too, among the people who come to listen to me, there are three kinds of vessels. Some are upside down: they will all go away empty-handed, and if you show them your treasures they will laugh at you. And because they have returned empty-handed, they will say, "How can you be so full? You must be deceiving yourself. You are a blind believer, a sentimentalist. You have no understanding." They are such intelligent people – but they have not received anything. How can they accept that you are more intelligent than they are? They will think that you are naive, a believer; that you don't know how to think, that you have no capacity to contemplate.

There are others who have placed their pitcher the right way up and are being filled many times over. Listening to me they feel that they have been filled. But even before they pass through the door they are empty again, they have forgotten everything. They are again the same, a pitcher full of holes.

Then there are a few who belong to the third type: they fill up, they have no holes, they are the right way up – but whatever falls into them is no longer mine; their minds deform it. They add their own interpretations to it, they put in their own meanings. They take something from here, but it is not what I gave them. They go back with a slightly adorned and rearranged vision of what they had come here with. I fall into their own rubbish.

It all depends on you. Sannyas simply means that you are ready to clean out your vessel, that you are ready to color your vessel with my color, that you are ready to plug the holes

in your vessel, that you are ready to keep your vessel the right
way up, that you are giving up all fear.

Sannyas is a rebirth, a new life. So far you have been living
your life in a certain way, and you have gained nothing from
it. If you had, you would not have needed to come to me or
to go anywhere else. It is obvious from your question that you
have found nothing in life so far. You have come here
searching for something, but you want to find it without
having to pay anything for it. You want to find it
without having to give anything. You want to find it in such
a way that no one comes to know that you have received
something. You want to own diamonds, but you don't have
the courage, the daring that is needed to own such things.

If you are not reborn,
Your inner abode remains forever dark.
However fine the paper you use,
The book of your life remains unwritten.

Nothing is gained by having fine paper until the truth
descends upon you. And without your being reborn...and by
rebirth I mean that your parents gave birth to you the first
time, but your second birth comes from the master. That is
why we revere the master over and above our parents —
because the body you have received from your parents, the
birth you have been given is mortal, it belongs to the physical,
it is gross. The direction of life you receive from the master
is subtle, it pertains to consciousness. Your body comes from
your parents, but you receive your soul from the master. Your
parents have given you one birth; the second comes through
the master.

Sannyas is the name of the courage that is needed to bow

down at the feet of someone else. And in this world there is no courage greater than this courage of bowing down. Don't think that standing tall is a great achievement. All idiots stand tall. There is no glory in swaggering around. The art lies in being able to bow down.

Lao Tzu pointed out that the big trees are rigid: when the hurricane comes, they collapse. When the hurricane comes, the small blades of grass, the small plants and the shrubs bow down and then rise up again afterwards. The typhoon cannot uproot the grass because the grass is flexible, but the big trees are uprooted because the big trees are very egotistical.

There is a storm blowing here. These are not talks that I am giving to you. This is a storm that will shake you to your very roots; it is a whirlwind. If you stand rigidly, you will not be able to benefit, you may only suffer a loss. You may collapse. If you bow down, you will never lose anything, you can only benefit. Then, the whirlwind will refresh you, it will renew you, it will sweep away the dust and the dirt from your life. You will rise again and flourish. This storm will be like the mythical life-giving herb; it will be a blessing.

Sannyas means that you say to the divine.... And right now the divine is still so far away, so you say it to the master instead. The master, the *guru* is only a *gurudwara*, a master-door. You make your request to the divine through this medium. You say to the divine: "I have not seen you, I am not familiar with you, I don't know your address or your whereabouts. But there is someone here who knows your address or your whereabouts, so I am sending my message to you through him. I am sending my prayers to you through him."

The master is a person who is like you and yet not like you; who is like you in some way and beyond you in some other way. The master is a person who has one hand in yours and the other hand in the hands of the invisible.

If you look with love, you will begin to understand about the master's invisible hand as well, and to see that the divine is peeping out here and there from the master. If you don't look with love, if you don't look with the eyes of surrender, then you will see only the gross form of the master that is available to your eyes. So there is no way you can see the master without becoming a disciple, because you are only worthy of this vision when you become a disciple, when you bow down, when you look with sensitivity, with love, with affection. Then the other side, the invisible world, also begins to become visible to you through the master. The master is only a window.

O musician, I am thy flute,
Breathe through me, play me.

Tunes lie dormant in my body,
Which by themselves cannot arise –
That is their frailty.
With the life-giving touch of thy lips
Fill my heart to its brim with honey.
Touch Ahilya,
Take away her ignorance, her lifelessness,
Reawaken her consciousness.

O musician, I am thy flute,
Breathe through me, play me.

You have no idea of the flute that is sleeping within you, so you go to a musician and ask, "Please play on my flute so I

can hear who is asleep within me, so I can consciously know
my potential." You gain the first glimpse of your potential
in the presence of the master.

Let my suffering find its voice,
Let my desolate garden of joy resound again.
Stir a tune in me, so filled with pain
That on hearing it
The three worlds lose all consciousness.
Move your fingers across my wounds,
And create new music in me.

O musician, I am thy flute,
Breathe through me, play me.

When I am silent, I am stifled,
Without music, I cannot live.
My song is only yours,
Who will play me if you do not?
Do not be so cruel, I implore you.
This I cannot bear.
Do not make me suffer more.

O musician, I am thy flute,
Breathe through me, play me.

For how long have I lain voiceless in the temple?
Do not withdraw, uphold my dignity,
My life is resting on this single hope –
That one day you may again pick me up.
Put me to your lips at least one more time,
Before my body becomes a corpse.

O musician, I am thy flute,
Breathe through me, play me.

Sannyas is a request that you make to the master: "I don't know who I am: please bring me to some consciousness, to some awareness. I don't know who slumbers inside me; please shake me up. *You* know. I have no idea where my treasure lies, but you do, so please show me the path to my treasure."

Sannyas is putting your hand into the hands of the master. It is a unique revolution and only daredevils can do it – because it is a very difficult thing to put yourself completely into the hands of someone else. And you only give when you give yourself completely. If you give only a little bit of yourself, if you give in a calculated manner – thinking that you will wait and see if anything happens, and that if nothing happens you will turn back again – then you have not really given yourself. If this is the case, then the distance will continue to exist even after you have become a sannyasin. And the gap, the difference will come from your side.

There are some sannyasins who have offered themselves with the idea of seeing what happens: if something happens they will remain sannyasins; otherwise if nothing happens – who can hold them? They will change their clothes in the train on the way home, they will hide their *malas* and so on. They will go back home, and arrive at their homes exactly the same as they were before they left. Such people exist. Now, I am not going to follow you with the police force! Here, it is one thing, but how do I know what you will do in Amritsar?

If you become a sannyasin in this way, the gap, the difference will remain, because you are being cunning. Who are you deceiving? Let there be at least one place where you don't become tricky, one place where you bow down your head in

complete trust and love, one place where you are
not dishonest, where you don't cheat.

So I am not saying that you must become a sannyasin. I am
saying that if you do, do it deliberately, decisively; with
complete understanding. Do it only if you have total courage.
And if you become a sannyasin, don't hold on to any ideas
about turning back – because if the idea of turning back
remains in your mind you will not be able to walk with me
at all. How can a person who wants to turn back ever move
ahead? Such a person will say, "If I take a few steps, then
later I may have to walk back that much – so I will just stay
where I am. I will just keep talking about going on – that I
will walk, that I will certainly walk – but the truth is I will
stay here where I am, because after all I may have to come
back."

But if you carry the feeling in your heart that you can go
back, you will not even be able to begin the journey. Sannyas
is a journey from which there is no return. Once you go, you
have gone forever. Then it will certainly happen. Then
you will certainly be one with the divine. Then you will be
able to catch the rays of my blessing instantly.

The second question is similar to the first one. Because it
is similar, it is necessary to understand this one too.

Osho,

*To what extent do orange robes, the mala and the master help in attaining
to the ultimate abode of the divine? And are they still needed after
attaining to that state?*

You have not yet attained to the ultimate abode of the divine, but already you are so afraid of orange robes, of the mala and the master, that even these thoughts comfort your heart. You think that it is okay: just take it all on for a short while, wear them, but then when you reach the ultimate abode of the divine you can give them all up. You will not reach the ultimate abode of the divine – because this type of mind does not reach to that state. This type of mind has not even begun the journey! It thinks of stopping even before it has started. It is calculating about the destination even before it has reached it. It is a very calculating mind; it cannot take you far.

The first thing: "attaining to the ultimate abode of the divine." The first thing is that all this talk of attainment of the ultimate abode of the divine et cetera is just the sign of a greedy mind. These are not the thoughts of a sannyasin. "Attaining to the ultimate abode of the divine"! You are unable to obtain a high position in the world so "Let us attain to the ultimate abode of the divine." You have no hope of winning anything in the elections, so "Let us attain to the ultimate abode of the divine." If Delhi seems so far away, "Let us attain to the ultimate abode of the divine." The ultimate status is a must for you!

Do you see the desires of your ego? Again and again your ego takes new forms. In the world it wanted wealth, fame and position. And even when it moves on from there in some way, still its basic tone doesn't change, its basic tone remains the same.

What are you looking for in religion? Are you searching for the ego there too? If so, your journey has gone wrong from the very beginning. The true meaning of religion is that there is no substance to any position – not even to "the ultimate abode of the divine." The very race for position is futile. The race for position is an ego trip. And there is no substance to ego either. You are walking around arrogantly here, and if you had the chance you would walk around just as arrogantly in the space of ultimate liberation.

Sit down sometimes and think about this: if you ever attained to *moksha* you would strut around there too, you would raise your seat a little higher than everyone else's. You would play the same game there too.

The search for religion means that you are tired of the ego, that you are no longer interested in the ego. When ego falls – that is sannyas. If your ego keeps taking newer and newer forms…. Sannyas simply means that you have really seen that there is no substance to any position, and when there is no substance to any position, what can there really be in "the ultimate abode of the divine"? – because the ultimate abode of the divine will be nothing but a bigger version of what is called "position" in the world. When there is nothing in wealth, what can there be in the ultimate wealth? If there is nothing here, there will be nothing there.

Your heaven is an extension of this world. Whatsoever you are asking for in this world, you will continue asking for those same things in heaven. You will decorate and polish your demands, but you will still ask for the same things. And what kind of ultimate divine state will it be while there are still demands, greed, desire and ego within you? You have not understood the meaning of "the ultimate abode of the divine."

It often happens that the enlightened ones say one thing and you understand something quite different. The enlightened ones say that the ultimate abode of the divine is that state where there is no ego, no greed, no illusion, no attachment. The name of that state is *parampad*, the ultimate abode of the divine. And when your greed hears this, you say "This is wonderful! Then let us attain to the ultimate abode of the divine. Why should we waste our time with small and insignificant positions?" And remember this: it is your greed which is saying this. You have understood everything completely the opposite way around. You have missed the whole point.

So the first thing is, you must not even talk about the ultimate abode of the divine. Give up talking about attainment. As long as the intoxication of attainment is there, you will not find the divine. The divine is already present within you; you don't have to attain to it. But because you remain occupied running after attainment, you keep missing it. You have been seeking; that is why you have missed. A person doesn't have to obtain what he already has. When all searching drops, when all running stops and you sit down peacefully, without any desires; when the winds are not blowing and the clouds no longer form and unform...in that moment you instantly find "Oh! here is the one I have been searching for."

Buddha became enlightened. Someone asked him, "What have you attained?"

He said, "I have not attained anything; I simply understood what I already had. I just understood it; I did not attain anything."

The ultimate state of the divine is already the case with you too. Wherever you are, there too is the ultimate abode of the divine. Wherever your soul is present, there too is the ultimate abode of the divine. Just look inside a little and see what a great throne you are sitting on! But you are wandering about like a beggar; you never return home, you never turn back to yourself. Sometimes you run after wealth, sometimes after position. And if ever you get tired of these, or regret them, then you immediately begin a new race — that now you must attain to heaven, that now you must attain enlighten-ment, that now you must attain to the ultimate abode of the divine.

Don't desire the ultimate abode of the divine or take sannyas because you want to attain something, because if this is the case, it won't be sannyas. Sannyas simply means that your greed has proved to be futile, that it has fallen away, that now you can enjoy what is. Attainment means it will happen tomorrow, it will happen in the future — but the divine is now, the divine won't happen tomorrow. The divine is here, now. Moksha is your intrinsic state; it is now, it is here. If you become calm, if the clouds of desire which are surrounding you disappear, then that light will manifest right now. That light has always been present. The sun is simply hiding amongst the clouds.

So firstly: in this "To what extent do the orange robe, the mala and the master help in attaining to the ultimate abode of the divine?" you seem to be wanting to use the master, the orange robe and the mala as a means. This is a mistake to begin with. To use the master as a means is a kind of exploitation. You are the overlord, and the master becomes your servant. You want to use the master to reach to the ultimate abode of the divine, so you step onto the master's ladder to climb up there. And you have no intention of even thanking the master afterwards, because in the last part of your question you say..."and are they still needed after attaining to that state?" How kind of you to climb my ladder; the ladder is blessed to have been graced by your presence! What would have happened to the ladder if you had not climbed it? You came with your lotus feet and climbed the ladder – the ladder will sing your praises for ages to come!

The relationship with the master is one of love, not of exploitation. If you form a relationship using the master as a means then you remain the overlord, you remain on top – simply making use of the master. This is immoral, this is ugly.

There is only one relationship you can have with the master, and that is of love. It is a relationship where, one day, the time will come for you to leave him – and that time certainly comes, because the master wants it to. Just as one day he had wanted you to cling on to him, a time comes when he wants you to let go of him, because now you yourself have become capable.

A mother holds her son's hand while she is teaching him to walk. But she is not going to hold on to his hand forever, because if she did, it would be harmful to him. One day she must let go of his hand, even though he doesn't want her to. The son will hold her *sari* and walk behind her around the kitchen and all over the house. She will say, "Please let go of me. You are able to walk by yourself now, so why are you holding on to me for support?"

One day the master wants you to let go of him, but by

this time the disciple doesn't want to let go. The disciple says, "How can I leave you? How can I let go of the one from whom I have received so much?" If both God and the master were to stand in front of the disciple, he would still wonder how he could leave the one from whom he has received so much. A moment comes when the disciple feels that he can abandon God, but he can never abandon the master, because until that moment he has never had any acquaintance with God. There has been no contact, no relationship with the divine. It is the master who has created, who has made this relationship possible: "If I must abandon someone, I will abandon God. As long as the master is there, he will create this relationship with God again, any time. It is better that the master remains, because he is the door, so then we can enter the temple any time we wish."

So this final hour of difficulty doesn't start from the disciple's side – it is not that the disciple wants to leave and the master wants to prevent him. This final hour of difficulty is that the master asks the disciple to let go of him, and the disciple doesn't want to. The very meaning of a disciple is that he has loved the master so completely, that how can he let go of him now? The very idea causes him great pain. Even if he has to abandon moksha, the disciple doesn't care. "If I can remain at the master's feet, that is enough for me." The disciple has received so much at the feet of the master that he cannot conceive that even moksha can give him anything more. And even if it could, the disciple cannot be so ungrateful as to let go immediately. In the beginning, the master has great difficulty in taking the disciple's hand, because the disciple wants to escape....

Now this gentleman is trying to escape and I would like to

hold his hand. His name is very sweet, Shyam Kanhaiya — "the beloved, dark Krishna" — but it appears to be just a name. At present, he has neither the desire to go towards Shyam nor the courage. I would like to hold his hand, but he is already preparing to leave me, asking: "Will I be able to leave it all later on? Once I have attained to the ultimate abode of the divine, will I be able to drop everything else quickly enough?"

If you try to take my hand when you are in such a state of mind, then you will not be able to take it at all, you will be too busy freeing yourself. You want to be free as soon as possible. And you will not be able to attain to the ultimate abode of the divine because such things don't happen in a hurry. These things require immense patience, great inner peace, infinite calm.

So firstly: it will be difficult to take Shyam Kanhaiya's hand in my hand. This will be the first difficulty. And if somehow, with great difficulty, that is done, then the second problem will be even greater. The second problem will arise when I see that the time has come for him to let go of me and take the final jump. This difficulty will be even greater. Right now his problem is due to his ego, and egoism is not such a big problem. How powerful can egoism really be? Egoism is like a nothingness, it is a negative entity, a shadow. It has no reality, it is like darkness. Right now, the idea of leaving the darkness is creating the difficulty. I am asking you to leave the darkness, I am standing in front of you with the light and saying to you, "Here is the lamp, hold my hand." Right now, you are grabbing at the darkness and finding it difficult to take the light.

Just imagine the day when you have the light and I ask you to let go of the light and enter the vast infinity of the divine. In that moment you will again say "No." You are creating such a difficulty about leaving the darkness, but you will create much more about leaving the light. How can you abandon the light, its festivity, its music and celebration, its bliss? In time, the master makes you give that up too.

This is very interesting. One day the master catches your hand and one day he frees you from him too. And the second struggle is the greater struggle, but when the master finally manages to free his hand from yours there is no end to the disciple's gratitude. The truth is, that the disciple is grateful when he places his hand in the hand of his master, but on the day that the master takes his hand away, however much he may suffer he will be even more immensely grateful — because the master's hand only contains a lamp, but when the disciple lets go of that lamp then the light of the whole sun becomes available to him. There was a drop of nectar in the master's hands: when the disciple lets go of that drop, then the whole ocean becomes available to him.

Then the disciple becomes even more grateful — because when the master was holding his hand it was out of his compassion, but now when he releases it, it is out of an even greater compassion.

And you ask: "Are they still needed after attaining to the ultimate abode of the divine?" Not the slightest need remains for them, but because of the disciple's gratitude to the master — just because of that feeling of gratefulness towards the master — the disciple will continue to care for them.

Sariputta, a disciple of the Buddha, became enlightened. And

Buddha sent him away, "Now you go. Now you can go. Now there is no need to stay with me. Make room for others. Go and spread the message from village to village. Give others what I have given to you."

Sariputta began to weep bitterly. He said, "Please don't do this to me."

Buddha replied, "Aren't you ashamed of yourself? You are a buddha and you are crying! You are enlightened now – what is all this weeping and crying about?"

But Sariputta continued to cry like a small child. He begged, "Please don't send me away. I would even prefer to accept that I am not enlightened. Please don't send me away. I would rather be unenlightened."

Buddha said, "You cannot deceive me by saying you have not become enlightened. These tactics won't work. You *have* become enlightened. Now, whether you cry or beat your chest, it is useless. You must go. It is necessary. Go and awaken others. How much longer will you cling to me?"

Sariputta had to go. He went away crying. He must have been a wonderful man, because to cry after having become enlightened is an extraordinary phenomenon. What gratitude he must have had! He left, but wherever he was, every morning and evening he would bow down in Buddha's direction. His disciples would say to him, "You are an enlightened one. Buddha himself has said that you are enlightened. So whose feet are you bowing down to now? What are you doing? Every morning, every evening, wherever Buddha may be.... If he is in Gaya, then you bow down in that direction, if he is somewhere else, then you will bow down in that direction."

Sariputta would always reply, "I have become enlightened because of his compassion. Whatever has happened, has happened through his grace. I can never forget his compassion."

You would say, "What is the need for that now?" You don't know, because you are such a businessman. You would say, "When the need was there I fell at your feet, but now the need is no longer there – so why should I still fall at your feet?" Have you even thought about what you are saying? Are these relationships based on need? If so, then you don't know what love is. Love is not a relationship of need, and it is in love that the flowers of the ultimate abode of the divine blossom. It is only in love that any flowers bloom. This is not a business deal – that when it serves your interest you greet a person saying, *"Jai Ram ji,"* – victory to thy inner self – and then when your interests are no longer being served you forget the greeting because you are no longer interested.

This is how you are, isn't it? When you pass someone on the street you greet them because of your self-interest. Even your greeting is false. You cannot even say, "Victory to the divine within" without some self-interest. You say, "I have some business to do with this man" – he is a bank manager or a deputy collector, or a commissioner. "I have some business to do with him. When my purpose has been achieved, then I'll show him! But right now I must greet him."

Do you greet the master in this way? If you do, then you are not a disciple and you have not taken the one you call your master as master.

"Orange robes and the mala and the master...." "Help" is
not the right word to use, it is not right to say that they
help. These are merely the symbols of your surrender. People
have attained to enlightenment even without wearing orange
robes; hence it is not right to say they help. Christ attained
enlightenment; Mahavira attained enlightenment without any
clothes at all. Buddha wore yellow clothes. So clothes are not
there to help you or not to help you. They are merely a
symbol of your surrender. You say: "Now I will live as the
master says. Now the master's color will be my color. Now
if the master says orange, then orange it will be." This is
merely a suggestion, a hint, an indication from your side that
"I am ready to color myself – even within. The outer is only
an indication that I am ready to be colored. How can I tell
you about the inner? Instead, I am informing with the outer."

What are you actually saying when you embrace someone?
Are you saying let bones meet bones? After all, it is the bones
that seem to meet. When two people embrace, their chests
meet, their skeletons and their skin meet. But is this what
you are wanting to convey? No. You are saying, "It is okay
for bones to meet, they are external, but we want our hearts
to meet, our souls to meet." What happens on the outside
is merely a hint about the inner.

When you take someone's hand in your hand, the physicality
of one hand in the other's hand does not give birth to love.
Yes, it may give birth to some perspiration – but you are
broadcasting a message: that this outer gesture is only
symbolic, that we want to meet inside in the same way that
our hands are meeting on the outside. The outer is only a
symbol.

These orange robes and the mala are signs that you have bowed down, that you have made your declaration to me and to the world that you are standing holding out your empty bag – open, so that if blessings shower you can let it fill up, you are ready to welcome them. You have opened your doors, and if the guest comes he will not have to turn away. You have become a host, you are waiting for the guest to come. This is all they indicate.

This indication brings results, deep results. We must express what is inside us in one form or another, because there is no separate language for expressing the inner.

Have you seen that when you feel surrendered to someone you bow down and place your head at his feet? Now, the head is external and so are the feet, so what are you doing? But this outer symbol brings information about the inner: that inside myself I am bowing down to this person. When you are angry with someone you want to do the opposite, you want to put your feet on his head. This is the reverse, because now you want to jump up and trample on his head and make him fall down. At the very least you want to take off your shoe and hit him on the head with it! This is a symbol too – a reverse symbol. You are saying: "Now I have ruined this man's reputation." Now what difference does placing your shoe on someone's head or hitting him with it make? How can a shoe insult anyone? But these are symbols and carry information about your inner state.

Orange robes are also symbols; they simply bring news about your interiority. There is no scientific reason for them. You won't become enlightened by wearing them, nor will you miss enlightenment if you do not. They are not causes, they are

simply poetic symbols. And I am not teaching you science,
I am teaching you the poetry of life.

Oh indestructible, oh deathless,
Oh offering of my eyes and heart,
When shall I see you?
Oh sweet stirrings
Of my oneness with breath...
You are without existence,
I am a rising of tiny hands.
You are the ultimate energy,
I am a longing, a wishing energy.
You are the immortal,
I am the moment that is offered to you a thousand times.
You are the very law of action,
And I am surrender, forever fresh.

They are simply indications that you have surrendered.

The third question:

Osho,

*In so many ways, in this way and that way, you go on saying the same
things. Does truth need so many words?*

Truth does not need even one single word. Truth can never
be expressed in words. Truth is beyond words. That is why
this effort is being made to say it in many different ways.
You may not understand it in this way, but perhaps you may
in that way. You may not see it from this direction, but
perhaps you will from another. If you cannot see it in this
way, then perhaps some other expression may help. Perhaps
Sahajo's, perhaps Daya's, or Mahavira's, or Buddha's...

perhaps the expression of Christ — I will use any means to help you to understand. If you miss this time, I will again find some other way to help you. But what I have to say is always that which cannot be said. I am always having to tell you about that which cannot be told. But if I were to remain silent, then there would be no possibility for you to understand.

Truth cannot be contained in words, but if the impact of the words continues to fall on you, then someone inside you will begin to wake up, and having awoken, will understand. Words are impacts.

Look at it this way. You set the alarm before you go to sleep. In the morning the alarm rings. By itself, the alarm is not enough to get you out of bed. Clever people hear the alarm, but they still refuse to get up. They always find a means of escape. They may dream that they are in the temple and that the temple bells are ringing, so if the alarm bell is ringing, they manage to ignore it in this way. And when they wake up at nine o'clock, they will wonder what has happened to the alarm. When the alarm was ringing before they had found an explanation, they had created a dream and covered up the sound of the alarm with it. By itself, the alarm cannot get you out of bed, but if you do want to wake up it can be of great help. It is as if someone is giving you a nudge.

Have you seen the new alarm clocks? They are different. The old alarm clocks rang for five or ten minutes. That was not helpful. Psychologists say that a man only wakes up when the alarm first rings. If the sound doesn't wake him up at once, then nothing will happen for the next ten minutes. If he hears it during the first minute and turns it into a dream, the dream will continue for ten minutes. The new clocks ring, then stop, then ring, then stop, then ring...so that if you miss the first time, then the second time may wake you; if not the second time, then the third. The clock still rings for ten minutes, but at two-minute intervals. It is more effective.

When psychological experiments were conducted, it was found that more people wake up in this way – because if you have deceived yourself with a dream, when the alarm rings again you will have to search for another dream. You have deceived yourself once, but how many times can you do this? In a while your capacity to dream will come to an end. You cannot go to the temple again and again. The idea will become boring the next time the alarm rings. You will wonder why you are going to the temple so many times – why the bell is ringing so many times. You will become suspicious.

That is why I don't keep speaking about devotion all the time, otherwise you will fall asleep. I don't talk on meditation the whole time, or on witnessing. Recently I spoke on Lieh Tzu. It worked for some people, it woke them up. For those who did not awaken, the matter ended there – there was no point speaking to them on him any longer. So then I speak on Daya, on Ashtavakra, on Krishna instead.

I speak in so many different ways.... Your question is right: what I say in so many different ways is the same thing, absolutely the same thing – I have nothing else to say. But your sleep is so deep that I must call you again and again. I can remain silent, but if you don't understand me when I speak, how will you understand my silence?

Truth cannot be contained in words, but if someone is willing to understand it can penetrate him even through words. Truth manifests only in silence, but if someone is not willing to understand, then the silence will appear to be completely empty; no message will come through it. Many enlightened ones have remained silent, but who has ever understood their silence? A few enlightened ones have spoken. If they speak to a hundred people, ninety-nine of them will not understand. But even if just one person understands, that is enough. Even if just one person wakes up, that is sufficient. Then a chain has been created: one person has awoken and that one person will awaken someone else.

When you awaken, don't sit down thinking that words are worthless. No, have this much compassion – that if you work hard with a hundred people and just one of them awakens, that is enough. Even the awakening of one person is a rare event on this earth – because if one person awakens, that one person becomes a temple of the divine. The milieu around him will spread, waves will arise, light will shower down, a fragrance will emanate. His music will echo far and wide, and someone else might awaken because of that music. A chain has been started.

Moreover, those words also belong to the divine, just like everything else. Truth is the divine's...and words...and nothingness.

As some weave patterns of henna,
Or adorn the forehead with a bridal mark,
You have created words.
"Prem" – love – two meaningless syllables
That you have given a meaning to.
"Main" – I – the sound of dark, cruel caves,

Has been given fresh life by you,
Has been filled with you.
The circle of an embrace,
Like making rounds about the sacred wedding fire,
The words of affection,
Like sacred mantras echoing at dawn,
You have created words.
Like one single leaf of the everlasting banyan tree,
Aloft on a torrent of waves,
You have created words.

Words belong to the divine as much as silence does. So if
you want to wake up, words will do it. If you want to wake
up, silence will do it. But if you don't want to wake up,
if you refuse to wake up, then nothing can help you.
Surely you are eager to wake up, otherwise why would you
have come this far, why would you have made such a long
journey? Somewhere there is a thirst in you, there is an
emptiness in your inner being, someone is calling you forth.

On the day you begin to understand silence, I will sit in
silence. I will say the same thing through my silence as I am
saying now in words. What I say will be the same: there is
nothing else to be said. But right now you cannot even understand my words. Words are gross, silence is subtle. Words
have form, silence is formless. Right now, you cannot even
grasp the form, your eye cannot even rest on the form. If you
were left with the formless you would be totally lost.

I can understand the difficulty of the person who has asked
this question. It arises because instead of using them to wake
up, you start accumulating the words I speak. This only

increases the load on your intellect. Your learning increases, your information increases. Your information increases, but not your knowing. Gradually, you become full of words; you start explaining to others — even though you yourself have not yet understood. Gradually, you become a great theoretician, a scholar, but you still have no acquaintance with the truth. This is your problem.

Remember this: not to make scriptures out of my words, not to transform my words into scholarship. If you do, not only will you not wake up, but on the contrary you will have made even more arrangements for sleeping. It is as if the alarm simply made you sleep more instead of waking you up. Such alarms can be made, they do exist.

A friend brought a radio for me, which was also an alarm clock. If you set the alarm for six o'clock, it will play the appropriate music, the *veena*. You don't wake even to a harsh noise; if the *veena* is playing you will think your mother is singing a lullaby. You will turn over, pull the blanket over you and become even more cozy. You will say, "This is great!" Your sleep might have been about to be disrupted on its own, but now it will be recalled.

Here, I am not singing you a lullaby. My whole effort here is to wake you up. That is why I sometimes even hit you, I sometimes even push you. Sometimes you feel hurt, sometimes you boil with impotent rage, sometimes you are angry. It is natural. When someone has to be woken up, the other must put up with that person's displeasure.

Have you ever tried to wake someone else up? Before he went

to bed the person might have told you to wake him up at
five in the morning, but when you do wake him, he will react
as though you are his enemy. He has told you to do it, but
no one likes to have their sleep interrupted. And it is a sleep
you are in, a spiritual sleep.

Listen to my words. Feel their hits. Use them to wake up. If
you don't wake up, at least don't accumulate my words, don't
become a scholar with them – just forget them. They were
wasted. I will speak again – listen to the hits of those words.
Don't come to me to become a scholar – because even sinners
may reach to the other shore, but the scholars never do.

A spoonful of sunlight or a pinch of fragrance,
Hold them if you can in your fist.
They may not have voices, but syllables can still speak,
Can still tell of hidden meanings at the right time.
A ladle of moonlight, a sip of a meter,
Hold them if you can in your fist.
When the grass grows, it has to grow upwards,
The flame that only faces downwards must die.
The Pancham raga, spring, the flowering of mango blossom,
Hold them if you can in your fist.
I give you burning hot coals. If you can hold them in your
fist they will wake you up, they will not send you to sleep.

A spoonful of sunlight, or a pinch of fragrance,
Hold them if you can in your fist.

But don't make knowledge out of them, otherwise the burning
coals will turn to ash. Knowledge is ash, and awareness is a
burning coal. When I am saying something to you, from my

side it is a burning coal. It all depends on you – whether you will hold it in your heart as a burning coal, whether you will allow the hits to work, whether you will allow them to wound you, whether you will wake up in shock, or whether you will turn it all into ash and hoard it in your safe, becoming a little more knowledgeable through carrying the burden, the load of it. It all depends on you. Whatever I say is out of my hands the minute I have said it. From then on you are the master as far as what use you make of it, how you use it is concerned.

The person who has asked this question must have been accumulating scholarship – that is why, suddenly, this nervousness. Don't gather knowledge. Either listen to me and wake up or, if you don't wake up, forget what I have said. Don't tie it up as a burden of memory. Don't carry a burden of memory. If you start carrying my words as a burden then it will become very difficult. I will be speaking to you again tomorrow, and your burden will become so heavy that what I say will not be able to reach you. It will stand like the Great Wall of China between you and what I am saying.

Those who might have collected much knowledge cannot hear me. Their capacity to listen has been lost. When it is time to listen they always say: "I know this, I have heard this. I already know this: it is written in the Upanishads, in the Koran. This is exactly what the Bible says." While I am speaking they are constantly figuring out where else this is written, where else they have read it, where else they have heard it....

While I am speaking don't spend your time working anything out, because with all this inner chattering you will miss.

The fourth question:

Osho,

What is the difference between character and individuality?

Character is something imposed from the outside; you have
superimposed it upon yourself, you have picked it up from
the outside. Individuality is a flowering from within; you
have not superimposed it upon yourself, you have not picked
it up, you have only allowed it to manifest.

Character is like plastic flowers; individuality is like the rose
on a rosebush. Individuality is alive; character is dead.
However holy or sacred it may appear to be — and it can
appear to be so — character is always dead, always superficial,
imposed from the outside, always false. There is a
truthfulness to individuality — it is your personal touch. It
comes from your own being, its roots are within you.

My entire teaching is in favor of individuality — it doesn't
care about character at all. My whole emphasis is on
meditation, not on morality — because, with meditation, what
is asleep within you will awaken of its own accord. With its
awakening, your character will also change, but this change
won't just be on the surface, it will come from inside you.
If something drops, it will drop because a ray of understanding has descended upon you. Ordinarily, we do just the
opposite: if we have to drop something, we practice doing
it.

A friend came to me. He is addicted to smoking. He had
wanted to stop for a long time. Someone told him that if
he couldn't stop smoking, he should become addicted to

something else so that this first addiction could be dropped. So he began to take snuff. He stopped smoking, but now he was sitting there all the time with his snuff box.

I asked him, "What is the point of this? First you abused your mouth, now you are abusing your nose. The abuse continues, nothing has changed."

He asked, "How can I stop?"

I replied, "Take up something else! If you start chewing tobacco, you will be able to stop taking snuff."

But is this really stopping? This makes no sense. People tell you you should stop smoking because it is harmful, but they don't understand why smoking has such a hold on you.

Have you ever noticed when it is that you smoke? It is always at times when you are sad, when you are restless, when there is no peace inside you, when you cannot figure out what to do and what not to do.... So then you light a cigarette, and blow the smoke in and out. It gives you something to do. When you are worried, you smoke more. When you are not, you smoke less. So the real question is not about cigarettes; the real question is how to be free from all cares, how to be rid of your worries. If a man stops worrying you could ask him to smoke a million times, you could offer him a hundred rupees for smoking one cigarette, and he will still say, "Do you think I am mad? Why should I smoke? Why should I inhale and exhale these fumes?"

But try to understand the person who smokes. Or, if you smoke yourself, notice that when you worry you smoke more.

You smoke less on the days when you are not worried. On the day that your heart is rejoicing you forget all about smoking. On the other days when your heart is not rejoicing – when you have quarreled with your wife or have had an angry scene with the boss in the office, or someone has pushed you in the crowd on the road, or something else has gone all wrong – you smoke a lot more, you will not feel comfortable until you smoke. This means that smoking is simply a way of covering up your anxieties. If you give up cigarettes but keep worrying, you will begin to put snuff into your nose or do something else. It makes no difference what you do.

Even young children do the same, only a little differently. If his mother is angry, the child will quickly put his thumb in his mouth. He is already smoking cigarettes! No one has given him a cigarette yet and he cannot buy them because he is still in his cradle, but he has already begun to smoke. This young man is tomorrow's smoker. He is smoking his thumb. What is really the matter? His mother is upset and he is worried about whether he will ever get to his mother's breast again. So he is creating a false breast; he is sucking his own thumb. He is saying, "There is no need to worry, I have a thumb. I will just drink that." He begins to suck and falls asleep sucking his thumb. Children often fall asleep shortly after they begin sucking their thumb. So whenever a child cannot sleep, he sucks his thumb.

Sometimes young children put a corner of their blanket into their mouth or their toy on their chest and then they fall asleep. These habits are already beginning to form – dangerous habits! Then, later, these habits will take new forms. As the child gets older they take on new forms of expression. But the root cause behind them all is still worry. If a mother really loves her child, the child will not form these habits. Usually, when the child puts his thumb in his mouth, the mother pulls it out again — and that makes him even more worried and he becomes even more nervous. So he quickly puts his thumb back in again. The mother is furious. She so strongly disapproves of him that now he is not even free to suck his thumb. So a feeling of guilt is born in the child. He keeps looking around: when the mother comes, he quickly pulls his thumb out and hides his hand. As soon as the mother goes, he begins to suck his thumb again. Sin has already entered his life. He begins to think that he has done something wrong. In the same way, people feel guilty when they smoke. They are scared that a parent will find out what they are doing.

You must understand what worry is and then relinquish it. When your worry is thrown out in this way a certain refinement appears in your personality, and then some other things fall away on their own.

Character simply means replacing one habit with another. Character means replacing one lie with another. Character means that you continue to color your outside, but you don't go within yourself, you don't catch a glimpse of your own inner being.

Individuality means looking for something that is already within you. If you are worried, go deeply into it. If you are angry, go deeply into it. If you feel sexual desire, recognize it; don't force an oath of celibacy on yourself. Nothing will be achieved by taking a vow of celibacy: your sexual desire will not change and the turmoil within you will only be increased. Your sexual desire will remain in its place and celibacy will be added to it. You will be more divided, more fragmented; there will be more conflict, and waves of confusion and worry will arise within you. No, you must understand the nature of the sexual desire.

Try to understand the difference. If you go to a temple and take a vow of celibacy this is character forming — because if you had understood that sexual desire is futile then there would have been no need to take a vow, the matter would have been over. But if you understand it to be futile, if you experience it to be futile, if one day you suddenly find out that there is no substance to it — not because Mahavira says so, not because Buddha says so, but because you have come to know it for yourself — on that day celibacy will arise in your life. This celibacy is the real flower. It is individuality, it is the rose blossoming on the bush.

Going to a temple to take an oath — in front of some holy man or some group of people — that from now on you will live in celibacy, is only a plastic flower. Inwardly, the thorns of sexual desire will continue to prick you.

Life is a river or a stream,
Not an ocean.
But there are two kinds.
One travels a long way
And, meeting ice,
It turns to ice
And moves no more.
It may be holy, it may be sacred
But it is not life's nature,
It has just formed a character.

The other, in which a fire flows,
Surges with joy, and thunders bravely.
Storms of love sweep through it,
Moving the branches of the trees on its banks.
Those who have been stained with soot
They too are washed and bathed
In the fluidity of this fire,
This stream is life's nature.

One is character: it is hollow, meaningless, imposed, no deeper than your skin. If you scratch character, you will find a mess underneath, total confusion. The taste of individuality, of one's nature, is always the same — no matter how much you scratch it. From the skin to the soul, individuality has only one taste; non-dual oneness. It has only one taste. No matter how deeply you dig into a person who has individuality, you will find only love — however deep you go. But don't try such a thing with the person who has only character. His love will be only superficial: if you scratch his skin a little, you will find anger, hatred, and hostility.

Stay away from the person of character. A person who relies on character cannot be trusted. He is a false person. He is like clothes which are not colorfast; if you wear them, you will always be afraid of water spoiling them and the sunlight bleaching them. Character is an impermanent dye that is not colorfast. And individuality is colorfast. But you can have this color only when it comes from within you, from your very being.

My whole effort is to give you individuality, your true nature, not character. Individuality is the soul.

The fifth question:

Osho,

I am a doubting type. I want to have trust but it does not arise. Only
doubts and more doubts continually arise in my mind. Please show me
the way.

Don't worry. It is natural to be a doubting type. Doubt is
man's nature. Don't condemn it. Whatsoever the divine has
given you has some purpose. Find out that purpose, let go
of the condemnation. Those who have chosen the journey
with me must give up condemnation. With me, there is no
condemnation for anything. If you have doubt, we will
make use of that doubt. If you have poison, we will make
a medicine out of that poison. Poison can be used as a
medicine; all that it takes is an intelligent man.

What is the meaning of doubt? Doubt simply means that
you are thoughtful, not blind; that you don't accept
everything and anything. That is absolutely right. What is
wrong with that? Why should it trouble you? There is no
need to accept absolutely everything.

I don't even ask you to accept the divine. All I say to you is
to look at life attentively. You will find that it is empty. If
you really look into life you will find that there is nothing
but ash there. And then the question will arise in your mind
that isn't some other kind of life also possible? If you are
truly a doubting person, put your own life under the scrutiny
of doubt. Doubt the love you have felt so far: ask whether
this is love or not. So far, you have only earned money: doubt
your wealth. Seek and find out whether it is true wealth, or
whether you are merely gathering potsherds and if death

comes tomorrow you will have nothing. Apply your doubt, your suspicion, in the direction of how you have been living your life so far. You will be astonished. If you apply your doubt towards your own world, you will not be able to remain a worldly householder for very long.

But what have you been doing? You have been doing exactly the opposite. You have placed your trust in the world and your doubt in the divine. Just change it around. Place your doubt on the world, and then you will suddenly find that your trust which was focused on the world has started searching for a new focus. Trust must focus somewhere.

So far, I have never seen a man who has no trust, and I have also never seen a man who has no doubt. They are always found together, and it should be so. Both are two aspects of the same coin. Doubt and trust are like night and day. What is the difference between them? A religious man puts his doubt upon the world and his trust towards the divine. An irreligious man focuses his doubt on the divine and his trust on the world. This is the only difference. There is no difference other than this. Both of these people have both of these qualities. It is up to you to choose!

I won't talk to you about trust right now, because you say trust doesn't arise. Leave it. Doubt arises easily in you, you enjoy doubting, so doubt the world. Fill your entire life with doubt. You will be astonished: as soon as you doubt the world you will start seeing everything becoming false, futile. Position, honor and respectability will all begin to seem pointless. Suddenly you will find a new direction opening before you for trust.

Doubts are the windows
Through which the intellect peers
Beyond her limits.
Truths she cannot yet speak rightly,
Come lisping from her tongue.
Doubts are the stairs,
And trust the highest floor.
Once doubt was thought a sin,
But now we love it,
And hate it not.
Time and again
Religion falls into darkness
And through doubt
We rediscover it
Again and again.

Doubts are the stairs, trust is the highest floor. Turn your doubts into a stairway. Doubt wealth, and you will begin to have trust in meditation.

A young man took sannyas yesterday. His name was Dhanesh, the lord of wealth. I have renamed him Dhyanesh, the lord of meditation. Hmm...! Now this finishes everything! Now he can move away from money and move towards meditation.

You have a lot of faith in the body – begin to doubt it. As soon as you doubt the body, how will you be able to avoid trusting the soul? So I don't say to you, like your so-called *mahatmas* do, that you should have no doubts, that you should have no suspicions at all. They don't know anything. I say to you: make right use of your doubts. There are many places in life where you must have doubts. The whole of life is worthy of your doubting. Peel back each and every layer, and look. With the help of these steps of doubt you will find that you have arrived at faith, at trust in the divine.

Learn to say "no." "Yes" will also come. When there is force in your "no," you will find that "yes" also comes.

So don't be afraid, don't be distressed by your worries. I am ready to give sannyas even to atheists because as I see it, atheists are often more sincere than believers. Believers are more often hypocrites. Atheists can also be hypocrites – at least not in India, but in Russia they are. It is difficult to be an atheist in India. Even an atheist pretends to be a believer here, because that is more convenient. Here, there is a crowd of believers all around, so being an atheist is really troublesome! In India only a really courageous person can be an atheist.

If you are a doubter, an atheist, full of mistrust, then the door of my sannyas is open to you. I tell you that you will not find anyone else in the whole world willing to give you sannyas – because such courageous believers who can include even an atheist have disappeared from this world. But this temple is open to all, you can come in. We will make a stairway from your doubts. You will reach the temple using these stairs. Always remember one thing: whatsoever the divine has given cannot be useless, even if you don't know what its use is. Search for the use. But whatsoever is, must have some use or other.

I have heard:

For many generations a special musical instrument was kept in a certain house. It looked like a *sitar*, but it had many, many strings and it was very big — and no one in the house knew how to play it. It took up so much room in the house — half of the sitting room — and it used to gather dust and dirt. If the children touched it, it disturbed the people of the household. If a rat jumped on it at night time, it disturbed their sleep. Finally, they decided to get rid of it, because what was the point of just keeping it there? So they picked it up and put it out with the rubbish.

Before they were even back inside the house they heard the most extraordinary music arising. They stood still, utterly charmed. Then they rushed back. A large crowd had already gathered. A passing beggar had picked up the instrument and had begun to play it. For an hour everyone stood spellbound. When the beggar finally finished playing the owners of the instrument tried to take it back from him, saying that it belonged to them. For the first time they had realized how unique the instrument was. No one had ever heard such music before.

But the beggar said, "An instrument can only belong to someone who knows how to play it. You threw it away. You have no claims on it anymore. What would you do with it if you owned it? It would only take up space in your house again. An instrument belongs to the one who knows how to play it."

I say unto you that life also belongs to the one who knows how to play it. Nothing is useless here. Even doubt is not futile. Don't throw it away, we will make a staircase of it. And one day, these stairs will take you to the truth.

The last question:

Osho,

I never thought my heart would be left behind in your assembly. I had the idea to go away after just a brief look.

It is good your heart has been left behind here – because if you had gone back after having had just a brief look that would have meant only one thing: that you have not looked at all. If you see me for even one moment, your heart will be left behind here. If you take just one single breath in synchronicity with mine, you will have to leave your heart behind, with me. If our eyes meet but once, your heart will remain here – it must. The whole arrangement here is that in some way your heart is left behind.

Who is this new stranger
Who has entered my world of dreams,
And spent a night under the shadow of my eyelids,
Who raises a temple in the lonely desert of my heart
Celebrating another passing year
In the burning ground of my longings,
Who lavishes me with a wealth of feelings
In my bare, empty poverty?
What clouds of deep monsoon have gathered in my sky?
Who sings wondrous songs of love in my courtyard?
Whose overwhelmingly desperate call
Dwells in the swirling overhanging of dense, dark clouds?
Who is the deceitful one, who is winning me
Through being defeated by me?
I have lost the diamond of my heart in this very first move.
Whose footsteps have startled my loneliness,
As if the inertness of my heart

was being freed from its curse?
Who is this Rama in whose feet
Lies hidden this benedictory touch?
Who is this new stranger
Who has entered my world of dreams,
And spent a night under the shadow of my eyelids?

Your heart has lain desolate for a long time, asleep. The *veena* of your heart has not known music for a long time. It is good that you have come. You thought that you would leave after just a brief look — this was a good try....

Miracles do happen in life. Sometimes, a ray enters your life unexpectedly. Sometimes, the divine knocks uninvited on your door. Without your knowing, without your waiting, sometimes your hand falls into the hand of the divine. In that moment, have courage. Don't be frightened. Begin your journey immediately with this unknown stranger. Don't take your heart and run away. Your intellect will tell you to run. The intellect is a great coward. It will say, "Why are you becoming entangled? Run away!" Don't run, because you will miss the moment of your destiny's dawn if you run away. You are fortunate that your heart has been caught here.

Since you came, my beloved,
This life feels like life.

If you remain a little courageous then a new light, a new vision, a new song will be born in your life.

Since you came, my beloved,
This life feels like life.
Since your compassion

Poured down on me,
Every season is as lovely
As the gentle rains of the Shravan month.
Before, what was my life
But just an excuse
To somehow go on living?
Life was a burden, breath a debt,
All to be repaid in some way.
But now that we have met,
All feels like a sacred celebration.

Stay. Don't run away. Life can become a celebration. Life can become sacred.

Without you, this carnival of life
Was like a desolate crematorium to me,
Each sorrow forever multiplying.
But now that we have met,
All feels like a sacred celebration.

This is what I want: that you don't run away from the world, that you don't leave the marketplace, that the crowds there become a pleasure to your heart, that you can see the divine in the crowd, that even the smallest details of your life become a worship, a reverence.

Before, my life was like a snake,
My heart as sad as poor Ahilya turned to stone.
Life was like an abandoned journey
That never reached the divine.
When it felt your touch
My petrified heart became alive.
My life was sadness,
But when you came it turned into a festival.

My life was a profound darkness,
But when you came, light came too.
For Radha's sake,
Krishna seems to have returned from Gokul.

If your heart is left behind here, let it be. Leave it here, Take
your intellect away with you — because I have no concern
with your intellect. If your love is left here, then the thread
of your very being has been left in my hands and I will be
able to transform you — it will not be at all difficult.
Transformation is certain: you can be assured that
transformation will happen, because all transformation comes
from your heart and all obstacles come from your intellect.
So take your intellect with you and don't bring it with you
when you return; leave it behind at home. And leave your
heart here.

I have colored your clothes, now I will color your heart. I am
a dyer. If you are ready, I will dye your heart the color of the
divine. And when your heart is colored, only then will you
find that your stone-like life has come alive for the first time,
that your consciousness has awakened, that a light has
descended into what so far has been an empty clay lamp.

This life is a potentiality — a potentiality of becoming the
ultimate temple. Don't be satisfied with less than that, don't
settle for anything less. Keep your discontent awake. Remain
discontented until the divine enters you completely. Be
content with the world and remain discontented about the
divine. This thirst will consume you, it will awaken you, it
will transform you.

Enough for today.

7

THE SHINE OF COUNTLESS SUNS

Said the master to Daya:

Take the vow of the tortoise,
Withdraw your senses,
And bring awareness to your breath.

Without utterance, with no beads in your hands,
Remembrance continues within.
Only a rare person experiences this,
It is the grace of the master, says Daya.

When the disciple chants the unchantable mantra,
Keeping awareness in his lotus-heart,
Pure knowledge manifests there,
Removing all stains of darkness.

Where there is no death and no blaze,
No cold and no heat, O my brother,
Seeing my home, my ultimate abode,
The unfathomable mystery of life is revealed, says Daya.

Seeing the peerless beauty of the beloved,
The light of ten million suns shines.
All of life's sorrows are erased,
And the essence of happiness is manifest, says Daya.

The shine of countless suns,
The miraculous light manifests,
It feels dazzling,
But the mind becomes cool and refreshed.

There is much light without lightning,
And it is showering without clouds.
Watching this ceaselessly
My heart is delighted, says Daya.

The world is a falsehood,
A deceptive well in the form of the body.
You are consciousness,
The abode of a marvelous bliss.

This person hurt me, that person hurt me,
But I have found no one
Who could soothe my aching heart.
The lamps have died from having no oil of affection,
Their wicks lie unlit.
The light-fairy is confined
To the desolate prison house of the black night.
Darkness rules in every household,
No ray of light smiles anywhere.
From where will the fire of oblation kindle?
Who will adorn me with the crown of light?
Who will offer luminous circumambulations
And turn my no-moon night into a full moon one?

The one who turns your no-moon night into a full-moon
night is the master. The one who fills your darkness
with light is the master. The one who gives you the clues
to your true identity is the master.

In today's sutras, Daya talks about the grace of her master and what has happened to her because of his grace. These aphorisms are unique, because they are the essence of meditation. If you can understand them, an abundance of light will shine in your life as well. If you can understand them, you too can be immersed in the ultimate bliss. As Daya says:

There is much light without lightning,
And it is showering without clouds.
Watching this ceaselessly
My heart is delighted, says Daya.

You have started your journey with the same seed as Daya. You have the same potential as she has. Your seed may not have fallen into the right soil, or found the right gardener; you may not have sown it in the right season or it may not have received the right amount of sunlight yet.... So it still remains a seed, but when it does sprout there will be the same shining of countless suns within you. When it sprouts, your heart too will be delighted. When "watching this ceaselessly" becomes your own vision, becomes your own experience, when this nectar showers on you, only then will you become aware of all the sorrows you have suffered so far in life: "This person hurt me. That person hurt me...."

Wherever you have gone, you have only received hurt. Your heart has never been delighted; you have received only thorns, even from those you have loved, and your heart has never been delighted. Sometimes wealth has hurt you, sometimes your position, sometimes relatives – your dear ones, your very own – sometimes strangers.... This one or that one, they have all hurt you. You walk around with wounds in your

chest. That is why you don't even look inside yourself —
because inside you there is nothing but wounds. The
awakened ones may tell you a million times to look inside
yourself, but you won't do it because you know that there
is no light there: no moon, no stars, no brilliance of countless
suns.... There is only a thick darkness there; the pus of your
wounds and the weeping, running sores of your pain which
you have accumulated through many, many lives.

As long as you think that you will receive happiness from
others this same thing will happen again and again:

This person hurt me, that person hurt me,
But I have found no one
Who could soothe my aching heart.

As long as you think that another person can give you
happiness you will receive only hurt. Happiness is your self-
nature. If it were possible to obtain happiness from
others you would have found it by now. For how many
lives have you held out your begging bowl in front of others
and begged? — and you have never even bothered to see that
they were begging from you too. You were begging from them
— beggars in front of beggars. You are begging your wife to
give you happiness; she is begging you to give *her* happiness.
This blindness goes very deep. If your wife had any happiness
to give to you, would she have asked you for it? If you had
happiness to give to her, would you have asked her for it?
We only ask for those things that we don't have. We give
others what we have; we ask for what we don't have.

If you open your eyes and look carefully, you will find that
everyone in the world is asking for happiness, everyone in
the world is begging for love. But people have neither love

nor happiness: the mistake is happening in the very asking. And because you go on begging outside of yourself, you don't even remember that what you are begging for is your very self-nature.

This revolution is called religion. On the day you remember: "I must stop begging; for once I must look inside myself, I must completely explore who I am. It is possible that what I have never found outside of myself may be within me...." It *has* to be within you. You would not have even looked for it if it were not already there, because we can only ask for something which is already present as an experience somewhere deep within us.

The whole universe is searching for bliss. If you had never known bliss, never tasted it; if you had never had a relationship with bliss, never.... No one can ever go on a search for the complete unknown — how can you do that? How can you search for someone when you have no idea about them: no address, no whereabouts? There has to be an echo somewhere deep within you. Somewhere, far beneath the darkness of your heart, a lamp burns. Sometimes, knowingly or unknowingly, your eye catches a glimpse of it. Sometimes it even happens that you think that this time your happiness is coming from the other — but that too is this same glimpse, and you are simply mistaking it.

Sometimes, listening to some music you felt happy. But how can music give you happiness? While you were listening to the music, something else was happening. Listening to the music, you drowned in your own juices — the music just became an excuse. Because of the music you forgot your cares, your family, the mad race of the world, your mundane problems. The music enabled you to forget the world. And as soon as one forgets the world, one begins to remember oneself, and because of this remembrance one feels happiness.

No one has ever received happiness from music. The happiness comes from within; the music is only an excuse. Similarly, sometimes one finds happiness from sex. This happiness also comes from within; making love is just the excuse. Whenever you have found any happiness, whenever even a ray of happiness has shone in your life – a small, brief glimpse – it has always come from inside you. But your eyes are focused on the outside, so whenever that ray comes you think it has come from somewhere outside of you. You are misunderstanding.

Have you seen a dog chewing an old bone? There is nothing in the dry bone, no juice, but the dog is completely engrossed as he chews it. If you try to snatch the bone away from him he will be angry. He will pounce on you and attack you. There is no juice in the dry bone, so what pleasure is he getting? When he chews the bone he is hurting his mouth, because he scratches the soft skin inside and it bleeds. Then he sucks on the blood and believes that it comes from the bone. This is natural because it wasn't there until he had the bone in his mouth. The logic of the situation is clear. The dog's logic is exactly the same as yours. If the dog could clarify his situation, he would say, "Until I put the bone in my mouth I knew no pleasure; I only knew this pleasure afterwards. So the pleasure must have come from the bone." And then he is not prepared to let go of the bone, even though the bone is just wounding his mouth; his own blood is flowing and then he is swallowing it.

This is exactly your situation. When you feel happiness from music it is actually coming from within you: it is your own juices that you are drinking. When you get pleasure from making love, this pleasure is coming from within you: you are savoring your own juices.

Whenever you have found happiness.... Perhaps you were in the Himalayas, looking at the lofty snow-covered peaks, and you were overwhelmed, speechless, and an exclamation of joy suddenly arose in your heart.... The happiness which flowed at this moment came from within you, the mountains were merely an excuse. The peace, the silence, the presence of the unprecedented beauty of the Himalayas freed you for a moment from your mad race for self-gratification. Once that desire has been broken, once your mind stops its activities for even one moment, the juices flow from within you.

The mind stops the flow of your juices. The mind is always interested in the other. Whenever the mind stops, your interest in others disappears and you immediately fall back to your own original source. And the stream of juices is there. *Raso vai sah* – in the divine is *rasa*, the juice.

The Upanishads say: The divine is rasa. You are made of this same stuff, this juice. The whole universe is made of the divine. From the pebbles and stones on the earth to the moon and stars in the sky, from the body to the soul – everything is made of the divine. The Upanishads say: The divine is rasa, the juice. So we are all made of rasa; rasa is our self-nature. Once we begin to recognize ourselves there will be nothing but happiness.

Religion means knowing oneself. The world is the search for happiness in the other, religion is the search for happiness in oneself. No one has ever found happiness in the world.

Those who have found happiness are the people who went within themselves – a Buddha, a Kabir, a Krishna, a Christ. Whenever someone found happiness in this world, it has been, without exception, for one reason alone: that the person has entered into himself. What method he used to do this may vary. Some have gone through dancing, some through music, some by the use of a mantra, some through tantra, some through devotion, some through meditation. But whatever means was used, it was only a means.

You have come here. Some have come by train, some by plane, some by car, some on foot. Maybe one person rode a horse and another came in a bullock cart. It makes no difference *how* you came here – you have arrived. The moment you arrive, how you came becomes unimportant. Some rode on their devotion, journeying through love; some rode on their knowledge, journeying through meditation – but it makes no difference. These are all means, means to awaken your self-remembrance within you.

Dry branches, dry leaves,
What kind of a tree is this?
The heart yearns,
Not finding the playful touch
Of the breeze of love.
Your life is like this:

Dry branches, dry leaves,
What kind of a tree is this?

Everything in you is dry because you are looking for the juice elsewhere, outside yourself. The juice comes from your very roots, it flows from your source. And you have completely forgotten your source — that is why you are dried up. You go on looking for something in the world, but you will not find anything. On attaining to the one, to your source, you will find everything.

Said the master to Daya:
Take the vow of the tortoise,
Withdraw your senses,
And bring awareness to your breath.

This is a matchless mantra for meditation! Understand it.

Said the master to Daya:
Take the vow of the tortoise...

The master said, "Daya, become like a tortoise." The tortoise has one special quality: it can draw all its senses in upon itself. The senses are the doors through which you go out. If you open your eyes, you will look outside yourself; if you use your ears, you will hear the sounds outside yourself; if you spread your hands, you will touch something. The senses go out. The hand cannot go inside you, the eye cannot see inside you. The eye that sees within you is another eye: it has no connection with your two eyes. That's why the wise talk about the third eye; they are speaking of a different eye, not related to these two at all.

And bear this in mind: the wise say there are two eyes for looking outwards and one eye for looking inwards. This too is very symbolic. Duality lies outside of you, non duality inside you. You don't need two eyes to see within: if you use two eyes it will cause a duality, a conflict; the world will be born within you. You need two eyes to look out and one to look within; two ears to hear outside and one to hear inside.

The third ear has not been talked about in the same way that the third eye has been, but it should be. Just as we have two hands to reach out, so we have one hand to reach in. The Zen masters have talked about that one hand: they say, "Clap with one hand." They ask their disciples to sit down and hear the sound of one hand clapping. Now how can one hand clap? It takes two hands to clap. But they ask their disciples to search for the sound made by one hand clapping. That hand is the inner hand.

There is one door to go in and two doors to go out. There are many senses for going outwards – there are eyes, ears, the nose, the hands...all the five senses. When you go inwards, the two eyes become one and your ears also merge into this one. Your hands and nose also merge into this one – everything becomes one.

Somewhere Kabir says that when he went inside himself he was utterly bewildered; he started hearing through his eyes! His ears could see, his hands could smell, he could touch things through his nose! People think that these are the paradoxical statements of some mystic – but they are not paradoxical statements, this is how it is, because inside you only the one remains, all your senses merge into one. This sutra is wonderful – pointing towards that one.

The master said to Daya, *Take the vow of the tortoise....* This must have been symbolic. Charandas, Daya's master, meant it as an allegory when he told her to take the vow of the tortoise. He used a concise expression to tell her to draw her senses within. "Contract your senses completely, turn your

outward going senses inwards, in the direction of your true
home" — because as long as the senses go out, your energy
will keep flowing outwards too, and how can the inner union
take place? If you go east, how can you meet the one who
lives in the south? If you go west, how can you meet the one
who lives in the east? And gradually, you become so used to
going outside yourself that you completely forget that there
exists a world inside you.

You know that people say there are ten directions. In reality,
there are eleven directions, but no one bothers to count the
eleventh. The ten are the eight directions around us, above
and below us. No one ever counts the eleventh direction
which is the inward direction. This real direction has been
forgotten.

Take the vow of the tortoise... means: Go in the eleventh direction.
Don't waste your energy now in going in the ten
directions; let your energy gather inside you.

The tortoise is unique in that respect. No other animal has
this ability. This is why the tortoise has become so important
in Hindu mythology: God has taken an incarnation as a
tortoise, and some very sweet stories have been written about
it. They say that the whole earth rests on the tortoise's back.
If you look at these stories superficially they appear to be
childish: how can the earth rest on the back of a tortoise?
But if you look at the deeper meanings of the story, new
understandings will unfold. They are actually saying that the
earth rests on those few people who have become like
tortoises — otherwise it would have been destroyed a long
time ago. Sometimes there is a Buddha, sometimes there is
a Mahavira...the world rests on them. You too live because

of them, even though you may never have met with Buddha
or Mahavira, you may never have bowed down at their feet.
The earth remains alive because of the presence of these
individuals. Somehow you also live, but you are dragging
yourself along.

Think about it: if you take away just a few names from
human history, those of Buddha, Mahavira, Krishna, Kabir,
and a few others like them, where would you be, what would
you be, what would your condition be like? You would be
reduced to nothing. Whatever small amount of humanity can
be seen in you is *their* gift. Whatever small amount of light
and brilliance is seen within you is their grace. Humans are
humans because of these few, otherwise they would all be
animals.

So when Hindus say that the earth rests on the back of a
tortoise, that is merely a symbol. There are two types of
foolish people in this world. Firstly, there are those who want
you to prove that such a tortoise exists. And then there are
those who get involved in proving that yes, a tortoise like
this does exist. Both are fools. It has nothing to do with any
tortoise, the earth rests on those few people who have become
like a tortoise. Those few have taken the entire burden of your
life on their backs. If there is any possibility of flowers
blossoming in your life, it is because of these few who have
drawn in their senses and gone beyond what their senses
knew.

So the master said to Daya: "Now you too become like a
tortoise, Daya."

...*Withdraw your senses,
And bring awareness to your breath.*

Withdraw all your senses. Withdrawing your senses doesn't
mean sitting down with your eyes closed. It doesn't mean
cutting off your hands or poking your eyes out. It means:
even if your eyes see something, there is no desire left in that
seeing. The eye will see because that is its nature. After all,
Daya will still differentiate between a door and a wall as she
is walking around. She will still differentiate between what
she should or should not eat. She will not start eating cups
and plates! Her eyes will do their work of seeing, but there
will be no desire left in her about seeing. When the interest
in form disappears, the eye has turned inwards, because
interest in form is the eye.

Our visible eyes have a use, and it is right that you should
use them in this way. Getting up, sitting down, walking,
eating and drinking – use them for the purpose they are there
for. But there is a desire hidden behind the eyes: the desire
to see. One has to become free of that desire to see.

What have you gained from seeing things over and over
again? Even if you saw beauty, what have you really gained?
Even if you saw the most beautiful person you could ever
imagine, what have you really gained? It was no more than a
dream. Whether you see a beautiful person in a dream or you
actually see them, makes no difference: in both cases, it is
simply a picture forming inside you. When the most
beautiful woman or the most handsome man stands in front
of you, what is really happening inside you? Your eye
functions like a camera, it creates a picture of the object
inside you. You don't really meet the beautiful woman. She
is outside you. How can you go outside? You are inside, the
beautiful woman is outside, and between the two the eye
brings a small picture of that beautiful woman inside you

and enlarges it out onto the screen of your brain – just like a film in a theater. And you are engrossed in that picture, but the picture is empty.

It is the same kind of madness with films. You are so happy to see those pictures – but there is nothing there. And it is not just with movies, people get very excited looking at naked photographs in magazines. Someone could ask: "What are you doing? Are you in your right senses or what? There is nothing on this page, just some colors spread out in a particular pattern – nothing." There is nothing on the film screen either – merely light and shadow. The screen is empty; there is no one there. But how eager you become when you watch it!

There is a secret behind this eagerness: all your life you have watched games like this on the screen of your mind. What else have you seen? A film is merely a trick invented by the human mind, it is merely an extension of the same process that goes on in the human mind. That is why films have such an influence on man: they have a deep affinity with the mind.

It never occurs to you that what you are watching in the movie house doesn't exist. No, you become so eager, so moved. Sometimes you cry, sometimes you laugh, sometimes you are sad, sometimes happy. Pictures are making you dance like a puppet. But this happens with a film screen – you become entangled with it in this way because this is just how you have been entangled with your inner screen for your whole life. The film is merely an extension of the same phenomenon.

Turning the eye inwards means that the eye is now only an

instrument for seeing and no desire to see form and beauty remains. Beauty is merely a photograph. The ears may hear, but there remains no desire for hearing. The hands may touch, but the madness for touching will not be a part of it. If all this madness can be dispersed, you will slowly find that the energy which used to drain out through your senses has started filling up the Lake Mansarovar within you.

Right now, you are empty within. Your condition is like this:

We are spinning days like cotton,
Carrying a book of complaints
Bound with a cover of grief.
Cut off from our surroundings
We are dancing like a spindle,
Resounding like a tambourine,
Laughing, but sadly.
Our friends have done us a favor
In giving us a love that is like a cactus.
We are all like empty bottles and glasses.

There is nothing inside you: "...like empty bottles and glasses." There is an absolute desert where that ocean of juice should be flowing within you — because the energy from which that ocean of juice is created is being constantly dissipated through your senses. The enlightened ones have said that the senses are like holes, and because of the holes your pot never fills up. Your energy is continually dispersing through these holes. And if you keep dispersing your energy in this way, you will always be as empty as you are now.

...Withdraw your senses,
And bring awareness to your breath.

If you can free all your senses from their outward journey your meditation will be released, because your meditation is caught up in these senses.

Try to understand it. You sit down to meditate, a beautiful woman passes by, and your awareness gets distracted; or someone jingles money near you and your awareness is broken. If someone sings a song nearby, again you are distracted; if someone talks about something relevant to you – your profession, the shop or the market, if someone says that the price of such and such an item is about to skyrocket – you hear it and immediately you are distracted. Why are you distracted? Because the desire is already there within you: it was touched and activated.

You must realize that you have only one energy and you can put it into meditation or into desires. If you put it into desire, your meditation is disrupted. If you put it into meditation, your desire is dispersed. The energy is one and the same; there aren't two energies. You have got the capital of only one energy; where you will invest it depends on you.

A worldly person is one whose total energy is going towards desires. A religious person is one whose energy has begun to travel in the opposite direction from desires – as though the Ganges has begun to flow backwards towards Gangotri, towards its source. This is all that is meant by meditation.

Meditation means that the energy that has gone into desires has begun to return towards its home. So when all your senses are relaxed and withdrawn, just as a tortoise draws itself in and waits, when you become like a tortoise.... A meditator becomes like a tortoise.

Look at Buddha sitting. How does he sit? He is like a stone
statue. One hand over the other, one foot over the other,
every door closed in every direction; his eyes are shut – he
is completely absorbed within himself. What is he doing
there?

This is a problem you generally face. People come to me, and
when I suggest to them to sit quietly once in a while, they
say, "What should we do when we are sitting quietly? Please
give us a mantra or something to do." They want a mantra
so they can keep making some noise. "Rama-Rama, Rama-
Rama, Rama-Rama...." Something...they won't be able to
sit still without having something to do. "Rama-Rama"
means "we are doing something" – but the nonsense within
them just continues in a new way. But if you tell them not
to do anything, just to relax, to put all "doing" aside for a
short while.... Meditation means relaxed non-doing.

The very meaning of meditation is: for a while, I will do
nothing. I will just allow my whole energy to lie still. The
first step in that direction is to bring awareness to your
breath. Buddha called this *vipassana, anapanasatiyoga*. This is
the greatest alchemy discovered in the history of mankind.
When desire – which is energy – withdraws from the senses
and enters within; when eyes are not interested in seeing, ears
are not interested in hearing, hands are not interested in
touching; when the whole interest has turned inwards
and you have become like a tortoise – then apply this energy
to your breath.

Daya says, *Bring surati, awareness to your breath.* Surati means
remembrance, meditation, awareness. Apply this awareness,
this consciousness to your breath. Breathing out, breathing

in – apply this to the circle of your breath. You don't need to sit with a rosary in your hands; with such a beautiful rosary of your breath going on, why do you need a separate rosary in your hand? Your breath forms a beautiful, natural rosary – out and in, out and in, out and in. Watch your breath as it moves out and in; don't do anything. When you breathe out, you should be conscious that the breath has left you. When you breathe in, be conscious that the breath is in. Don't miss it, don't forget it. In the beginning you will forget over and over again; take hold of your consciousness again and again and apply it to your breath.

Remember: you don't need to breathe hard, you don't need to soften your breath. Don't change your breathing at all: let it continue naturally and bring all your awareness to your breathing. This is not *pranayama*. In this process, there is nothing like making the breathing faster or deeper, or filling your lungs to capacity and then emptying them – because if you engage in this you have started working, you are active again, you have lost your relaxed state, you have entered into a new type of turmoil. Pranayama...now you will calculate and count: how long the breath is to remain expelled and how long it is to be held in! Expelling, retaining – this is shop keeping, accounting. The mind has become busy, it has found a job to do.

The mind always wants work. Beware of it! The mind wants work. The mind says: "Give me any work, I am ready for it" – the mind dies when it has nothing to do. When the mind dies, you begin to live. When the mind has been erased, you are born.

The mind says: "Give me any work, I will survive under any

work conditions." The mind doesn't care what it does. It needs to do something, anything, because mind means the sense of being the doer: "Pranayama will do! If I am not allowed to run a shop, that doesn't matter, if I cannot go to the cinema, that doesn't matter. I am allowed to practice pranayama – this is great! Patanjali has recommended it, the yogis have always done it. Let's get started.... A mantra is a good thing. I cannot use dirty language, I cannot have worthless thoughts...Rama-Rama – this is a beautiful name. Let me repeat this one!"

The mind says: "Give me any job, and I will manage to live through it because then I will be able to continue being the doer." The mind is a doer. *You* are the witness. The state of witnessing is born only when the state of doing disappears completely. So don't do even this much – breathing faster or more slowly, like this or like that, in a particular way. Don't do anything! All techniques are a madness, but if they have the support of tradition then they don't appear to be madness. If a man sits moving his rosary, we don't call him mad. But if he were in Russia, he would immediately be sent to a mental asylum. "Are you mad? What are you doing?" they would ask him.

A woman was traveling in a bus with Mulla Nasruddin. They were strangers, but by chance they were sitting on adjacent seats. The woman began to feel a little restless, because Mulla was moving his head from side to side all the time. She was already feeling dizzy because of the bus climbing the mountains, and here was this man sitting next to her and shaking his head. Even when she tried not to look at him shaking his head it was difficult, because he was right next to her. She couldn't avoid him.

She was a good, gentle woman, who never interfered with other people. She restrained her curiosity for a long time, but eventually she couldn't control herself. "Sir," she said, "what exactly are you doing? Is this some religious practice – shaking your head like this, to the left and the right?"

Mulla replied, "No, it is not a religious practice at all." But he continued shaking his head even while he was talking.

The woman asked, "Then what are you doing?"

Mulla replied, "This is how I keep track of time. One second this way, another second that way. In this way I have no need to buy a watch." And he kept shaking his head. "It is so cheap and convenient," he said. "There is no need to ask anyone the time."

The woman became curious. She asked, "All right, tell me what the time is right now."

Continuing his shaking, Mulla replied, "Half past four."

The woman looked at her watch and reported, "Wrong. It is a quarter to five."

Mulla began shaking his head a little faster and said, "It seems my clock is running slow."

You will call this man mad. But had Mulla replied, "I am repeating Rama's name – one Rama this way, one Rama that way," it wouldn't have been considered mad. Many forms of madness are justified in the name of religion. That is why fewer people go mad in religious countries than elsewhere, because they have the escape route of religion. There is no need to go mad — why should they choose such a costly affair? More people go mad in irreligious countries because they cannot do the things that people can do here and in other religious countries, in the name of religion. Once you adopt a process that can appear to be religious, no one will call you mad.

This sutra is very precious: bring your awareness on your breath without doing anything to it, leaving it as it is.

Bringing awareness to your breath is very useful. Firstly, it is your breath that links you to your body. Your breath is the bridge. Your breath is the thread that ties you to your body. So if you become aware of your breath, you will immediately realize that you are not the body, that you are separate. That is the first thing.

The second thing: Ordinarily, we consider breath to be life. When someone stops breathing, we assume that he has died. There can be no other conclusion, even for a medical doctor. This is his whole criterion: if the breath has stopped, the man has died.

What is your criterion for believing in death? It is just this, isn't it? — that life is over because the breathing has stopped. When breathing begins, life begins, when the breath goes, life goes. So breathing and life have become synonymous. Ordinarily they are, but when you become aware of your breath you will realize that "I am not the breath either." The one who is aware of it is quite separate from his breath — totally separate from it. The breath moves in front of him. It is like a scene that he is witnessing. And the seer is always separate from the seen.

This small sutra is very precious:

...Withdraw your senses,
And bring awareness to your breath.

But before you apply awareness to breath, you must first become a tortoise. Otherwise, your awareness will not be able to attach itself to the breath — because you will have no awareness. Awareness is a very subtle energy. Either it keeps flowing out through your senses, and then it is not really under your control...your senses are causing your awareness to wander who knows where, to what places. The bird of awareness has flown away through your senses, it is not in your grasp, it is wandering in faraway places. It has gone in many different directions following each of the senses so it has become fragmented. And then whatever each sense is telling you about the world, that is what you think life is, that is what you think truth is. But the senses have no way of knowing the truth. The senses are blind. Only the witness inside you has the possibility of knowing the truth; no one else has. If you listen to your senses, you will not become a tortoise, and then the senses will continue to lead you astray.

Haven't you seen a rope lying on the path on a dark night and thought it was a snake? You may have even run away, your heart beating madly, alarmed and fearful. Your eyes saw it. You say, "I saw it with my own eyes! There was a snake there." Then you take a light and you discover that it was only a rope. The eye is very easily deceived. Even in the slightest darkness your eyes can be easily deceived.

You may see your shirt hanging up in your home at night and think that a thief is standing there. When you turn the light on, you realize it was only your shirt. The eye cannot be trusted that much. It needs light. It cannot be trusted even on the outside – you need light even there – so how can you trust it inside? You need light there as well. That inner light comes from witnessing, from remembrance. The inner lamp is lit with remembrance.

The information the senses give you is simply a matter of habit. You see what you have become used to seeing.

You may not have noticed this, but if a woodcutter were to come into this garden he would not see the flowers at all. He would see only the wood. He would think about which tree he could cut down and sell in the market. If a gardener came, a connoisseur of flowers, he wouldn't see the wood, he would see only the flowers. "What beautiful flowers" he would think. If a poet came he would not even see the flowers directly, he would see the beauty of the flowers. His focus would be on beauty. If a painter came he would see colors – unique colors which you don't see. Generally, you think that when you and a friend come into a garden, you are seeing the same as your friend is seeing. Don't make this mistake – because if your friend has trained his eyes for some other purpose, he will see one thing and you will see something else.

The senses are nothing but a training. Through them we see what we have trained ourselves to see. The ears are the same: we gradually hear what we have trained them to hear. Taste depends on training. Have you noticed? – the first time you drank coffee it tasted horrible. You have to train yourself to drink coffee. The first time you drank alcohol, you probably didn't like it at all.

Mulla Nasruddin's wife was always nagging him to stop drinking. He wouldn't listen, he wouldn't hear her. One day she went to the tavern. Mulla was a little frightened because she had never been to the tavern before, and it wasn't right for a lady from a decent household to go to such a place. But now nothing could be done about it. She sat down beside him and said, "Today I will also drink. If you won't listen to me, it must be because there is something good about alcohol. I want to try it."

Mulla couldn't say, "You shouldn't drink alcohol because it is a bad thing to do" — this was what his wife was always telling him. He was in trouble. What could he say except, "All right"?

He poured some wine into a cup and said, "Drink!"

She took a mouthful and spat it out straight away. It was so bitter, so sour! "How can you drink such a rotten, foul-smelling thing?" she asked.

"Just listen to you!" the Mulla replied, "and you always thought I was having fun here!"

One has to practice. When you train yourself, even bitter things taste sweet. It is only a matter of training.

One day Mulla Nasruddin told me, "Once I was going on a train and the girl sitting on the seat opposite me was a radio announcer."

I asked him, "How did you know? Did you ask her?"

"No", he said, "I didn't ask her."

"Then how did you know she was a radio announcer?"

He replied, "When I asked her the time, she said, 'It is a quarter past nine. Always use Godrej locks and sleep with peace of mind.' Then I knew that she was a radio announcer."

Habits form. If you examine your life you will realize that everything you see, hear and understand is a matter of training and has no relationship with the truth. When your senses are trained in one particular way, it becomes difficult for them to take any other path.

Children see the world in a certain way. You know that, because you were once a child and there are probably children in your home now. They see things in their own particular way. Adults see them in a different way. Old people see them in a third way. If you are old, you will know this. If you are honest, you will remember that you saw the world one way when you were a child and a different way when you were more mature. The world is the same. Now you are old and you have a third way of looking at the world.

So the senses cannot be trusted. Your perception is akin to your passion. When you were a child you were not interested in beautiful men or women, or in money. You were completely involved in your toys and games. That was your world. When you became an adult your games and toys were left behind and you became interested in beauty, in the body, in wealth and position. Then came old age and even those toys were left behind. That is why an old man and a young man cannot communicate with each other. Even a father and his son find it difficult to talk. They cannot, because they both speak different languages. Their way of looking at life is different. Do you think a mother and a son are able to communicate? It is very difficult. Neither the son understands the father, nor the father the son – not at all – because the son cannot see from the father's vantage point. And the father has seen things from where the son now stands but found them all to be meaningless. Now it is difficult for him to see things that way again.

If you look carefully, you will see that your experience changes every day. And when your experience changes, your eyes will see differently. When you are young, you see bodies. When you are old, your body becomes decrepit and decayed and you begin to see death in every single body. You glimpse death even in the youngest body, because you know death is coming. When you look at even the most beautiful body, you see graves and the flames of the funeral pyre.

A woman took her two children to visit a female friend. When her friend saw the younger child she said, "His eyes are like his mother's, just like yours."

The mother replied, "And his forehead is just like his father's."

The older child said, "But he has got my pajamas."

When everything belongs to someone else – his eyes to his mother and his forehead to his father – why should the older child keep quiet? His younger brother is wearing his pajamas! Everyone thinks that *his* way of seeing things is the correct way. The boy is not interested in his brother's forehead or his eyes. He is simply annoyed that he is wearing his pajamas!

If you try to remember this a little every day, you will find that you can escape from this habit. Your soul doesn't belong to your childhood, your youth or your old age – because the soul has no age, and the soul has no habits either. The soul is just pure awareness.

To withdraw your senses like a tortoise means to put all of your old habits to one side and then to see. If you see in accordance with your old habits, everything will be seen as wrong: you will see only what you have learnt to see, your vision will not be pure. There will be glasses, colored glasses, over your vision. The world will appear to be colored.

...Withdraw your senses,
And bring awareness to your breath.

Gradually, take your energy away from your senses. If you cannot do this for twenty-four hours a day, at least do it for a couple of hours every day. And I suggest that you will even benefit if you simply sit like a tortoise for some time – exactly like a tortoise. Put down a mattress and sit on it like a tortoise, drawing your hands and legs inwards. Sit like a child in the mother's womb, in *garbhasana*, the womb posture. Just imagine yourself as a tortoise, with all your senses contracted, and your head drawn in as well. If you wish, cover yourself with a sheet. Be completely closed in upon yourself. Now bring your awareness to your breath. You will find great bliss and your awareness will increase enormously. A very deep consciousness will be born in you. Don't expect all this to happen on the very first day. Have a little patience.

I call this *kurmasana*, the tortoise posture. Make this posture, because the posture of your body also supports the shaping of your inner state. Sit contracted, exactly like a tortoise, covered with a sheet – a hard shell formed around you, a shield, withdrawn inside yourself, and your eyes shut. Begin to watch the breath as it goes slowly in and out. The breath goes out: watch it go. The breath comes in: watch it come in. Don't even say that the breath is going out, or that the breath is coming in. Just keep watching. Sometimes you will fail. At times you will forget because of your old habits. When you remember again, don't get angry and cry out, "I am a worthless sinner because my mind has strayed!" When you remember, bring your mind back to the breath, without any regrets. There is no need to repent. If the mind strays, it strays. Accept that as well. Come back again quietly to your meditation. Otherwise, what happens? First the mind wanders, then you begin to repent – and it strays off in your repentance. This will be double trouble.

In the beginning, the mind will certainly stray. Success will not happen immediately. You are going against the practice of many lifetimes; it will take some time. Accept distraction as natural and then, when the mind wanders, let it. When you remember again, bring your awareness back to your breathing – without any feeling of repentance, without any guilt; without thinking that you have blundered or greatly sinned. Nothing has happened. It is natural.

Without utterance, with no beads in your hands,
Remembrance continues within.
Only a rare person experiences this,
It is the grace of the master, says Daya.

Without utterance, with no beads in your hands.... And Daya says there is no need to hold a string of beads in your hand, that there is no need to utter words with your tongue:

Without utterance, with no beads in your hands,
Remembrance continues within.

Just let there be awareness within you. And don't let Daya's use of the word remembrance mislead you. You think remembrance means sitting down and reciting "Rama-Rama, Rama-Rama, Rama-Rama." That belongs to the tongue. We are talking about what Nanak calls *ajapa jap*, unchanted chanting.

Without utterance, with no beads in your hands,
Remembrance continues within.

Let your remembrance remain, let your awareness remain. There is a little trouble with words. When we say "Let your remembrance remain there," the question always arises in our minds, "Remembrance of whom?" Remembrance of yourself, awareness of yourself.

If remembrance of someone else remains, your mind is continuing. Let the awareness of "am-ness" be present there. The awareness that this is you, should remain. It shouldn't be allowed to be lost. No curtain should cover it, no word should come and cover it.

Only a rare person experiences this,
It is the grace of the master, says Daya.

And Daya says that what can be experienced in this state has been experienced only by some very rare people. She is right. This experience is very near, very close at hand. If you reach out just a little, it can be yours. But you don't reach out. This wealth is yours, but you have never claimed it.

...It is the grace of the master, says Daya.

Daya adds, "I couldn't have done this by myself; this has happened because of the master's blessings, the master's grace." It is necessary to understand this too. In every possible way you must give up your sense of being a doer. If you keep the idea that you are meditating, then the sense of being the doer has already come in through the back door. You can sit in the tortoise posture, and still feel arrogant because you are meditating. You wonder whether someone might be watching you meditating. When you are finished, perhaps you look around to see if anyone saw you or not, whether they knew what you were doing or not.

If you bring even a tiny sense of the doer into the meditation you will have missed again. Ego has entered, the mind has returned. That is why the disciple says: "Whatever is to happen will happen because of the master's grace: my actions can achieve nothing. Nothing can happen because of my doing; by my doing only the world has happened. My actions have only spread a web of sorrow over life. This ray of happiness cannot happen through my doing." So the disciple says: "This is the master's doing, the master's grace."

...It is the grace of the master, says Daya.

You must realize that this is not something that the master literally gives to you. This is just the way the disciple feels and it is very helpful for him. The master's grace is the same towards everyone – to the one to whom something is happening and also to the one to whom it has not yet happened. If this had happened because of the grace of the master, then it should have happened to all of his disciples. This sense of the grace of the master is a device on the path of the disciple: it doesn't allow any ego to be created in him. And when this ego is not created, then no obstacle stands in the way and the thing happens. That it happens through the grace of the master only means: "It will not happen because of me, because of anything I have done. Out of my doing only ego is created, and the ego has to be destroyed, the ego has to be dispersed."

Now this is difficult. If you work without a master and something begins to happen, you will naturally feel, "I have done it." There is no one else there. It will bring out an arrogance in you.... If you are doing it in a surrendered state at the feet of your master, then whenever something happens you will remember the master – that it happened through his grace. Your ego will not harden. It will get no nourishment, it will dry out and disperse.

When the disciple chants the unchantable mantra,
Keeping awareness in his lotus-heart,
Pure knowledge manifests there,
Removing all stains of darkness.

Keeping awareness in his lotus-heart.... So first bring awareness to your breath. When awareness of your breath is accomplished and you begin to see the coming and going of your breath with an attitude of witnessing, when the rosary of your breath revolves in front of you, then remove your awareness from your breath and apply it to your lotus-heart.

Have you sometimes seen a lotus flower with its petals closed? When you open the petals, you will find a small empty spot within them. The lotus-heart is like that too. When it opens, there is an empty space within. When you open a rose there is an empty place there too, just like the lotus flower. Sometimes, when the lotus closes at night, the black bee gets caught in that empty space. The bee sits there all day, totally engrossed, drunk with the honey, and does not feel like flying away. When the lotus shuts at night, the black bee still remains sitting, and gets caught in it.

There is an empty space inside your heart, just like there is inside the lotus. You have to lock the black bee of awareness inside your empty heart.

First, bring awareness to your breath. You will experience two things: "I am not the body" and "I am not the breath." This is a negative experience; you have found out what you are not. Your second task is to find out, "What am I?" You have found out that "I am not the body." This is a big discovery. You have discovered that "I am not breath either." This is an even bigger finding. The negative work is over, but now you must find out who you are.

So see your heart as a lotus. It is just a symbol so that you can understand the whole thing better. Now take your awareness into your beating heart, to where the breath comes and sets the heart in motion, to where the thread of the breath lingers. You have seen the breath, now go beyond the breath, deeper, into the beating of your heart.

See your heart as a lotus. In that empty space within the lotus where the black bee is sometimes caught... sit in a meditative posture in that empty space. Put your awareness right there, your consciousness, your remembrance.

When the disciple chants the unchantable mantra,
Keeping awareness in his lotus-heart...

This is what Nanak calls unchanted chanting: no chanting is taking place and no one is chanting. Then the real chanting begins. Now for the first time you hear the sound of existence – it is called *omkar*. Now you hear the sound of *om*; now, you are not doing it. And this sound is not coming from outside of you. Sitting in the tortoise posture, you have left your ears and all other senses far behind. The sound that you are hearing inside yourself has always been there, but you couldn't hear it because of the noise outside....

It is like a *veena* being played very softly inside a house: if there is a great noise outside, then you will not hear the *veena*; or like when someone plays the flute softly and it cannot be heard because of the noise of the market. This is the situation with this inner sound. The yogis call it *anahat nad*, the unstruck sound. This sound is already resounding there within you – it is the music of your heart, and for the first time you start hearing it. This is the unchanted chanting. You are not the doer of it, you are simply a witness. You simply hear it, you simply experience:

Unnecessarily hermits have invited this blame
For the meaningless use of their rosary beads,
This name is so precious,
It should be recited countless times.
What is the joy of it if it is recited with counting?

Once, I was a guest at someone's house. My host brought
out his account book to show me. I asked him why. He said,
"I would like you to look at it. It is not an account book,
I have written 'Rama-Rama' in it at least ten million
times by now."

This man is dangerous. If he ever meets God…which is
impossible because even God will be afraid of him, thinking,
"This man will come with his account books in his hands."
So I told him a story:

I have heard that one day a pious devotee died. And on the
same day a sinner who lived across the road from the devotee
also died. The angels came to drag the pious man to hell and
the sinner to heaven. The pious devotee was very angry. He
was sure that there must have been some mistake somewhere.
So he said, "Please go back and check. There seems to have
been some mistake. This sort of thing happens all the time
on earth in the government offices – but now the same thing
is going on here too! You have simply mixed things up. I have
recited the holy name all my life. Every morning and evening
I sang devotional songs, *bhajans*, I did everything – I omitted
nothing. Day and night I chanted the name of Rama. Can't
you see the shawl I am wearing? It has the name of Rama
written all over it! How dare you try to take me to hell! I
have never seen that sinner chanting Rama's name at all."

The angels replied, "There has been no mistake. But if you
wish, you can come along with us and lodge a complaint."
So the man went with them.

With great arrogance, he said to God, "What is going on
here? What sort of justice is this? This is sheer injustice. I

have done so much chanting, I have sung so many devotional songs — I always got up at three in the morning to sing them. The whole village is my witness, because I used a loudspeaker. This is not just my word, the whole village is my witness. You must have heard me too. It isn't right to send me to hell. The other man never sang any devotional songs. On the contrary, he used to come to my place saying, 'Brother, let me sleep. Don't make so much noise at three o'clock in the morning, or at least don't use the loudspeaker. If you want to chant in your own home, I have no objection.' This man was always creating obstacles for me and now he is the one who is being taken to heaven!"

God replied, "That's why. He was on my side. You have been tormenting me the whole time, so I cannot let you live in heaven. If you do, I will have to move to hell. You will bore me senseless. You did not allow me a moment's peace. At three o'clock in the morning I too am asleep and you created so much nuisance with your microphone and loudspeakers."

This man who has written the name of God ten million times is dangerous. He even keeps accounts with God.

Unnecessarily have hermits invited this blame
For the meaningless use of their rosary beads,
This name is so precious,
It should be recited countless times.
What is the joy of it
If it is recited with counting?

In reality, this name is such that if you utter it you are making a mistake. Don't try it. It is only when the stream flows within you, naturally, when the sound of omkar rises

within you day and night, continually – then, and only then
has the real chanting begun. The real chanting is unchanted.

When the disciple chants the unchantable mantra,
Keeping awareness in his lotus-heart,
Pure knowledge manifests there,
Removing all stains of darkness.

Pure knowledge manifests there.... Pure knowledge doesn't come
from the scriptures or from learning. It comes when you are
freed from your body, your breath – everything – and sit with
your consciousness centered in the lotus-heart. *Pure knowledge*
manifests there. Pure knowledge is born there: understanding,
experience, *samadhi, satori,* or whatever you want to call it. Pure
knowledge is born there, and with that knowledge, all
bondages are severed, all your sins disappear...

...Removing all stains of darkness.

All dirt is washed away, that is why this is called pure
knowledge, because all dirt disappears.

People ask me how they can wash away the dirt of their past
lives' actions. This is difficult. You won't be able to clean
away the stains, because if you try to wash them, you will
only make them dirtier. This dirt has accumulated because
of your own doing. It won't disappear by your doing, by your
washing it. This dirt from your past actions has accumulated
because of your doing in the first place. Now you want to
do more, you want to do something else. They can be
cleansed only when you become a non-doer. The stains
of your past actions will go only when you drown in non-
action, when you become a non-doer. Then the divine will

wash them away, you cannot wash them. You knew how to spoil yourself, and you have done that well. Now don't spoil things any further by trying to correct things.

Please don't try to clean up this web of your past actions. Descend into your awareness, then all your impurities will be washed away in the rain of that awareness. In this way, within a moment, you will become as pure as you should be – something you could not become even after lifetimes of effort on your part. Your effort cannot be greater than yourself, it can only be the same as you. Whatever you do will have your imprint on it, your signature on it. That is why I teach you no actions and no rites – just meditation. Drown in meditation.

Meditation means that you stand in front of the divine just as you are: dirty, bedraggled, with all your imperfections – just like a child who has been playing outside in the dust and dirt then comes and stands in front of his mother with his clothes torn and covered with mud. Stand in the presence of the divine the way a child stands before his parent. As soon as you do, you will be cleansed. As soon as you stop, you will be showered on.

...Pure knowledge manifests there,
Removing all stains of darkness.

So don't be caught in calculations, the way so many others are caught. They say that they have accumulated these stains of past actions over many lives, therefore enlightenment cannot happen in just one day, in just one moment. They have accumulated these stains of past actions over many lives and it will take many lives to wash them away, to erase them.

That way you will never be free; that way liberation is impossible, it can never happen, because it will take so many lifetimes to wash them away. And, of course, you will not be sitting idle all this time, you will go on doing things, so the stains from your actions will also go on increasing.

No, your doings have no relationship with your liberation – the relationship is with your surrender. Bow down and say to the divine: "Wash me if you want me to be washed, keep me dirty if you want me to remain dirty. Do as you wish." But you can only say this when you reach the lotus-heart, not before that. Before that, you have no trace of the divine. Until then you will say this in front of the temple idols that you have made. They are your doing, your making. Where will you find the divine in them? The divine is enthroned in the lotus-heart; its throne is in that empty space.

Where there is no death and no blaze,
No cold and no heat, O my brother...

Daya says: "My brother, this phenomenon takes place in the lotus-heart, where there is no death and no fire." Death does not exist there, nor pain, nor time:...*no cold and no heat, O my brother.* Nothing is cold there, nothing hot. All dualities have come to rest, all dualities have fallen. There, two eyes have become one.

...Seeing my home, my ultimate abode,
The unfathomable mystery of life is revealed, says Daya.

Seeing one's ultimate state, the mystery of life becomes clear – that we have been unnecessarily distressed, worrying whether to give up evil, whether to become a good person, a *sadhu*; whether to do this or that, to go to this temple or that one, to follow this scripture or another one, this religion or a different one.... And we have been wandering around to no purpose.

...Seeing my home, my ultimate abode,
The unfathomable mystery of life is revealed, says Daya.

The scripture of all scriptures, the veda of all *Vedas*, the deepest secret, the mystery of all mysteries has been found. What is that mystery? The mystery is that human beings are bound by their own actions and are unable to be free because of their further actions. If a person becomes a non-doer, a witness, he is free, he is free here and now.

Seeing the peerless beauty of the beloved,
The light of ten million suns shines.

And seeing the beauty of the beloved in the nothingness of the lotus-heart... *Seeing the peerless beauty of the beloved...* seeing the incomparable beauty of the beloved, the most precious *one... the light of ten million suns shines* — as though ten million suns have arisen.

All of life's sorrows are erased,
And the essence of happiness is manifest, says Daya.

Your sorrows will be erased and the essence of happiness, the key to your happiness, will become manifest. The key of that happiness is our intrinsic self-nature. Because we asked others for it, we remained poor and wretched. Because we became beggars, we remained beggars. But our nature is to be an emperor. We have been forever wandering because we never looked within ourselves.

All of life's sorrows are erased,
And the essence of happiness is manifest, says Daya.

The shine of countless suns,
The miraculous light manifests,
It feels dazzling,
But the mind becomes cool and refreshed.

The shine of countless suns.... So many suns rising together! For birth after birth there has been only darkness in your life. You have lit millions of lamps and they have all died. You trusted these lamps, and none was of any use to you. Those you considered to be your dear ones turned out to be strangers. All your boats proved to be paper boats.

The shine of countless suns.... And now the light of countless suns has suddenly appeared: *The miraculous light manifests.* And this light is miraculous.

What is miraculous in this light?

...It feels dazzling,
But the mind becomes cool and refreshed.

The miraculousness is that it is both light and fire – on the one hand the eyes are dazzled and on the other hand the mind is becoming cool and refreshed. A cool fire; hence miraculous! The divine is a cool fire.

The Jews have the sweetest story about this. When Moses saw God on Mount Sinai, he could not understand what was happening – because God appeared as a fire in a living bush, and the bush did not burn. A flame appeared and its blaze began to rise upwards towards the sky, but the bush remained fresh and green. Its leaves remained green, its flowers did not wither. Nothing burned. Moses could not understand what was happening. A cool fire? It had never been seen.

The Jews have no explanation for this story. The story is supposed to have happened to Moses, but then the Jews didn't bother much to investigate its significance. But this Mount Sinai is nowhere else...it is the name of the ultimate height of consciousness within man. That is why all religions have chosen their places of pilgrimage on high mountains. These are symbols. Badrinath and Kedarnath are the pilgrimage sites high on the Himalayas. And the concept about Kailash is that Shiva lives there, that it is the god's abode. These are symbols, these are symbols of the heights of the soul. When your consciousness reaches to its ultimate height, its highest peak, that is Kailash – and that is where Shiva resides. If you search for it in the Himalayas you will not find it anywhere. It is within you. Sinai is also about the inner mountain peak, and you are the bush Moses was talking about. The divine fire will arise within you and you will be left utterly astonished: *The shine of countless suns....* It will be as though thousands of suns rose together within you:

...The miraculous light manifests,
It feels dazzling,
But the mind becomes cool and refreshed.

And the miracle is that this glaring light will make your eyes close, but your mind will be cooled.

There is much light without lightning...

And the miracle will be that although there is no lightning, the sky is full of light. There is no sun and yet it feels as though thousands of suns have risen.

There is much light without lightning.... The source is not visible anywhere, but there is an abundance of light, so it is a light without a source. The first thing is that the light is cool. The second thing is that the light has no source. Any light which has a source runs out. This light never runs out. If you fill a lamp with oil and light it, sooner or later the oil will run out and the lamp will be extinguished. If the oil is enough for one night, the lamp will burn all night. If it is enough for a month, it will burn for a month.

Scientists say that the sun has been burning for billions of years, but that it will not burn for ever — perhaps just four or five million years more. It is becoming cooler day by day. Its light is running out, its oil is running out, its energy is waning. One day the sun will also cool down.

The divine is the only light which will never burn out, it is eternal — because it has no other source, no fuel, no oil, no cause beyond itself.

There is much light without lightning,
And it is showering without clouds.

And Daya says this is what is happening. There are no clouds to be seen and yet it is raining. Where is this shower of bliss coming from, when there are no clouds to be seen? There is no lightning anywhere and yet the sky is so bright! It is a very symbolic statement.

Watching this ceaselessly
My heart is delighted, says Daya.

And now Daya tells us that she is totally engrossed; her heart is dancing, and she watches on and on. What she sees within herself, this experience, this realization, this face-to-face meeting is enough to keep watching for the whole of eternity. Its bliss never ends, its delight never ends.

There is much light without lightning,
And it is showering without clouds.
Watching this ceaselessly
My heart is delighted, says Daya.

The world is a falsehood,
A deceptive well in the form of the body.
You are consciousness,
The abode of a marvelous bliss.

The world is a falsehood, a deceptive well in the form of the body.... Whatever we see in this world is changeable, ephemeral; now it is here and now it is not — just like a dewdrop. *The world is a falsehood....*

It is like the source of water which a thirsty person imagines he sees in the desert because of his own thirst. It is a projection. There is no source of water, but it becomes visible because of his own thirst, it becomes projected because of this thirst. He is so thirsty that he assumes that there must be water there. When you are very thirsty, you start imagining things. Whatever your deepest passion, desire and longing is, you start searching for it on the outside, assuming it must be there, it should be there, because you want it so deeply. It is your longing forming on the outer screen.

So Daya says, *The world is a falsehood....* Everything continues to change in this world; there is nothing you can hold on

to. In fact, whatever you see are your own dreams – in reality
they have no existence. They are lies – like a garden in the
desert.

...A deceptive well in the form of the body.

The water that you imagine you are seeing in this well of
the body is your own false belief. It isn't really there. There
is no water in this body which can give you contentment.
There is no water in this body which can quench your thirst.

There is an incident in the life of Jesus. Once he came to a
well by the side of the road. He was exhausted. A woman was
there drawing water. She must have been an outcast. He said
to the woman, "I am thirsty, please give me some water."

The woman replied, "Forgive me, but you seem to belong to
a noble family. I am a poor untouchable wretch. No one
drinks the water I fetch. Please wait a while, someone else is
sure to come along and will get you water. You can take water
from that person."

Jesus said, "Don't worry. Remember this: if you give me
water, I will give you such water that when you drink it, your
thirst will be quenched forever. The water you give me can
only quench my thirst for a short time. It cannot be
quenched for ever. But I have another kind of water and
I will give you that. As soon as you drink it, your inner thirst
will be quenched."

The world is a falsehood,
A deceptive well in the form of the body.

The well of your body is empty; totally dry and barren. There is no water there. You see water in the body because you are thirsty. A thirsty person can see water anywhere. A thirsty person assumes there must be water wherever he looks.

Have you noticed? You believe a thing to be there if you really want it badly enough. If you are waiting for a letter from someone, then as soon as you see the postman coming you will go to the door and imagine that the letter has already come, that it has already arrived. If you are waiting for someone and even a gust of wind touches the door you will run to it, thinking that the guest has arrived.

You see whatever you badly want to see. If someone tells you that there is a cremation ground on the way to a certain place, you will see ghosts and spirits as you pass that spot — and you may have passed along that same road many times before and never seen any ghosts, any spirits. Because you had not been told about the crematorium you didn't project anything. Once you find out about the crematorium, the trouble begins. You won't be able to pass that way in the same manner again. There will be troubles, you will invite troubles. It is your beliefs and fears that become the ghosts.

The world is a falsehood,
A deceptive well in the form of the body.
You are consciousness,
The abode of a marvelous bliss.

Daya says: *You are consciousness, the abode of a marvelous bliss.* Consciousness is your self-nature, the divine is your self-nature; you are the abode of a marvelous bliss! *Raso vai sah:* That indeed is the juice! *Sachchidananda:* Truth, consciousness, bliss.

But you know this only if you go inside yourself. There is only one place of pilgrimage worth going to, only one temple worth entering, only one peak worth attaining and only one depth worth reaching: you are That. The Upanishads say, *Tattvamasi, Svetketu!* This means: Svetketu, That art thou.

But I can understand your difficulty. It is everyone's difficulty. Until you have had this experience, these things will seem farfetched. Until now, you have had only one experience of life: sorrow, pain, hell. You have forgotten the very language of heaven — you don't even remember how to rejoice. And what goes on in the name of religion is absolute hypocrisy; it is a web woven by priests and *pundits*. You find nothing in the world and the temples have all fallen into the hands of hypocrites. There is nothing to be found in the world, or in the temples. Man is caught in a noose.

Here, I am not going to point you to some outer temple. The outer temples have not delivered the goods. And here I am not going to tell you about any outer scriptures either; the outer scriptures have also not delivered the goods.

There is only one thing worth doing here: to dig within yourself. There is only one thing worth learning here: learn to know your own self.

Put aside all rubbish and go within yourself. There will be hindrances, obstacles; the habits of many lifetimes will stand in the way. But they can all be overcome, because they are all contrary to and not in tune with your self-nature. It may be difficult to find that which is in tune with your self-nature, but it is not impossible. And it may be difficult to demolish that which is contrary to your self-nature — but it is not impossible. If you want, you can certainly get there.

The destination of your pilgrimage is not far away. It is in the closest place – it lives in your heart.

When the disciple chants the unchantable mantra,
Keeping awareness in his lotus-heart,
Pure knowledge manifests there,
Removing all stains of darkness.

Let me repeat these three things so that you remember them well. One: Learn to be a tortoise. There is a great secret hidden in becoming a tortoise. Become a tortoise for at least one hour each day out of the twenty-four. As you become that tortoise, you will find that the divine has begun to descend in you. That is the meaning of the mythological incarnation of the divine as a tortoise.

The second thing: Once you become a tortoise, then bring your total awareness to your breath. And when you slowly begin to experience that you are not the body, you are not the breath.... And remember, I don't mean that you are to repeat: "I am not the body, I am not the breath" – otherwise any realization will be false. Just wait, let it happen of its own accord. There is no hurry anyway.... The danger is that we can learn to repeat like parrots. You will sit like a tortoise, applying your awareness to your breath for half an hour, or perhaps even less, and then you will begin to parrot: "I am not the body, I am not the breath." That will falsify the whole thing. Don't repeat anything. Just sit. Let it happen, let it enter your experience. One day it will come, and on that day all your doors will open. On the day that "I am not the body, I am not the breath" enters your experience – enthrone this awareness in the emptiness of your lotus-heart.

On that day, tell yourself: "I am a lotus." Turn your remembrance, your perception, your awareness into a black bee and place it in the middle of the lotus. Then, all else happens there on its own.

Seeing the peerless beauty of the beloved,
The light of ten million suns shines.
All of life's sorrows are erased,
And the essence of happiness is manifest, says Daya....

There is much light without lightning,
And it is showering without clouds.
Watching this ceaselessly
My heart is delighted, says Daya.

Enough for today.

8

RUNNING WITH YOUR WHOLE HEART

The first question:

Osho,

Yesterday you said that those who search will miss. And one of your famous books is called, "Those Who Search Find." What is the truth? Please explain.

Mulla Nasruddin and his friend were traveling home on a certain path. Suddenly, his friend grabbed Nasruddin's arm, saying, "Quick! Run! Escape!" and dragged him into a nearby hotel. Breathing heavily, Mulla followed him nervously. Then he asked, "What's wrong? Are the people who do vasectomies coming? Why are you so agitated?"

His friend said, "This is even more dangerous than a vasectomy. Did you see my wife coming this way talking with my girlfriend?"

The Mulla carefully looked out and said, "Praise be to Allah for saving me in such a beautiful manner."

His friend asked him, "Why did you say that Allah has saved you so well?"

Mulla replied, "You were wrong on one point. Your wife is not talking to your girlfriend. My wife is talking to my girlfriend."

But both the things can be true simultaneously; there is no contradiction in this. "Those who search find" and "Those who search lose" can both be true at the same time. There is no contradiction. Try to understand this. The one who never searches will never find anything, but the one who only goes on searching will also never find anything. There comes a day when you must seek and there comes a day when you must stop this seeking and simply sit down. "Those who search find" is the first step. Half of the journey involves searching. The other half takes place when you stop searching.

Buddha searched for six years. He toiled ceaselessly. He did whatever he could, whatever his teachers told him to do. He practiced yoga, he recited mantras, he followed great asceticism, he fasted, he was devout, he meditated... he did everything. He drowned himself completely in all of these activities, but with no result.

One day, he decided that he had tried everything, that he was tired and it seemed that there was no sense in doing any of these things — because when you are doing something, the doer remains. The one who is searching remains in the search. Whatsoever you do, yoga, asceticism, meditation — they all create an ego. You think, "I am meditating: I am a meditator. I am practicing devotion: I am a devotee." You continue to build a subtle ego. And the essence of all religions is that as long as there is ego, you will not find the divine — because the ego itself is the obstacle. As long as *you* are, you won't find the divine. Its arrival is possible only when you disappear.

When you stop standing between the divine and yourself, only then can the meeting take place. You are there, remaining stubbornly present like a rock. Once you earned money, so you were a wealthy man. Now you are earning devotion, so you are a devotee. But the "you" remains. Admittedly, it is a little better than before: this ego is more like gold, the old ego was only sticks and stones, rubbish. This new ego is precious. The old ego was ordinary; this new one is extraordinary. The first one was the ego of a worldly person; the second is that of a religious person. But ego is still ego.

So, after continuously searching for six years, he was tired in every way, but his ego was not. The ego never tires of doing things. It never tires from running on and on. But one day, after six years' relentless searching, Buddha saw that everything was futile. He had found nothing in the world, and nothing in this *sannyas*, this renunciation. That night he even dropped sannyas from his mind. He sat down under a tree. He didn't meditate, or practice devotion or asceticism, or any kind of chanting. That night he simply slept.

It was a wonderful sleep. He had never slept like that before, because there had always been some desire or other in his mind – sometimes the desire to obtain wealth, sometimes the desire to attain to the divine, sometimes the desire to possess the world, sometimes the desire to possess the truth.... When there is desire, there are dreams, and when there are dreams, there is tension. And how can there be sleep when there is tension, how can there be rest?

That night, for the first time, he rested. And in that rest truth descended upon him. When his eyes opened the next morning.... The Buddhist scriptures say something wonderful, they say, "Eyes opened in the morning." They don't say that he opened his eyes in the morning, because now there was no one in him to open the eyes. When the sleep was complete, the eyes opened. The eyes opened just like a flower opens in the morning, and Buddha's opening eyes saw the last star setting. *The world is the last morning star.* The last star was about to set. As the sparkling, shimmering star was beginning to disappear, the last traces of his self, the last touch of ego also shimmered and dissolved. In that instant, enlightenment happened.

Later, whenever people asked Buddha how he attained enlightenment, he would say, "It is a difficult question to answer, because I did not attain enlightenment through my doing. I attained enlightenment the day I did nothing. But it is also true that if I had not done what I did, this state of non-doing would not have arisen."

Understand this. The truth was not attained directly because of his six years of ascetic fervor. But if Buddha had sat under the tree without those six years of ascetic practices, that moment of relaxation would not have been possible either. You can go and sit there – the tree is still in Bodh Gaya – and you might decide not to do those six years of hard work, because there was no substance to it, it did not achieve anything…. Buddha achieved enlightenment through sitting. He sat down. You too can sit down and be like Buddha on the outside: still. But inside? – you will not have known the experience of spending six years doing ascetic practices without attaining anything, you will not have realized that nothing can be attained through doing, and so it is futile to do anything. You will be lacking that experience. And even if you do lie down under the *bodhi* tree, the tree will not be the same tree of enlightenment for you as it was for Buddha.

So what can we say? Did Buddha become enlightened through doing or through non-doing? We must answer: both together. He attained because of doing and non-doing — both. Through doing he attained to the state of non-doing and through non-doing he attained to the truth. Hence "Those who search, find" is the first step. It took the Buddha six years. Sometimes, when I say to you, "Don't search, or you will miss," I am talking about this final step — so you don't just go on searching, turning six years into sixty years and six lifetimes — because if you only go on searching, then too you will never arrive.

You have to run to reach your destination, but then you must also stop — because if you get addicted to running, even as you are approaching your destination you will run past it. You won't stop even when you reach it! You can reach the destination only if you stop. If you are a skilled runner, a good runner, and forget how to stop — if you have simply kept running for many lives, you will not know how to stop even when you reach your destination. You will go on running past it. You will meet your destination only when you stop. But only the person who has run with his whole heart, with utter totality, will know how to stop.

So both statements are true at the same time. Many times it will seem to you there are contradictions in my statements, but whenever it is so, know that you are making a mistake somewhere. However contradictory my statements may appear to be, they can never be truly contradictory. There has to be a thread in there somewhere which will join them all together. There has to be a bridge somewhere which you are

not seeing, there is a connecting link which is not visible to
you. Whenever you find two of my statements are
contradicting each other — and you will find thousands
of contradictory statements in my talks — if you search
carefully, you will always find that there only appears to be
a contradiction, in reality there is none. Both things can be
there simultaneously. And I also want to tell you that
something can happen only when both are there simultaneously.

The second question:

Osho,

*You told us not to support the mind and to be natural about life. Are
they both possible at the same time or are they separate activities? Please
be compassionate and explain this.*

You ask, "Are they both possible at the same time?" They
are both possible only when they are together. They will never
be possible if they are separate from one another because they
are not really two things, but just one: the two sides of the
same coin. I have talked about one side at one time, and about
the other at another.

Understand this: "You told us not to support the mind and
to be natural about life" — both of these create the two sides
of the same coin. The mind is unnatural. What is mind?
It is born whenever you go against your self-nature. The mind
is created through effort. That is why animals don't have
minds — because they cannot go against self-nature. They
never go astray. They are just as nature has made them. Hence
they have no need for minds. Human beings have a mind: it
is man's glory and his difficulty — both. It is man's glory that

he has mind, and this is also his only problem, his only turmoil. The mind means that human beings can go against self nature if they wish. This is man's freedom.

Have you ever seen an animal doing *shirshasana*, a headstand? I don't mean in a circus, because circus animals have been perverted by human beings. Let us not talk about them. Have you ever seen an animal performing a headstand in the jungle? An animal cannot even imagine doing a headstand. And they must laugh when they see you performing a headstand: "What on earth has happened to these people? They were standing quite well on their feet and now they are standing on their heads!"

Man searches for ways of going beyond nature, of rising above nature, of being different. When sexual desire arises, man tries to impose celibacy on himself. When anger arises, he tries to suppress it and smile. This is also the man's glory, this is his beauty. But whenever he goes against nature, sorrows, tensions and restlessness are born. Whenever you are in accord with nature there is relaxation, there is restfulness in life.

So the mind is something you have created. This is why very young children don't have a mind. It takes time to create the mind. The mind is created by the society, by the family, through education, through collective conditioning, through culture and civilization.

Have you ever tried to recall your earliest years? If you have, you can remember back to when you were three or four years old, but not before then. Why? – because then you had no mind, so you cannot remember before then. Your memory goes back to that point and becomes stuck. You need to have a mind to remember, so you remember only after your mind started being born. If you look back, you can remember when you were four or five. Before that everything is dark, the page is blank. The mind had not yet been created, the mechanism was not yet ready.

So the mind only becomes properly active by the age of four or five. Then it goes on becoming increasingly skillful. An old man has an old mind. We forgive children when they make mistakes. We say, "They are only children." Why? We are saying, "The poor things don't yet have a mind. They are still children. Their minds are not yet developed and conditioned to that extent. It will take a while; at this point they can be forgiven." We also forgive a mad person, because he is mad. When a drunkard causes trouble we forgive him too, because he is drunk. Why do we do this? When he is drunk, it means his mind is unconscious. Right now, the mechanism that keeps control is unconscious, so he is like a child.

Once a drunkard abused Akbar. Akbar used to go out riding an elephant. The drunkard climbed onto the roof of his house and showered abuse on the emperor to his heart's content. Akbar was amazed to see this weak, scrawny man talking so courageously. He had the man caught and brought to the court. After being locked up all night, the man was summoned in the morning and asked why he had been so abusive.

He fell at the feet of the emperor and said, "I didn't abuse you. It wasn't me who abused you."

Akbar said, "Are you calling me a liar? I saw you with my own eyes. There is no need for any other witness. It was you. You abused me."

The man replied, "I didn't say that I wasn't that person. I was drunk. It was the alcohol which abused you. Please forgive me. It wasn't my fault. If there is any fault, it was that I drank alcohol. Punish me for that, but not for abusing you."

The man's words appealed to Akbar. What is the point of punishing a drunk? He should be forgiven. A mad person can be forgiven. If a mad person kills someone and it can be proved in a court of law that he is mad, then that is the end of the matter — because how can you expect someone who doesn't have a mind to act in a responsible way? So a child, a mad person and a drunk can all be forgiven because either they don't have a mind, or the mind is suspended, or it has become unconscious for the time, or it is deformed.

The entire human civilization and culture is based on the mind. Mind is the basis of our humanity. Understand this. Animals don't have a mind and enlightened ones don't have a mind. There is some similarity between the two — some. There is a great difference, but also some similarity. The enlightened ones have gone beyond the mind and the animals don't yet have a mind. The enlightened ones are like children. The mind has not yet been born in a child and the enlightened one has put his mind aside. This is a great revolution — to put the mind aside — because if your goodness has its roots in your mind, what kind of goodness will that be? It will disappear the moment you drink a little alcohol. If your virtue has its roots in your mind, it cannot be very deep. Real virtue has to be natural. That is the difference between a so-called virtuous person and an enlightened mystic. A virtuous person is one who is good through constant effort. An enlightened mystic is good without any effort, naturally. A virtuous person can turn into a bad person, an enlightened one can never become evil – there is no way. But at a certain point, a virtuous person can turn into a bad person.

Understand it this way. There is a good person who says that he has never stolen anything. You ask him, "What would you do if you found one hundred thousand rupees lying by the side of the road? Would you pick them up? There is nothing to fear, no one is watching you, there are no police around. Would you pick up the money?"

The man may say, "Never, I am not a thief."

But then if you said, "What if it were ten million rupees?" the man might begin to think. There is always a limit. He may be able to control himself up to a hundred thousand rupees, because his mind would tell him that it is more important not to be a thief than to have a hundred thousand rupees, but at ten million, or a hundred million rupees, his conviction will begin to shake.

One day Mulla Nasruddin was riding in a lift and there was only one other person there, a beautiful woman. The opportunity was too good to miss. He said, "Will you sleep with me tonight if I give you a thousand rupees?"

The woman was angry. She said, "What do you think I am?"

Nasruddin replied, "What if I give you ten thousand rupees?"
The woman took his hand and said, "Okay."
Again Nasruddin asked, "And if I give you ten rupees?"
She retorted, "What do you think I am?"

He replied, "Now I know! Now we are just bargaining. If you consent to ten thousand, it is merely a matter of settling a price. I know what you are, I understand how far your virtue extends. Now we are merely bargaining...because there is also the matter of what I can afford. Where would I get ten thousand?"

The virtuous person has a limit, the enlightened one has no limits – because the mind sets boundaries, but meditation doesn't. The virtuous person is good from his mind; the enlightened one is good through meditation – naturally, spontaneously. This is the difference between conduct and consciousness. Conduct depends on the mind and consciousness is freedom, ultimate freedom. The person who lives through his innermost consciousness is a religious person and the one who lives through a code of conduct is a moral person.

Now understand your question: "You told us not to support the mind and to be natural about life." To be natural means that you understand all that you have been doing through your mind. For example, you may be an angry person and you may have somehow suppressed your anger by using your mind. Now this compassion is not real – it is an imposed one, superficial, a painted one. On the outside you show compassion, on the inside you are angry. Now this state cannot bring a revolution into your life. You will remain as hollow as you are now, as hypocritical as you always were. I tell you not to suppress your anger, but to understand it. Because by understanding it a moment comes, a time comes, when you become free of anger and don't have to impose compassion on yourself. When you become free of anger and compassion has arisen within you of its own accord, I call this naturalness.

Many times you impose your own meanings on my use of this term naturalness. I am aware of that too. These are dangerous matters: when I ask you to be natural, you think that you must become an animal. I understand your difficulty. You have never known any other way of being natural. "Natural" has only one meaning for you: the moment you remove your mind you fall to the lowest level, some trouble gets created. Somehow you are keeping yourself under control – otherwise you would have run away long ago with your neighbor's wife. "And now he tells me to be natural!"

Have you heard this story?

A very rich man went to a psychologist to ask for some advice. He said, "It is very difficult in my office because no one wants to work. They sit around all day with their feet on their desks. Some read the newspaper; everyone gossips. When I go there they pretend to work, but in fact they do nothing. One day I even asked them, 'Brothers, whenever I come here you are startled and begin to work, but as soon as I leave you stop again. How can things go on like this? Do you want me to harass you twenty-four hours a day? How many people can I harass at one time? The office is too big.' So what do you think I should do?"

The psychologist said, "Do one thing. Put some signs around the office. They will bring great results. The signs should say, 'Don't put off until tomorrow what you can do today, because tomorrow never comes. Do it now!'"

The man put up the signs. The following day the psychologist came to see if there was some outcome from the signs. The rich man was beating his hand against his head. He said, "Outcome? Plenty! The cashier has disappeared with all my money, the clerk has escaped with the typist, and the office boy has threatened to beat me with his shoes as soon as I come out of my office. He has always wanted to do it, but has never implemented the idea thinking, 'I'll do it tomorrow.' Now I am afraid to leave my corner. Great signs you suggested! They have certainly brought results!"

I also know that when you hear me tell you to be natural the question always arises in you: So what shall I do? I am a cashier at an establishment, should I run away with the cash? Or I have been planning to murder someone for a while; I have not done it thinking that it is such a bad thing to do. Now that I have to be natural, I wonder – should I commit that murder? Should I steal something, should I cheat? What shall I do?

Try to understand what happens in your mind as soon as I ask you to be natural. These are the things your mind has suppressed.

When I ask you to be natural, you should sit down for an hour and meditate on what you would do if you were natural. Make a list, write all these things down. In doing this, you will understand many strange things about the mind. All the things that you would want to do if you were natural are suppressed within you. They are like pus, they are your wounds.

I am not asking you to be an animal. When I tell you to become natural I mean don't suppress, rather, understand. If anger is suppressed inside you then understand your anger, meditate on anger. Don't hide it in a dark corner deep within yourself. Don't put it in the basement, bring it into the light – because when light falls on your anger, it will disperse. And when your anger disappears, the energy that was attached to it is what turns into compassion. And this compassion is natural, spontaneous.

Brutality is natural for animals, and saintliness is natural for the saint. But saintliness comes from meditation, never from repression. You can be a good person through repression, but you will be sitting with your diseases festering inside you. There will be utter hell within you. You may smile on the outside, but your inside will remain full of tears. It will change nothing for you. You may become a better citizen, society may bestow many honors upon you – but these are all external things. Inside, you will have no sense of honoring yourself, no respect for yourself. You will reproach yourself, hate yourself, condemn yourself – because although you may be able to deceive the whole world, how can you deceive yourself? I also understand that you can take only the meaning that you are capable of.

A washerman's donkey fell under a truck and was killed. The driver of the truck tried to console the owner. He said, "Don't worry, brother – trust me. I will replace him."

"No, no," said the washerman with tears in his eyes, "You cannot replace him."

The driver asked, "Why can't I replace him?"

The washerman replied, "You are not as strong as he was. He used to carry heavy loads of washing from my home to the washing *ghats* – back and forth. You won't be strong enough to travel from the ghats to my home and back again."

When the washerman's donkey died, there was only one thing the owner could think of – his donkey. He couldn't do anything without that donkey. The truck driver offered to replace him. The washerman must have studied the driver carefully and decided he would be of no use to him at all; he was not as strong as the donkey was. The washerman had his own level of understanding, his own desires. The donkey that had just died had totally supported him.

I have heard about a villager who bought a clock. One day the clock stopped. The man opened it up, and there was a dead mosquito inside. He began to cry loudly. Another man asked him, "Brother, why are you crying like this? What is it? Has someone died? You are wailing so loudly."

He replied, "Yes brother. Someone has died. The driver of my clock is dead."

A villager cannot possibly know how a clock works. The poor man opened up the clock and saw a dead mosquito inside. He said, "That explains it. That is why the clock has stopped."

Every individual has his own level of understanding. If something is said that is beyond that level, you will translate it into your own terms of understanding. You do the same here. I say one thing here, you translate it into another. I say: "Be natural," and you start thinking that this is a difficult matter: "Should I become wicked, a sinner, a criminal?" You have suppressed your feelings of crime and wickedness: you are sitting cross-legged on them. As soon as you move a little, they raise their head like a snake. You dare not move because of the possibility of sin. But what kind of a life is this? It is a life of sorrow. Whatever you suppress has to be suppressed every day, and whatever you suppress will wait to take its revenge, it will explode in a moment of weakness.

So a good man can murder someone, even though you had never thought him capable of committing such a crime. You cannot even imagine that he might murder anyone. He seemed to be a straightforward and good man. But the appearance is not the real person. Inside him, there is something else.

Many times your friends have deceived you. You could not even have imagined that they would deceive you, or prove to be dishonest. Man is one thing on the inside and another thing on the outside. Because of your mind you appear to be one thing on the outside, but are something else on the inside. When I tell you to be natural, I am saying: Look again at what you have suppressed. Because of suppression there is neither freedom from it, nor transformation, nor revolution. If you want to revolutionize your life, observe every single thing that you have suppressed. Through this constant observation, this continuous watching, the recognition of anger becomes your liberation from it, the recognition of greed becomes your liberation from it, the recognition of sexuality becomes your liberation from it.

I don't even hint that you should take the vow of celibacy, because that would be false. If you go to the so-called saints and monks, they will ask you to take some vow or other, especially the vow of celibacy. I don't talk to you about the vow of celibacy. I tell you: Look at your sexual desire with penetrating eyes, focus your full awareness on your sexual desire. Recognize it fully. It is in that recognition that you will become free of it. Knowing is liberation and ignorance is bondage. If you look at your sexual desire with a totally penetrating eye you will become free from it. And celibacy is the fruit of that freedom.

Celibacy is not something you take a vow about. A celibacy that is based on a vow is false, hollow, imposed. And a celibate who has taken a vow will always be scared, nervous: "I hope I don't see a woman!" Now where can you run to? — women are everywhere! And how can you run away? — because the woman is inside you as well. Half of you comes from woman — where can you run to? Your mother has made one half of you and your father the other half: you are half woman and half man. Woman lives within you. How can you escape from her? You may escape to the forest, you may sit hiding in a cave, but the woman within you, who is a half of you, will arise in your dreams.

You have read many stories about seers and so-called saints who were besieged by the *apsaras*, the dancing girls from the court of the god, Indra. Where are these apsaras? Why should they bother? What interest can they have in seers and saints?

Just think about it — can't these apsaras find some healthy young men? These dry and withered seers and saints, almost dead, waiting to die — all they can do is somehow turn their beads devoutly, that's all — they don't have the strength for anything else! What apsara would pay attention to these poor creatures sitting in their caves? Go and try it for yourself. Do you think that if you go and sit in a cave in the Himalayas some Hema Malini is going to come to you? No one will come! Keep sitting there, waiting and thinking that some apsara will come.... No one will come. I tell you that even if the seers and saints go and knock on the apsaras' doors, those doors won't open. The police will come and take those holy men away.

But these stories tell a truth, they cannot lie, because they are created from the experience of many centuries. These apsaras don't come from the outside — they are the inner woman who takes shape in your intense imagination. She doesn't come from outside of you, she is a part of your imagination. When a man is hungry for many days, his imagination will see food wherever he looks.

I have heard:

Heinrich Heine, a famous German poet, has written that once he lost his way in a forest. For three days he had no food. He continued to wander, lost. And then, on the night of the full moon, as he wrote in his diary: "I was astonished. It appeared as if a loaf of bread was swimming across the sky. I had never felt like that before. I have spent my whole life writing poetry. I have always seen beautiful faces, beautiful women in the face of the moon, but that night it looked like a loaf of bread. I was amazed. I rubbed my eyes with my hands to see what had happened to me...."

But when you are hungry even the moon turns to bread. If your stomach is empty you will see food everywhere. You have suppressed your sexual desire...now how long can you sit in a cave? — because it will raise its serpent's head. And this sexual desire can arise so powerfully that you may feel that the woman is standing there, right in front of you. She may seem so real that you could touch her, caress her. The so-called seers and saints were not deceived. There *was* a woman, but it was an image of their own intense imaginations, it was a projection.

So you won't become a celibate by simply taking a vow of celibacy, or become a charitable man by taking a vow to be charitable. You won't become peaceful by taking a vow not to be angry. These things will still affect your mind.

So when I tell you to be free of your mind, I mean for you to bring your awareness to each and every process which un-settles you: your sexual desire, your greed, your attachment, your envy. Understand them, recognize them, go deeply into them. If you can experience them deeply they will lose their hold over you, and you will lose your hold on them — because when you watch them with awareness you will find that they are nothing, they are futile. The realization of futility is the key to liberation.

You have been angry many times, but what substance does anger have? What have you gained from it? What I am saying about it cannot solve your problem. You will have to enter the whole process of your own anger totally and see if there is any substance to it or not. If you accept this just because

I am saying it is so, it will be just another repression. You must pass through your own process.

You should take it as if no one has ever been born before you, as if you are the first man, as if you are Adam. Adam had no scriptures, no saints. He was very fortunate indeed. There was no tradition. No one had left anything behind for him. Whatever he found out, he found out for himself. When anger arose in him, he must have known anger, recognized anger firsthand. There was no one to tell him that anger is bad: to stop it, to control it. There was no one to tell him anything. Imagine that you are the first man on the earth: there has been no saint before you, no sage or seer to explain anything to you. Move on, imagining yourself to be the first man, so that you can recognize all your life processes completely. True recognition cannot take place if you begin with a bias – if you are beginning from the premise that sexual desire is bad, then you have already accepted it.

People come to me. I ask them, "Why do you accept that sexual desire is bad when you don't know this for yourself?" They say that the saints and seers have told them this. Let the saints and seers say so – what difference does that make? They might be wrong! After all, how many saints and seers are there? There are more non-saints and non-seers.

Do you believe in democracy, or not? Then test it by taking a vote. Most votes will be in favor of sexual desire. Ninety-nine out of a hundred will go in favor of sexual desire. This one man may be deluded – why is there such a desperate need to accept what he says? When ninety-nine percent of people say that sex is their very life, there must be some depth to sexual desire, some strong hold, some irrepressible grip.

You won't be able to find release from this irrepressible grip by just taking a vow or observing some rules, you must go deep down to its unfathomable depths. You must apply the energy of meditation to it. You must go into it in an unbiased way. Good or bad, don't make any choice. Know it, recognize it, and let your decision come out of this process of knowing and recognizing. Then that decision will become your release.

When I ask you to become natural, all I mean is that you shouldn't suppress your life processes, you shouldn't become inimical to them. They are all just steps you have to climb. It is by climbing these steps that a human being reaches to the divine. You can turn these steps into stumbling blocks or you can use them as a ladder. It all depends on you.

It often happens this way: try to understand this. Everyone's diseases are not similar. One person may have a lot of sexual passion in his life, but he may not be very greedy. He cannot be, because his sexual desire uses up all his energy. So this man will conquer greed early without much difficulty. He may even begin to preach to others that there is nothing to greed: "I have given it up just like that! I took a vow and the matter was finished." Don't fall for this story, because his life situation is different from yours. Each person's life situation is as different as their fingerprints.

Whenever someone went to Gurdjieff he would say: "First of all, search for the biggest disorder in your life, your greatest disease. Everything else will depend on that" — because it often happens that a man fights with very small diseases and goes on enjoying the pleasure of beating them, but these are not the real problems. It is necessary to identify the real problem. It is possible that sexual desire may be the most irrepressible, the most powerful passion in a person's life. That person can easily give up wealth, or position. He can easily give up anger. But from this you shouldn't deduce that it will be easy for everyone to give up anger. If anger is the basic problem in your life, you can easily give up sexual desire. Everyone has to find out which is the basic problem in his own life situation.

I have heard:

A woman was buying toys at a toy shop. The shopkeeper was a young woman. She handed the doll to the customer and said, "Look at this doll. As soon as you put it to bed, it will close its eyes and sleep like a real child."

The woman laughed. She said, "My dear, it seems that you have never had the experience of putting a real child to sleep."

A real child doesn't fall asleep so easily. If you try to make her sleep, she will open her eyes and be wide awake. The harder you try, the louder she will scream. The woman was right when she said, "My dear, it seems that you have never had the experience of putting a real child to sleep."

At times it often happens that those who have put dolls to sleep are ready to advise others: "You too can put them to sleep. There is nothing to it. It is easy." But don't fall into the delusion that something which was easy for someone else will be easy for you too; that something that was difficult for someone else will also be difficult for you. Someone else's advice is seldom of any use. It often causes harm and provides no benefit.

That is why you will find many contradictions in what I am saying — because I give different advice to different people. My focus is on the person, not on the advice. I say one thing to one person and something else to another one. Sometimes I say something which shows the contradiction very clearly. My eyes are on you, not on what I am saying. I don't care about principles; they are not important. People are not made for principles, principles are made for people. People are not made for the scriptures, the scriptures have been made for people.

My attention is on you. When I look at you, I tell you what seems to be meaningful for you. It is not necessarily right for another person as well.

Don't catch hold of it and start applying it to the other person. Don't think that if I have said something to you, then that is that: now you know the truth. Truth incarnates differently for each person.

Mulla Nasruddin shouted loudly from the sitting room while his wife was working in the kitchen, "Hey, something is burning in the kitchen. What is it?"

"My head," his wife answered angrily.
Mulla replied, "That's all right then. I thought it was the vegetables, or some other food."

Everyone has their own values. To the Mulla, the vegetables are more valuable than his wife. If her head burns, that is nothing to worry about.

Bear this in mind: meditate on whatever is most valuable to

you. First of all, find out which of the six enemies mentioned in the scriptures — sexual desire, anger, greed, attachment, pride, envy — which one of them is your chief enemy. Begin with that one. Once that has been settled, the remaining five can easily be got rid of. Once you have been released from that root disease — if you can conquer that number one enemy — the rest will follow. Focus on your chief enemy. And don't be in a hurry: meditate on it every day. Don't try to escape it; try to be natural. If you are feeling that it is dangerous to be natural outside, that the consequences will be too big....

For example: say anger is your main enemy. If you start expressing it spontaneously as and when it comes, you may lose your job, your wife may divorce you, your parents may throw you out of the house, all sorts of problems may arise.... So sit down in some solitary place in your room and become angry there. Close all the doors and windows. Be absolutely angry. Keep a symbolic image of the object of your anger, just as you keep a symbol of God, a statue. If you are angry with your boss, make a drawing of him on a piece of paper and then take your shoe, and hit him to your heart's content. At first you will be puzzled: What are you doing? What is this madness? But soon, within a few minutes, you will find that you have started feeling enthusiastic, that you have started having fun.

In Japan they have done these experiments in a big way. Following the advice of psychologists, some large Japanese companies have set up effigies of their owners. It is natural for the workers to feel resentful towards their bosses, so when a clerk is displeased, he can go to a separate room where the effigies are — of the foreman or of the manager or of the owner – and hit them. When he comes back, he feels happy, lighter. He works faster, with more interest. Gradually he even begins to feel pity, "Oh I beat that poor man needlessly!" Some goodwill towards the man may even arise in him.

You should try this. In the West many experiments of this sort are taking place and have proved to be very effective. Instead of beating your wife, keep a pillow with her name on it, or if you wish her photograph, and beat that. In this way no violence will take place, but your whole anger will be released. After a while you will find that you are shaking with anger: your hands and feet will be trembling, your eyes red, your teeth clenched. When your anger reaches this stage and you begin to burn with the flames of its fire, sit down with your eyes closed and watch this burning – because only now can you see your anger. You cannot see things their seed form, you can only see them when they blossom fully. Meditate on your anger at this stage.

Mahavira is the first Indian mystic to include *raudra*, the raging, and *aart*, the wretched, among the four forms of meditation. Mahavira gave a name to what is happening now in the West. The meditation on anger he calls raudra, and the meditation on sorrow he calls aart. If you are sad, don't suppress your sorrow: go into your room, beat your chest, roll around, and live out your sorrow in its entirety. And when the clouds of sorrow draw in upon you from all directions, then sit down peacefully in their midst and become a witness. You will be astonished. The key has come into your hands. And in this way gradually you will find that one day you have become natural – not like an animal, but like a sage. You will have gone beyond the mind.

The third question:

Osho,

*Pleasure, love, meditation, understanding, surrender — none of these seem
to be helping me. Yet you have accepted me: this is already your great
compassion. I leave it all up to you.*

Listen! Listen once more:

If you can do even this much, everything can happen. If you
can just allow, let to, everything can happen. If you can trust
even this much, if you can have even this much faith, everything can happen. Because trust is a great alchemy, it is a great
revolution.

Let the story not end having just attained to love
Extend the plot by bringing in a tide.
Having launched the boat of love, now drown,
Extend the life of remembrance and drown.
To what avail if you find your destination
On the first expedition?
How can you say that you have walked
If you have not stumbled and wandered off your way?
Walk in such a way
That your destination can be proud of you,
That your footsteps are honored like lighted lamps.
Enough of being wounded,
Of facing storms and pounding waves,
Bedeck the stream with bell anklets, and drown.
Create one final storm and drown.
How can I tell you? Your drowning is your crossing over.
Losing this way for the sake of the other is your victory.
Bury your heart to protect the comfort of the other's heart.

Offer your life
So that the other's sacred fire ritual can be completed.

Listen! Listen once more:

How can I tell you? Your drowning is your crossing over.

If you can gather the capacity to drown in me, if you can do only this much – to enter into a let-go, a complete let-go, a total let-go – then in this very surrender you will find that a revolution has already happened. In this very surrender you will become integrated, whole – because you have let go of every last bit of everything you have. You have crystallized yourself totally, fully; in doing this one thing all your parts have united to become one indivisible whole. And in this undividedness, in this indivisibility, you will have the first taste of your soul. Hence surrender is a key, and trust is a key without equal.

The god of the waves will ask for a sacrifice,
Decorate the wealth of your dreams,
Offer the libation of your tears – and drown.
Drown your desires, and then yourself.
Forget the other shore, first plunge into every whirlpool,
Kiss every wave as you embrace it.
Where you drown will become a holy place of light,
Where you are laid to earth will become a temple.
Let there be pain but no tears, O my friend,
Live your life this way.
Having awakened the man of your heart, drown.
Having helped the new sun dawn, drown.
Do not struggle: all must go one day,
You must drown one day, whether you like it or not.

Life is a guest who does not stay for long,
One day you must bid it farewell with a song.
Breath is a game of chess, which you are bound to lose,
By drinking poison you will find deathlessness — try it!
Look at the present dark state of humanity.
Trample on time and drown.
Having decorated a crown of song, drown.
Having awakened the man of your heart, drown.
Having helped the new sun dawn, drown.

Surrender means that you have tried everything, as much as
you can; you have failed in every possible way…. This is what
I was just telling you about in the story of Buddha. For six
years he tried in every possible way, and when nothing
happened he gave up and just sat down. This is the meaning
of trust, the meaning of surrender: "I couldn't manage it —
so what to do? I have done everything, it is time to stop."
But then don't keep coming back to it again and again. Once
you have stopped, stay that way. Then leave it in the hands
of existence, then live according to the will of existence.
Move as it moves you. And if this movement is good, so
be it; and if it is bad, so be it. If it makes you a good person,
a virtuous person, so be it. If it makes you a bad person, then
be a bad person, then let go of it all unconditionally. Then
don't judge, thinking: "If it makes me good, then that is great,
but if it makes me bad, then I will hinder it." Such an attitude
won't do.

To surrender means that whatsoever happens, whether it is
good or bad, let it be so.

Having awakened the man of your heart, drown.
Having helped the new sun dawn, drown.

And nothing is lost by this drowning.

Do not struggle: all must go one day,
You must drown one day, whether you like it or not.

Sooner or later, death will come and you will drown. To be a
disciple means that you have drowned in the master before
death comes. The ancient scriptures say "The master
is death." Sometimes there are such amazing statements in
the ancient scriptures – "The master is death"! The very
meaning of the master is that you die in the master, you
drown in the master. Then whatever happens, will happen.
You no longer exist. Now the bookkeeping is no longer in
your hands.

The question is from Swami Mohan Bharti.

So I only say: Drown, Mohan.

The fourth question:

Beloved Osho,

I am alone, I seek a fellow traveler,
I search for you by night and by day.
Come into my heart, settle in my eyes.
Come into my colorful nights of love.
How beautiful is this fragrant night
But you are not by my side.
I am alone, I seek a fellow traveler
I search for you by night and by day.

This is important, it is worth understanding. As long as you
think you are alone you will keep searching – but you will
not find. Because your search is due to your loneliness, you

will search for the wrong thing. You are not interested in the divine, you are just trying to fill your loneliness. You are not interested in the search of the divine; you are alone, and you simply want a companion, a fellow traveler. *You* are important. You don't want to be a fellow traveler to the divine, you want to make the divine your fellow traveler.

I constantly say that there are two kinds of people in the world. The first kind are those who are ready to go with the truth, and the second kind are those who want the truth to come with them. There is a great difference between the two. Do you want to be a companion to the divine, or do you merely want to make the divine your companion? There is a great difference. Don't think that it is just a question of a few words changing place, that nothing else is different. If you want to make the divine your companion, you want to use the divine.

You are alone. At times you have tried to fill your heart with your wife but it has not happened. At other times you tried to fill your heart with your friends and again nothing happened. Sometimes you tried to fill it with position and prestige, and still nothing happened. In the club houses, in the crowd, in the bazaar, in the shop, you have tried to fill your heart in a thousand different ways, and every time you were defeated, your heart was never filled. So now you say you want to fill it up with the divine. "I am alone, I seek a fellow traveler...."

But this is not the attitude of a devotee. A devotee's attitude is quite different. And there is a great difference between loneliness and aloneness. There is an aloneness that comes when you are filled with bliss. Aloneness means you are filled with your own presence. You are engrossed in the awareness of yourself, alone. We call this solitude. And there is the loneliness that comes when you are afflicted by the absence of the other, you have no awareness of your presence; the other person is absent and his absence pierces you like a thorn. There is a vast difference between loneliness and solitude, aloneness. In loneliness, one cries. Sitting in aloneness you are blissful, delighted, joyous.

The song that you have written is a song of loneliness. "I am alone, I seek a fellow traveler." There is a weeping in it, there are tears in it, there is an emptiness in it.

"I search for you by night and by day,
Come into my heart, settle in my eyes.
Come into my colorful nights of love."

You still think about the divine in the same way you think about your wife or your beloved. Not much has changed. You have imposed the same old lust, the same old attachment, the same old desire upon the divine.

"How beautiful is this fragrant night
But you are not by my side."

You are sad — because the night is so fragrant, life is so happy.... But you are sad, because your beloved is not by your side.

"I am alone, I seek a fellow traveler,
I search for you by night and by day."

You can go on searching, but you won't find it. One thing is certain, you will not get it even though you go on

searching forever. You can search in the evening and in the
morning, in the day and the night. You can go on searching.
This is what you have been doing for many lives: you have
not given up this habit, this old addiction. You continue
searching, but there is something fundamentally wrong with
your search.

I want to say to you that you should become blissful in your
aloneness, you should become joyous in your solitude.
Turn your solitude into *samadhi*, into superconsciousness.
Don't weep. Don't be a beggar. Don't beg the divine to give
you anything. Whoever begs, misses. As soon as you beg your
prayer is spoiled, defiled.

I want to say to you that on the day you sit in supreme
bliss, flowering like a lotus, fragrant, the divine will come
searching for you. On that day the divine will come to you,
entering through the door of your bliss – not through your
tear-filled eyes but through your song, through your exquisite
fragrance.

You are searching for God, but because you are searching you
will not find him. Do something so that he comes looking
for you; only then will you find him. Where can you really
search for him? Think about it! Do you know where he is?
You can search in the morning and in the evening, but where
will you search? You are sure to search in all the wrong places,
because you don't know his correct address. You don't even
know what he looks like.

Even if you do meet him, how will you recognize him? Just
think: even if the divine came and stood at your door today,
would you recognize him? No, you would not. You would

not be able to because you have never seen him before, so how can you recognize him now? So far, no one has introduced you to him, and you have never met him. If he suddenly appeared at your door today, you would simply shut your door again. You would say, "Go away. What are you doing here? Is something the matter? Why are you standing here?"

You cannot recognize God, and you cannot search for him. Where will you search for him? How will you recognize him? No. You should do something that will make him search for you.

That is the difference. The one on the path of knowledge is searching for the divine, but it is the divine who searches for the devotee. A devotee is engrossed in his own bliss. He dances, he is happy in his ecstatic joy. And keep this in mind: even if the devotee sometimes cries his tears are tears of joy, not of sorrow, not of pain or sadness, not of complaint. They are tears of his gratitude, they flow from his fullness. He knows that if he doesn't flow through his tears, there is nothing else he can do. He has no other way to flow. He flows through his voice, he flows through his dance, he flows through his tears. Sometimes he laughs, sometimes he cries.... Do you remember? – Daya has said: *He laughs...he cries, he rises and falls.... This is very paradoxical.... He puts his feet in one spot but they land elsewhere.... This is very paradoxical.*

A devotee is in drunken ecstasy, he lives in rapture. He has drunk the wine of his own bliss. The divine comes looking for him. The feeling of the devotee is not that "I am alone." The feeling of the devotee is something different.

From the first ray of dawn, to the last touch of night,
A soft, exuding fragrance stays with me.
I am never alone.

Understand this difference, reflect on it well. Your question
is: "I am alone, I seek a fellow traveler, I search for you by
night and by day." This is the talk of a lover, not of a devotee.
A devotee talks more like this:

From the first ray of dawn, to the last touch of night,
A soft, exuding fragrance stays with me —
I am never alone.
My eyes are all three measures of time,
The stars are jewels on my lofty forehead,
The emperor of time himself carries
The palanquin of my progress on his shoulders.
I am the last brink of darkness, receive my light,
Embrace me with your infant hands.
I am the truth that stands unmoving
And beyond all arguments,
Accept me — simply, naturally.
From the churning deliberation of questions,
To the humble salutations and offerings of love,
Your final promise walks with me
And I am never alone.
My feet have touched the limits
In every direction and beyond,
Life and death are forever balanced in my breath,
Dreams blossom as flowers on the earth,
My imagination is the very covering of the horizon.
The soft, fragrant breeze along the lane
Returned, thus lost,

And as I slept restfully through the storms
Its fragrance sullied my body again
That had been washed clean by the tides.
From the recurring, piercing pain
To the downpouring of falling tears,
Some remembrance, demolishing all barriers,
Walks along with me –
I am never alone.

The devotee feels: "I am never alone." The devotee feels: "I am suffused with the divine from all directions."

From the first ray of dawn, to the last touch of night,
A soft, exuding fragrance stays with me...

Where does this realization that "I am never alone" come from? It comes from drowning within one's own self, from descending deep into oneself.

There is a story about the life of Hazrat Mohammed. Abu Bakar, one of his companions, and Mohammed were being chased by their enemies. There were thousands of enemies, whereas Abu Bakar and Mohammed were all alone. They hid in a mountain cave as their enemies searched for them. Horses were galloping around everywhere. Mohammed sat, absolutely unconcerned, whereas Abu Bakar was trembling with fear. Eventually he said, "My lord, you are so composed. The situation is perilous. There are so many enemies. For how long can we escape? We don't have much longer to live. The sound of horses' hooves is coming closer every moment. There are only two of us and a thousand of them."

Mohammed laughed. "You fool!" he said. "Two? There are

three of us. There may be a thousand of them but there are three of us."

Abu Bakar looked all around. He said, "What do you mean? Are you joking? There are only two of us. I can't see anyone else."

Mohammed said, "Look again, look carefully. We are three. You have forgotten to count God."

From the first ray of dawn, to the last touch of night...
I am never alone.

There is a similar incident in the life of St. Theresa. She wanted to build a church – a big church. So one day she gathered all the people of the village together. She was a poor ascetic, a penniless woman. She said, "We must build a big church, like no other church on this earth." But the people said, "You are crazy! How can we? How much money do you have?"

In the currency of that country she had the equivalent of one *paisa*. She took it out and said, "This is what I have. The church will be built. It must be built. I will invest all that I have."

The people began to laugh. They said, "You are mad! You have only one paisa and you think you can build the church with that?"

She replied, "You only see my hand and the paisa in it. You don't see God standing next to me. One paisa from Theresa and the boundless wealth of God...there will be no limit to the size of this church."

From the first ray of dawn, to the last touch of night...
I am never alone.

And the church was built — it still stands today. And people say that there is no other church like it in the whole world. It was built out of the trust of this one devotee. It was built out of that feeling that "I am not alone."

Give up talking about loneliness. Otherwise you will keep wandering around forever. If you enjoy crying, that is something else. It is another matter if you have begun to enjoy this running around — but you will not find the divine this way.

The first step towards finding the divine is to settle down wherever you are, as you are; to be blissful, delighted, ecstatic. Your fragrance will bring him to you. He will come, drawn by the fragile threads of your fragrance. Your noise will not reach him, but the fragrance of your life will. God will come, like a bee to a flower. Just work on your worthiness.

The fifth question:

Beloved Osho,

Am I to dance in the meditations or is it my body that has to dance?

Right now, you are not, so only your body can dance. One day, when you arrive, then *you* can also dance. As of now, you are not; there is only your body.

Why do you raise such questions at this point? Although you have heard about the soul, you have not yet known it. Although you have read about the soul, you have not yet experienced it. Right now, you are just the body. Right now, the soul is just a dream. You cannot make a dream dance. How can you make something dance which doesn't exist? Right now, it is enough if you let the body dance. Let what you have dance. Begin with the body.

People come to me and say that they want to take *sannyas*, but they want "inner sannyas." They say, "What is the point in outer sannyas?" I say to them, "Where is your interiority? I am ready, I will give you inner sannyas, but where is your interiority? Right now there is nothing but your outside. Where is your inside? I can color your inside – if it is there! But right now there is no inside, so I will begin by coloring your clothes. That, at least, is a symbol, a beginning."

When the outer is colored, slowly slowly we will color the inside as well. We have to begin somewhere, and it has to begin from where you are. It cannot begin from where you are not. You talk of the inner, but what is inside you? Have you ever closed your eyes to see what is inside you? Even when you close your eyes, they still only see what is outside you. You close your eyes and you still see the shop, the market-place, your friends, your family – but all these are on the outside, you are not seeing the inside yet. You close your eyes and your thoughts begin to move. All this is external.

Thoughts are as external to you as objects are. You will know the inside when no remembrance of objects remains there, no stream of thoughts; when only you, only consciousness remains. Then you will know your inside. If you know that, you are already a *sannyasin*. Right now, you have no idea of the inside. But man is very dishonest; he is not interested in moving and so he starts talking about the places where he is not. He says "inner sannyas."

Now you ask: "Am I to dance in the meditation or is it my body that has to dance?" You already believe that you are separate from your body. If you have come to know this, it doesn't matter whether you dance or not. But look at it: do you really know this? The very purpose of your dancing here is so that, in some way, you can come to know your interiority. The dancing is just a starting place for that. Once you find your interiority, after that it is up to you. It has happened in both ways: some danced, and some did not. Meera danced, Daya danced, Sahajo danced, Chaitanya danced. Buddha didn't, Mahavira didn't. Once it has happened inside you, you will not even need to ask. Then, whatever comes naturally from within you.... If that is dancing, dance; if it is not, don't. But these questions will only arise after you have reached inside yourself. You are raising questions that are hypothetical, academic.

One day Mulla Nasruddin rushed to the hospital, got off his scooter and went inside. He asked the doctor if a bed was available so that his wife could give birth to their baby. The doctor said, "You can't just walk in like that. You need to inform us beforehand. Fortunately, there is an empty bed. Bring your wife in. Where is she?"

Mulla Nasruddin said, "Don't worry. I only wanted to check the arrangements. I wanted to make sure she would be able to get a bed when the time comes."

Then the doctor asked, "When is your wife going to have the baby?"

Mulla Nasruddin said, "What are you talking about? I don't even have a wife yet. I am thinking of getting married."

The clever person makes all the preparations beforehand. Even though he is not yet married, he has already started preparing for the birth of his child.

Don't be in a hurry. Let the wedding take place first. The time will come for your soul, but right now first dance with your body. I know what you mean. You don't want to use your body to dance. You are looking for an excuse, thinking, "Let my body keep sitting and my soul can dance." Where will your soul dance? If you had a soul, the question would not arise. It is not that you don't have a soul, but just that you don't yet know it.

Always remember, begin your journey from where you are. Don't stop your journey by finding these kinds of excuses.

Become a flower,
And you will gain a fragrance.
Release it, be colorful,
Sing, color the world,
Adorn your beloved's hair —
For she has come to you
So beautifully dressed.
Become a flower,
Oh, become a flower.
Become a flower,
And you will gain a beauty,
You will gain a smile.

Let it radiate, and behold
Beauty will come to both heaven and earth.
Barren hearts
Will overflow with delight,
And you will become a home to many a poem,
You will be a sun of divine brilliance on this earth.
Become a flower,
And you will gain benediction.
The divine will meet you
Even before it meets with devotees.

But how can a person become a flower? He cannot become one in the ordinary sense. Man is not a plant. But when a person is full of delight, he becomes a flower. He radiates joy, just like a flower opening. When you are blissful, you become a flower; when you are sad, your petals close. Hence my emphasis on dance – because all your petals will open up when you dance wholeheartedly.

Become a flower,
And you will gain a fragrance.
Release it, be colorful,
Sing, color the world....
Become a flower,
And you will gain a beauty,
You will gain a smile.
Let it radiate, and behold
Beauty will come to both heaven and earth....
And you will become a home to many a poem,
You will be a sun of divine brilliance on this earth.
Become a flower,
And you will gain benediction.
The divine will meet you
Even before it meets with devotees.

Dance, don't be shy. Don't give way to small shynesses. If you give your body joy, then the shadow of your bliss will fall onto the heart that lies behind the body. Gradually, it will also become blissful, it will also begin to sway. When the heart sways, its shadow will fall onto your soul that is hidden behind the heart, and then the soul too will sway, the soul too will dance.

The sixth question:

Osho,

Are you only here for your disciples?

Is this why I am not allowed to meet you?

A disciple means one who has come to learn. And only the one who has come to learn can be taught. The one who has not come to learn will waste my time as well as his own. There is no need for us to meet. If you have come to learn, the doors are open for you.

But many times it happens that people come wanting to teach. The name of the gentleman who has asked this question is Brahmachari Sagun Chaitanya. I have seen his photo as well as his letter. He appears to be a pundit, and an extremely knowledgeable one. He is a brahmachari, a religious person practicing celibacy. He appears to know the scriptures very well.

Please don't be angry with Laxmi because she stopped you from meeting me. It is I who have stopped it. I have no interest in erudition. I have no interest in useless theories or idle talk. If you know, you know. Why waste my time and yours? If you don't know, then come. But then come feeling that you don't know.

It is very difficult to point out something to someone who is pretending to know. It is very difficult to awaken someone who is pretending to be asleep. And the most subtle ego in this world is that of knowledgeability, of erudition, of scriptural knowledge. I have no interest in these subtle egotists. If you know, you are indeed blessed. Why inconvenience yourself here? What will you find here? You already know, the matter is finished. But if you don't know, then leave all your rubbish outside the door when you come here. The very meaning of preparedness to learn is to come with an acceptance that you don't know, that you are ignorant. Then my doors are open to you.

A famous Russian mathematician by the name of P.D. Ouspensky went to see George Gurdjieff. Ouspensky was a world-famous mathematician. His book *Tertium Organum* was famous the whole world over. And nobody knew Gurdjieff; he was simply a mystic, a nobody.

When Ouspensky went to see Gurdjieff, it was like a renowned person coming to meet a nobody. Ouspensky was full of arrogance. Gurdjieff looked at him from head to toe, picked up a blank piece of paper and gave it to him. Gurdjieff told Ouspensky to go into the next room and write all that he knew on one side of the paper, and all that he didn't know on the other side. Ouspensky didn't understand what Gurdjieff meant. Gurdjieff replied, "We won't talk about what you already know. That would be a waste of time. We will only deal with what you do not know. So go into the next room — and let it be clear, because your face radiates knowledgeability."

It was a cold night, the snow was falling – a Russian night! When Ouspensky went into the next room, he began to perspire. The paper trembled in his hand. He tried very hard to write what he knew. But he must have been a very honest man. He couldn't think of a single thing that he could say he knew. "The soul, the universal soul, deliverance...what do I know?" He had written books, but the books were written based on secondhand information; it is not necessary to know anything to write a book. Most books do not come from knowing, they come from knowledgeability. He was shaken.

After an hour he returned and handed the blank piece of paper back to Gurdjieff, saying "I don't know anything. Please say what you have to say."

Gurdjieff replied, "We can begin. That will do."

People come here every day – so-called sannyasins, pundits and scholars of the scriptures. I have no interest in any of them, I don't even have one single moment for them. They should understand this very well. If they know, the matter is finished: they have my blessings. You know, so the matter is finished – may the divine bless you. But if you don't know, then come like a blank sheet of paper. Only then can something be done.

One thing is certain: why would anyone who knows bother to come here? What is the point of it? I don't go anywhere. You have come to me, so it is clear that you don't know. You have simply fallen into the false illusion that you do know but that is merely an illusion: nothing has happened to you, no shower of bliss has fallen upon you, no song has come to you, no moon has arisen. The light that you have been searching for has not yet dawned; you are still filled with darkness. That is why you are searching. But you are a great egoist, so you cannot accept that it has not happened to you.

Many times people come to me. Once a gentleman came who had been a sannyasin for thirty years. I had been avoiding him for a long time, because there was no point in his coming to meet me. But he kept persisting, so I said, "All right, I will see him."

I asked him straight away whether he had found it or not.

He replied, "What a question! At the very beginning, the first thing you ask me is whether I have found it or not."

I said, "I want to be clear from the start. If you have found it, the matter is over; if not, we may be able to do something together."

He began saying that no, he had not really found it; perhaps just a little....

I replied, "It has never happened that one has found just a little of God. This sounds just like surgery: you have his hand or his foot or, if nothing else, his appendix! The divine is indivisible. Truth is indivisible. You cannot break it into pieces. You have found a little bit...what are you saying? Have you run away with God's underwear or what? What is the matter?"

"No," he said, "I have not found him yet, I have only had a few glimpses."

I said, "Be honest. If you have had a glimpse, keep moving in that same direction. Why waste your time here? If you have had a glimpse, the matter is over. Keep moving in that same direction, and don't waste your time anywhere else, not with me either. You have had a glimpse – keep moving on."

Finally he said, "Why do you keep insisting? I have not even had a glimpse. I am ready to listen to you."

I said, "Now we can talk. Now it is clear – otherwise we would only argue."

People come to me and say, "You have said this, but such and such a scripture says something else." What can I tell them? Am I responsible for what is written in their scriptures? If what I say seems right, correct your scriptures. If what I say seems to be wrong, it is up to you and up to your scriptures. I have no trouble with this, not the slightest difficulty. You and your scriptures! – you can keep them! If you were getting something from them why did you come to me? You are not getting anything from them but you will not accept the fact. If I am different from your scriptures, but what I am saying appeals to you, then amend them. There are so many scriptures in the world. I am not here to keep account of what is written where.

The face of the friend who has asked this question shows his erudition and also shows that he has a mind which is always involved in arguments: "It says this in the scriptures, it doesn't say that in the scriptures." He is a disciple of Swami Chinmayananda. Naturally, as he is the disciple of a pundit, he reaches to the same heights that his master reaches to! So my door is closed to him. Come here with a light heart, come here when you have put your erudition aside. Then you will find my doors open.

Naturally your question itself says it. You ask: "Are you only here for your disciples?" Water is here for the thirsty, the master is here for his disciples. If you are a disciple, I am here for you. If you are not a disciple, then neither you are here for me nor am I here for you. The matter is finished. No connection is possible – and nothing will happen without a connection.

I want to say this to you:

There are altitudes beyond the great heights
Where your ambitions are hovering like eagles.
You have an ego that claims to know it all,
But there are truths beyond its reaches.
True, you have crossed some depths
But this is not the end,
There are depths beyond them.
What you had thought to be the destination
Was always just a place to rest that night.
Like the onion peels
There are layers upon layers.

One has to move on using the first as a stepping stone for the second. Certainly, one first comes into contact with pundits, because it is not possible to make direct contact with the one who knows. The first is a necessary precondition for the second. First, a person comes in contact with the scriptures, then he comes in contact with the true master. The first is the precondition for the second. But keep this in mind:

There are altitudes beyond the great heights
Where your ambitions are hovering like eagles.

If you are in search of those altitudes, if that is your desire,
then my doors are open to you. And my doors are open only
to those who really are on the search. If there is a thirst inside
you, a call, only then am I ready to shower on you. Otherwise your clothes will get wet for no reason at all; you will
be angry with me and you will say, "It has rained unnecessarily. Now I must go home and dry my clothes." I don't want
to inconvenience you in this way.

Opening up again and again, the cloud
Filled the earth's heart,
A bird kept calling from forest to forest,
"O beloved, O my beloved."
Thus love was endlessly showering with an open heart,
Thirst was longing as before, wordlessly,
The earth kept quietly, slowly, soaking up,
Henna fragrance filling the paths.
"O beloved, O my beloved" –
A bird kept calling from forest to forest.
They are flowing –
Carrying mountain-peak water on their heads,
Time is being drenched
Capturing a shower and a fragrance in the moment.
Rice plants dance
As the sickle of the horizon captures them.
"O beloved, O my beloved!" –
A bird kept calling from forest to forest.

When you become like a bird wandering from forest to forest
and calling out, "O beloved, O my beloved!" – only then are
you a disciple.

What is the meaning of a disciple? A disciple is one who is eager to learn, so eager that he is willing to lose everything – his erudition, his ego…all that he has done so far. If you set down your burden, I will take your hand in my hand. Otherwise, I have only a small amount of time, and in that small amount of time allow me to shower upon those whose throats are thirsty. Don't come and waste my time unnecessarily. I am only interested in those who are ready to receive.

The last question:

Osho,

From what I was to what I have become,

I did not even notice it…
Locking your eyes into mine, you stole my life.
The strings of my heart sing songs of Holi,
You have drenched me in color.

The question is from Anand Sita. If you come in this way something can happen, something can take place. Come like this – ready to be obliterated, ready to drown. If you come prepared to die, you will receive a new life.

I am not interested in giving you knowledge, but a new life. Nothing less than that is worth anything. But to be reborn, you must first experience the crucifixion.

Lakes unfold the boat sails,
Drunk with elixir, comes spring with joyous gait.
The wind is blue, the flowers red and yellow,
Half-sleeping dreams open their wings and soar up high,
The hands of the tesu trees hold gleaming torches,

Lakes unfold the boat sails.
Golden pollen showers everywhere.
A honeymoon feel caresses the butterfly's every limb,
The silver snow-shawl slips from the mountain peaks,
And lakes unfold the boat sails.

Here, I am unfolding boat sails. If you want to travel, get in
the boat. I am not interested in debates or arguments. Here,
we are preparing to go to the other shore. If you have that
sort of courage.... And you cannot see the other shore from
here, so you must trust me. And then I might be just a
madman – who knows? I might make you leave this shore
and there may not be any other shore, and you may have to
drown in the middle of the ocean with me. So all these
dangers are there.

This is why the cunning are unable to walk with me. Don't
come as a calculating man, come in your innocence. Only if
you are a gambler can you come with me. You must let go of
this shore that you know so well. Your Hindu shore, your
Muslim shore, your Jaina shore, your Christian shore – is well
known to you, familiar. Your shore of the scriptures: the
Vedas, the Koran, and the Bible is well known to you. Your
shore of the tenets, of the society, is familiar to you. You have
spread your roots well, you have buried your pegs deep into
the ground, and I am telling you that I have untied my boat
– the sails have been unfurled, the journey is beginning. Come
and sit with me.

And I am not interested in discussing whether the other shore
exists or in proving that it does, because it cannot be proved.
Come with me and I will show it to you. I have seen it, I will
take you there. You are interested in debating whether the

other shore exists, and if it does then what color it is — yellow, green, red, or black.... I am not interested in all this. The color of the other shore is not like any color you know. Those colors all belong to this shore. The forms you know belong to this shore, they have nothing to do with the other shore. The language we speak is the language of this shore, there is no language on the other side. Silence is the language of the further shore. If you are ready to go, let us set off immediately.

It is dangerous, but the one who is ready to pass through dangers is the one who I call a sannyasin. The danger is that this shore is being left behind without knowing whether you will reach the other shore or not. You have trusted a madman.

This is possible only in great love. Such trust can happen only in extraordinary love.

The disciple is someone who has fallen in love with me, who is ready to drown with me — not just to enter the water, but who is ready to drown with me. If I say that I am going to hell, the disciple wants to go there. If it is possible for him to go to heaven, but without me, he won't go. With me he will be happy — even to go to hell. To be a disciple takes great courage, unprecedented courage.

Sita has asked: "Osho, from what I was to what I have become, I did not even notice it...." You will not notice, one doesn't notice. This revolution takes place so silently, that not even footsteps are heard when it happens. If you are willing to open yourself, it occurs in silence. There is no sound at all.

"Osho, from what I was to what I have become,
I did not even notice it…
Locking your eyes into mine, you stole my life.
The strings of my heart sing songs of Holi,
You have drenched me in color."

The disciple is one who is eager to look into my eyes, the
disciple is one who says, "Pour yourself into me. I am empty,
empty in every possible way. Fill me up." Such a readiness
is disciplehood.

Now, this is a straightforward matter. I am interested in such
empty vessels, I am interested in disciples. If you become like
Sita, then come. Otherwise, may God bless you wherever you
are. May God bless you, whatever state you are in.

Enough for today.

9

THE GOLDEN ALCHEMY

How shall I please you, Lord,
By what name shall I call you?
When the wave of your compassion washes over me,
I will have found my shelter.

The river of this phenomenal existence is fearsome,
So how to cross it?
O my Lord, hear me again and again,
This is forever my request.

You are the ruler of the three worlds,
And my body is a captive of these thieves.
Hear the entreaty of Daya,
Your servant, your humble subject.

I have no ascetic disciplines, no spiritual practices,
Have undertaken no pilgrimages, no vows, no charity.
Like an innocent child who relies on his mother,
I depend wholly on you.

The child may make a million mistakes,
Yet his mother will never abandon him.
Taking him in her lap, she fondles and nurtures him,
Doubling her love for him as each day passes.

Peace comes to the chakvi bird
As blissfully it feeds on the first rays of the sun.
Daya is your slave, O Krishna, O Moon of Braj,
Never leave her sight for even one moment.

You have become my refrain,
Like the moon's rays are for the staring chakor bird.
I have no one else to quarrel with
But you, O Mohan, O youthful son of Nanda.

The glory of your name is infinite,
As even a tiny spark of fire
Burns the greatest forest.

Where I am,
The morning is a reddish dark
And night is fair-complexioned.
Where I am,
Sunshine's feet stumble
And there is only rain.
Where I am,
Every fragrant flower is imprisoned
And only steel roams free.
Where I am,
There is endless mud, there is moss,
But there is no lotus.
Where I am,
People hesitate to open up
And love is unknown.
Where I am,
All avert their eyes from their mirrors
And everything is a lie.
Where I am,
No inner song comes to wrinkled lips,
Where I am.

This is the condition of man: the false is true, and the futile is meaningful. Where lotuses were meant to blossom there is nothing but mud and moss. Such is the state of man. Living in darkness, we have accepted darkness as light. After all, man needs some consolation if he is to live. If you accept darkness as darkness, you will be restless. If you believe that darkness is light, the darkness does not become light because of this, but your mind finds some peace.

Man has invented so many lies. Most of the time man lives with the support of his lies. Truth is difficult. The search for truth is difficult, the path of truth is covered with thorns. This is not because truth has any need to be difficult, but because we have become so used to lies. A person who has only known mud for lifetime after lifetime finds it impossible even to imagine that a lotus can be born out of the mud. And a person who has only lived in darkness, in the night – whose eyes have become used to this darkness – cannot open his eyes even if the light comes. His eyes will be dazzled; the light will feel very painful.

This is why we hear a lot of talk about searching for the divine, but no one searches. We hear a lot about going in, but no one goes in. The enlightened ones shout at us to wake up, but we never awaken. And even there we play false games. We say, "We will awaken, yes, we must awaken, but how can we right now? How can we today?" Even there we have created great philosophies of falsehood. We say, "We have woven the web of our past actions through many lives. It will take time to break it. We must strive with our spiritual disciplines, we must exercise self-control, we must observe religious vows and rules, we must go on pilgrimages, we must fast. If we can earn enough virtue, our sins will be erased. Then, and only then, will it happen."

These are all man's tricks so that he doesn't have to change. The reality is, if you want to change, the blessings of the divine are available to you in this very moment.

When rays of light enter the darkness, how can the darkness object? Can it say, "I am thousands of years old, millions of years old, how can I disappear just like that — just because the light has arrived? I am not a new darkness, I am not a child; I am old, ancient, I belong to eternity! Let the light ray come and hit against me, but it will need many lifetimes to destroy me." No, the darkness doesn't say anything like that, it can do no such thing. What power does darkness have? This is the art of a devotee. This is the key, the essence of a devotee: "I am the darkness, I have made many mistakes — that is certain. I have stumbled many times, and yes, I am darkness — this is my identity, my ego. If your light can descend on me, this darkness will disappear right now. With your grace it can happen immediately."

"The devotee doesn't seek to change his actions. Rather, he invokes the grace of the divine.

Today's sutras are related to that call for divine grace. They are unique. But first you must keep in mind that the basis, the foundation of a devotee is grace, not effort. Effort belongs to man, grace belongs to the divine. Effort is your doing, grace is your waiting — not your action. Effort is what you do, effort is where you succeed or fail. Grace is where you don't exist, where only the divine is. And there, there is no way that you can be unsuccessful.

Look at it like this. As I see it, your world is your effort, it *is* effort. You build a house, a shop; you build a position and your prestige — and this is all your effort, your endeavor. It would not have happened unless you had done something – and you did.

The world is man's effort, because it is an expansion of man's ego. What about religion? Religion is not man's effort. Religion means to be tired of one's efforts, bored; to be distressed by them. Even when you succeed, your success is still only dust. If you build a house, it is still simply an inn. Even if you complete your house, you still don't find your home. It is still only an overnight stay, and when the morning comes you depart. Here, even success is failure; wealth can only impoverish you. Here, no fame, no name or position can fill your inner heart, can overwhelm you with delight. Here, everything is a deception.

Whatever man does through effort is what is called *maya*, the illusory. Whatever is not done through human effort is called the divine. So this is the basic concept of the devotee: it will happen by calling out, by longing, by prayer, by worship. But you need not understand prayer and worship to be an effort. People have turned them into efforts. They say, "We are *doing* prayer." This is wrong. How can anyone *do* prayer? One can be in prayer, but one cannot do prayer. You will miss if you do it. In doing, *you* have entered. If it happens, that is different.

So there are neither formal rules for prayer nor any formal words for it. Prayer is informal. It happens in a certain state of feeling. Sometimes it happens through tears and no words come. Sometimes it happens through dance and there is no trace of tears; sometimes through a smile, sometimes through humming a song. And it is not fixed, that song will not be the same every day. If you hum the same song every day it will become false. Just whatever emerges, whatever comes, whatever arises naturally.... You sit down for some time, and let whatever happens happen. At times you cry, at times you sing, at times you laugh, at times you dance, at other times you do nothing, you just sit peacefully. This is exactly what Daya says: sometimes the devotee laughs, sometimes he cries, sometimes he sings – how paradoxical! Sometimes he stands, sometimes he sits, sometimes he falls – again and again he falls. How paradoxical!

It is said that when Moses saw God on Mount Sinai, he fell down seven times. The sight was so immense, so unprecedented – what else could one do but tremble? One is shaken to the very roots. He fell down seven times, fell and rose again, fell and rose again. He was only able to stand up fully the eighth time – and even then his feet were trembling.

The divine is such an immense experience that you will go crazy. You will be like a drunkard. And this wine is not like ordinary wine where the intoxication wears off after a while. Wine made from grapes is a false wine, because its intoxication wears off after some time. The color that quickly fades is not a fast color. The color which never fades is what we call "fast," isn't it? The divine is the real wine. We are deceiving ourselves when we make wine from grapes.

You will be surprised to know that the person who discovered wine was a very saintly person. His name was Dionysius. He was a Greek. He discovered wine. It is a strange thing that a saint should have discovered wine. Even today, wine is made in the Greek monastery named after Dionysius. Western thinkers don't mention this, because it seems so strange to them that a saint should have discovered wine – but it appeals to me. Only a saint can discover wine, only one who has known the real thing can make a copy. You cannot make a copy unless you know the real thing. You cannot make counterfeit currency unless you have real money – otherwise how will you know what it looks like? It appeals to me. A saint *must* have discovered wine. He must have seen the real thing, and feeling pity for the poor people who were unlikely ever to know it, he made a copy of it for them. I have no difficulty with this, it seems very logical to me.

Only enlightened mystics can discover wine. A mystic who had tasted it must have thought that others should also taste it in one form or another. And it is true: today he will only know a copy, but tomorrow he may begin to search for the real. How long can a person drink false wine? One day he will begin to think about finding a wine that will intoxicate him forever. And on that day, his journey to the divine will have begun.No bliss is possible in this life without discovering the wine of the divine.

Somewhere in this darkness lurks unease,
Like me, the night cannot sleep.
So helpless, so sad,
There is no one else like me in this whole world.
Perhaps no one has ever missed life
The way I have.
Perhaps no one has ever washed laughter's feet
With endless tears
The way I have.

But this is the state of everyone. Sometimes you may also have felt that no one is as sad as you are, no one is as wretched and dejected as you are. It isn't just you, everyone is suffering. And everyone thinks no one else is as wretched as he is. But we cannot see the sorrow of the other; the wounds of his sorrows are hidden in his innermost being. We only see the outer decorations, not the inner wounds, not the inner sores. But we can see our own sores.

People laugh even though they have no reason for laughing. They smile. What else can they do? If they didn't smile, they would have to cry the whole time. So somehow they impose a false smile on themselves.

Around 1920, Maxim Gorky, a great Russian thinker, went to America. Wherever he went in America, he was shown the ways America had discovered to amuse itself. No other country in the world had discovered so many ways. The person showing Gorky around thought that he would be greatly impressed, and indeed he did appear to be so. After showing him everything, the guide waited anxiously for Gorky to say something. Instead, tears came to Gorky's eyes. The guide asked, "What is wrong? Why are you so sad?"

Gorky replied, "People who need so many things to amuse themselves in order to live must be very sad. How can they not be?"

The sad person goes to the cinema, the sad person goes to the pub, the sad person goes to the circus, the sad person watches the cricket match. They are all sad people. A sad person needs some way to distract himself. He calls it entertainment. His mind is weary, always on the run. A sad man discovers a thousand ways to laugh for a little while.

A happy person drowns in himself. Only sad people need

entertainment. A happy person is beyond mind; there is no need to entertain it. When you have no mind, what is there to entertain? A happy person is so engrossed in himself, so immersed, so enraptured in his own being, his own being is so sufficient for him that nothing else is needed. He lives in supreme satisfaction and contentment.

The search for the divine means only this: "I want something so that I no longer need to search for my happiness outside of myself, so that I can find my happiness within myself, so that the fountainhead of my happiness can burst forth within me."

When this moment comes, the drop instantly becomes the ocean and all boundaries immediately dissolve. On that day you are neither the body nor the mind; on that day you are the universal self. The day the divine descends into the devotee, the devotee becomes the divine.

And always remember that the most fundamental point about a devotee is that he never says, "I did this, I took vows, I observed the precepts of religion, I fasted – therefore you must come to me." No. This is not the talk of a devotee. This is the talk of a shopkeeper: "You must come to me because I did this for you." This is not the language of a lover, this is the language of a deal. It is as if you are saying, "If you don't come to me, I will take you to court. I have fasted for so many days and so far nothing has happened."

Your so-called ascetics are trying to find the divine using their own strength, and their strength is only a proclamation of their ego. So you will find a great flush of ego on the faces of your so-called yogis, *mahatmas* and monks – a great pride. The lamp of the ego is burning there.

A devotee is humble. He says, "Nothing happens through my doing. Whatever happens is because of the divine." What room is there for pride, for arrogance, in this? The devotee says, "I have no claim to being worthy." He simply says, "I know my unworthiness." Every day he presents his unworthiness before the divine and says, "I am unworthy, but please come – because if you ask me to be worthy, then the whole thing is beyond me. And if you require that I am worthy, then what of your compassion? This is what I am – good or bad, this is how I am. Accept me, make me your own."

The prayer of a devotee arises from his humility. Ego arrogantly says, "I have done so much, I have done this and that." The devotee says, "I have only one strength – that you have made me. My strength is only one: that you may not have forgotten me, no matter how easily I forget you. My strength is only one – that you are my source. I have come from you so I can call out to you. You made me – however I am."

If you can understand this concept of devotee, then these verses of Daya are absolutely unique.

When you are with me,
I am connected with the world
In a thousand ways.
When you are not,
What is the world to me?
The devotee says:

When you are with me,
I am connected with the world
In a thousand ways.
When you are not,
What is the world to me?
A thousand storms and typhoons may gather,
My boat may be tossing helplessly,
And I may be rowing with the strength of trust,
But if you are not in the boat
When I bring it to the shore,
What is it to me
That I touch the land?

The devotee says, "Even if I attain to *moksha*, salvation, if you are not there, what use is this salvation? Even if I find the other shore, if you are not there, what use is that other shore to me? If I am rowing this boat and you are not in it, then why should I row, what is the point in it?

But if you are not in the boat
When I bring it to the shore,
What is it to me
That I touch the land?

You are my sun, my moon,
My mornings and evenings,
My polestar.
If you are not there, who will destroy
The darkness of my life?
When you are there, everything is bright,
If you are not there,
That brightness means nothing to me.

So the devotee will not wait for his *kundalini* to awaken, nor

for his *sahasrar*, his seventh chakra to open. He doesn't wait
for light to illuminate his interiority. He simply says, "Come,
O Lord, whatever else is following in your wake is all right.
I desire nothing but you. Even if I have to live in the darkness
with you that is acceptable. Without you, I cannot live even
in the light."

Spring blossoms because of you,
Moonlight shines because of you,
Beauty lives because you are,
Music plays because you speak,
The earth is bedecked because you are adorned.
What good are adornments to me
When you are not adorned?
Upon your alchemical touch,
My heart of iron turned to gold.
Stumbling at your door,
My sins turned to virtues.
Your door is my place of pilgrimage,
What good are Kashi and Haridwar to me?

The devotee says: "The trouble of transforming my sins and
earning virtue are both beyond me. I cannot manage that. I
simply surrender at your door."

Upon your alchemical touch,
My heart of iron turned to gold.

The devotee says to God: "You are the golden alchemy. If
you touch me, I will turn to gold. I cannot become gold
through my own efforts. I have lost the way because of my
own efforts, my actions have led me astray. Because I think
I am the doer, I have lost my way."

Stumbling at your door,
My sins turned to virtues.
Your door is my place of pilgrimage,
What good are Kashi and Haridwar to me?
You are *riddhi* and *siddhi*, prosperity and fulfillment,
The omens and all that is auspicious.
Wherever you settle becomes the city of the gods,
And every moment, the shade of the wish-fulfilling tree.
But when you are not with me,
Even if all the powers of heaven were in my hands,
It would be as nothing to me.

The devotee has no desire for heaven, for salvation, for
paradise, for bliss, for the nectar of immortality, for truth.
The devotee's desire is to enthrone his beloved in his heart.
And the devotee is doing a wise thing, because everything else
follows after that.

There is a famous saying of Jesus: "Seek ye first the kingdom
of God, and all else shall be given unto you." First seek the
divine, and the rest will automatically follow. If you keep
searching for everything else you will not get it and you will
miss the divine as well.

The devotee is actually very wise in his foolishness, while the
so-called learned people — the *pundits* and the priests, the
yogis and the mahatmas — are totally foolish in their so-called
wisdom. They seek trifling things, futile things. The devotee
goes to the root. He invites the emperor to his house and
then the ministers and other servants follow. He doesn't
waste his time inviting everyone — the minister, the prime
minister, the servants, the doorkeeper, the chief of the army!
He doesn't worry about them, he invites God directly. He

calls to the most important one and the rest automatically follow. That is why I say that there is great intelligence in the devotee's so-called foolishness.

Listen to Daya's words:

How shall I please you, Lord,
By what name shall I call you?
When the wave of your compassion washes over me,
I will have found my shelter.

How shall I please you, Lord...? The devotee says, "I want to please you. But how are you pleased? Tell me the art – because I don't know it at all. Tell me what I should call you, what your name is, where you live – because if I try to find your name and address I will be sure to get it wrong. Anything I do is wrong. I can only do wrong. Even if I try to please you, I will only manage to displease you. I cannot manage to do things right; I am only used to being wrong. I am an expert at being wrong. For life after life I have only nurtured the wrong and the futile. How can I nurture you? What shall I call you?" Daya says, "Tell me how to win your heart." Do you hear how beautiful this is?

How shall I please you, Lord,
By what name shall I call you?

"And I don't know your name or where you live. The names I know are scholarly – just words taken from the scriptures. Tell me your real whereabouts, so I can call you.

When the wave of your compassion washes over me,
I will have found my shelter.

"And when you show your kindness to me, *When the wave of your compassion washes over me*...when the wave of your compassion rolls in my direction so that I drown in the wave; when your grace, your compassion drowns me, only then... *I will have found my shelter.* Without you, I am an orphan; a lost traveler who has no idea of where he is going, who doesn't know the paths, and who has a long, long acquain-tance only with what is wrong."

Pay attention to this, meditate on it. Whatever you have done so far has been wrong. Understand this. When you gathered wealth, wrong happened, and even if you now renounce this wealth, that too will be wrong.

Because you are wrong, as soon as you touch anything it will go wrong too. Just as iron turns to gold with the touch of the alchemical stone, things turn from gold to iron as soon as you touch them. Whatever you touch turns to dust.

You have been gathering wealth because of your ego. You wanted to show the world who you were, how wealthy you were. Now the futility of wealth has become obvious: having amassed wealth, you now know that there is no substance in it, and so now you want to prove something else to the world. Your disease remains the same. Now you say, "I will renounce everything and show the world who I really am." You can give up your wealth, you can renounce everything and stand naked on the streets, but your old sickness still persists. The name of the sickness has changed, but not the sickness. Its appearance has changed, but the sickness has not. And this second sickness will be far more dangerous than the first, because it is more subtle.

Everyone can see the sickness of a rich man, even a blind person can see that he is mad, but the sickness of the renunciate is visible only to someone with a very deep vision – otherwise it cannot be seen at all. The same madness has merely taken a new direction.

Whatsoever you have done so far.... Up to now you were obsessed with sexuality, now you have taken the vow of celibacy and have started suppressing yourself from every direction. This will make no difference. Whatever you will do with your present understanding can only be wrong.

I have heard:

One night Mulla Nasruddin and his friend left the pub completely drunk. It was midnight and all the roads were deserted. But when they came to a crossroads, they suddenly stopped. Pointing to the traffic lights, Mulla's friend said, "My friend, what a beautiful woman!"

Mulla looked closely, then said, "She is really something. Gorgeous. She is a celestial nymph, not a woman. Look how her face glows. I am amazed – how could this beauty hide herself away for so long in Pune? You stay here. I'll go and try to win her over."

For ten minutes, he talked about all kinds of things to that beautiful woman. When he returned, the other drunk asked him, "How did it go? Did you make any progress?"

Mulla replied, "It wasn't too bad. Everything else is fine, she is indeed amazingly beautiful, but she appears to be dumb. She has not said a word. But don't worry, she has agreed to come with us, because I saw her wink."

When a man is drunk, out of his senses, whatever meanings
he derives will come from his unconsciousness. All his
interpretations come from there. If you are unconscious, it
makes no difference whether you accumulate wealth or
renounce it, whether you create a household or run away to
the jungle. Your unconsciousness cannot be so easily broken.
Hence the devotee says, "It is beyond me, I am helpless."

How shall I please you, Lord,
By what name shall I call you?
When the wave of your compassion washes over me,
I will have found my shelter.

"I can do nothing, I am an orphan and will always be an
orphan. You must do something."

So the devotee only appeals, only surrenders. He puts his ego
at the feet of the divine. This takes a great deal of courage,
extreme courage – because generally man's mind tells him that
perhaps something would have been attained, something
would have happened had he done the right thing, had he done
this or that, had he calculated things differently, had he
used another method. Try to see the difference clearly. You
can change your method, you can change your mathematics,
but how will that change you? You are the one who is to be
changed, but you are also the one who wants to affect
the change – and how can you change yourself? It is as if you
are trying to lift yourself up by your own bootlaces.

There is a great strength in what the devotee says. The
devotee says, "I will be lifted up only if *you* pick me up. *When*

the wave of your compassion washes over me.... Nothing will happen by my trying to lift myself up by holding onto my own bootlaces. I cannot lift myself up and be lifted up at the same time. That is impossible. It cannot happen. *You* must raise me up."

And for centuries it has been the devotees' experience that if you leave everything totally to the divine it will raise you up. But it must be totally. There mustn't be the slightest thought that, "It will be good if existence lifts me up, but if it doesn't, then I will try to raise myself by my own bootlaces. If it doesn't help me, I won't just sit here waiting for ever. I will rise up one way or another."

If you think like this you will be continually looking out from the corner of one eye to see whether existence is supporting you or whether you need to do something for yourself, whether you should become your own savior. If existence is not protecting you, you must protect yourself. If even a small amount of this desire remains, no relationship is possible with the divine. If you miss the divine, it will not be because of the divine, but because of your own dishonest heart. Hidden somewhere within you, the feeling always remains that if nothing else works out, then "I" will still be there. You have kept your faith in yourself – and faith in the divine comes only when you have completely let go of any faith in yourself – only then. But you still have faith in yourself. Even though you have suffered for many lives, still you have not lost your faith in yourself.

People come to me. They say they don't have enough self-confidence to practice devotion. I tell them that only those who no longer have any confidence in themselves are able to practice devotion. Confidence means: "I am enough on my own, I don't need anyone else." If you have really discovered that you lack confidence in yourself, you have come to a wonderful door. Open that door now and fall to the ground, saying, "I just have no confidence in myself, I don't trust myself. I have tried to lift myself up many times and been defeated every time – defeat after defeat, defeat after defeat! How can I be confident? Everywhere I go I run into · a wall. So far I have not found the door to you – so how can I believe in myself?"

Pay attention to this. An ascetic moves with the support of his self-confidence, a *yogi* moves with the support of his self-confidence, a learned person depends on his self-confidence. They rely on *sankalpa*, on their own self-will and determination. The devotee surrenders everything. He says, "If I do not exist, if I am not, how can I have confidence in myself? I am just a *shunya*, a zero, a nothing. I will only have a value when you move next to me as a figure, a number. Without you I am worth nothing."

When the wave of your compassion washes over me,
I will have found my shelter.

"Without you, I am nothing but a zero which has no value." When you add a one to zero, the zero becomes a ten. If you add a zero to ten, it becomes a hundred, and then a thousand. Do you see? – if you put a zero next to one, or a one next to a zero, its value goes up ten times, so a zero equals nine! One is one, and when you add it to zero, it becomes ten. So a zero is the same as a nine. If you add the divine to your zero, you will become priceless, precious. Your value will be beyond all calculation. The account books and registers will all be too small to hold you, because your number will be beyond reckoning. When one is joined with the divine, when one places his zero behind the divine, the matter is over. Now you are of infinite worth, you have come in contact with the alchemical stone.

The river of this phenomenal existence is fearsome,
So how to cross it?
O my Lord, hear me again and again,
This is forever my request

The devotee says, "I plead, I beseech you, I cry out to you, I call to you. My eyes are full of tears: I can see nothing, I have only my tears, and I offer them at your feet. I wash your feet with my tears."

The river of this phenomenal existence is fearsome...

This world is terrifying, because we have known nothing except how badly we have been missing, how we have kept missing, slipping, falling. We have wandered, slipped and fallen. We have never been able to raise ourselves up. Blow after blow, sorrow after sorrow – and still we don't drop our dreams.

I have heard that Mulla Nasruddin once said to his psychiatrist, "Doctor, I dream the same dream every night. I am catching fish. Small fish, big fish, fish of different colors and kinds – but there are always fish. Always. All night, every night. It worries me."

The doctor said, "Yes, it is a matter for worry, Nasruddin, but the thing is that you think about the fish all day long too. And whatever you think about during the day floats into your dreams at night. Do one thing: start thinking about beautiful women before you go to bed. Why waste your time thinking about fish when you can be surrounded by lots of beautiful women? Change your dreams and dream of beautiful *apsaras* instead of fish."

When Nasruddin heard this, he was angry. "What?" he cried, "and lose all those fish?"

Those fishes are in a dream, but still he is afraid of losing them – "And lose all those fish?" You have nothing but your dreams.

People ask me "Why don't you ask your *sannyasins* to renounce the world?"

I tell them, "These fish that you have are all the stuff of dreams. Even if you renounce them, where will that get you? Is there anything in the world worth renouncing? If there was something worth renouncing then there would be something worth attaining as well. Understand this: if there was something in the world worth renouncing, if there was something real in the world that needed renouncing, then that in itself would be the proof that there is something in the world worth attaining. I ask you: What is there to renounce? What really exists in this world? – ideas, just ideas and creations of your own imaginations."

Look how angry the Mulla was! He immediately started to leave the doctor's office. So the doctor said, "Brother, at least pay me for my advice before you leave."

Mulla replied, "Who is listening to your advice? I should pay only if I take your advice."

We are too stubborn even to give up our dreams. Look carefully inside yourself. Your whole world is nothing but dreams. You consider someone to be your wife or your husband. That is simply a matter of belief. Once you believe it, it is there.

There is a gentleman here who is greatly troubled by his wife. Who isn't troubled in fact? But this gentleman is rather innocent, so he says it. Whenever he comes to see me he only laments about one thing – his wife! So I told him, "Now change the object of your complaining. Stop weeping about your wife, now start weeping for the divine." He has a lot of money, everything one could possibly need. I told him, "If this is how you feel, give your wife half of your property and be free of her."

He replied, "How can I be free of her? What are you saying? Do you support divorce? This is a relationship of lifetimes."

So I asked him, "Were you born with her? A relationship that goes beyond lifetimes? Are you twins? What is the matter?"

He said, "No, I am not her twin, but when I married her we circled around the sacred fire seven times."

I told him, "Bring your wife here, I can undo those seven circumambulations. Go around in the opposite direction. I have known you for the past twenty years and you have done nothing but cry and lament. There must be some other things you can cry about. Your eyes are swollen from crying

— "My wife! My wife!" And nothing is gained from this weeping and wailing. Had you cried this much for God, you would certainly have found him long ago."

I don't ask you to renounce the world and run away. What is there to renounce? Just recognize that everything in the world is just your belief. Your wife is a belief, your husband is a belief, the relationship of brother and sister is a belief, father and son are a belief — all are beliefs. If you have believed in it, it is okay, but there is nothing more to it than that. The shop, the bazaar, fame, position and prestige — all are your beliefs. They are all a dream. The world is a dream that you dream with open eyes. Don't place any higher value on it. Don't think of it as real. It is neither worth grasping nor worth renouncing. As it doesn't exist, what can you grasp, what can you renounce? The world is only worth waking up from. Pay attention to this statement.

And how will you wake up? You are only used to sleeping. Life after life, you have only poured yourself the draught of sleep.

So Daya rightly says, *The river of this phenomenal existence is fearsome.* "I have suffered greatly. There is fear everywhere. I fall wherever I go. There is nothing but nets and nooses all around." If you hate someone, that is a noose; if you love someone, that is a noose. If you are angry, that is a noose; if you feel compassion, that too is a noose. If you set up a shop, that is a noose; if you sit in a monastery, that is a noose. There is nothing but nooses.

The river of this phenomenal existence is fearsome,
So how to cross it?

Daya says, "I can't think of any way to cross this river. My capacities have been badly damaged. I no longer have any faith in myself. So far I have kept going with the support of my faith, thinking that one day I will find the path and the door. But no, I can't do it."

The day you gain the deep conviction that you cannot do it, that you won't be able to do it; the day this realization penetrates your being like an arrow, in that moment the feeling that arises in you is called prayer. Then whether you utter the name of Allah or Rama or Krishna makes no difference; then all names belong to it. Then whether you utter any name or not, wherever you bow down your head you will be bowing down at the feet of the divine. Then wherever you are sitting is the place of pilgrimage.

O my Lord, hear me again and again...

Daya says, "I can only pray to you, that is all. I send you my petition. If you listen to me that is good, otherwise I will just keep saying it again and again, for life after life – asking you to hear my request":

O my Lord, hear me again and again,
This is forever my request.

The devotees, the enlightened mystics have used the word *sahib*, lord, very sweetly. They call the divine "Lord."

O my Lord, hear me again and again,
This is forever my request.

You are the ruler of the three worlds,
And my body is a captive of these thieves.

Hear the entreaty of Daya,
Your servant, your humble subject.

"You are my *thakur,* the master of the whole universe, you are
the Lord, and I have become only a home for robbers...*and*
my body is a captive of these thieves. In my body live only thieves,
swindlers and enemies. I have nurtured only enemies. I have
fed only those who are destroying me. So far I have only
drunk poison. I am committing suicide.

You are the ruler of the three worlds,
And my body is a captive of these thieves.

"Here I am, with nothing inside me except these thieves.
Sexuality, greed, anger, illusion and infatuation with the
unreal, envy...all of these lurk within. This is my wealth.
Even if I wanted to invite you to come, how could I when
they are there? I can make no claims to being worthy. I can
only have faith in your compassion. I am not worthy; I
am unworthy in every way. I have no knowledge, no meditation, nothing. I have only these thieves within me. Please
understand my pain and don't examine my worthiness."

Hear the entreaty of Daya,
Your servant, your humble subject.

"I can only make a humble request. I am your slave, your
humble subject. But however I am, whether I am good or bad,
I am yours. Please hear my humble request."

I have no ascetic disciplines, no spiritual practices,
Have undertaken no pilgrimages, no vows, no charity,
Like an innocent child who relies on his mother,
I depend wholly on you.

The whole essence of devotion is contained in these two statements. There are so many verses in Narada's *Bhakti Sutras* – he wrote that many. But these two statements contain the whole essence of all those sutras:

I have no ascetic disciplines, no spiritual practices...

Daya says: "I know nothing about *sanyam*, self-control, asceticism. I know only indiscipline. I know nothing about yoga and everything about *bhoga*, pleasure. I know everything about going astray, and nothing about arriving. I have no ascetic disciplines, no spiritual practices.... *I can achieve nothing through my spiritual practices.* I try, but each time my efforts slip from my hands. I have tried many times and I can't do it. *I have no ascetic disciplines, no spiritual practices...*so I cannot boast about my spiritual practices or how much ascetic discipline I have."

...Have undertaken no pilgrimages, no vows, no charity...

"I have not given any great wealth – because I have nothing. I have only worthless pennies, what help can they give? These coins of the smallest value are so insignificant; one can only give charity if first one has something to give."

Charity happens so rarely – only sometimes when a Buddha, a Mahavira, a Krishna, or a Christ give. Those whom you call "patrons of charity" are not really so, but in your eyes they appear to be. Someone donates a hundred thousand rupees, and you call him a patron of charity – because a hundred thousand rupees have a great value for you. Rupees have a value for you, so he seems to be a hero. If you knew that rupees were only potsherds, would you still think that? What kind of giving is this? Can you give away trash to charity? How can you give away what wasn't yours in the first place?

A wealthy man came to a Zen master carrying a bag filled with a thousand gold coins. "I have brought you a thousand golden coins," he said.

The master replied, "Fine," and did not raise the matter again. When someone brings you a thousand gold coins, he is hoping that you will thank him by saying, "My profoundest gratitude. You are such a kind person, so very generous...." The master said nothing, as though he had received nothing. Not even once did he take a good look at the bag.

The wealthy man said, "Sir, do you realize the value of a thousand gold coins? It is not easy to collect so much money."

The master replied, "What do you mean? Do you want me to thank you? If you do, then take this bag and be on your way, because anyone who wants thanks does not yet see that wealth is useless. I cannot accept money from such a person. Take it away!"

The wealthy man became worried, "No, no," he said, "it is not like that at all. I have already given it to you."

The master said, "Take your words back! You have given it to me? How can you give away what is not yours? Giving has a claim in it: "This was mine." There was gold on the earth before you arrived; it will be here after you have gone. You didn't bring it with you and you cannot take it away. How can it be yours? Pick up the bag and stop this nonsense.

The gold cannot be yours, it belongs to whosoever finds it."

The world belongs to its real owner. We come here empty-
handed and we go away empty-handed. The situation is very
strange. There is a saying that we come into the world with
closed fists and we go away with open fists. When a child is
born, his fists are closed. When an old person dies, his fists
are open. So we lose even the little that we bring with us.

What is yours? How can you give it away? The devotee
understands the questions, "What do I have to give? How
can I take any vow?" – because a vow smacks off the ego's
arrogance. Your pride boasts, "I have taken a vow of celibacy,
a vow of non-violence, a vow of truthfulness." You become
arrogant because you have taken so many vows. You think
that your vows make you religious, but your arrogance itself
is the barrier between you and the divine.

I have no ascetic disciplines, no spiritual practices.
Have undertaken no pilgrimages, no vows, no charity,
Like an innocent child who relies on his mother,
I depend wholly on you.

Daya says, "Like a young child who relies on her mother, I
rely on you. Something will happen only if you do it; but
if you don't, that too is your will. I will continue to entreat
you again and again, that is all that I can do. That is as far
as I can reach – that I will keep on calling, calling, and one
day you *must* hear me. One day you will have compassion
on me. One day the wave of your compassion will flood over
me."

The longing of a devotee says, "Give me another life before

I die. Give me another life before I die because this present life is not really a life. You have played a great trick on me. You have deceived me by placing me in this body."

It is like giving a toy to a child. The child asks for a car and we oblige him by giving him a small toy car. That makes him very happy. He fits the key and lets the car go.

If you think that this life is a true life, then you are mistaking a toy car for a real car. You will not be able to go anywhere in it.

Give me another life before I die.
In the effort to live
This life so far has passed without living,
Going by in endless ponderings
Without fulfilling my intents.
Day after day, I have been broken,
Sometimes by circumstances,
Sometimes by my state of mind.
Agreeing to the persuasions of convenience
I have often turned my face from voiceless truths.
All my individuality has gone,
My mind has not created me.
Take back this silk, these gems, this clothing,
And give me a mirror.
Do you hear?

Take back this silk, these gems, this clothing,
And give me a mirror.
Give me another life before I die,
Give me a mirror so that I can see myself
Without veils.

Give me courage, so that I can write exactly as I see,
Not just compose life's epic with dew-washed lyrics.
Whenever smelted steel challenges me
I must not turn my back and hide.
Give me the strength to say what is,
Give me the strength to know what is,
Give me the strength to live what is.
Enough of falsehood!
Take back this silk, these gems, this clothing.
Give me a mirror so that I can see myself,
So I do not run away or turn my back to save myself,
So I do not escape.
I have written many false poems, but I shall write no more.
I will not compose life's epic with dew-washed lyrics.

"Enough of dreams. Let me be completely honest when I
write the poetry of my life."

Whenever smelted steel challenges me
I must not turn my back and hide.
I cannot enjoy the benefits of glory.
May my wish for fulfillment not remain barren,
May I not wither before becoming a seed,
This, O this assurance I ask of you –
Give me another life before I die.
Take back this silk, these gems, this clothing,
And give me a mirror.

The devotee says, "I need a mirror in which I can see myself.
Become my mirror so that I can see myself in you. I will keep
calling out until you do. Like a small innocent child...."

...Like an innocent child who relies on his mother,
I depend wholly on you.

Try to understand the condition of a child. For nine months, the child lives in its mother's womb — it has no knowledge of itself, no worries about hunger or thirst, no responsibility; it is completely carefree, everything is done for it. This is how the devotee begins to live.

For the devotee, the whole of existence becomes the mother's womb. He says: "I am living in existence, what is there to worry about now? I am surrounded by existence on all sides — why should I worry? It is surrounding me in every direction — with the wind, with the moon and the stars, with the sun, with the trees, with its people, its earth, its sky. It is surrounding me everywhere." Existence becomes a womb and the devotee is happy to be lost in it without a worry.

...Like an innocent child who relies on his mother,
I depend wholly on you.

The child may make a million mistakes,
Yet his mother will never abandon him.

However many mistakes the child makes, no mother ever abandons her child.

The child may make a million mistakes,
Yet his mother will never abandon him.
Taking him in her lap, she fondles and nurtures him,
Doubling her love for him as each day passes.

Whenever the child makes a mistake, the mother calls him to her, puts him in her lap, caresses him and loves him.

Jesus has said: "God is like a shepherd who returns home in the evening with his sheep. On arriving, he suddenly finds that ninety-nine of his sheep have come home, but one is still lost somewhere in the forest. He leaves those ninety-nine where they are, and runs off into the forest. He searches in the darkness calling out in faraway valleys for the lost sheep, even risking his life as he does so. At last he finds the sheep and brings it home. And when he finds it, do you know how he brings it home? He brings it home on his own shoulders." So Jesus too says, "God is the shepherd."

The child may make a million mistakes,
Yet his mother will never abandon him.

The child may make many mistakes, but the mother will always forgive him.

Taking him in her lap, she fondles and nurtures him,
Doubling her love for him as each day passes.

And have you noticed that a mother especially loves the child who is a troublemaker, who comes home after getting into difficulty, who makes trouble around the neighborhood? The greater his mistakes, the more his mother's love flows towards him.

There were hundreds of seekers in the *ashram* of the Sufi *fakir*, Bayazid. A new seeker arrived and soon he created a lot of trouble. He used to steal things and drink alcohol. He had other bad habits too: for example, he was also a gambler. In the end all the disciples were complaining about him again and again. Even Bayazid's things started disappearing. But Bayazid just listened to the endless complaints saying, "Yes, we will see, we will see."

Finally, it was all too much. The disciples gathered and said to Bayazid, "This is impossible. What is happening? Why do you let him stay here? Why don't you just throw him out?"

Bayazid replied, "Listen, you are all good people. Even if you left this place, somehow or other you would still find God. But if this man misses me, if I throw him out, there will be nowhere else for him to go. So do one thing: if he bothers you that much, you can go. But he and I are bound together now, and I must live with him.

"And think about it, no one else but me will accept him. I agree that he is a thief, a drunkard, and a gambler. He steals my things as well – he doesn't even spare me, his teacher. But if existence tolerates him, it would never forgive me if I did not tolerate him. Existence has not yet stopped giving him breath. The sun showers the same light on him now as it always has. Existence has not taken the moon and the stars away from him. If it is prepared to tolerate him, who am I to interfere? It is God's wish, God's world. And what is really ours? What can he really steal from us?

"So if you want, you can go, but I cannot let him go. If I let you go, I can answer God by saying, 'They were all good people, they would have found you anyway.' But how could I show my face to God if I sent this man away? What would I say when he asked me, 'Where did you send him? Where is he? How could you abandon him?'"

The child may make a million mistakes,
Yet his mother will never abandon him.

So Daya says, "You are the source. We come from you. We are your children. It is true that we have made many mistakes. We have made nothing but mistakes, and we acknowledge that. But that is no reason to abandon us. It cannot be that because of something like this a mother will no longer remain a mother. So we entreat you, please hear us." *O my Lord, hear me again and again, this is forever my request.*

Peace comes to the chakvi bird
As blissfully it feeds on the first rays of the sun.
Daya is your slave, O Krishna, O Moon of Braj,
Never leave her sight for even one moment.

This is her prayer; and she is not asking for much. Just as the chakor bird gazes constantly on the moon, Daya is not asking for much. *Daya is your slave, O Krishna, O Moon of Braj, never leave her sight for even one moment.* She only asks him not to leave her sight for one single moment. This is her only request. It is not a big demand: she doesn't ask for vast treasures, for salvation or for heaven.

The devotee never asks for anything. He simply says, "Only this much I ask you: that I should not forget you, that I should not become oblivious of you, that the memory of you may constantly prevail in me."

Try to understand this difference. The one on the path of knowledge falls far short in this regard because he only wants something. He wants bliss, salvation, spiritual merit, eternal life – his whole life is filled with wanting. The devotee says, "I don't want anything. Just don't let me forget you. Even if I am in hell, no matter, just let your remembrance be with me. It is enough for me if you are open to my prayers."

Daya is your slave, O Krishna, O Moon of Braj,
Never leave her sight for even one moment.

You have become my refrain.... My eyes are waiting only for you.
You are my light, you are my life, you are my salvation.

You have become my refrain,
Like the moon's rays are for the staring chakor bird.
I have no one else to quarrel with
But you, O Mohan, O youthful son of Nanda.
It is so sweet. Daya says, "Why should I bother anyone else? Why should
I quarrel with anyone else?"

You have become my refrain,
Like the moon's rays are for the staring chakor bird.
I have no one else to quarrel with
But you, O Mohan, O youthful son of Nanda.

"Now I will quarrel only with you. Only you exist, no one
else but you. If nothing happens, then I will quarrel with you,
I will argue with you, I will complain to you."

Understand this difference. You complain, the devotee also
complains, but there is no prayer in your complaint. In the
devotee's complaint, there is prayer. You go to God asking
for something and complaining that you want things to be
this way and that way....

A great Western thinker, Emerson, said that the essence of
all human prayer is that people go to God asking that two
and two should not be four. You have stolen something, but
you don't want to be punished. You have sinned, but you
don't want to suffer. All human prayers ask that what

must happen should not happen. Instead something else should happen, what you want to happen should happen. You want the system to be different for you, you want a change in the system.

Your prayer is your desire. Your complaints are full of anger. The devotee also complains sometimes, but that complaint is full of great love. Listen to these words:

I have no one else to quarrel with...

"Now who else shall I quarrel with? There is no one else, only you exist for me. If I must quarrel, I should quarrel with you; if I love, I should be enthralled with you. If I am enamored, it should be with you; if I am annoyed, it should be with you."

You have become my refrain...

"Now everything is focused on you. Just as the eyes of the chakor bird are focused on the moon, my eyes are focused on you. Don't turn away from me."

There is one more verse. It is unique. I don't know why Maitreyaji did not include it with these other verses. Perhaps he thought it is too problematic and left it out. Maitreyaji chooses these verses: he may have thought that it was too problematic a verse. But I cannot leave this verse out. I enjoy trouble.

The verse is:

It took you no time to save great sinners,
The lowest of the low.
Will Nanda lose some wealth, O Lord,
Now that it is my turn?

Do you hear this? It is very amusing!

It took you no time to save great sinners,
The lowest of the low.

Even great sinners crossed over, were saved in no time at all.
Will Nanda lose some wealth.... "Will your God lose anything,
if I also cross over?" This is an act of great courage: "Will
your father Nanda lose anything?"

Will Nanda lose some wealth, O Lord,
Now that it is my turn?

"You are stopping only me – greater sinners than I am have
already made it to the other shore!" Only a devotee can speak
like this. Only a person in whose heart there is nothing but
love can say such things. Only a devotee can have such
courage.

There is another verse also that Maitreyaji has left out:

I have become wretched calling you for so long,
And you, O Lord, responding not.

"I have been calling out for so long, but you never listen to
me. Are you hard of hearing? Can't you hear properly?"

Are your ears becoming deaf?
Or have you merely forgotten your old glory?
"Have you forgotten your old promise? – *Sambhavami yuge*
yuge! Yada yada hi dharmasya.... 'In every age, whenever
religiousness is in decline, I will come – again and again.'
Have you forgotten all this talk? Am I to face this difficult
situation all alone?"

Are your ears becoming deaf? "Has something gone wrong with
your ears, are you going deaf?" Only a devotee can say this.
And these are such sweet words…. *Or have you merely forgotten
your old glory?* By "glory" she means, "You were so renowned
for carrying out your promises, and now you have forgotten
all about them. Have you decided to let your good name and
reputation sink in disgrace? Once you were famous for
helping sinners cross to the other shore. You were the one
who could take them across the ocean of birth and rebirth;
you had a great reputation for delivering sinners. So what is
so difficult about me? Greater sinners than I am have already
crossed over." *Will Nanda lose some wealth, O Lord, now that it is
my turn?*

You have become my refrain,
Like the moon's rays are for the staring chakor bird.
I have no one else to quarrel with
But you, O Mohan, O youthful son of Nanda.

This is her nagging, her goading, her quarrel – a quarrel of
love.

Have you seen how lovers often quarrel? And as they quarrel,
their delight in their love increases, it doesn't decrease.
Psychologists even say that when a woman and a man, a
husband and a wife, the lover and the beloved stop quarreling,
then know that their love has finished, because peace has
come at last. As long as they quarrel, they are in love. You
can only fight with people you care about. Quarrels come in,
if caring is there. If you don't care, what quarrel can
there be? You don't fight with just anyone. If your wife nags
you to give up cigarettes or alcohol, it is because she cares,
she loves you. So you continue to fight over even the smallest
things, but every fight only deepens your love. These quarrels

prove only one thing: that there is still a longing in the person about how you should be; a desire to refine you, to beautify you.

Quarreling is not necessarily a sign of enmity. Friends also quarrel. And there is a pleasure in quarreling. This love of Daya's is the ultimate love; there is no greater love than this. Devotion is the ultimate love, so the devotee quarrels with the divine. Only a devotee can dare to quarrel. Those on the path of knowledge are afraid, because their relationship is that of a bargain. These so-called wise ones are scared that God may become angry. But the devotee says, "If he wants to get angry, let him!" – because the devotee trusts that God will understand. If existence itself doesn't understand, who will? The devotee knows that what he is saying is said because of love. There is no enmity in this quarreling, only a deep friendship, a deep love.

You have become my refrain,
Like the moon's rays are for the staring chakor bird,
I have no one else to quarrel with
But you, O Mohan, O youthful son of Nanda.

Although we have parted many times this life
The pictures abiding in my eyes have not become as dust.

Melting, my entire ego
Is flowing towards you.
Every happiness I know
Has something to do with you.
Only the dreams we conceived together
Are mine amidst countless strangers.
When all commotion ends,

Only then do I hear your voice.
I choose the color
That was your favorite.
Wherever your eyes have rested – even just once,
I have wandered those paths time and again at dusk.
On every picture I see, in any place,
Your image descends.
In every word I hear,
Your name emerges.
The fragrance of your body in my breath,
And the spark in my heart,
Oh my life, my love!
My every pore, is grateful to you.

The devotee says, "On every picture I see, in any place, your
image descends. In every word I hear, your name emerges."
All names become his name, all forms his form. The whole
of existence fills up with the ocean of his presence. And the
devotee begins to live in a unique world: a world of prayer,
of love and complaint – even quarreling – where one is free
to sulk and cajole, to take offense and to try to win the other
over.

Looked at from the outside, the devotee will seem mad.
Those who look only from the outside never understand the
devotee. There is only one way to understand a devotee: one
must become a devotee oneself. There is no other way. This
taste is inner; if it catches you it catches you, but you
will not understand it at all from the outside. Those who
have only studied devotion from the outside, never having
experienced it for themselves – whatever they have said about
the devotees is absolutely wrong. If you ask a psychologist
about Meera, or Daya or Sahajo, he will tell you that these
women are insane, sick.

But I say to you, if these women are sick, their sickness is better than your health. If these women are mad, their madness is a hundred thousand times better than your wisdom. Leave your wisdom and buy this madness. Because this psychologist who says that they are mad people.... Just look at him – no juice in his life, no light, no peace, no music. His life is insipid, dry, a desert; there is no oasis anywhere. And in the lives of these devotees there is nothing but flowers, only greenery, only fountains. So if to be a devotee is to be mad, then all right – be mad!

Devotion has slowly disappeared from the world, because people have mostly come to believe in what is said about things from the outside. Love too has vanished from the world. Whatever was sublime in the world seems to be disappearing while only the superficial remains. And if your life then loses all meaning, what is surprising about it? People seem determined to take everything away from you. The web of logic is destroying all the riches of life.

The greatest wealth is devotion; all other riches are below it, because devotion means your relationship with the divine, your relationship of love with the divine, and only a relationship of love can give color to your life. Love means color. Only a relationship of love can bring a dance in your life, can make flowers blossom in your life.

The glory of your name is infinite,
As even a tiny spark of fire
Burns the greatest forest.

Daya says, "I know that the glory of your name is boundless. *The glory of your name is infinite, as even a tiny spark of fire burns the*

greatest forest. Just as a small spark burns the greatest forest –
the whole forest – similarly even your smallest spark, as tiny
as this, when it falls inside me can burn away my entire
darkness, my whole forest. All my sins, all my past actions,
all the mistakes I have made throughout my infinite lives
– all will be burned away. May a small ember of your
compassion fall into me."

So the devotee waits. Devotion is love. Devotion is waiting.

Take a few steps towards devotion. Nothing will come from
just understanding Daya's words. If even a small thirst
awakens in your life after hearing these words, that is the
most that can happen from just hearing them. Take a few
steps in this direction, gather some courage to be mad. If
you cannot be mad even for God, you will never find him.
Being mad only means that we are ready to lose everything,
even our wisdom.

What I call *sannyas* is exactly this state of madness and
ecstasy. My sannyas is not the old type of traditional sannyas.
It doesn't take you away from life, it joins you more fully
with life. It isn't a sannyas of detachment, but of love. It isn't
a sannyas that teaches escapism, it is a sannyas of standing
firm, with your roots sunk deeply into life. Life belongs to
existence, so where can you run to? If you run away from this
creation of the divine, indirectly you will only be running
away from the divine itself. To appreciate its creation is to
appreciate the divine. To appreciate a song is to appreciate
its writer. To appreciate a statue is to appreciate its sculptor.
To condemn the statue is to condemn the sculptor.

Hence I insist that this is God's world. He is present in every fiber of the world. Dance a little, be ecstatic, expand yourself. Go beyond the limits of your intelligence a little, and you will suddenly be surprised to realize how you have been missing the divine so far. You have been missing what is so close, so near.... This is what is surprising, this is the miracle! There is no miracle in finding godliness, the miracle is that you have been missing it for so long. This should not have happened. As Kabir says, "I cannot help laughing when I see that the fish in the ocean is thirsty." You will laugh when you realize that we are swimming in the ocean of existence and are still thirsty. We are its waves, yet we are thirsty. The fish is born in the ocean, lives in it, and is finally dissolved back into the ocean — it is a wave in the ocean. How can it be thirsty? The very idea is ridiculous. But we are such fish in the ocean and we are thirsty.

There is an ancient Hindu story:

Once, when a certain fish heard the word ocean, she became very curious and began to wonder where the ocean was. She searched far and wide, asking people about the ocean. Whenever she asked the other fish, whosoever she asked always replied, "My dear, we have heard about it. The *puranas*, the scriptures, our teacher, all talk about the ocean, but we are only ordinary fish and we don't know where it really is! Or perhaps it existed once upon a time, but not any more. Who knows, it might be just poetry, something imaginative people dream of. We have never seen the ocean."

The fish became very restless...and she has been living in the ocean this whole time, and the other fish she is inquiring from are also in the same ocean. But how is she to know? Something that is too close is missed.

You need some distance to know. There is only one way for her to know the ocean: some fisherman must catch her and put her on the seashore. Only when she is writhing on the beach will she realize where the ocean is.

Now any fisherman can catch a fish and throw it onto the shore, but there is no boundary to existence, no shore, and so there is no way we can be thrown outside it. Wherever we are, we are a part of the divine. That is why we go on missing it.

You cannot find the divine through logic, through thought, through searching. You will only find it when you disappear. Devotion is the art of disappearing.

I wish I weren't a musk deer,
For then, why would my feet be wandering day and night?

The musk deer bears a fragrance in his navel and he goes on chasing it. As Kabir says, "The musk resides in the navel." The musk resides within the deer itself, but the fragrance seems to come from somewhere outside. How can the deer know that the fragrance comes from within himself? His nostrils open outwards, the fragrance emanates from his body, returns and fills his nostrils. The musk deer chases madly after this smell.

I wish I weren't a musk deer,
For then, why would my feet be wandering day and night?
If I were just a flower
I could be blossoming somewhere,
Not suffering this dreadful thirst.
I too carry the fragrance in me, but in vain —
It keeps me forever restless like the wind.

Enchanted by the mantra of narcissism
I pursue myself.
How many places have I traversed?
But this desert never ends,
With no trace of a water source in sight,
And the sun never setting.
How can I bear this double anguish?
For how long can I refrain from asking
For shelter from the shadow?
This measure of time – how helpless, how powerless.
Hurt by dreams, my consciousness is almost dead.
Poisonous frustration bites me
Like a female serpent,
Crushing me in its coils.
For how long can I live like this,
Licking the dewdrops of my ego?
Oh what is this that is suddenly happening to me?
What invisible hand is touching me?
My breath came back to go away again,
Or are the clouds gathering to call me away?
If only someone could tell me,
Is this my new life or my death?

The musk deer wanders in search of the fragrance which is hidden within him. He runs and runs; there is no end to his journey – there cannot be. In the end, the deer gets tired and falls down.

Oh what is this that is suddenly happening to me?
What invisible hand is touching me?
My breath came back to go away again,
Or are the clouds gathering to call me away?
If only someone could tell me,
Is this my new life or my death?

Through this non-stop wandering, the situation has become that of near-dying – and who knows whether death is death or the beginning of a new life? If we can't know life, how can we know death? If we have missed life, it is certain that we will miss death. Life lasts for seventy years and you cannot wake up. Death happens within moments; how will you wake up? That is why you have been born again and again and you have missed again and again – you missed life, you missed death. But the one you are searching for – "I wish I weren't a musk deer, for then, why would my feet be wandering day and night?" – that musk is within you.

The divine cannot be outside you. The divine is the sum total of both the inner and the outer. The divine is as much hidden within the seeker as in the outer where he is seeking. Nothing will be gained by going to Kailash or to Kaaba, to Girnar or to Jerusalem, because the one you are searching for, that ray of consciousness, resides within you. Find it there.

There are two ways this can happen. One is the way of hard work, effort. Few can follow this path. It is quite possible that you will not be able to do it – only once in a while someone reaches through the path of effort, only one in a hundred reaches through effort. Only the one who knows the art of making the effort, without allowing any ego to form because of it, reaches through this path. This is rare, difficult – only once in a while a Mahavira, a Buddha, has done it. The danger is that your effort almost always strengthens your ego. Only a very skillful person can avoid the presence of ego in his efforts. Effort without ego…only then one reaches. But this is the trouble. First, it is difficult to make an effort, and then it is even more difficult to make it egolessly. It is like trying to turn poison into the nectar of immortality. Effort added to the ego is like a bitter gourd — and grown on a neem tree, it only becomes even more bitter.

Most people have attained the realization of truth through grace. There is one advantage about the path of grace, the advantage is that ego cannot arise in it. Then you are not the doer, the divine is the doer and therefore effort is not a problem. So the dangers of the path of effort do not exist on the path of grace.

Daya is talking about the path of grace. Leave yourself in the hands of the divine. May its will be done — you simply become an instrument, a means to it.

The glory of your name is infinite,
As even a tiny spark of fire
Burns the greatest forest.

"If even a small spark falls onto me, O Lord, I will burn like the forest and turn to ash." The moment the devotee is burned to ash, to nothingness, the moment he has been erased, he becomes the divine. The death of the devotee is the birth of the divine within him. The death of the devotee is the coming of godliness. Devotion is a lesson in death, because love is a lesson in death. Only those who are able to die ever know love, and only those who are determined to die the great death ever know devotion.

Be determined: it can happen. And until it does, you will remain the same orphan that you are now. It can happen, it is very close to you. If you open your doors and windows even a little the divine will come inside; just as the rays of the sun and the fresh air enter as soon as you open the doors of your house. Don't sit with your doors shut. Sway, dance, sing, give thanks to life. If you can thank life, you will know that whatever you have already received, even that is enough. What you have is enough. If you can give thanks for that, you will receive more and more. Your gratefulness will bring more and more. The greater your gratitude, the more will come onto your side of the scales. The more your gratitude, the more you will be worthy and the more you will be filled with the blessings of the divine.

The path of devotion is the path of the heart. Only the mad succeed there, only those who can laugh and cry with their whole heart, those who are not afraid to drink the wine of the divine — because when you drink that wine you will lose all your senses, you will lose all control over your life. Then you will walk when he makes you walk, you will stand when he makes you stand. Even though it is he who is making you walk, he who is making you stand up, your life goes on very beautifully, very blissfully. Right now, your life is nothing but sorrow: then your life will be nothing but bliss. But this happens only when your life is not under your control. And that is the fear.

The only thing that stops you from moving towards devotion is this fear that you will lose control and no longer remain your own master. If you want the divine to be your master, you cannot remain the master yourself. *Lord...this is forever my request....* If the divine is to be your lord, you must give up your lordship over yourself. If you want the divine to be your master, you must get off the throne. Get off the throne! As soon as you do, you will find that he has always been sitting there. You couldn't see him because you were sitting there. Get down and bow in front of the throne and you will find that his boundless radiance, his infinite light, his grace has filled you from all sides.

Ramakrishna used to say: "You are unnecessarily rowing. Unfurl your sails, put down your oars. His winds are blowing. He will take your boat to the other shore."

Devotion is sailing with the wind, the path of knowledge is working the oars. In rowing, naturally it is you who will work. But when the sails fill with the winds of God and the boat takes off – you don't have to do anything. Surrender, unfurl your sails! Nothing done on your own has succeeded so far. Stop relying on yourself. Walk with his feet, see with his eyes, live according to him. Let your heart beat with his heart.

These verses of Daya are unique. They can bring a revolution into your life.

...As even a tiny spark of fire
Burns the greatest forest.

If even a tiny spark of these verses falls into you, your darkness will be completely destroyed.

Whenever I have liked myself,
I remember only you.
Whenever I feel happy with my image in the mirror,
Your image arises
In my thrilled eyes.
Whenever I feel greedy for happiness
I think only of you.
Whenever a new song has come to my lips
Only your voice comes into my remembrance.

Whenever I have stolen the moon,
I remember only you.
You are the witness to my nights, restless with creativity,
You are the strength of my creating hands.
Whenever I have defeated time,
I remember only you.
Whenever I have liked myself,
I remember only you.

If you can give up your ego just once, you will be amazed.
When you look at yourself in the mirror, you will
only see God. What to say about others? — you will certainly
see God in them, but when you look at your own image in
the mirror, then too you will only see God. When you close
your eyes and look within yourself, you will see him. When
you walk, the sound of your footsteps becomes the sound of
his foot-steps. When you sing, it is he who is singing. When
you dance, it is he who is dancing. Once your ego is gone,
his energy becomes your energy. Once your ego disappears,
his life becomes your life.

Enough for today.

I 0

COMPLETING THE CIRCLE

The first question:

Osho,

Why is there jealousy in love?

If there is jealousy in love, then your love is not love. If this
is the case, then some sickness is masquerading as love.
Jealousy is indicative of an absence of love.

It is like saying that the lamp is lit but there is darkness all
around it. There should be no darkness if the lamp is burning.
The absence of darkness is proof that the lamp is lit.
The proof of love is that there is no jealousy. Jealousy is like
darkness, love is like light. Use this as your touchstone: as
long as jealousy remains, your love is not love. Some other
game is taking place in the name of love, your ego is on a new
trip: the joy of possessing the other in the name of love,
exploitation of the other in the name of love, using the other
person as a means.... And using someone as a means is
the greatest immorality in the world, because every person
is the divine. Every person is an end unto himself – not a
means. So never use anyone as a means – even by mistake. If

you can be of some use to someone else, that is good, but never use anyone for your own purposes. There is no greater insult possible than using someone as a means. It means that you have turned the divine into your servant. If you can, become a servant, but never make servants out of others.

Real love will dawn only when you understand that the divine is present everywhere. Then there is nothing for you to do but serve. Love is service, not jealousy. Love is surrender, not ownership.

You have asked, "Why is there jealousy in love?" I can understand the questioner's difficulty. In ninety-nine cases out of a hundred, the love we know is only another name for jealousy. We are very clever. We are very skilled in denying there is filth by spraying some fragrance over it. We are adepts at placing flowers over our wounds. We are great artists in making falsehood appear to be truth. So what is there is jealousy, but we call it love. Thus jealousy prevails in the name of love. What is actually there is hatred, but we call it love. Something totally different is there.

One "goddess" has asked another question. She says, "I cannot do the Sufi meditation, and I don't allow my husband to do it either, because in the Sufi meditation you have to gaze into the eyes of others. There are many women here, and if my husband looks into the eyes of another woman, and it leads to something totally different, what will become of me? As it is, I don't get along very well with my husband anyway."

We continue to pretend that we love even those we don't get

along with very well. We pretend to love even those we have never liked. Our love is, rather, some other arrangement for us – for our security, for our economic well-being, to make our lives more convenient. You may lose your husband, so there is some worry. You may have gained a house by taking a husband, you may have gained wealth...your life has found a certain structure. It is up to you if you are content with this structure, very good, but because of this structure you are missing the divine – because the divine is only attained through love. There is no other door through which you can meet the divine except the door of love. Whosoever misses love will miss the divine.

How can fear and love exist together? If you are so afraid of your husband looking into the eyes of another woman, then love has not happened between you. Your husband has not looked into your eyes, nor have you looked into his eyes. You have not seen the divine in your husband, nor has he seen the divine in you. Do you call this a relationship of love?

When love happens, fear disappears. Then even if your husband looked into the eyes of every woman in the world it would make no difference. He will find only you in every woman's eyes. He will find your eyes in every woman's eyes – because every woman will reflect you. He will be reminded of you no matter what woman he sees.

But love never happens. Somehow we go on holding ourselves together, so that we don't fall apart.

I have heard:

Mulla Nasruddin was in a lift. The building was twenty-seven

storys high. The lift was already crowded when Mulla and
his wife entered on the second floor, and when an extremely
beautiful woman entered on the fourth floor, there was
absolutely no room left at all.

Somehow the woman managed to squeeze herself between
the Mulla and his wife. As the lift slowly ascended towards
the twenty-seventh floor, Mulla's wife became increasingly
anxious. Mulla was pressed against the woman, and the
woman was pressed against him. There was no way that either
of them could say anything because the lift was so crowded.

Mulla's joy only made his wife even more anxious.
And Mulla's joy... it was as though he were in heaven! Again
and again he drooled as he gazed at the woman. Then,
suddenly, the woman screamed and slapped Mulla's face. "You
decrepit old man! How dare you? How dare you pinch me?"

There was a pindrop silence in the lift. Rubbing his face,
Mulla got out with his wife on the next floor. At last he was
able to speak again. "I don't understand what happened," he
said. "I didn't pinch her."

"I know," replied his wife in delight, "I did."

Such are your relationships of love. You keep watch over each
other. It is a form of enmity – where is the love in it? How
can you guard over each other in love? There is trust in love,
there is a confidence, an unprecedented faith. These are the
flowers of love – faith, trust, confidence. If a lover doesn't
have these, then love has not blossomed. Jealousy, envy,
enmity, spite anger – these are the flowers of hatred. You
carry the flowers of hatred while thinking you have planted

a tree of love. You bear the bitter neem fruits thinking that
you have planted a mango tree. Get rid of this delusion.

So when I say to you that love can become a path to take
you to the divine, you listen to me but you don't trust it,
because you know your love. Your life is a hell because of
that love. If I am talking about that love, then I am certainly
saying the wrong thing. But I am talking about another kind
of love – the kind that you have been searching for, but have
not yet found. You can find it – that is your potentiality –
but until you do find it, you will cry, weep, suffer in agony
and remain distressed. Until the flower of your life blossoms,
until the fragrance of love spreads from that flower of
life you will remain restless, discontented. Until then,
whatever you do you will still remain dissatisfied, you will
still be restless. Until you blossom, you will not be fulfilled.

Love is a flower.

Love is a great religious phenomenon. It is the opposite of
jealousy. Love is very close to prayer. Once love begins, its
next step is prayer. Once prayer begins, its next step is the
divine. Love, prayer, the divine…these are the three steps of
the one temple.

The second question:

Osho,

Who am I, and what is the purpose of my life?

You are asking me? Dear sir, don't you know who you are?
And can anyone else's answer be of any use to you? It will
be borrowed. No matter what answer I give to you, it

will never be your answer. You will have to find your own answer. The question is yours, and only your answer can solve the question. If I say to you, Tattvamasi Svetketu – that you, Svetketu, are the embodiment of brahman – what will that achieve? I can tell you that you are the soul, the eternal, the very embodiment of deathlessness – what will that achieve? You have heard these kind of answers many times. You know them by heart. You yourself give such answers to others. When your son asks you, you explain to him that he is the soul, the witness, sachchidananda, ultimate bliss.

Other people's answers can be of no help to you. At least as far as "Who am I?" is concerned, the question requires that you descend into your own self. The well of the self is very deep. You can find the source of its water only if you go down to the very bottom. It is a deep well, and you must go there alone. No one else can come with you. Who can travel inside you? – no one. This journey must be undertaken on your own. This is a flight of the alone, to the alone.

All religions tell you to enjoy aloneness – because how can you go into yourself until you enjoy aloneness? You must go there alone. This is why all the religions tell you to light the lamp of meditation. Only that lamp can accompany you, nothing else – neither wealth, nor position, nor prestige. Only the lamp of meditation can go there with you, just you and the lamp of meditation. Then you can descend into the deepest well. And this well is certainly very deep. Your depths are unfathomable. You are as deep as existence itself, so how can the well be any less deep? How can it be any smaller? When you peep into the well you will not be able to glimpse the water – it is too far down. The journey is long. The journey into oneself is the longest journey.

This seems contradictory because we always think, "Me? I'm right here. All I have to do is close my eyes to find myself." If only it were that easy. Certainly one reaches by closing one's eyes, but by just closing your eyes your eyes don't really close: you close them, but your dreams of the outside world continue, the outer transactions go on. Your eyes close, but the images of others continue to arise — friends, your loved ones, your relatives and kin. You close your eyes, but you are never alone. If you could be alone, you could go into yourself even with your eyes open.

The question is of removing the crowd. You will have to put aside all your scriptures, all your doctrines — because you will never be able to go inside yourself with such a burden. Such a burden will make it impossible. This journey is possible only when you are weightless.

And remember: no one else can go with you, no one else can give you the answer. Often answers are an obstacle. Because you have accepted these borrowed answers you don't go within yourself, you don't search. If you have already accepted that the soul is there inside you, why would you even try to find it? These borrowed answers, these beliefs, don't allow you to experience your life.

So the first thing I say to you when you ask, "Who am I," is that you exist. How could you ask this question if you didn't? You must be someone. And whatsoever you are, ABC, whatever your name is, you are conscious — otherwise how could this question arise? Rocks don't ask such things. You are conscious. I am deriving this conclusion from your question. I am not answering your question, merely clarifying it, analyzing it — because if the question is diagnosed properly, the treatment won't be hard to find. The diagnosis is the important thing. If the diagnosis is correct, then it will not be difficult to find the right medicine. If the diagnosis is wrong, you can use as many drugs as you like but they will never benefit you; they may even cause you harm, because if you take the wrong medicine it can harm you.

I am diagnosing your question, analyzing it. I want to hold the pulse of your question in my hand.

The first thing: you are not a rock. A rock doesn't ask a question. I have met many rocks. A rock never asks, "Who am I?" You are consciousness, therefore questions arise. Plants don't ask, trees don't ask. They are more alive than rocks, but still questions don't arise in them. It takes more than just having life to ask a question. You are something more than life. Animals and birds don't ask questions. They are more evolved than plants, they can fly, they can move around; if someone attacks them, they can protect themselves. They are afraid of death, but they know nothing about life.

You are asking about life: "What am I? who am I? what is the goal of my life?" You are more than the birds and the animals. You are alive, you are consciousness – and consciousness is the ability to contemplate, the power of reflection. You have turned in upon yourself to ask, "Who am I?"

This is an important question, but don't ask me. Make this question *your* meditation. Every day, close your eyes in solitude and let the question, "Who am I?" resound within you. And remember, don't let answers interfere with your asking. Borrowed answers will interfere, stale answers will get in the way, the answers you have heard from others will block you. Don't let them. Such answers come from your mind, they are not you; they are knowledge, not realization. If you already knew the answer, would you have asked the question?

So, it is clear that you don't know. Take your knowledge and put it to one side. It is only worth two cents; it has no value, it doesn't create knowing. You have read the Upanishads, the Gita, the Koran, the Bible, and that didn't solve anything – otherwise you would have already found the answer. You must ask "Who am I?" not using the answers that other people have provided – whether they are from Krishna, Mohammed, or Mahavira – or the answers I have given you.... Get rid of them, get rid of them all. Hold on to your question. Refine it. Put your whole life-energy to the question "Who am I?"

No answer will come. Complete silence will reign. The deeper you go with your question, the more profound the silence will be. You will begin to be concerned that perhaps there is no answer, because you will be in a hurry to get an answer. The answer does not come so quickly. Using the sword of your question, you will first have to behead all borrowed answers.

Zen monks say that if you meet the Buddha on the path of meditation, cut him into two pieces with your sword. They worship Buddha every day, but they still tell every disciple that if he meets the Buddha on the path of meditation, he should not feel shy or diffident, but immediately pick up his sword and cut Buddha into two pieces.

It is necessary to be free of others on the path of meditation. Only when you are free of the other can you see yourself, otherwise your eyes are always caught up with the other.

It makes no difference who this other is – your brother, your sister, your wife, your husband, Buddha, Mahavira, Krishna. The other is always the other.

There will come a time in this inquiry when only the question, "Who am I?" remains, and then stillness will reign. In your bones, in your flesh and marrow, only one question will resound: "Who am I?" Only one arrow will pierce your being... and it will go deeper and deeper: "Who am I?" Your anxiety will increase, your restlessness will grow, because you will not be able to see an answer anywhere; the ocean will be all around you and the shore will be nowhere to be seen. This is the moment when all your courage will be required. If you can pass through this moment, you will arrive at the answer.

When does one reach the answer? – when no answer remains, when you become completely ignorant. "When no answer remains" means that you will be totally ignorant, like an innocent child. You will not know anything. All your erudition, your wisdom, your mind will be gone. Only one question will remain: "Who am I? who am I?" – one final obsession.

In the end the question will no longer be in words, only an awareness – "Who am I?" It will not be you who repeats "Who am I?" In the beginning you repeat the words; at first with your lips, then on your tongue, then in your throat, then deep down in your heart. Then you will not have to repeat anything, but merely experience "Who am I?" A question mark will be there in your very being – it is not that there will be words. You will go beyond the words and there will be nothing but a thirst: "Who am I? Who am I? Who am I?" If you can endure that thirst.... Then, once all your answers have fallen away, the question will also fall away. When there is no answer coming, for how long can you keep asking the question?

Remember, don't be in a hurry. Don't drop the question from your side, otherwise the whole thing will be useless. Don't drop it on your part. Don't make an effort to drop it, telling yourself that it is enough, it is time to finish. It can take years. Go on asking, one hour a day. And one day, suddenly, you will find that everything has stopped – the answers have gone, but so has the question. Only you remain – the pure you. No words will form, no thoughts will arise. At that moment you will realize that you have found the answer. The answer will not come like a written note on a piece of paper. The answer will not come as if someone is saying to you, "Listen, my son. This is the answer." The answer will not be an answer, it will be an experience. You will know, there will be a flash of lightning. You will have seen. That is why we call this moment *darshan*, seeing. You have seen who you are. Your eyes turned towards you, towards your self. You have met yourself. You have come face-to-face with yourself.

And the moment you know who you are, you will also know the goal of your life. To know life, is also to know its purpose. To know the source, is also to know the destination. To know yourself, is also to know the divine – because you are a ray of the divine. If you know even one ray, you can understand the mystery of the entire sun. If you know even one drop of the ocean, you will understand the mystery of all the oceans. The whole ocean is contained in one single drop. The whole of existence is contained in a single you.

The question is not our understanding of isness,
We must avoid that,
We have no choices
But to create a new foundation.
Who are we? where do we come from?
What do we have to become...?
To search for the essence of these questions
Is a waste of time.
Whatever answer is found
Will only be a delusion.
The pain of our inferiority and futility
Will never be diminished.
We are what we must become.

Understand this:

We are what we must become.
We must carry other's loads.
When did the butterfly ever ask,
"Where have my wings come from?"
When did the thorn ever ask,
"Where did my prickliness come from?"
Why should we try to fathom out alone
The enigma of our truth?
What concern is it of ours
That we struggle with this pursuit
Day and night?
We are not an expression,
Merely a medium;
Not heroes,
Merely a sequence of events in a story.
These cannibalistic questions
Gnaw at our bodies.
The more we think, the more we waste away.

Which path to take, where should we go...?
Abandon these dilemmas –
Some cruel, murderous animal is chasing you – run!
The techniques are different, but the outcome is the same,
The end, dear brother, is where the beginning is.

You ask: What is the goal of life? "The end, dear brother, is
where the beginning is....We are what we must become."

These things appear to be somewhat contradictory, "We are
what we must become." You are already, right now, what you
must become. The seed is the flower; it is simply a different
manifestation. Today the doors are closed, tomorrow they
will be open. Now the petals are asleep, tomorrow they will
be open. The seed already is what it has to become.

That is why you cannot produce all kinds of flowers from
one kind of seed. A lotus plant will produce a lotus flower
and a rosebush will produce a rose flower. No matter how
hard you try, a lotus plant cannot produce a rose flower. We
are only that what we have to become.

Your future already lies within you. Your potential rests
within your seed. "The end, dear brother, is where the
beginning is." We arrive at the place from where we begin.
This is one of life's absolute truths.

The Ganges arises at Gangotri in the Himalayas, and flows
down to the ocean. If you ask "How can she reach her source?
She began at Gangotri and ended at Gangasagar, in the
ocean," then you didn't see the whole thing in its entirety.
You didn't see the circle. The Ganges will rise again into the
sky in the form of vapor at Gangasagar, it will again turn into

clouds, it will again rain on the Himalayas and descend again at Gangotri. The circle is complete. When the Ganges again descends at Gangotri, the circle is complete, the journey has been completed.

"The end, dear brother, is where the beginning is." That is why all the sages say that when you reach *siddhawastha*, the ultimate state of awakening, you become a small child again.

"The end, dear brother, is where the beginning is." When you reach sagehood, you will become simple — as though you are ignorant. The ultimate state of knowing is like ignorance.

The Upanishads declare: When someone says "I know," know that he does not know. When someone says "I do not know," know that he knows.

Socrates said: "When I was young, I thought I knew everything. As I grew older, I was astounded to realize that I didn't know everything! I would have been content just to have known a little — that would have been more than enough. Now that I am really old, I am sure that I know nothing. I am completely ignorant."

The ultimate realization of one's own ignorance is also the ultimate moment of knowing. Why?

"The end, dear brother, is where the beginning is." But don't parrot other people's answers. You will have to search for your own Gangotri.

Why are you so sad?
Your life has become a mere serving girl.
If there is no freshness in your thoughts,

Your life is stale.
Open your windows, it is morning,
Let the bounteous light enter.
Your heart is restive, wanting to sing,
Let it sing some new melody.

Why should you repeat what others say, why not sing your own song! Why live on what is borrowed from others. Why not express your own individuality!

Don't ask me who you are. Go within yourself. You exist, that much is certain. Even if you doubt everything else about yourself, this much is certain – that you are.

A great Western thinker, Descartes, has said there is only one thing in the world that cannot be questioned – your existence. Why can't you doubt it? Because even if you doubt it, you must exist in order to be able to doubt. Who doubts? You cannot doubt your own soul. You must at least accept your own existence before you can begin to say, "I doubt that I am; I have no faith in it." But who is it who has no faith? Who is this doubter?

There is only one truth in the world which is beyond doubt – your own existence. Step into this unquestionable truth a little. Follow this stairway a little.

And the inquiry "Who am I?" is astounding. If you make this inquiry it can take you deep into the well of your own being. That well contains clean, crystal-clear water, and when you drink it, you will be content forever.

The third question:

Osho,

Why shouldn't we connect directly with the divine? Why should we take a master as a go-between?

How kind of you. What great compassion you have for the master. The idea is good. Just do it.... But what have you come here for? And why do you need to ask even this? — because your search for the master has already begun. Why do you ask me? It means there is a need to ask someone.

A young man once came and asked me whether he should get married or not. I said, "In that case, you should."

He said, "In that case? What does 'in that case' mean?"

I replied, "If you are asking, then you should get married."

He said, "But you have never been married."

I told him, "I never needed to ask anyone!"

The meaning of your asking is clear. If you cannot find the answer to this question by yourself, how will you ever find the divine? If you need to depend on others in such small things, how can you undertake this infinitely vast journey alone? And it is true: the journey *is* done alone. If you can go on your own, good. But you can't. And do you think that the master goes with you on your journey? No one can go with anyone else — not even the master. Then of what use is the master? The master is there to encourage you, simply to encourage you.

When I was a child, I was taken to the man who used to teach swimming in the village. I wanted to learn swimming. I had always loved the river. I must have been very young at that time – about six or seven years old. That man in our village who taught swimming was a wonderful man. He loved the river very much. He is old now, perhaps eighty, but I suspect he is at the river at this very moment. From four in the morning until ten, and then from five in the evening until nine at night, he was always at the river.... The river was everything to him, the heart of everything. He had only one interest: teaching swimming to anyone who came to him.

When I met him, I asked, "Do I have to learn to swim by myself, or will you teach me?"

He replied, "No one has ever asked me this question. The truth is that no one can teach anyone else how to swim. I will drop you into the water. You will be frightened and you will thrash about using your hands and feet. That is how one begins. I will stand on the bank to give you the courage to realize that you won't drown. If need be, I'll save you. But so far the need has never arisen."

So I said, "Do this, just stand on the bank. I'll jump in by myself. There will be no need for you to throw me into the water. And if that need doesn't arise, then you don't need to save me even if I begin to drown – because I want to learn by myself."

He sat down. I jumped into the river. Naturally, I went under a few times. My mouth was full of water. I thrashed about with my hands and feet. At first there was no structure to my thrashing. Gradually I found that too. I learned to swim in about three days. And I didn't even need him to hold me once.

The truth is that descending into religiousness is like swimming. You already know swimming: you simply need to get into the water. You will thrash about with your hands and feet a little; at first your movements will be haphazard, unstructured, nervous. Then, gradually, you will become more confident. Why? That confidence is bound to come because the river never drowns anyone. The river holds you up.

Have you noticed that a living person can drown, but a dead body always floats? This is strange. The living person certainly knows something and because of this he drowns. The dead person floats, while the living person drowns. The living person must drown himself; the river doesn't drown him because it cannot drown even the dead, dead things always float. There is a natural lift to water. Water is wonderful; it has a mystery hidden within itself which the scientists have often searched for but have never found. There are many other secrets hidden in this mystery, including the entire mystery of religion. I have not chosen the symbol of swimming at random. It is a conscious choice on my part that I use swimming as a symbol.

Three hundred years ago a scientist, Newton, discovered gravity. You have heard that an apple fell down while Newton was sitting in a garden. He wondered why things always fall downwards, never upwards. Why? Why downwards? If you throw a stone, it will come down again. Everything does. Why? What is the secret behind it? He thought and searched and eventually discovered the theory of gravitation: that the earth pulls everything to itself. It has a special power which pulls everything down.

His idea has been expanded a great deal since then. Today's science virtually rests on the foundation of his discovery. It could not stand without it. The theory of gravity became the basis of modern science. But this theory is incomplete. Nothing exists in life without its opposite.

There was another man living in Newton's time – a poet, a thinker, a wise person, a sage. One day he jokingly said something against Newton, but at that time no one paid any attention to what he was saying.

He asked, "Mr. Newton, it's true that the apple fell from the tree and down on to the earth. But I want to ask you one thing. Tell me, how did it get up there in the first place?"

Every day the tree grows upwards. The apple fruit was hidden in the seed; one day it blossomed and then it became a fruit at the top of the tree. The man was saying, first find out how it got there. How it came down again is a secondary matter. How did it get up there? This is no small matter.

In Lebanon, there are cedar trees which are five hundred, six hundred, and even seven hundred feet high! Water reaches up to the topmost leaves even when the trees are seven hundred feet tall. The water current reaches there. Something raises the water that high.

No one paid much attention to what this poet said. Who cares what sages say? People ignore poets because they are only poets – let them be! But I say to you that he said something far more important than Newton and, in the future, science will agree with him more.

This is already happening Scientific circles have started to discuss a new theory: levitation. Gravitation is the force that pulls things down; levitation is the power which pulls them up. And it should be so because life is always equally balanced: life and death, day and night, heat and cold, love and hatred. Have you ever seen anything that exists without its opposite? There is no such thing. Man and woman, childhood and old age, knowledge and ignorance, a good person and an evil person... nothing exists without its opposite. In electricity, positive and negative exist together: if you try to separate them, they cannot exist on their own, both cease to be. So why should gravity be any exception? It is not. There are no exceptions. There must be a principle which pulls things upwards.

There is a principle behind what the poet said, which the sages have always known. In their language, the principle is called *prasad*, grace. Gravitation and grace. Attraction and grace. Grace pulls things upwards. Water uses the principle of grace to lift things up. It never drowns things on its own.

It is not hard to swim; you simply need to have a trust in the water. After thrashing around with your hands and feet for about two to three days, you will gain this trust and know that there is no need to be nervous, that the water doesn't drown you. As soon as your doubt fades you begin to swim. Faith comes and you swim. You acquire both faith and the ability to swim at the same time. Now all you will need is a little more acquaintance with water, a little more familiarity with this capacity that water has.

When you dip a pitcher into a well, it fills with water and feels very light. As you pull it out of the water, it begins to get heavier. In the water you can lift a man twice your own weight. Water creates weightlessness.

There is no art to swimming. And notice this too about swimming: once you know how to swim, you can never forget it — no matter how hard you try. Do you know of anything else that you can never forget? All the things that are learned can be forgotten, but not swimming. Swimming is not a learning; rather, it is a truth of life. Once you have become acquainted with it, you cannot forget it. It isn't something trivial which slips out of your memory. It is not that you know swimming and then one day you enter the river and begin to shout, "Help! Help! I knew how to swim, but now I have forgotten." This is impossible.

Once you have known the divine, you can never forget it. Once you have entered meditation, you cannot undo it. Once you have tasted love, you cannot turn away from it. Once the ray of prayer descends upon you, you cannot forget it. The divine is not something you learn; it is our intrinsic self-nature.

In swimming, when your intrinsic nature and the intrinsic nature of the water fall into a harmony you can just lie there, not moving your hands and feet, and the water will keep you supported. There is no need to move your body even a little. A harmony has happened, a perfect tuning has taken place.

A similar thing happens with the master when you want to attain to the divine. The master does nothing: his presence acts as a catalytic agent, his presence gives you courage. If you have sufficient courage, you won't need a master. People have known the divine without having a master — not many, but some. So don't lose courage: if you want to know without having a master, it can be done.

But be careful that it is not just your ego saying, "I will know without having a master." If it is your ego, then you will not be able to know. In that case you will drown pitiably, you will sink badly. So examine this carefully within.

Look at it this way: the master is doing nothing for you except taking away your ego, except chopping away your ego. In reality, you are the absolutely beautiful, the absolutely good, the absolutely true. *Shivam* – absolutely good: you are Shiva, godliness. The master pulls away the ego that is covering you – and this ego is nothing but a delusion, a belief. This belief drops away in the company of the master, this delusion is washed away. Once this happens, you are beautiful from head to toe.

If you can do it on your own, then certainly go ahead. There is no problem. And I know this is not an altogether meaningless question. What goes on in the name of a master is enough to trouble any reasonable person – all the hypocrisy, cheating and lying that can happen. The type of people who make claims to the name of "master" naturally lead you to ask such a question.

Everyone is a patient,
Patients are patients,
Even doctors are patients.
Hence we cannot help each other.
Helpless,
Everyone is sick.
Some in their eyes, some in their ears,

Some in their bodies, some in their minds.
Such a vast hospital
But no one to nurse –
Everyone is sick.

Sometimes it seems that such a master is traveling in the
same boat as you yourself, that there is no difference between
the two. He himself has not attained, so how can he help you
to attain? Such people have neither a glimpse of the divine
in their eyes, nor the peace of the divine in their lives; the
fragrance of the divine is not found in their being, nor does
any authenticity arise from what they say. Their songs are
stale; they have already been sung by someone else. They have
not sung their own song yet so how can they awaken your
song which is sleeping inside you?

A true master is someone whose own life-flower has
blossomed. It is difficult, it is rare; it is not so easy to find
a master. You are trying to avoid the master and I am saying
to you that even if you want to find him it is not
so easy. And then, even if you do find him, don't take it
for granted that he will accept you! In the same way that you
search for the true master, so the master searches for the true
disciple.

A disciple means a humbleness to learn, a surrendering in
order to learn, an ability to bow down in order to learn. If
you remain conceited, even if you have found the real master
he will not be able to accept you. It is not that he doesn't
want to – he does – but there is no opening for him. You
are standing tall in your arrogance, you cannot be transformed. You cannot be transformed without your coopera-
tion.

What then is the meaning of a master? The only meaning is: the divine is invisible, and even if we want to find some way to recognize it, where can we find this? So if even a small reflection of the divine can be available somewhere, that will bring some reassurance.

The real moon in the sky is too far away. Haven't you seen – when a small baby starts crying for the moon, his mother fills a plate with water and puts it outside the house. The moon is reflected in the plate and the child is delighted that he has found the moon.

The master is the same; like a moon in a plate. The actual moon is very far away. Perhaps our eyes cannot yet see that far; we may not be able to tolerate the direct manifestation of truth. Truth may be too vast, too bright.... Do you remember how Daya has said time and time again that it is like a thousand suns arising, the light is so dazzling? If you are not prepared for it you will panic. The divine is vast – it cannot fit into your tiny courtyard. If you have not first broken down your walls you will be shaken, there will be an earthquake in your being.

The master is a reflection of the infinite in the finite. The master is like you and at the same time he is not like you at all. You can hold the master's hand, but you cannot hold the hand of the divine. The divine has no hands. You will keep groping, but you cannot get hold of its hand. It is formless, it has no attributes. The master has form, the master has attributes.

I am a small, negligible piece of bamboo,
I know who I am.

But at the touch of your lips
A song bursts forth from my throat,
Your breath fills me with melody,
I sing your song,
And I echo your tune.

What is a master? A piece of bamboo which has agreed to
be a flute, which has become eager to resonate with the voice
of the divine.

I am a small, negligible piece of bamboo,
I know who I am.
But at the touch of your lips
A song bursts forth from my throat,
Your breath fills me with melody,
I sing your song,
And I echo your tune.

Near the master you will come to learn the language of the
divine. The meaning of a master, in human language, within
human limitations, is only this much: a small glimpse of the
divine.

The master is a door. You can also enter without using the
door – that too is possible. It is up to you. One person comes
as a guest, someone else can come as a thief. The guest enters
through the main door, the guest is welcomed by the
host who stands at the door inviting him in and offering him
somewhere to sit down. The thief, on the other hand, enters
in the night, in the dark, breaking down the wall of the house.

Thieves reach to God too – it is not a big problem. And there
is nothing wrong in stealing the divine. Who else can we steal,

if not God? He himself is a thief! That is why Hindus have
given him the name Hari. *Hari* means one who steals away, a
thief, a kidnapper. He is a thief; he steals people's hearts. So
if you want to steal from him, to pick his pocket, there is
no harm in it. It is your choice: if you want to make a
hole and break into his house, do it. If you want to
jump through the window, do it. If you want to jump over
the fence, do it. Do as you wish. But you can also enter
through the front door. The master is the front door. You
can enter in a simple way, in an easy way.

Remember one thing:

Even the bountiful ocean sent me away thirsty,
Where in this frugal world can I find water?
Once, I believed the ocean was never miserly,
Because wherever there is water, it is the gift of the ocean.
But it has neglected me so much
That requesting water from the river makes me uneasy.
I had heard from the sky that the world is a lovely place,
That the love we find here
Is a balm for the wounds of a thousand lives.
But in some way, the world's love has hurt me so badly,
That I do not like any of the kindness here.

I know your difficulty. You have formed many relationships
in life and have always been deceived, and so you are afraid
whether to enter this new relationship with a master now or
not.

But in some way, the world's love has hurt me so badly,
That I do not like any of the kindness here.

You have become afraid. And with a master, no other form of relationship is possible except that of his kindness, his compassion. And you have seen many sorts of compassion, but each time you were deceived. You have tried many doors, and always found only a wall. You have tasted many loves and found them all to be poison and the only result to be a hell. Now you are frightened – even of the master's love.

"...I do not like any of the kindness here." The ocean is vast, you can go to it but can you drink its water? You cannot.

Even the bountiful ocean sent me away thirsty,
Where in this frugal world can I find water?

One starts thinking: "If even the ocean leaves me empty-handed, with nothing to drink, where else can I go?"

Once, I believed the ocean was never miserly,
Because wherever there is water, it is the gift of the ocean.
But it has neglected me so much
That requesting water from the river makes me uneasy.

But keep this in mind, it is the river's water that is drinkable. Although the ocean's water is in the river, it is only in the river that the water is drinkable. The river runs into the ocean, but its water is sweet.

The divine is like the ocean, the master is like the river. The master is a small lake. Whatever the master has received he has received from the divine. You cannot drink the divine directly – no one can drink from the ocean directly – but when the divine comes to you through the master the water becomes drinkable.

The master is an alchemy. You cannot eat soil – or can you? No one but a small young child even tries to. You cannot eat soil. But whatever you eat is made from the soil. Wheat, rice, grapes, apples, pears – all are made from the soil. But you cannot eat the soil directly.

The tree does a great job – it transforms the soil in such a way that you can digest it. The tree is a medium in between. It prepares the soil so it becomes suitable for your stomach.

And it is the same with a master.

You cannot digest the divine directly – it becomes digestible through the medium of the master. If you have decided to go without a master, then go with pleasure; but where will you go? Which direction will you take? Who will you search for? Whosoever or whatsoever you start searching for has been named by some master or other. Will you search for God? Then you are accepting what some master has said. You will be accepting what the Upanishads, the Vedas, or the Koran have said. Will you search for the soul? You are already accepting some master's statement, accepting what Mahavira or Krishna have said. Will you search for *moksha*, or *nirvana*? You are already accepting what some master has said. What will you search for? Whatever you search for, you will be accepting some master's statement. And if you are going to accept some master's statement, then accept the statement of a living master – because dead masters are good for a little worshipping, but they cannot be of any more use than that.

People are clever: they just want to worship others, they don't want transformation. If this is the case, then it is okay, then find a dead master. But if you see through a living master's eyes, you will begin to have a direct recognition of the truth. If you pulsate in the heart of a living master...and this is what *satsang* means – that you sit down with the master, join your song with his song, drown your wave in his wave, pulsate a little with his heart, walk a little with him, flow with his current, swim in his stream....

What is the meaning of the master? Just this: a telescope is available to you.

Come closer to my eyes. See a little through my eyes. When you do, you will begin to understand what your eyes should be like. Participate a little in my celebration and you will learn what kind of a celebration your life should be. What other reason can there be for accepting a master?

The fourth question:

Osho,

For the past three years I have wanted to take sannyas, but have never been able to do so. What could be the reason?

A small joke: One bright moonlit night, an extremely shy young man was sitting with his beloved under a tree. It was the full moon of autumn and everything was very still. The young man was shy, full of modesty and very bashful. The silence began to be oppressive. The young man said nothing. Finally, gathering all his courage, he stammered, "May I...may I...may I kiss you?"

The young woman lifted her eyes and looked at him. There was an invitation in those eyes, a thanksgiving. But the young man had already buried his eyes deep into the ground. The

silence returned and was even heavier this time. After half
an hour the young man asked again, "May I…may I…may I
kiss you?"

The young woman looked at him again, but this time he was
staring at the moon in the sky and the stars in order to
escape. There was another long silence. Finally, after another
half hour, when the matter had begun to be very heavy indeed,
the young man asked, "Have you suddenly gone deaf? Or
dumb?"

The lady said, "No, neither. But have you become paralyzed?"

This is what I can say to you. "For the past three years I have
wanted to take *sannyas*…." Have you become paralyzed? What
are you waiting for? And your name is Gobardhandas, which
means the servant of Krishna — the one who used to care for
the cows… such a nice name! Be careful not to turn it into
"Gobardas" — a slave of cow dung! Three years…how long
will you continue thinking about this? Your life will slip
away! It is a very sweet name, Gobardhandas. Have courage,
otherwise, I say to you that you will be nothing but Gobardas
in your dying moments.

Now you are asking me: "For the past three years I have
wanted to take sannyas, but have never been able to do so.
What could be the reason?" There is no reason. It must be
your lack of courage. Sannyas means courage, bravery. You
must be prepared to be mad. Doesn't Daya say again and
again that the devotee sometimes laughs, some-times cries,
and sometimes sings — that is how the devotee is. His feet
land here when they should land there. It is very paradoxical!

Sannyas is a different kind of lifestyle. One lifestyle is that of the world: the shop and the office, your wife and your children, wealth, position and prestige – this is the way of the world. To bring the ray of sannyas into this way of life means that you have begun to change its very foundation. Now meditation has become more valuable than money. Now the divine has become more valuable than your wife or your husband. Moksha, salvation and release have become more valuable than position or prestige. The foundation of your life has changed. Now everything will be in a chaos. Disorder will reign, everything needs rearranging.

So sannyas is not a small event; it is big. No wonder one feels scared. So one thinks to let life continue as it is. You can, but one day death will come and snatch everything away.

Sannyas means that you have decided to earn something which death can never snatch away from you. To earn something while keeping your own death in context is sannyas. *Samsara* means forgetting about death and earning something. But death will take away all the things that you have earned and reduce them all to the same level as the things that you have never earned. Whether you have earned or lost something, it will all mean the same. Whether it is *Diwali*, the festival of wealth, or *diwala*, bankruptcy, it will all mean the same. It makes no difference to death.

The person who lives his life in the full awareness of death is a *sannyasin*. And whoever forgets about death, whoever lives forgetting death, is a worldly person. It is a difficult thing to live and keep death in front of you. Even to think that one must die is extremely distressing. The mind says: "I will die? Everyone else must die, but not me. Other people may die, but somehow I can save myself from death." To ignore death is the way of the world. And keeping death constantly in your awareness, always in sight, forming a lifestyle in accordance with death, is sannyas. As soon as you bring death into your calculations, all your other values will change.

There was a young man who often visited Eknath. He asked the same question again and again: "You are always so peaceful, so joyous, so blissful. How do you do it?" Eknath listened, but never answered.

One day the young man asked the question again, adding, "I can't believe it. Sometimes, at home, I think that although you smile a lot when you are with others, you may not smile at all when you are on your own. At night you may be just like us. Who knows, it may all be just a pretense — because how is this possible? I am not like this, nor is anyone else I know. How can such bliss shower on you? And I can't see anything that might give you such bliss: you have no wealth, no position, no prestige, no fame. What do you have? You are only a naked *fakir*. You have one loincloth, but you are so happy."

On that day, Eknath knew that the right moment had come. He said to the young man, "Show me your palm." Eknath took the man's hand and immediately he became very sad.

The young man looked worried. He asked, "Why has your expression changed? What is wrong? What do you see in my palm?"

Eknath said: "I see a sudden break in your life-line. Seven more days...you have only seven more days to live. After that, when the evening sun sets on Sunday, your life will set too."

The man stood up. Eknath said, "Hey, where are you going? I still have to answer your question."

"To hell with my question!" the young man replied. "Glory to Rama, and good-bye! Is this the time for philosophical discussion?"

He was covered in sweat. When he had first arrived, he had climbed the stairs with a strong dignified step. But as he left, he needed to hold on to the wall. He was suddenly old. His whole life had been shaken up because he had come face-to-face with death. He had made so many plans — what he wanted to do, and what he didn't want to do. Now they had all disappeared. It was as though he had been building a house of cards and suddenly a gust of wind had blown it apart.

He went home and got straight into bed. His wife and children began to cry. The news spread throughout the whole village and all the neighbors gathered. If Eknath had said it, it must be true. Eknath would not lie. His death was certain.

By the third or the fourth day, the young man was half dead. He couldn't get out of bed. His strength had gone, he had no interest in food. Whenever someone talked about food he would say, "Who cares?" He asked forgiveness from all his enemies. He said to the people against whom he had court cases, "Brother, please forgive me, it was all a mistake." He let go of all his quarrels and admitted to all the acts of deception and fraud that he had ever committed. Death was coming — what was the point now of all that quarreling and cheating? Why continue it? Such are the joys and diversions of life! After all, who and what is mine, who and what belongs to others? Even when his wife was sitting next to him, she seemed to be just the same as everyone else. Even his own son looked like a stranger. Close companions and strangers were all alike. No relationships mattered anymore. As death approached, everything seemed to be falling apart. Only one thing concerned him: the seventh day was coming closer and closer, death had almost arrived. Now what was there left to do or not to do?

On the seventh day, he couldn't rise from his bed, he couldn't talk, there were large black circles under his eyes. Over and over again, he asked how much time remained before the sun would set.

And as the sun was just about to set, Eknath arrived at his door. His wife fell weeping at Eknath's feet. The children began to cry. Eknath said, "Don't be distressed, there is nothing to be alarmed about. Take me inside." He went inside and asked, "My brother, have you committed any sins during the past seven days?"

The man opened his eyes with great difficulty. "Sin?" he asked. "Are you mad? With death standing in front of me the whole time, where is the space to commit sin?"

Eknath said, "Your death is not coming yet. This was just my answer to the question you had been asking me so often. In this same way death constantly stands beside me, in front of my eyes. When can I sin? And if there is no sin, there is no sorrow. If there is no sin, there is no worry. If there is no sin, there is no restlessness. If there is no sin, the fragrance of virtuous deeds automatically arises. Get up! Death has not yet come for you."

The man got up quickly. His eyes immediately changed. He patted his son on the back. "You have put me in a fine fix," he said to Eknath. "I have asked forgiveness from all those people I have been quarreling with my whole life. Now I will have to see to them again.... Wait until tomorrow! I tried to settle all my court cases. 'The matter is over,' I told them, 'take as much land as you want, live there...any farm you want. There is no point to our quarrels.' You have put me in a fine fix! Is this any way to answer my question? I asked you a simple, innocent question, and you have made everyone cry for seven days – and I almost died."

And from the following day, the man became as he was before.

When death descends into your life, that is sannyas. If you accept death, that is sannyas.

You may not have the courage, but gather courage. Whether you accept death or not, it will come. It is going to come. After seven days, or seven years, or seventy years – what difference does it make? Death is going to come, that much is certain. Nothing else but death is certain. If you can see death, then gather courage. Sannyas is the search for that wealth which death cannot take away from you.

The fifth question:

Osho,

Isn't devotion just a figment of the imagination? Isn't that too a kind of dreaming?

If you rely on your intellect, devotion will seem to be only a dream. Now what to make of this: when Daya is talking to

Krishna, she is not only talking with him, she is quarreling and bickering with him. She appeases him, she consoles him. Sometimes she even sulks.

One question constantly occurs to thinking people throughout the world: "What is the meaning of life?" And no answer to this question has ever been found, because whatever meaning there is in life comes from the heart and not from the intellect. And the heart understands the language of dreams, not the language of mathematics. The heart understands poetry, love, beauty. The way of the heart is different, its world is another world.

Devotion belongs to the world of the heart. If you ask the devotee, then it is a different matter. The devotee will say:

It is not the paths, but the horizon that is foggy,
Whatever goals there were
Have all become futile.
How can the words be at fault
If all meanings have been lost?
Our dreams might have taken us home,
It is the truths that have led us astray.

"Our dreams might have taken us home, it is the truths that have led us astray." Doctrines, logic, mathematics…. If you ask the devotee, he will say that all these things have led man astray. Without them, man would be a waterfall of juices, full of songs. He would dance, be joyous; his life would be a celebration, the divine would be present.

After all tumult sleeps,
Listen to the word that awakens
If you will.

A soft music slowly arises

Covering the stillness,
The way a magical blueness trembles
On the pure mirror of a lake.
After all truths vanish,
Weave the awakening dream
If you will.
Every procession follows a few slogans,
The crowd has no personality.
The most-listened to are rumors,
Truth does not exist in a majority.
Once the high tide has receded,
Choose what remains on the shore
If you will.

Oh sculptor, do not work so much on the statue,
Natural beauty dies with refinement.
This beautiless, dejected, sad incompleteness
Makes the youth in a work of art eternal.
Only that which is incomplete has a future,
Its every moment is a new sensation,
Contemplate this
If you will.

After all truths vanish,
Weave the awakening dream
If you will.

In the language of the intellect, devotion is a dream. In the
language of the heart, devotion is true, truer, the truest.
There is no greater truth than devotion.

Now it is *you* who is to decide what sort of a person you are.
If you are an intellectual type devotion will not appeal to
you, leave it alone. Don't worry about what doesn't appeal

to you. Then, your path is different. Walk on the path of knowledge and meditation and you will move through a refinement of the intellect. But if you like the path of devotion, if it appeals to you, if your heart becomes delighted listening to devotees, if your heart moves when it hears the language of devotion, then stop worrying about what the intellect says, stop listening to the intellect.

After all truths vanish,
Weave the awakening dream
If you will.

Then give up all this talk of doctrines, truth and so on. Instead, put your focus towards pulling together the threads of devotion, and you will discover that an individual reaches the divine even through dreams. But you will have to learn to dream of the divine.

The dream too is a power. Just as logic is a power, so too is the dream. Logic is the basis of science, dreaming is the basis of devotion. Logic is the basis of spiritual discipline, dreaming is the basis of love. These are the only two ways. Either expand your imagination to the point where it becomes capable of seeing the divine, or disperse your imagination so totally that it is altogether lost, and that which is manifests itself in front of you.

If your path is through the intellect, you will experience the truth. If your path is through devotion, you will experience the divine, the beloved. It is one and the same: those on the path of knowledge call it the truth, devotees call it the divine. It is up to you. But it feels to me that the devotees enjoy things more because they make the truth beautiful, they turn the truth into their beloved. Truth is no longer a mathema-

tical calculation, it is not like "two and two are four." Truth
becomes like your own son, your own beloved, your own
lover. The truth becomes steeped in love.

If your heart is moved, if your heart is stirred when you hear
the songs of the devotees praising the divine, don't be afraid.

Again a face has settled in my eyes,
Again some lost horizons have emerged,
Again some setting suns have risen,
Again the thorny paths are strewn with silk.
Since seeing those eyes,
My shoulders are winged,
Again my dreams fly midst unseen longings.
Whichever place in me was touched,
As new I have become there.
Again mysterious arms embrace me,
Again a face has settled in my eyes.

If the face of the divine settles in your eyes and it appeals
to you, then don't be afraid. And you cannot avoid choosing
between either the heart or the intellect.

Moving rock-like memories
Ever so slightly
This way and that
For a brief moment,
Oh, it has arisen,
A dream has arisen.
After many, many days,
The moon has arisen.

…Let it arise. If the dream of the divine arises, then don't
condemn it as a mere dream. Even dreams are beautiful.

Take it like this: even dreams come true if you pour the whole
of your being into them, and even truths remain only a
falsehood if they are borrowed and stale, if they belong to
others, if they do not contain your whole being in them.

The sixth question:

Osho,

*The title you have given to this series of discourses appears to promote
detachment and a life-negative attitude. Please explain why there is this
negation on the path of all-embracing love, juiciness and ecstasy?*

It may have appeared so to you, but there is no negation
there. *The world is the last morning star* doesn't carry a life-
negative attitude in it, and it doesn't contain any message
to renounce the world. It only declares the facticity of the
world. There is neither affirmation nor negation in it. *The
world is the last morning star.* There is no condemnation in this.

These beautiful words cannot be words of condemnation in
any way. They simply state that the world is like this, that
it is like the last morning star – here for a moment, then
gone. It is the truth, not a condemnation. If someone calls
a bubble a bubble, stating that it exists for a moment and
then will burst the next moment, is that being negative? If
someone tells you that you exist now and that death can
come in a moment, is that being negative? Is it negative to
call the ephemeral "ephemeral"? No – it is merely accepting
the fact. This is how the world is. But people understand
things in their own way....

The question is from Yoga Chinmaya. He has a leaning
towards negation, so if his mind finds any support for

negation anywhere he doesn't let go of the opportunity, he holds on to it tightly. He has the old-fashioned approach – negation of the world. *The world is the last morning star* – he must have felt that this is a good opportunity: "So – Daya also sees things this way!"

But no, Daya is not saying this at all. Daya is simply saying that this is how things are.

One day I met Mulla Nasruddin. He was coming from the direction of the river and carrying a basketful of fish. So I asked, "Where did you catch them, old fellow?"

Mulla replied, "I have found a wonderful place, and some kind gentleman has put up signs so that I can remember exactly where it is. As you go down the hill towards the river, there is a sign in both Hindi and English which says, 'Private, No Entry.' Then there is another board which says, 'Trespassers will be prosecuted.' A little further on another sign says, 'No Fishing.' And this is where I always go fishing."

Mulla believes that the kind gentleman has placed these signs there for his guidance....

We take our own meanings to suit our own interests. We hear what we want to hear. *The world is the last morning star* – there is nothing of negation in this, it is merely a reminder that this is how things are. Your world is not eternal, and you should not think that it is. Even if you accept it as eternal, it won't be. The world comes and then it is gone; it is like a line drawn on water. If you wait here, accepting that the world is eternal, you will know nothing but sorrow. If you have a desire for the eternal, don't search for the eternal in the world. The eternal is somewhere else, hidden; somewhere beyond it. You will see the eternal only when you stop looking in the world.

So, when we say "The world is the last morning star," this simply means that there is also the polestar, the symbol of the eternal. Don't remain entangled only in the world, otherwise you will remain deprived of knowing this polestar. If your eyes are fixed on this world, how can you see what is beyond it? If your mind knows that this world is not eternal, it will have already begun to leave it, to move away from it, to go beyond it — because our whole life-energy desires the eternal, the unchanging, the everlasting. We are searching for that which will remain forever. To search for that which is here today and gone tomorrow is only a waste of time and energy.

The path of devotion is the path of juiciness and ecstasy. Where can there be negation in it? If we see someone trying to squeeze oil from sand and tell him that he would be better off extracting oil from sesame seeds, we have not stopped him from finding oil, we are not negating anything. Remember that. If I say to you, "My dear sir, the desire for oil is good; by all means extract oil, but you would be better off looking for it in sesame seeds. Sand will never produce oil, and may even damage the mill," I am not denying or negating anything, I am merely pointing out that oil cannot be found in sand. It exists, but in sesame seeds. Joy and ecstasy exist — but in your being with the divine, not in your being with the world.

The world is sand. For life after life you have worked like a slave, turning your mill. Nothing ever comes from your efforts, but you won't stop. It has become a habit and you can think of nothing else to do. So you continue to grind sand.

The last question:

Osho,

There is an intoxication in your words; hence I am afraid.

There is an intoxication, but in my words you will simply receive a small taste of it. If you became afraid of my words you will miss out on the real intoxication, because the real intoxication lies in the experience. If there is some intoxication in what I say, it is only because these words are coming steeped in the inner wine. They bring a little taste, they overwhelm you.

I am a connoisseur of wine, a trader!

And I can understand your fear. You are afraid that this wine is such that your ego will drown in it, that you will disappear. You are afraid of disappearing.

A friend has asked:

I am drowning midstream in the ocean of this phenomenal world,
There is now no other refuge in the world.
My boat laden with the burden
of my sins nears the whirlpool,
O lord, run, save me quickly before I sink.

You have come to the wrong person. My entire work is to drown you. If you are delaying your drowning, I will hasten the process and make you drown more quickly — because one who drowns is saved. One who drowns arrives: your drowning midstream takes you to the shore. The whole work here is about drowning. I am here to entice you so that you too can become a drunkard.

One day, Mulla Nasruddin was singing the praises of alcohol to me – the "other" alcohol. He said, "Not just human beings, but even animals believe in alcohol."

"What do you mean?" I asked him.

He replied, "I went fishing one day. Because I had forgotten to bring some flour to put on the hook, I looked for some earthworms instead, but I couldn't find any. So I found a snake with a frog in its mouth. I quickly snatched the frog out of the snake's mouth, cut it into pieces, and used it for bait. But then I felt sorry for the snake. Poor thing – I had taken its food. Seeing no other way to compensate the snake, I took a bottle from my bag and poured a few drops of wine into its mouth. Its ecstasy was really worth seeing! The way it waved its head, the way it raised its eyes in its intoxication, the way it swayed...."

"Then," the Mulla said, "I was so engrossed in catching fish, that I forgot all about the snake. An hour later, I felt something tapping at my shoe. I looked down and was amazed to see the same snake with two frogs in its mouth. The snake was saying, 'The same again, bartender.'"

That story was about the false wine, and we are talking about the real wine.

It is natural to be afraid. You are living in a certain way, and I will disturb it all. You have cultivated a certain kind of world, and I will put it all into chaos. But I want to say to you that the world that you have cultivated is...*the last morning star.* You only are imagining that you have managed it — nothing is managed. And what I am pointing at is the polestar: if its light enters into your life, you can come into contact with the eternal.

Don't be satisfied until you have made that contact. Don't settle for less than the divine. Let the search continue until your cup is full with the wine of ultimate liberation. You will have to continue. Those who have stopped early without finding their destination, have turned an overnight stay into their home. They will be sad, they will suffer. They are the worldly people.

Here the effort is to turn you all into *sadhjan,* to turn you all into drunkards. The day that you rise and fall down, the day that your feet land where you did not intend them to land, the day that you laugh, cry, sing and glorify the divine — on that day the flower of your life, which has waited for so long to open, will blossom. Your lotus will unfold all its petals, and your fragrance will be released into the air. That is moksha, the ultimate liberation. And that moksha is bliss. Everything else is sorrow, pain and anguish.

Gather courage, be brave. This wine is not to be missed.

Enough for today.

About Osho

Osho defies categorization, reflecting everything from the individual quest for meaning to the most urgent social and political issues facing society today. His books are not written but are transcribed from recordings of extemporaneous talks given over a period of thirty-five years. Osho has been described by the *Sunday Times* in London as one of the "1000 Makers of the 20th Century" and by *Sunday Mid-Day* in India as one of the ten people – along with Gandhi, Nehru and Buddha – who have changed the destiny of India.

Osho has a stated aim of helping to create the conditions for the birth of a new kind of human being, characterized as "Zorba the Buddha" – one whose feet are firmly on the ground, yet whose hands can touch the stars. Running like a thread through all aspects of Osho is a vision that encompasses both the timeless wisdom of the East and the highest potential of Western science and technology.

He is synonymous with a revolutionary contribution to the science of inner transformation and an approach to meditation which specifically addresses the accelerated pace of contemporary life. The unique Osho Active Meditations™ are designed to allow the release of accumulated stress in the body and mind so that it is easier to be still and experience the thought-free state of meditation.

Osho International Meditation Resort

Osho International Meditation Resort has been created so that people can have a direct experience of a new way of living — with more alertness, relaxation, and humor. It is located about 100 miles southeast of Mumbai in Pune, India, on 40 acres in the tree-lined residential area of Koregaon Park. The resort offers a variety of programs to the thousands of people who visit each year from more than 100 countries. Accommodation for visitors is available on-campus in the new Osho Guesthouse.

The Multiversity programs at the meditation resort take place in a pyramid complex next to the famous Zen garden park, Osho Teerth. The programs are designed to provide the transformation tools that give people access to a new lifestyle — one of relaxed awareness — which is an approach they can take with them into their everyday lives. Self-discovery classes, sessions, courses and meditative processes are offered throughout the year. For exercising the body and keeping fit, there is a beautiful outdoor facility where one can experiment with a Zen approach to sports and recreation.

In the main meditation auditorium the daily schedule from 6:00 A.M. up to 11:00 P.M. includes both active and passive meditation methods. Following the daily evening meeting meditation, the nightlife in this multicultural resort is alive with outdoor eating areas that fill with friends and often with dancing.

The resort has its own supply of safe, filtered drinking water and the food served is made with organically grown produce from the resort's own farm.

An online tour of the meditation resort, as well as travel and program information, can be found at: www.osho.com

This is a comprehensive website in different languages with an online magazine, audio and video webcasting, an Audiobook Club, the complete English and Hindi archive of Osho talks and a complete catalog of all Osho publications including books, audio and video. Includes information about the active meditation techniques developed by Osho, most with streaming video demonstrations.

The daily meditation schedule includes:

Osho Dynamic Meditation™: A technique designed to release tensions and repressed emotions, opening the way to a new vitality and an experience of profound silence.

Osho Kundalini Meditation™: A technique of shaking free one's dormant energies, and through spontaneous dance and silent sitting, allowing these energies to be redirected inward.

Osho Nadabrahma Meditation™: A method of harmonizing one's energy flow, based on an ancient Tibetan humming technique.

Osho Nataraj Meditation™: A method involving the inner alchemy of dancing so totally that the dancer disappears and only the dance remains.

Vipassana Meditation: A technique originating with Gautam Buddha and now updated for the 21st Century, for dissolving mental chatter through the awareness of breath.

No Dimensions Meditation™: A powerful method for centering one's energy, based on a Sufi technique.

Osho Gourishankar Meditation™: A one-hour nighttime meditation, which includes a breathing technique, gazing softly at a light and gentle body movements.

Books by Osho in English Language

Early Discourses and Writings

A Cup of Tea
Dimensions Beyond The Known
From Sex to Super-consciousness
The Great Challenge
Hidden Mysteries
I Am The Gate
The Inner Journey
Psychology of the Esoteric
Seeds of Wisdom

Meditation

The Voice of Silence
And Now and Here (Vol 1 & 2)
In Search of the Miraculous (Vol 1 &.2)
Meditation: The Art of Ecstasy
Meditation: The First and Last Freedom
The Path of Meditation
The Perfect Way
Yaa-Hoo! The Mystic Rose

Buddha and Buddhist Masters

The Book of Wisdom

The Dhammapada: The Way of the Buddha (Vol 1-12)
The Diamond Sutra
The Discipline of Transcendence (Vol 1-4)
The Heart Sutra

Indian Mystics

Enlightenment: The Only Revolution (Ashtavakra)
Showering Without Clouds (Sahajo)
The Last Morning Star (Daya)
The Song of Ecstasy (Adi Shankara)

Baul Mystics

The Beloved (Vol 1 & 2)
Kabir
The Divine Melody
Ecstasy: The Forgotten Language
The Fish in the Sea is Not Thirsty
The Great Secret
The Guest
The Path of Love
The Revolution

Jesus and Christian Mystics

Come Follow to You (Vol 1-4)
I Say Unto You (Vol 1 & 2)
The Mustard Seed
Theologia Mystica

Jewish Mystics

The Art of Dying
The True Sage

Western Mystics

Guida Spirituale (Desiderata)
The Hidden Harmony
(Heraclitus)
The Messiah (Vol 1 & 2) (Commentaries on Khalil Gibran's
The Prophet)
The New Alchemy: To Turn You On (Commentaries on
Mabel Collins' Light on the Path)
Philosophia Perennis (Vol 1 & 2) (The Golden Verses of
Pythagoras)
Zarathustra: A God That Can Dance
Zarathustra: The Laughing Prophet (Commentaries on
Nietzsche's Thus Spake Zarathustra)

Sufism

Just Like That
Journey to the Heart
The Perfect Master (Vol 1 & 2)
The Secret
Sufis: The People of the Path (Vol 1 & 2)
Unio Mystica (Vol 1 & 2)
The Wisdom of the Sands (Vol 1 & 2)

Tantra

Tantra: The Supreme Understanding
The Tantra Experience
 The Royal Song of Saraha
 (same as Tantra Vision, Vol 1)
The Tantric Transformation
 The Royal Song of Saraha
 (same as Tantra Vision, Vol 2)
The Book of Secrets: Vigyan Bhairav Tantra

The Upanishads

Behind a Thousand Names
(Nirvana Upanishad)
Heartbeat of the Absolute
(Ishavasya Upanishad)
I Am That (Isa Upanishad)
The Message Beyond Words
(Kathopanishad)
Philosophia Ultima (Mandukya Upanishad)
The Supreme Doctrine (Kenopanishad)
Finger Pointing to the Moon
(Adhyatma Upanishad)
That Art Thou (Sarvasar Upanishad, Kaivalya Upanishad,
Adhyatma Upanishad)
The Ultimate Alchemy, Vol 1&2
 (Atma Pooja Upanishad Vol 1 & 2)
Vedanta: Seven Steps to Samadhi (Akshaya Upanishad)
Flight of the Alone to the Alone
(Kaivalya Upanishad)

Tao

The Empty Boat
The Secret of Secrets
Tao:The Golden Gate (Vol 1&2)
Tao:The Pathless Path (Vol 1&2)
Tao: The Three Treasures (Vol 1-4)
When the Shoe Fits

Yoga

The Path of Yoga (previously Yoga: The Alpha and the
Omega Vol 1)
Yoga: The Alpha and the Omega (Vol 2-10)

Zen and Zen Masters

Ah, This!
Ancient Music in the Pines
And the Flowers Showered
A Bird on the Wing
Bodhidharma: The Greatest Zen Master
Communism and Zen Fire, Zen Wind
Dang Dang Doko Dang
The First Principle
God is Dead: Now Zen is the Only Living Truth
The Grass Grows By Itself
The Great Zen Master Ta Hui
Hsin Hsin Ming: The Book of Nothing
I Celebrate Myself: God is No Where, Life is Now Here
Kyozan: A True Man of Zen
Nirvana: The Last Nightmare
No Mind: The Flowers of Eternity
No Water, No Moon
One Seed Makes the Whole Earth Green
Returning to the Source
The Search: Talks on the 10 Bulls of Zen
A Sudden Clash of Thunder
The Sun Rises in the Evening
Take it Easy (Vol 1 & 2)
This Very Body the Buddha
Walking in Zen, Sitting in Zen
The White Lotus
Yakusan: Straight to the Point of Enlightenment
Zen Manifesto : Freedom From Oneself
Zen: The Mystery and the Poetry of the Beyond
Zen: The Path of Paradox (Vol 1, 2 & 3)
Zen: The Special Transmission
Zen Boxed Sets

The World of Zen (5 vol.)
Live Zen
This. This. A Thousand Times This
Zen: The Diamond Thunderbolt
Zen: The Quantum Leap from Mind to No-Mind

Zen: The Solitary Bird, Cuckoo

of the Forest
Zen: All The Colors Of The Rainbow (5 vol.)
The Buddha: The Emptiness of the Heart
The Language of Existence
The Miracle
The Original Man
Turning In

Osho: On the Ancient Masters of Zen (7 volumes)*

Dogen: The Zen Master
Hyakujo: The Everest of Zen–
With Basho's haikus
Isan: No Footprints in the Blue Sky
Joshu: The Lion's Roar
Ma Tzu: The Empty Mirror
Nansen: The Point Of Departure
Rinzai: Master of the Irrational
*Each volume is also available individually.

Responses to Questions

Be Still and Know
Come, Come, Yet Again Come
The Goose is Out
The Great Pilgrimage: From Here to Here
The Invitation

My Way: The Way of the White Clouds
Nowhere to Go But In
The Razor's Edge
Walk Without Feet, Fly Without Wings and Think Without Mind
The Wild Geese and the Water
Zen: Zest, Zip, Zap and Zing

Talks in America

From Bondage To Freedom
From Darkness to Light
From Death To Deathlessness
From the False to the Truth
From Unconsciousness to Consciousness
The Rajneesh Bible (Vol 2-4)

The World Tour

Beyond Enlightenment (Talks in Bombay)
Beyond Psychology (Talks in Uruguay)
Light on the Path (Talks in the Himalayas)
The Path of the Mystic (Talks in Uruguay)
Sermons in Stones (Talks in Bombay)
Socrates Poisoned Again After 25 Centuries (Talks in Greece)
The Sword and the Lotus
(Talks in the Himalayas)
The Transmission of the Lamp
(Talks in Uruguay)

Osho's Vision for the World

The Golden Future
The Hidden Splendor

The New Dawn
The Rebel
The Rebellious Spirit

The Mantra Series

Hari Om Tat Sat
Om Mani Padme Hum
Om Shantih Shantih Shantih
Sat-Chit-Anand
Satyam-Shivam-Sundram

Personal Glimpses

Books I Have Loved
Glimpses of a Golden Childhood
Notes of a Madman

Interviews with the World Press

The Last Testament (Vol I)

Intimate Talks between

Master and Disciple – Darshan Diaries
A Rose is a Rose is a Rose
Be Realistic: Plan for a Miracle
Believing the Impossible Before Breakfast
Beloved of My Heart
Blessed are the Ignorant
Dance Your Way to God
Don't Just Do Something, Sit There
Far Beyond the Stars
For Madmen Only
The Further Shore
Get Out of Your Own Way

God's Got A Thing about You
God is Not for Sale
The Great Nothing
Hallelujah!
Let Go!
The 99 Names of Nothingness
No Book, No Buddha, No Teaching, No Disciple
Nothing to Lose but Your Head
Only Losers Can Win in This Game
Open Door
Open Secret
The Shadow of the Whip
The Sound of One Hand Clapping
The Sun Behind the Sun Behind the Sun
The Tongue-Tip Taste of Tao
This Is It
Turn On, Tune In and Drop the Lot
What Is, Is, What Ain't, Ain't
Won't You Join The Dance?

Compilations

After Middle Age: A Limitless Sky
At the Feet of the Master
Bhagwan Shree Rajneesh: On Basic Human Rights
Jesus Crucified Again, This Time in Ronald Reagan's
America
Priests and Politicians: The Mafia of the Soul
Take it Really Seriously

Gift Books of Osho Quotations

A Must for Contemplation Before Sleep
A Must for Morning

Contemplation

India My Love

Photobooks

Shree Rajneesh: A Man of Many Climates,
 Seasons and Rainbows
through the eye of the camera
Impressions... Osho Commune International Photobook

Books about Osho

Bhagwan: The Buddha for the Future by Juliet Forman
Bhagwan Shree Rajneesh: The Most Dangerous Man Since
Jesus Christ by Sue Appleton

Bhagwan: The Most Godless Yet the Most Godly Man by
Dr. George Meredith
Bhagwan: One Man Against the Whole Ugly Past of
Humanity by Juliet Forman
Bhagwan: Twelve Days That Shook the World by Juliet
Forman
Was Bhagwan Shree Rajneesh Poisoned by Ronald Reagan's
America? by Sue Appleton.
Diamond Days With Osho
by Ma Prem Shunyo

*For any information about Osho Books & Audio/Video Tapes please
contact:*

OSHO Multimedia & Resorts Pvt. Ltd.

17 Koregaon Park, Pune–411001, MS, India
Phone: 020 4019999 Fax: 020 4019990
E-mail: distrib@osho.net Website: www.osho.com

JAICO PUBLISHING HOUSE
Elevate Your Life. Transform Your World.

Established in 1946, Jaico Publishing House is the publisher of stellar authors such as Sri Sri Paramahansa Yogananda, Osho, Robin Sharma, Deepak Chopra, Stephen Hawking, Eknath Easwaran, Sarvapalli Radhakrishnan, Nirad Chaudhuri, Khushwant Singh, Mulk Raj Anand, John Maxwell, Ken Blanchard and Brian Tracy. Our list which has crossed a landmark 2000 titles, is amongst the most diverse in the country, with books in religion, spirituality, mind/body/spirit, self-help, business, cookery, humour, career, games, biographies, fiction, and science.

Jaico has expanded its horizons to become a leading publisher of educational and professional books in management and engineering. Our college-level textbooks and reference titles are used by students countrywide. The success of our academic and professional titles is largely due to the efforts of our Educational and Corporate Sales Divisions.

The late Mr. Jaman Shah established Jaico as a book distribution company. Sensing that independence was around the corner, he aptly named his company Jaico ("Jai" means victory in Hindi). In order to tap the significant demand for affordable books in a developing nation, Mr. Shah initiated Jaico's own publications. Jaico was India's first publisher of paperback books in the English language.

In addition to being a publisher and distributor of its own titles, Jaico is a major distributor of books of leading international publishers such as McGraw Hill, Pearson, Cengage Learning, John Wiley and Elsevier Science. With its headquarters in Mumbai, Jaico has other sales offices in Ahmedabad, Bangalore, Bhopal, Chennai, Delhi, Hyderabad and Kolkata. Our sales team of over 40 executives, direct mail order division, and website ensure that our books effectively reach all urban and rural parts of the country.

SINCE 1946